A Parent's Guide to Mandarin Immersion

中英双语教育 – 家长指南

By Elizabeth Weise

A Parent's Guide to Mandarin Immersion
中英双语教育－家长指南

Chenery Street Press
San Francisco, California

The author wishes to thank the following for permission to reproduce copyrighted material.

Madeleine Adams: A Student Profile
Sarah Beth Chionsini: A Cantonese Immersion Experience
Carmen Cordovez: *Una familia trilingüe: Español, Inglés y* 中文
Anya Hauptman: A Student Profile
Jamila Nightingale: Being Black and Bilingual

Cover design: James Smith of GoOnWrite.com
Layout and design: Craig Johnson, Remex Publishing, San Francisco

ISBN 978-0-9903659-0-7

To Starr King Elementary School

Monolingualism is the illiteracy of the 21st century.

Gregg Roberts
World Languages and Dual Immersion Specialist
Utah State Office of Education
Salt Lake City, Utah

At the National Chinese Language Conference
in Boston, Massachusetts
April 8, 2013.

Contents

Portland Public Schools, Oregon 1998
Minnetonka, Minnesota 2007
Los Angeles Unified School District 2007
Pioneer Valley Chinese Immersion Charter School,
    Hadley Massachusetts 2007
Utah's immersion program 2009
Washington Yu Ying Public Charter School, Washington DC 2008
Deutsch-Chinesische Grundschule, Berlin 2011
Mandarin Chinese Language Immersion Magnet School,
    Houston 2012

Once you've made the leap

Final thoughts

Resources

一
yī
1

Welcome to Mandarin Immersion

As my two daughters neared school age, I knew that I wanted them to become conversant in both Mandarin Chinese and their native English. I have been fascinated by Chinese since high school. While my ancestors came from Germany and England, their father's family comes from China. More importantly, as adults we wanted them to be able to move easily between cultures and languages.

This put our family on the ground floor of a growing, but little known, movement in education dedicated to raising a generation of bilingual children. I'm talking about language immersion programs that begin in kindergarten or first grade and continue into middle school, high school and beyond.

Historically, Americans haven't felt the need to speak anything but English. New immigrants were encouraged to quickly throw off their mother tongues. Today, more than 1,000 U.S. public and private schools offer the standard elementary school curriculum with a twist—at least half the day is taught in another language. Spanish is the most common and for years French immersion was a strong second. Now Mandarin is gaining ground. There were at least 170 Mandarin immersion programs in the United States at the beginning of the 2014–2015 school year, with another 22 in Canada.

In these programs, the standard elementary curriculum is offered, but for between 50% and 100% of the day it is taught not in English but in Mandarin. Generally a class will have both a Chinese-speaking teacher and an English-speaking teacher, with students switching between the two depending on the language in which a given subject is taught. For example, math, science and social studies might be taught in Mandarin and art, physical education and English language arts in English.

Mandarin is popular for many reasons. I asked parents with children in Mandarin immersion programs across the country why they chose this type of education for their children and got the following answers. You might find yourself reflected in some of them:

- Mandarin is so difficult for an English speaker to learn well unless you start young.
- I'm pessimistic about the future of the United States economy and I want my kids to have opportunities to live/work elsewhere.
- It is a language that demands hard work and diligence to master, which are important qualities for kids to develop.
- My parents spoke Chinese, but never taught me. I'd like my children to learn the language.
- I think it is important for Americans to take the time to learn another language.
- Once we were committed to an immersion program, we decided to go with what we perceived to be the harder language to take advantage of my daughter's young, adaptable brain.
- We believe it expands the mind and facilitates learning.
- The school district was offering it for free! Any parent who would pass up this opportunity is a fool in my mind.
- Our child is very visual and art-focused; we thought characters would be more interesting to him than just learning the alphabet.
- Our daughters are adopted from China. We want them to have access to their culture and country.
- I spent years studying French and never once used it. I want my children to speak something useful.
- I know if my kids are in a Mandarin immersion program they'll be in class with children whose families value education.
- I have a gifted child but my school district doesn't offer any gifted programs. This is the most academically challenging program I could find for her.

As you tour your local Mandarin immersion school (or begin agitating to create one in your local school district), know that you're not alone. There are at least 20,000 U.S. children who walk into classrooms every day in which Mandarin, not English, is the dominant language of instruction.

Remember that putting your children in immersion at the tender age of five is about giving them options when they're 25. No one expects they're all going to become Chinese linguistics professors, work as investment bankers in Shanghai, or do biotech research in Singapore. Instead, our hope as parents is that our children's language skills will offer them a wider view of the world and a broader palette of possibilities.

Despite thinking this all sounds like a good idea, you may want more information than is offered by the school in a flyer or a website. How does immersion work? Why does it work? What happens to kids who go through it? How much Chinese do they learn? How do they perform academically compared to kids who spend their school days learning only in English? Are there any downsides, any trade-offs?

Or maybe you've already got kids in a Mandarin immersion program but you still have questions. You love your child's teachers, but what goes on in the classroom day-to-day is still a mystery. And sometimes you don't quite understand what other parents want or expect out of the program—or even what *you* want or expect.

This book is for you. In it, I've tried to explain how immersion works, give some background about Chinese and Chinese immersion and generally answer the many questions parents ask. Mostly I hope it will be helpful both to families contemplating immersion for their children and also those already in immersion schools.

You don't need to speak Chinese or be a teacher to understand any of it. It's meant for parents who just want to understand what they're signing on for. When I use Chinese, I give the character, the *pinyin* pronunciation and the English meaning. I've used simplified characters throughout the book, as those are the most commonly used worldwide.

In my family's case, we began in one of the first classes of the San Francisco Unified School District's (SFUSD) Mandarin immersion program, launched in 2006. Two years before that I started attending meetings SFUSD was holding about the possibility of starting a Mandarin immersion program. Eventually Mandarin immersion programs were launched in two elementary schools and in the 2012–2013 school year, a middle school. I helped found the Mandarin Immersion Parents Council in 2008 to support our program. We launched a website, miparentscouncil.org, to publish information for families in the program and eventually I became the webmaster.

As our program grew and expanded, so did Mandarin immersion across the country. When we began there were very few that we knew of—San Francisco's Chinese American International School, of course, then one in Portland, Oregon, two in Silicon Valley, a cluster in Minnesota and one in New York City. Today it seems like new Mandarin immersion programs are announced every month.

My day job is as a reporter for *USA Today*, so I have a natural inclination for collecting and sharing information. I started doing that first for our PTA, then for our Mandarin immersion parent group, then for our blog. It began with meeting notes, moved on to profiles of other schools and finally expanded into interviews with experts in the field of Mandarin immersion. As our oldest daughter entered fifth grade and middle school loomed, I decided I needed to pull everything I'd learned together into a book, to offer a road map for the parents who were increasingly coming to the blog for information and e-mailing for advice.

I write this book as someone who deeply loves (but these days, sadly, barely speaks) Chinese. I fell in love with the language, culture and literature of China in my Catholic Jesuit high school, Seattle Prep. At the time it featured an accelerated program named for Mateo Ricci, the 16th century Jesuit who was one of the first Westerners to master classical Chinese. Though our school sadly didn't actually teach Chinese, it was named for Ricci to honor his wide-ranging interests and deep appreciation for other cultures.

But it was there, in tenth grade geometry, that I was first introduced to Chinese. My classmate Tim Louie spoke Cantonese at home and his parents sent him to Saturday Chinese school. One day during a lull in class he showed me how to write the Chinese character for "horse," 馬. He patiently walked me through writing it correctly, stroke by stroke. I was hooked and wanted to learn more.

I didn't get the chance until college. I first studied about China at the University of Lund in Sweden and continued at the University of Washington in Seattle, where I got as far as third year Mandarin. I later worked as a tour guide in China and then for China Books and Periodicals in San Francisco. In 2008 I got to go to Beijing to cover the Olympics for *USA Today*. And yet, in spite of all these experiences, I never developed the level of fluency that I desired. (I should have moved to China to study.)

Still, it was lucky happenstance my daughters' father learned Mandarin from his parents. His dad is from Sichuan province and his mom from Zhejiang province. However, at home our girls hear only English. For me, the opportunity to raise children who are bilingual in a language I love has been a gift beyond measure.

I write as an English speaker who cannot presume to address the issues and concerns Mandarin-speaking parents might have about immersion schools. I am writing for the most part for families who don't speak or read Chinese, although I hope some of what I've gathered is helpful for those who do.

Here's how Tara Williams-Fortune, one of the leading researchers in immersion education today, puts the promise of immersion:

> Becoming bilingual leads to new ways of conceptualizing yourself and others. It expands your worldview, so that you not only know more, you know differently.[1]

It's not an idle promise. Julie Haley's children started in Chinese immersion in kindergarten and graduated in eighh grade. They learned grit and perseverance, how to work hard and not to give up. As a parent it wasn't always easy but looking at them today, she knows it was the right decision.

Watching my son, who's in high school now, he feels like his mind is capable of doing anything, having done something this difficult. It's given him a huge confidence in his abilities. He's gained this amazing sense of resilience. The other day he said to me, "Mom, learning this language and this other culture has given me insight. It made me realize that I see the world from one perspective but it's not the only perspective." It blew my mind.

To all of you—welcome to a wonderful journey you'll be taking with your children for the next nine years and more. It is one I believe will prepare them to be true citizens of the world, whether their future holds international travel, overseas work or simply the openness of mind that comes from speaking a second language.

As parents, that's something we very much want for our children. An immersion education allows us to give them that gift.

1. Tara Williams Fortune, "What the research says about immersion." *Chinese language learning in the early grades: A handbook of resources and best practices for Mandarin immersion* (New York, Asia Society, 2012).

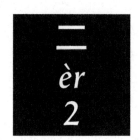

A History of Language Immersion

Language immersion has always existed. It's how all children learn to speak the language of their parents and their community. Children who live in an environment where two or more languages are spoken often grow up speaking both fluently, simply by being exposed to them in daily life.

We in the United States are the outliers in this respect. Until very recently multilingualism was actively discouraged. Here languages typically are taught beginning in high school for an hour a day. These generally have included French, German, Spanish or Latin, and there was little real expectation of fluency. If students graduated with the ability to read a little, it was considered satisfactory.

This is very different from the rest of the world. Most children in industrialized countries begin to study a second language, generally English (the most common second language in the world), in elementary school, usually in second or third grade. It's simply *expected* that English is a subject that must be mastered right along with math, history and science. Students in Germany or China or Israel could no more imagine a school day without an English class than they could imagine a day without a math class. Everyone studies a second language. Educated people are expected to be able to move effortlessly between multiple languages, including English.

Marjorie Diaz, a parent, speaks only her native Spanish to her children. They speak English with their father and are learning Mandarin in school. Her reasons for wanting her children to speak three languages stem from her observation that those with power and prestige do so automatically:

> Look at the famous, rich people. Julio Iglesias' kids all speak at least three languages. I really don't think they miss out on English and I am hoping that what they will gain should be more than enough to compensate for a missing word here or there. The reality is that in Europe, the elite and royalty have been speaking and obtaining education in at least trilingual environments, so we are really behind but slowly catching up.

A study of the top 25 industrialized countries found that 20 begin mandatory study of world languages (usually English) by fifth grade, with three others starting in middle school.[1] In the European Union, there's a push to get every student to study two foreign languages, one of which you can be sure is English.

The United States is the only industrialized country that waits until high school and then only grudgingly offers instruction in other languages. Only 12 states make foreign language compulsory in high school. Just 30% of high school students here study a foreign language, mourned Maureen McLaughlin, director of International Affairs for the United States Department of Education, in a 2013 speech at the Asia Society's Chinese Language Conference in Boston.

This practice comes at a cost. How many people do you know who took three or four years of Spanish or French in high school and yet couldn't hold a conversation to save their life? That is not the case elsewhere. The next time you meet someone educated in another country who speaks English fluently, ask them how much English they studied and for how long. Almost all will have begun in grade school and taken at least one English class a day through high school. Beginning in high school they are required to read original materials, not only in their native language but also in English. At the college level there are few universities in the world where being able to at least read English isn't expected. In many, most of the textbooks are in English.

The ability to move back and forth between multiple languages simply is expected in the international business and academic world. When I attended the University of Lund in Sweden, we were routinely given academic papers to read in English, Swedish, Danish and Norwegian. And, on one distressing day, in Dutch. When I went up to the professor and said I couldn't read Dutch, he looked at me with the disdain of a European who had learned to read German and English before he was 12.

"You Americans, you really have no languages, do you?" he said dismissively. "Well, get yourself a dictionary and see what you can make of it. There's really no other choice; certainly I don't have time to translate it for you!"

We have the Canadians to thank for immersion

Children in North America were rarely intensively schooled in languages until 1965 when a new kind of language immersion arose in the town of St. Lambert, Quebec.[2] At the time Francophone rights groups were pushing for more use of the French language. It was becoming apparent to English-speaking parents in the primarily French-speaking province of Quebec that their children needed to speak French. The traditional method of teaching French to English-speaking students was the hour-a-day class many of us grew up with. But these Canadian parents knew this had not made them fluent in French, so they looked for another method that would give their children a better chance at becoming bilingual.

They read up on bilingual education and discussed the issue with scholars at McGill University in Montreal, then made an audacious proposal to their local school board. Their monoglot, English-speaking children would enroll in a school in which, from the first day of kindergarten, they would be taught entirely in French. Only in second grade would the students begin to be taught some lessons in English. Not until sixth grade would half of their children's classes be in French and half in English.

The parents called this program "immersion."

It worked. The students spoke English natively because that's what they spoke at home. Perhaps more importantly, given that they lived in a French-speaking province, they also were able to speak French. Not, it turns out, as fully fluently as children from French-speaking families. But very, very well. They were able to get jobs in the province that required French. They were also able to pass French proficiency tests required for many jobs within the Canadian government. As a report produced by the Canadian Council on Learning in 2007[3] put it:

> French-immersion students do not typically show native-like proficiency in speaking and writing skills, although their linguistic deficiencies are generally not a serious obstacle to their effective use of French for academic or interpersonal purposes.

Even more interestingly, not only did these children become fully functional in their increasingly French-dominated province, but—and this surprised everyone—they did better in English than their English-speaking friends as they moved up through the grades. The report explains:

> During the first years of their immersion programs, early total-immersion students tend to score lower than students in English school on English-language testing of literacy skills (such as reading comprehension, spelling and written vocabulary). However, most studies indicate that they show improvement in these skills after the first year of English-language arts instruction (introduced in grade 3 or 4). In a recent Ontario study, early-immersion students in grade 3 and grade 6 were found to perform as well as their English-school counterparts on English reading and writing skills. In addition, a recent report based on data from the Programme for International Student Assessment (PISA) suggests that 15-year-old French-immersion students perform better on reading assessments than non-immersion English students,* even when tested in English.

Here's where it's crucial to read the asterisk. The Canadian report adds:

* It is important to note that factors other than French-immersion education likely play a role in these differences. These factors include self-selection, parental-educational attainment, and greater availability of immersion programs in more affluent and urban communities where literacy tends to be higher.

This is significant for parents looking at Mandarin immersion because our experience is quite similar in terms of the types of families who are drawn to immersion. In French immersion in Canada: English-speaking students learned to speak, read and write French in almost native fashion, even though they spoke English at home. They were also fully fluent and functional in speaking, reading and writing English.

Parents who wanted their children to be bilingual tended to be more motivated, more activist, more educated and more literate. As a consequence, their children tended to do better in school than children in English-only programs.

The programs were all "one-way," meaning there were no French speakers in them. This allowed teachers to use French at levels that were comprehensible to these non-native students.[4]

Canada and Chinese immersion

However, Canada isn't all about French. Few Americans would immediately name the Canadian prairie city of Edmonton, Alberta as home to North America's largest and most vibrant Mandarin language immersion network. However, that is exactly where you would find it. In 1982 the Edmonton Public School system launched an experimental English-Chinese language program at the kindergarten level. It had 33 students. The program was so successful that the next year, the beginning of the 1983–1984 school year, the district formally established the English-Chinese Bilingual Program. A grade was added each year and the first class of high school seniors graduated in 1995.

By the 2013–2014 school year, the program had grown to include five elementary schools, four junior high schools and three high schools. Over 1,800 students out of the district's 86,500 students are in Mandarin immersion.[5] The entire 12-school program is supported by the Edmonton Chinese Bilingual Education Association,[6] a non-profit, parent-run group.

In grades one through six, students learn English language arts, science and social studies in English. Subjects taught in Chinese are Chinese language arts, mathematics, art, health and physical education. In junior high, which is grades seven through nine in Canada, students take Chinese language arts. In senior high school, grades ten through twelve, they take courses designed to improve listening, speaking, reading, and writing skills, with emphasis on conversational skills. They also study short stories, novels, plays and poetry. In high school, Chinese language arts fulfills the language requirements of the International Baccalaureate (IB) program. Students have the option of taking the IB Chinese exam in twelfth grade.

Edmonton has made a name for itself in China. In 2013 students from Edmonton won first prize in the group category at the sixth annual Chinese Bridge, an international Chinese language and culture competition held in Kunming in Yunnan province.

Edmonton has invested heavily in immersion in other languages as well. The district has 11 French immersion elementary schools, five junior highs and two high schools. There are also four schools offering Arabic immersion, four German, three Spanish, two Ukrainian and one each for Hebrew and American Sign Language. Forty-five out of Edmonton's 202 total schools have immersion programs—22% of schools in the district.

Canada is also home to five Mandarin immersion programs in or near Vancouver, British Columbia; three in Calgary, Alberta; and one in Toronto, Ontario.

The "best kept secret" in education

In the wake of the Canadian experience, this type of immersion education for young children has spread around the world. Swedish-speaking students in Finland are immersed in Finnish, Hungarian speakers in English and Australians in French. English speakers in Ireland, Wales and Hawai'i are immersed in Irish, Welsh and Hawaiian respectively.

Now it is an idea whose time has come in the United States. Immersion is "the best kept secret in this country," says Nancy Rhodes, director of Foreign/World Language Education at the Center for Applied Linguistics in Washington D.C. It offers a remarkable opportunity for students to achieve high levels of ability in another language while still learning the U.S. core academic curriculum. What is surprising to her is simply that there aren't *more* immersion schools.

In the United States, Spanish immersion schools are the most popular by far, with hundreds nationwide. The nation's first Spanish immersion public school program opened in 1971 at Linwood Howe Elementary in Culver City, California. It was originally offered in just one kindergarten classroom. Today two elementary schools in the district offer Spanish immersion to more than 850 students.

Even the White House wants your child to learn Mandarin

Signing your child up for Mandarin immersion at the age of five or six may feel like a complete leap of faith, but it's one more and more parents are taking. Mandarin immersion programs existed in only nine elementary schools prior to the fall of 2000. By the fall of 2014 there were 170 schools offering such programs. While there are an estimated 137,000[7] schools in the United States, it's still a pretty impressive number.

Several things have led to this increase. "One major stimulus is the rising economic and political power of China, which has led many businesses, educators, and parents to request programs that can provide students with much higher levels of proficiency in Chinese," according to a study by the Asia Society, a nonprofit education organization.[8]

Another was the realization that we as a nation had too few people who could take part in the world's conversations. Efforts to change that began to take on urgency after the attacks of September 11, 2001. Lest you think you're off on some quixotic quest to raise bilingual children, know that the White House itself is behind you:

> ...under the direction of the President of the United States, the Secretaries of State, Education and Defense, and the Director of National Intelligence (DNI) have developed a comprehensive national plan to expand U.S. foreign language education beginning in early childhood (kindergarten) and continuing throughout formal schooling and into the workforce with new programs and resources.[9]

Chinese is one of the languages the initiative specifically addresses. Experts realize the real shot at fluency comes from education of grade school and middle school students, and immersion. This is a massive shift because historically Chinese studies in the United States by non-native speakers were only undertaken at the college level. Those programs were created at the turn of the 20th century, in part to teach China-bound missionaries to speak Chinese.

It wasn't until 1957 (Sputnik, anyone?) that more than just a few colleges offered Asian studies programs. Congress passed the National Defense Education Act Title VI of 1958 (now Title VI of the Higher Education Act) in 1958, aimed at bringing non-European languages into U.S. graduate schools.[10] Even so, in 1960 there were only 1,844 students studying Chinese in U.S. colleges. [11]

Chinese studies didn't exist for younger students outside of Saturday schools meant to teach reading and writing to children from Chinese-speaking families. However, in line with the emphasis on teaching non-Western languages in colleges at the time, two foundations began to fund programs at the elementary and high school level in the 1960s, though because immersion didn't exist yet neither promoted it.

The Carnegie Foundation funded seven university centers for teaching Chinese, which in turn supported 200 Chinese programs in high schools in the 1970s. Unfortunately by 1980 only two of these remained.[12] The Geraldine R. Dodge Foundation (of NPR fame) took a different approach beginning in 1983. It established 55 high school Chinese programs, a Secondary School Chinese Language Center at Princeton University, and the Chinese Initiative for Children in 11 elementary schools in New Jersey.[13] However, the Princeton Center ceased to operate in 2002 and it's unclear how many of those elementary and high schools still offer Chinese.

"Neither of these major initiatives has had a lasting effect on Chinese language teaching in the United States in terms of *programs*, although they did have positive effects on introducing the language to American school children," according to the authors of *Teaching and Learning Chinese: Issues and Perspectives.*[14]

A great leap forward in elementary Chinese language teaching came with the creation of the Foreign Language Assistance Program (FLAP)[15] in 1988. It offered school districts grants to fund foreign language instruction in elementary and secondary schools. It was the only federally funded program for foreign language teaching that focused on K–12 schools. It was further expanded in 2006 when the National Security Language Initiative was created, which focused specifically on "critical foreign languages—specifically Arabic, Chinese, Japanese, Korean, Russian and languages in the Indic, Iranian and Turkic families."[16]

Most of the grants funded in 2006 and 2007[17] focused on one of those critical languages, with the majority proposed for Chinese. This perhaps explains the huge leap in Mandarin immersion schools in 2007 (see *Chapter 3: Mandarin Immersion in 2014–2015*) and beyond. Many school districts won FLAP grants to create or build out programs. Examples included Portland, Oregon, which expanded its program from one to two classrooms per year, and San Francisco and Tulsa, which launched Mandarin immersion programs.[18] Unfortunately, the FLAP grant program was eliminated by Congress in 2011 as a budget-cutting measure.[19]

In 2012, of all U.S. college students taking a foreign language, only 4% were studying Chinese. Those numbers are expected to increase in the coming years as interest in China rises. When the College Board asked high schools whether they would be interested in an Advanced Placement Chinese test, 2,400 said yes. The first AP Chinese test was administered on May 19, 2007[20]. In 2013, 12,672 students took the exam.

Another big push came as a result of the National Security Language Initiative, launched in 2006. It was designed to "dramatically increase the number of Americans learning critical need foreign languages such as Arabic,

Chinese, Russian, Hindi, Farsi and others, through new and expanded programs from kindergarten through university and into the workforce."[21] Four different federal agencies sponsored it: the U.S. Departments of Defense, State, Education, and the Office of the Director of National Intelligence.

"An essential component of U.S. national security in the post-9/11 world is the ability to engage foreign governments and peoples, especially in critical regions, to encourage reform, promote understanding, convey respect for other cultures and provide an opportunity to learn more about America and its citizens. To do this, Americans must be able to communicate in other languages, a challenge for which most citizens are totally unprepared."[22]

One of the things to come out of the initiative was the Language Flagship program. These promote the idea of beginning language training early, so that by the time students reach college they are advanced enough to be able to complete course work in the chosen language. The motto of Language Flagship is "global professionals." You can read about how these work for students of Chinese in *Chapter 6: Immersion and Your Child's Academic Career.*

One of those programs went to Brigham Young University, which got $1 million from the National Security Education Program to create the Chinese Flagship Center,[23] which works to implement K–12 Chinese education. You can read more about that below and in *Chapter 22: Immersion Consortia: The Support Schools Need.*

The other player in all this has been the Chinese government, through Hanban and the Confucius Institute. Hanban is the Chinese abbreviation for the 国家汉语国际推广领导小组办公室, the Office of Chinese Language Council International, a non-profit affiliated with the Chinese Ministry of Education. Its mission is to provide Chinese language and cultural teaching resources worldwide. Hanban is very much like Germany's *Goethe Institut*, France's *Alliance Française* and Britian's British Council, all of which promote the study of their respective languages internationally and encourage international cultural exchange and understanding. However Hanban is more directly linked to the Chinese government than the other groups. Hanban also has a large program to bring Chinese teachers to the United States that is used by many immersion schools. There are also 100 Confucius Classrooms nationally, which are model sites for developing Chinese language teaching in the United States.[24]

Being monolingual no longer cuts it

While this push towards Mandarin is gaining ground in the United States, there has been an interesting development in China—it is increasingly taken for granted that foreigners will speak Chinese. When I first began traveling in China in the mid-1980s, merely attempting to say anything more complex than *Ni hao!* (Hello) was greeted with huge enthusiasm by the Chinese people I met. That was still the case as few as 10 years ago. But today, Beijing is awash in college students and recent graduates from the United States and the world over, many of whom speak respectable, and some quite excellent, Chinese.

When visiting in 2012 I had my first experience of interacting with a Chinese person who was surprised I didn't speak Chinese. She put up with my halting efforts to ask directions in Chinese and quickly switched into English. She said she hadn't realized I didn't actually speak Chinese.

"After all, so many Americans are in Beijing," she told me, as if being there presumed one spoke Chinese. Once upon a time it didn't. Today, increasingly, it does.

While English is unlikely to cease to be the world's *lingua franca* any time soon, the days when Americans could confidently presume English was all they would ever need to speak appear to be coming to an end.

1. Asia Society, *Meeting the Challenge: Preparing Chinese language teachers for American Schools*. (New York: Asia Society, 2013) 8.
2. Marjorie Bingham Wesche, "Early French Immersion How has the original Canadian model stood the test of time?" In *An Integrated View of Language Development. Papers in Honor of Henning Wode*, Wissenschaftlicher Verlag (Trier, 2002)
   http://www.fmks-online.de/_wd_showdoc.php?pic=509
   Accessed March 7, 2014
3. Canadian Council on Learning, *Lessons in Learning: French–Immersion Education in Canada*, May 17, 2007.
   http://www.ccl-cca.ca/pdfs/LessonsInLearning/May-17-07-French-immersion.pdf
   Accessed March 7, 2014.
4. Stephen Krashen and Douglas Biber, *On Course: Bilingual Education's Success in California*. (Ontario, Calif., California Association for Bilingual Education. 1988) 30.
5. Edmonton Public Schools Facts and Statistics. 2013–2014.
   http://news.epsb.ca/facts-and-statistics/
   Accessed Feb. 23, 2014.
6. Edmonton Chinese Bilingual Education Association.
   http://www.ecbea.org/index.php
   Accessed March 7, 2014.
7. William Schmidt and Curtis C. McKnight, *Inequality for All: The Challenge of Unequal Opportunity in American Schools*. (New York, The Teachers College Press, 2012) xii.
8. Asia Society, *Chinese in 2008: An Expanding Field*.
   http://asiasociety.org/files/Chinesein2008.pdf
   Accessed March 7, 2014
9. National Security Language Initiative.
   http://www.aplu.org/NetCommunity/Document.Doc?id=50
   Accessed Jan. 14, 2014.

10. Jianguo Chen, Chuang Wang, Jinfa Cai, (eds), "Teaching and learning Chinese: Issues and perspectives," *Chinese American Educational Research and Development Association* (Charlotte, Information Age Publishing, 2010)
11. Shuhan C. Wang, "Sustaining the rapidly expanding Chinese language field," *Journal of the Chinese Language Teachers Association* 47:3 (October 2012): 27.
12. Jianguo Chen, Chuang Wang, Jinfa Cai, (eds) "Teaching and learning Chinese: Issues and perspectives," Chinese American Educational Research and Development Association (Charlotte, Information Age Publishing, 2010)
13. Jianguo Chen, Chuang Wang, Jinfa Cai, (eds) "Teaching and learning Chinese: Issues and perspectives," Chinese American Educational Research and Development Association (Charlotte, Information Age Publishing, 2010)
14. Jianguo Chen, Chuang Wang, Jinfa Cai, (eds) "Teaching and learning Chinese: Issues and perspectives," Chinese American Educational Research and Development Association (Charlotte, Information Age Publishing, 2010) 16.
15. Rebecca Richey, *The Foreign Language Assistance Program (FLAP)*, Learning Languages. (Fall 2007 Volume XIII, Number 1) http://www.ncela.us/files/uploads/2/Richey_FLAP_brochure.pdf Accessed Jan. 14, 2014.
16. Rebecca Richey, *The Foreign Language Assistance Program (FLAP)*, Learning Languages. (Fall 2007 Volume XIII, Number 1) http://www.ncela.us/files/uploads/2/Richey_FLAP_brochure.pdf Accessed Jan. 14, 2014.
17. Rebecca Richey, *The Foreign Language Assistance Program (FLAP)*, Learning Languages. (Fall 2007 Volume XIII, Number 1) http://www.ncela.us/files/uploads/2/Richey_FLAP_brochure.pdf Accessed Jan. 14, 2014.
18. Audra Pace, *FLAP grant provides critical language support programs*, District Administration: Solutions for school district management (March 2010) http://www.districtadministration.com/article/flap-grant-provides-critical-language-support-programs Accessed April 22, 2014.
19. *Speaking in Tongues*, "Foreign Language Assistance Program on the chopping block: A major threat to K–12 language instruction in the U.S. (2011) http://speakingintonguesfilm.info/guest-blogs/foreign-language-assistance-program-on-the-chopping-block-a-major-threat-to-k-12-language-instruction-in-the-us/ Accessed Jan 14, 2014.
20. The College Board, AP Advanced Placement Program, AP Chinese Q & A. http://www.collegeboard.com/prod_downloads/about/news_info/ap/qanda_english.pdf Accessed Jan. 14, 2014.
21. National Security Language Initiative. http://www.aplu.org/NetCommunity/Document.Doc?id=50 Accessed Jan. 14, 2014.
22. National Security Language Initiative. http://www.aplu.org/NetCommunity/Document.Doc?id=50 Accessed Jan. 14, 2014.
23. The Chinese Flagship Center, *K–12 Programs.* http://chineseflagship.byu.edu/k-12 Accessed Jan. 14, 2014.

24. Asia Society, Asia Society Confucius Classroom Network.
http://asiasociety.org/education/chinese-language-initiatives/
asia-society-confucius-classrooms-network
Accessed Jan. 14, 2014.

Mandarin Immersion in 2014–2015

Today, schools that are home to Mandarin immersion programs come in all shapes and sizes and are scattered across the United States. There's Dutchtown Elementary in Hampton, Georgia, Southeast Elementary in Jenks, Oklahoma and Monte Vista Elementary in South Jordan, Utah. You can spend nothing but your energy at Doss Elementary in Austin, Texas or over $40,000 a year at Avenues: The World School in New York City. You can send your child to Martin Luther King Jr. Elementary in Cambridge, Massachusetts, San Francisco's José Ortega Elementary, or Cherokee Elementary in Lake Forest, Ill. The numbers keep growing. By the fall of 2014 there were at least 170 schools[1] in the United States that offered Mandarin immersion programs to K–12 students. Of these, 152 are elementary schools and almost half of the programs were begun in the 2010–2011 school year or later.

While enrollment figures for each program are impossible to come by, even a cautious back-of-the envelope calculation results in a very large national enrollment. A conservative figure of 120 students per program (six classes times 20 students per class) results in 20,400 students sitting in a Mandarin immersion classroom on any given day nationwide. A more reasonable multiplier of 150 students per school (some are higher, some will be lower, so this is a guesstimate average) results in 25,500 students nationwide.

How we got here

The first Mandarin immersion school in the nation, San Francisco's Chinese American International School, opened in 1981. It wasn't until 1991, with the opening of Pacific Rim International School in Emeryville, California, that a second appeared. The next didn't come along until 1996 when the first two were joined by two more, Potomac Elementary in Potomac, Maryland, the nation's first public Mandarin immersion program, and the private International School of the Peninsula in Palo Alto, California. Things stayed somewhat steady, with a few programs opening every year or so. Then in the fall of 2007 immersion took off with an influx of federal funds,[2] with 15 new programs that year and 12 the next. For the nation, it looks like this:

Fall of	Programs founded	Total programs
1981	1	1
1991	1	2
1996	2	4
1997	1	5
1998	3	8
1999	1	9
2000	1	10
2002	2	12
2003	2	14
2004	2	16
2005	3	19
2006	5	24
2007	15	39
2008	12	51
2009	17	68
2010	17	85
2011	22	107
2012	32	138
2013	21	159
2014	11	170

It's easier to see it as a graph, opposite.

These numbers illustrate some interesting trends nationally. Three of the first four Mandarin immersion schools were all in the San Francisco Bay area. That's not surprising. According to the U.S. Census, the area's population was 23% Asian in 2010.[3] In the case of the Chinese American International School in San Francisco (1981), the immersion program came from the desire of a non-Chinese-speaking mother who had adopted a son from Taiwan to give her child the language. San Francisco's 30% Chinese-American population was a major factor in its early success, though now the school is very popular among non-Chinese parents as well.

Originally opened in Berkeley, the Pacific Rim International School (1991) is additionally a Montessori school all the way through high school, emphasizing "joyful, meaningful and integrated learning." That combination of the rigor of learning to read, write and speak Chinese together with the more free-form Montessori method, is perhaps a unique American version of the perfect school.

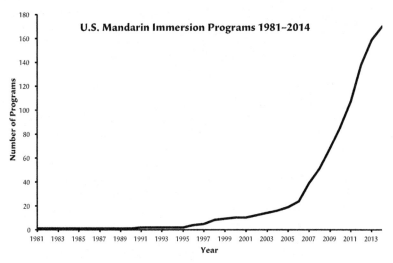

U.S. Mandarin Immersion Programs 1981–2014

(Y-axis: Number of Programs, 0 to 180; X-axis: Year, 1981 to 2013)

The third of the trio, the International School of the Peninsula (1996), originally began as a French language school in 1979. It added a Mandarin immersion track in 1996. That's not uncommon among private immersion schools; they began with another language and then added Chinese when interest began to rise.

Also in 1996, the first public Mandarin immersion program was launched at Potomac Elementary School in Potomac, Maryland. It was very much aimed at high achieving, non-Chinese speaking parents who wanted a "value add" to their children's education.

Add the 1998 opening of public Woodstock Elementary School in Portland, Oregon, and you've got the full range of motivations. Woodstock's program was definitely aimed at getting better-resourced families to look at a school with low test scores and falling enrollment.

During the expansion boom in 2007, California launched five programs in five different school districts. In Minnesota the same thing happened, with four schools opening in four different school districts. In 2008 California started another four programs, and in 2009 four more.

Also notable in 2009 was the launch of Utah's Dual Language Immersion program. That year saw 25 immersion schools open in the state, eight of which offered Mandarin. The state launched another six in 2010, three in 2011, seven in 2012 and two in 2013, bringing the total number of Mandarin immersion schools in Utah to 26. Because its immersion program is coordinated statewide by the Utah State Office of Education, Utah is the single largest curriculum and policy builder in the field of Mandarin immersion in the United States.

The double-digit expansion of new Mandarin immersion programs doesn't appear to be slowing down. In 2012, an astonishing 31 programs launched and 2013 saw the addition of another 21.

Where they are

In 2013 there were Mandarin immersion programs in 26 states and the District of Columbia. California, Utah and New York had the largest number of programs.

Mandarin immersion programs by state:

38	California
28	Utah
12	New York
9	Minnesota
8	Arizona
8	North Carolina
8	Oregon
7	Colorado
7	Maryland
7	Michigan
5	Georgia
5	Illinois
4	Delaware
4	Washington
3	South Carolina
3	Texas
2	Massachusetts
2	New Jersey
2	Wisconsin
1	Idaho
1	Louisiana
1	Missouri
1	Oklahoma
1	Rhode Island
1	Washington D.C.
1	Wyoming

California has the most with 38. Astoundingly, 8% of the state's private schools offered Mandarin immersion, according to data from the California Department of Education's 2012–2013 Private School Affidavit Data.[4]

Next comes Utah with 28. New York has 12, Minnesota nine, North Carolina and Oregon both with eight. From there the numbers fall.

California's programs cluster in the San Francisco Bay and Los Angeles areas, with only a few in the eastern parts of the state. They consist of 51% public schools, 40% private and 8% charters. Utah's programs are all in public schools and scattered statewide, as their program is statewide.

Of Colorado's seven programs, four are at one of the Global Village Academy's campuses, a network of charter schools that launched in Aurora, Colorado in 2007. All of Delaware's four programs are public, part of the state's master plan for world language immersion programs. Minnesota's nine programs are all public while both of New Jersey's are private.

Mandarin immersion by city

New York City has the most programs, with 12. There are schools in Flushing, Brooklyn, Manhattan and Queens. The first was Shuang Wen (Public School 184), a K–8 launched in 1998. Beginning in 2007, the New York City Department of Education started to convert its Chinese bilingual language programs into immersion programs open to both Chinese and English speakers. By 2014 there were seven elementary schools, a middle school and two highly regarded high schools, the Dual Language and Asian Studies High School in Manhattan and Queens High School for Languages Studies. Manhattan is also home to two private programs, Bilinguals Buds and Avenues: The World School.

Portland, Oregon, comes in second for programs, with eight. The city has five elementary schools, two public, one charter and one private. There are also two middle school programs, one public and one private, and a public high school. I have included two schools in the western suburb of Beaverton in this tally. One, the Northwest Chinese Academy, is a private school. The other, Hope Chinese Charter, is a school in the Beaverton School District but has a Portland address.

San Francisco has five programs, offering parents a choice of four different elementary schools, two public and two private, and a public middle school. A public high school program is scheduled to launch in 2015-2016. The private programs are both K–8 while the public schools feed into a public middle school Mandarin program. The city also has six Cantonese immersion public school programs, four in elementary school, one in middle school and one in high school. They are a legacy of the city's strong Cantonese immigrant community and extremely popular, in part because of their high test scores.

Two cities have four programs; Los Angeles, California and Minneapolis/St. Paul, Minnesota. Four cities have three; Atlanta, Georgia; Berkeley, California, Denver, Colorado and Excelsior, Minnesota (Minnetonka Public Schools).

Public or private?

The vast majority of Mandarin immersion programs in the United States are in public schools.

Type	#	%
Public	138	82%
Private	31	18%

With charter schools broken out, the numbers are:

Type	#	%
Public	118	70%
Charter	20	12%
Private	31	18%

An analysis of the types of Mandarin immersion programs launched over time yields interesting results. Half of the first ten programs (1981–2000) were private schools, when there was little knowledge or interest in Mandarin immersion nationally. The next 29 (2001–2007) included 17% charter schools. Most appear to be cases of parents wanting a Mandarin immersion programs for their children but not being able to convince the local school district to create one, so they did it themselves. The final 130 schools (2007–2014) have percentages pretty similar to the entire nation: 72% public, 16% private and 11% charter.

There are three religious schools offering Mandarin immersion in the United States. Zeeland Christian School in Zeeland, Michigan, which will celebrate its 100th anniversary in 2015, offers both Spanish and Mandarin immersion, as well as English. All Souls Catholic School was founded in 1924 and closed its doors in 2010 due to low enrollment. The Archdiocese of Los Angeles, in Alhambra, California, decided to re-open it as the nation's first Catholic dual-language immersion school, offering both a Spanish and a Mandarin track. Reid Temple Christian Academy in Glenn Dale, Maryland launched a Mandarin immersion program for the 2011–2012 school year. The school itself was founded in 2005.

Elementary, middle and high schools

In general, charter and private schools tend to be K–8, while traditional public schools tend to be K–5. In Utah, where kindergarten is not mandatory, many programs are 1–5. Most programs were so new in 2014 that there were just ten middle school programs for Mandarin immersion students, as few had produced a crop of sixth graders. The ones that did exist were in:

- Pasadena, California
- San Francisco, California
- San Jose, California
- Rockville, Maryland
- Minnetonka, Minnesota
- New York City, New York
- Chapel Hill, North Carolina
- Portland, Oregon

High schools with Mandarin immersion programs explicitly linked to K–8 programs, so that the language progression is continuous, are still rare. The only ones I could find with clear progressions were in Portland and New York City. However more are coming. In 2015 both San Francisco, California and Minnetonka, Minnesota, are scheduled to launch program for their newly-graduated eighth graders.

Other programs, such as Potomac, Maryland, simply send their immersion students to the appropriate level of Chinese in the regular foreign language track in high school. Unfortunately, this often means students have only one year of Chinese at their appropriate level in high school before their knowledge surpasses what's offered.

There are four K–12 schools nationally. They are the two Pacific Rim International School campuses in Emeryville and San Mateo, California, Pioneer Valley Chinese Immersion Charter School in Hadley, Massachusetts, and the International School of Indiana in Indianapolis, Indiana.

Percentage of day in Chinese

By definition, a language immersion program must offer at least 50% of its academic day in the target language, in our case Mandarin. Sixty-five percent of U.S. Mandarin immersion elementary school programs teach 50% of the academic day in Mandarin and 50% in English. That figure is based only on schools that contain elementary school programs, as in all programs the percentage of the day taught in Mandarin drops to 30% beginning in middle school. Of the 157 such programs in 2014, 102 were 50/50.

Thirty-five percent of programs offered some variation of a progression that began with more Mandarin in the lower grades and gradually moved to 50% of the day in Mandarin in the upper grades. Some schools begin in kindergarten with 100% of the day in Mandarin, some 90%, some 80%. When they get to 50/50 varies by school.

Trilingual immersion programs tend to offer the largest percentage of the day in Mandarin, followed by a smaller percentage in another language, usually Spanish or French, and a still smaller percentage in English. The thinking seems to be that the most difficult to master language requires the greatest amount of time.

Simplified or traditional

The vast majority of Mandarin immersion programs use simplified characters. These are the less complex form of characters, based on handwriting shortcuts, that were adopted by China in 1964. They are also used in Singapore. Traditional characters, the original and more complex form of characters, are used in Taiwan, Hong Kong and by many in the Chinese diaspora.

Of the 170 programs open in 2014, 84% (143) used simplified in 2014, while 15% (26) used traditional. Private schools were the most likely to teach traditional characters, with 31% using the older forms. In public schools, the number was only 11%.

Some programs teach both, beginning with one or the other in the early grades and then gradually introducing the other form in the upper grades. In these programs, students are generally expected to be able to read both but write only one.

Strand versus whole school

Most Mandarin immersion programs are strands within a larger school. That means the school has multiple classes per grade level, some of which are in the immersion program and some of which are part of the school's regular English-language program. For example, at José Ortega Elementary in San Francisco, each grade has three classes. One of them is a Mandarin immersion classroom and two are "General Education," the district term for plain-vanilla English language instruction.

About 15% of immersion programs are in whole school environments, meaning the entire school is devoted to Mandarin instruction.

In breaking down strand versus whole school, I removed middle and high schools, as none of them are whole school environments. I looked instead at the K–5, K–8 and K–12 schools.

Out of the 158 schools that begin Mandarin immersion in kindergarten or first grade, 85% (135) are strands within a larger school.

One-way and two-way immersion

Immersion programs come in two types, one-way and two-way. One-way means the program is set up to teach English speakers the "target language" (in our case Mandarin.) Two-way means the program is meant to go both ways. Students who enter speaking only Mandarin will learn English, while students who come in speaking only English will learn Mandarin.

Schools adopt two-way immersion when they have a large cohort of English language learners (ELLs in education-speak). Most Spanish immersion programs are two-way, because most U.S. communities have Spanish-speaking students who need to learn English. Most Mandarin immersion programs are one-way because few communities have enough Mandarin speakers to make up half the students.

Of Mandarin immersion schools, 83% are one-way programs (131) and 17% (27) are two-way. This is based on the same set of K–5, K–8 and K–12 schools I use above, as the issue doesn't really exist in middle or high schools.

However, these numbers are somewhat deceptive. A true two-way program has a balance of English and Chinese speakers. Many two-way programs seek an ideal mix of 33% Mandarin speakers, 33% English speakers and 33% bilinguals. Few programs in the United States meet that ideal configuration, though some in New York City and the San Francisco Bay area come close.Not surprisingly, given that according to the 2010 U.S. Census 36.2% of Chinese immigrants lived in California, the majority of two-way schools are in that state. California is home to 46% of two-way programs.[5]

However, although 27 programs actively describe themselves as two-way, it's unlikely they truly have an even mix of Mandarin and English speakers. This is in stark contrast to most Spanish immersion programs in the United States, which are typically fully two-way, offering the chance for Spanish-speaking students to learn English and English-speaking students to learn Spanish.

Utah is a special case. There, the immersion programs are explicitly designed to be two-way, but because of the low number of Mandarin-speaking students in Utah school they are de facto one-way.

Multi-language schools

There are 37 schools that offer Mandarin and another language through immersion. Spanish is the most popular, with 27 schools offering both. French is next with 12 schools offering both, followed by Japanese with six, German with five, Russian with three and Vietnamese with 1. Almost all have names that use the words as "international" or "language," rather than Chinese. Eighteen of these are private, twelve are charter schools and six are public.

There are several schools that offer three or more languages. Combinations include:

Mandarin, Spanish, Japanese
Mandarin, Spanish, Russian
Mandarin, Spanish, French, Japanese
Mandarin, Spanish, French, Russian
Mandarin, Spanish, French, German
Mandarin, French, German, Japanese

The International Baccalaureate

Internationally, the IB program is known as a rigorous curriculum recognized by universities around the world. It was originally created in private schools in Switzerland in 1968 as a way for international secondary schools to set standards so universities would have a better sense of the qualification of their graduates. It is known for strong academics and an emphasis on creative and critical thinking. Schools in the United States have adopted it to offer rigor and depth. When graduating from high school, students receive an IB diploma

The IB program exists in three forms. The Diploma Programme for students in the final two years of high school, the Middle Years Programme for students aged 11 to 16, and the Primary Years Programme for students aged 3 to 12

As of 2014, 14 schools that offered Mandarin immersion programs also offered IB programs. It is not surprising that these two programs overlap as both are attractive to families that value education and an internationally-focused curriculum.

The future

For 2015–2016, six new Mandarin immersion programs in schools have been announced. In Jenks, Oklahoma the program has reached middle school and in Minnetonka it will have reached high school. San Francisco's public Mandarin immersion program will also reach high school in the 2015-2016 school year but the site of the program had not yet been announced by the time this was written. Coming programs include:

- Global Ambassadors Language Academy, Cleveland, Ohio, Charter
- Global Renaissance School, Saratoga Springs, New York, Private
- Global Village Academy, Douglas County, Colorado, Charter
- Minnetonka High School, Minnetonka, Minnesota, Public
- Sino-Trojan Academy at East Intermediate School. Jenks, Oklahoma, Public

More are sure to come. But adding these six brings the total of Mandarin immersion program in the United States to 176 by the fall of 2015–2016. Presuming 150 students per program, that's almost 27,000 students nationwide studying at least 50% of the day in Mandarin.

Cantonese immersion here, Chinese immersion worldwide

In addition to Mandarin immersion, there are seven Cantonese immersion schools in the United States, including three elementary schools, one K–8 school, a middle school and one high school. All but one are within the San Francisco Unified School District. West Portal Elementary School's Cantonese immersion program, the first in the world, was launched as a strand at the school in 1984. Sacramento, California's Elder Creek Elementary School also offers Cantonese immersion. That program began in 2011.

Internationally, schools are difficult to find outside Asia. Australia is home to at least three Mandarin immersion programs and Budapest has one, the *Magyar-Kinai Altalanos Iskola*.[6] A Chinese-English bilingual free school, to be called the Marco Polo Academy, will open in North London in the fall of 2014.

Singapore schools offer a Mandarin strand for students coming from Mandarin background families. See *Chapter 24: Going to School in Singapore* for more details. Hong Kong is home to multiple private schools that teach in both English and Mandarin. Immersion schools for both English-speaking and Mandarin-speaking students are beginning to emerge in China, mostly in cities such as Beijing and Shanghai.

Coming soon

It's difficult to know if Mandarin will continue to be a strong part of the U.S. educational system, as Spanish and French are today, or if it will peak and then fall away as Japanese and German have done. Given that U.S. parents are beginning to realize the worth of speaking two languages, coupled with China's ever-growing place on the world stage, it seems unlikely there will be anything but growth in the foreseeable future. Only a lack of teachers, because there are few teacher training programs that feature Chinese immersion as an area of specialization, seems likely to slow the introduction of new programs.

1. Please note that there exists no master, "official" list of immersion schools in the United States, or internationally, for that matter. I have been keeping a list of these schools since 2007 and have attempted to include them all. However

information is often not readily available. If I have missed a school, my apologies. Feel free to contact me to update and correct the current listings. You can find the current listing here: http://miparentscouncil.org/full-mandarin-immersion-school-list/

2. See *Chapter 2: A History of Language Immersion.*

3. Metropolitan Transportation Commission, "Bay Area Census San Francisco Bay area." http://www.bayareacensus.ca.gov/bayarea.htm Accessed Nov. 9, 2013.

4. California Department of Education, "Private Schools." http://www.cde.ca.gov/ds/si/ps/index.asp Accessed May 20, 2014.

5. The Asian Population: 2010, "2010 Census Briefs," March 2012. http://www.census.gov/prod/cen2010/briefs/c2010br-11.pdf Accessed April 22, 2014.

6. Thanks to Joan Fang, whose son attends the Mandarin immersion program at Bergeson Elementary in the Capistrano Unified School District in Orange County. She volunteered to input the schools the Mandarin Immersion Parents Council had collected into a spreadsheet. Her work made it possible to analyze information about the programs. Thanks also to the database of the Center for Applied Linguistics in Washington D.C., which contributed to the list.

How Mandarin Immersion Works

Mandarin immersion means that students don't just learn Mandarin, they learn *in* Mandarin. They don't have a Mandarin class; they have classes *in* Mandarin—math class, science class, social studies class, art class—all taught entirely in Mandarin Chinese. Their Mandarin teachers will use no English in the classroom. They don't learn fractions, they learn 分数, *fēnshù.* That's the difference between immersion and the one-class-a-day language program you had in high school.

Immersion has a very specific definition in education:[1]

- Students are taught subjects in Mandarin for at least 50% of the school day in elementary school.

- Teachers are fully proficient in the language they use for instruction (i.e. either English or Mandarin.)

- Support for English is strong and present in the community at large.

- Mandarin and English are clearly and constantly separated during instructional time. Teachers use one language or the other, but never both, in class.

In a standard U.S. elementary school, most students have a single classroom and a single teacher for the entire school day. In immersion schools students typically have two teachers, one who teaches in Mandarin and one who teaches in English. Depending on the school's immersion model the students might spend 50 to 90% of their day with the Mandarin teacher learning regular elementary school subjects in Mandarin: language arts, math and social studies, etc. Except that the language arts is Mandarin language arts. For English time they switch to a different classroom and an English-speaking teacher, who teaches them English language arts and whatever other subjects their school teaches in English.

Some programs begin with 100% immersion and English isn't introduced until second or third grade. Sixty-five percent begin with half the school day in Mandarin and half in English. Even in an elementary class considered 100% immersion, subjects like gym, music and art are generally taught in English.

Can students who don't arrive at school speaking Mandarin actually learn in Mandarin? And more importantly, if they learn material in Mandarin can they make use of it in English? The answers are yes and yes, though parent support helps this process a great deal as we'll see.

All the research shows immersion really does work. There's ample evidence that what a child learns in one language is available to them in another.[2] Children can and do learn concepts in one language and then access that information in another. It sounds like an academic question until you sit down with your third grader and realize that he's learning division in Mandarin and can easily tell you what 27 divided by 3 is when you ask him in English, even though he learned it in Mandarin. However, he might not be able to *explain* division to you in English. If they can add in Mandarin, they understand addition. If they learned they have to raise their hand before they ask a question in class in Mandarin, they know it no matter what language their teacher is speaking. If they learn mixing red and blue makes purple, they know the concept in both languages.

What *is* different, however, is even when they understand a concept, they don't always have the vocabulary to explain it in both languages. This is where parents come in. When our younger daughter was in third grade we spent a week or so in the spring going through a packet of math questions for the standardized test all public school students in our state take each year. The test, and practice questions, were in English. She'd been studying math since kindergarten but it had all been in Mandarin.

One of the questions was, "Which of these shapes is a pentagon?" Below were drawings of three different shapes.

"That one's a *sānjiǎoxíng*, that one's a *liùbiānxíng* and that's a *wǔjiǎoxíng*," she said, pointing to the triangle, the hexagon and the pentagon. She knew the geometric forms and could easily have passed the test—except the test was in English.

What she *didn't* know was the English word for 五角形, or *wǔjiǎoxíng*.

Thankfully, that was easily fixed. I asked her what *wǔjiǎo* meant and she correctly said it meant "five sides." *Xíng*, she told me, meant "shape."

All I had to do was tell her that "penta" meant five. Then I asked her which shape was a pentagon. "五角形! That's a pentagon," she told me.

We all learned to speak through immersion

Whether in Mandarin, Spanish, French or any other tongue, language immersion programs make use of children's innate ability to learn languages. Put a child with people who only speak to each other and to the child in a given language and that child will learn the language. Immersion simply means being surrounded—immersed—in a language so that you begin to pick it up. It is a skill innate to all humans, we are born primed to learn language.

To a baby, it doesn't matter if mom is speaking English, Mandarin or Romanian, it's a language and they begin to babble in it between four and six months. It's not about sounds: it's about communication. Babies raised by parents who use sign language babble with their hands. The progression is steady. Around a year or so babies start saying their first words: mama, dada, milk. They use these to request, demand or exclaim. By 18 months they typically know between five and 20 words.[3]

At age 2 most toddlers have learned about 150 to 300 words and start using two- or three-word phrases like "give milk!" or "pick up!" By age 3 they know between 900 to 1,000 words. They still can't say much, but their "receptive ability"—their ability to understand what is said—is excellent. If you tell a 2½-year-old, "Go to the table and get the red ball and bring it to Daddy," he or she will be able to do it. That doesn't mean he or she could say that sentence, just understand it.

This difference between *productive*, or spoken, and *receptive* language is something that you'll see a lot of in immersion. Students have much higher levels of receptive than they do productive language. In first grade you might hear a teacher say this in Mandarin, "Okay children, today we're going to talk about the seeds we planted last week. Can I get two volunteers to go over to the windowsill and bring the milk cartons on the green trays over so we can take a look and see if our seeds have sprouted?"

Not one of those students, whether they speak Mandarin or English at home, could say that paragraph. But they would understand it well enough that any of them could do exactly what the teacher asked and know what they were going to do that day.

Back to our toddlers. At this point, they do not understand all the individual words they hear and how they're composed into sentences. They just know that if you want X, you say Y. When our daughters were this age, they would always put their arms up and say, "Carry you!" They meant, "Pick me up and carry me!" That's because when we asked if they wanted to be carried, we always said, "You want me to carry you?" They got the important parts—*you* and *carry*—and figured out pretty early on if they said those words, they'd get picked up.

Between ages 4 and 5 vocabulary makes a big leap. Children at 4 use between 1,500 and 1,600 words and compose four-to six-word sentences. They start to use articles like "a" and "an" and "the," as well as more adjectives, adverbs and conjunctions. They're beginning to sound fluent, in a child-like way.

By the beginning of kindergarten most children know more than 2,000 words.[4] Once they enter school their language takes off; it's estimated school-age children learn about 3,000 new words per year.[5]

They accomplish this without being "taught" how to speak by a teacher or sitting down in a class and learning grammar. This is why many researchers don't use the phrase "language learning" but rather "language acquisition," because children don't learn languages, they acquire them.

Immersion is a brilliant way of taking advantage of this baseline human ability. If you take a 5-year-old and have her spend three, four or five hours a day with an adult who only speaks to her in Mandarin (or German or Punjabi or Swahili), she will start speaking that language without an accent, just as she learned to speak the language her parents speak to her at home. That, in a nutshell, is how immersion schools work. Beginning in kindergarten, students spend between half to all their school day with teachers who speak only to them in Mandarin.

This is not effortless, mind you. But learning to speak their home language wasn't effortless either. Anyone who's spent time with a 2-year-old throwing a tantrum because he can't make you understand what he wants with his limited language will realize this. Learning a language is tiring. It's work for kids when they're 2, it's work for kids when they're in kindergarten and it's work in any language they encounter.

But they have a talent for it.

What does it look like in the classroom?

From the day your child enters school, teachers in their classes that are in Mandarin will speak to them only in Mandarin. They'll speak just as you'd talk to a toddler, in short, simple sentences with lots of hand motions and acting out. Remarkably quickly, the students will be learning not just Mandarin, but normal school subjects (in Mandarin), such as math, science and social studies, depending on your school's program.

This is what sets immersion apart from traditional language classes. As two of the experts in the field, Myriam Met, an immersion consultant, and Chris Livaccari, the former director of the Asia Society's Chinese Language Initiatives and current Chinese Program director at the International School of the Peninsula in Palo Alto, put it:

> There is no better way to learn a language successfully in a school context than in an immersion program. Since the language teacher and the content-area teacher are one in the same, students are exposed to a much richer palette of language and a more sophisticated range of concepts than they would be in traditional foreign language programs.[6]

To start, teachers use what's called "comprehensible input." This is a teaching method in which students are surrounded with spoken language, almost all of which they can quickly understand, so they don't feel lost. To facilitate that understanding, the teachers use what's called Total Physical Response or the Natural Approach, in which they act things out in an exaggerated way, making their meaning clear—pretty much what you do when you're talking to a baby or a toddler who's just learning to speak.

When the teachers use new words or grammatical structures, the students naturally figure them out from context, just as babies work out what all the grown-ups around them are talking about merely by listening. This is very different from how languages traditionally are taught, with vocabulary and rules memorized and then practiced until they become automatic.

It's also a lot more fun. For example, this is what the first day of kindergarten might look like:

小朋友，你们好吗。

Xiǎopéngyǒu, nǐmen hāo ma.

Hello children (literally "little friends"), how are you?

The teacher smiles, is very welcoming.

请进来。

Qǐng jìnlái.

Please come in.

The teacher uses her arms to usher the children into the classroom.

把你们的书包放在这里。

Bǎ nǐmen de shūbāo fàng zài zhèlǐ.

Put your backpacks here.

With a big smile she takes a backpack from one of the children to show everyone what it is.

书包

Shūbāo

Backpack.

She holds up the backpack and has them all say the word several times. A Mandarin-speaking child (or one who's got older siblings in the school) says very proudly, "书包 means backpack. She means backpack. We put our backpacks over there!"

请你们坐在这里。

Qǐng nǐmen zuò zài zhèlǐ.

Please sit down here.

She sits down cross-legged on the rug at the front of the room and pats the spaces on either side of her.

这里!

Zhèlǐ!

Here!

Here! Here! She says, waiting for the first child to sit down next to her. When one does, she beams.

好!

Hǎo!

Good!

She smiles broadly.

Your child is just 10 minutes into Mandarin immersion and has already learned to understand these words and phrases:

Come in

Backpack

Good

Here

By the end of kindergarten, students will be able to follow complex stories and understand most of the words they hear, or figure the others out from context. That's exactly where they'd be in English instruction as well. Adults use all sorts of words that 5-year-olds don't understand. Kids tend to ignore the ones they don't know and pay attention to the ones they do, unless it's really clear they're missing something, in which case they demand an explanation. If you asked most kindergarteners in an English language classroom the meaning of what every single word their teacher said in the course of a day, they probably couldn't tell you a good number of them.

By April, the teacher in a Mandarin class is passing out pictures from the book and asking questions like these, in Mandarin:

"Who has the picture with the boat? (Student raises hand and shows the pictures.) "Right, Jet has the picture with the boat. Who has the picture with the trees? Right, Sabrina has the picture with the trees."[7]

The students aren't expected to speak a lot here. They're just expected to understand and answer with Mandarin words they know. So a classroom discussion might look like this:

"Who has red hair in our class?" the teacher asks.

"Leo," a couple of children might say.

"Leo has red hair. It's redder than Eleanor's in fourth grade," a child from a Mandarin-speaking family might answer.

"You're right, Leo has red hair," the teacher says. To the Mandarin-speaker she says, "I think Leo's hair is redder than Eleanor's hair, too!"

Some words to the wise

Your child may know "backpack" and "sit here" and "Whose lunchbox is this?" but that doesn't mean they're suddenly fluent speakers of Mandarin. Students in immersion, especially in the early grades, don't talk a lot. It's the difference between *productive* and *receptive* language again. Stephen Krashen, an expert on language acquisition, writes:

> Children often go through a silent period of several months before they begin to speak a new language. This silent period is a time during which they are building competence in the second language—when they begin to speak, it is not the beginning of their acquisition, just the beginning of showing off their competence. This idea also helps explain the feeling of uneasiness many people have in language classes when they are asked to speak in the second language right away.[8]

So don't expect that your child will suddenly be able to chatter away on demand with waiters in Chinese restaurants. I've been guilty of that myself. Our children are not trained seals. Give your kids—and the waiters—a break and don't ask them to perform in Mandarin until they do it on their own. In French immersion schools in Canada, students are not required to start speaking in French until the middle of first grade, giving them a year and a half "silent period" for it all to soak in, just as babies soak in language for a year or two before they begin speaking.

Do you see the theme here? If you let nature take its course, children will pick up the language all by themselves, as long as they're exposed to enough of it. No need for us to push them along—they'll get there on their own.[9]

Ssshhh. Don't tell!

A big "secret" in many immersion schools (at least to the kindergarteners) is that the Mandarin teachers actually do know how to speak English. Some parents, watching their little 5-year-old go off to an immersion classroom, wonder if the teacher can't just speak a *little* bit of English to help the child along. However, Mandarin teachers work hard to never speak English in front of their students, especially at the beginning of the year. This teaches the students they have to speak in Mandarin to their beloved, but sadly "monolingual," teacher to be understood. So you might ask a question as a parent in front of some students and the teacher will answer you in Mandarin, asking the children to translate. Or the teacher might wave for you to step away from the children so she can speak English freely. Many classrooms have signs (in English) that say, "Chinese only here, please!" to remind parents.

This is important and it's not just for show. If students realize their teachers speak English, they'll feel free to use English words when they can't think of the Mandarin ones. It trains them that they can "get away" with not using Mandarin, and that's a bad habit to get into. When they were babies learning English at home, they had to find a word their parents could understand, and they got rewarded by huge smiles, praise and the ability to communicate. They couldn't just blurt out a word in Swahili and get what they wanted. Your child's Mandarin teacher is doing exactly the same thing you did when you had a baby at home. So do your part and don't let the cat out of the bag.

There is another reason for Chinese speakers to never use English in the classroom. Speaking English sends a subtle and possibly more damaging message, say researchers who observed Chinese language classes in England. It teaches students that English is the language of authority and that English has more social importance than Chinese. In the end, they concluded, any English in the classroom "helps to reinforce the status of English as the dominant language of society."[10]

Remember the goal of immersion is to make students realize Chinese is a valid method of communication—so valid, in fact, that one of every seven people on the planet uses it. So, no English during Chinese time!

This isn't your high school Spanish class

As you can see, immersion schools don't teach language the way most of us learned it in high school or college, with translations and grammar and vocabulary lists to memorize and verb conjugations to drill. But if you were to attend a language class today, chances are it would look a lot like what these kindergarteners are doing. Language experts have come to the conclusion that this kind of teaching, being immersed in language you can understand for the most part, is the best way to acquire a language. As Krashen says:

> Memorizing vocabulary words, studying grammar and doing drills make a very small contribution to language competence in the adult and even less in the child—the only true cause of second-language acquisition is comprehensible input.[11]

You won't find your child coming home with pages of translations to do or grammar exercises to complete. Instead, their exercises will be the same kinds of things that children in China or Taiwan get. This doesn't mean they won't be taught Chinese grammar. They will be, just as they're taught grammar in English (during English language arts class,) but only to explain difficult parts that aren't readily apparent.

For example, we don't spend a lot of time teaching English-speaking children that in English the subject comes first and then the verb and then the object (i.e. She saw the cat). They know that just from talking. Instead, we teach them things that are less clear, such as when to use "lay" and when to use "lie," or the rules for when you use "who" and "whom."

Chinese has these same sorts of persnickety grammar bits kids have to learn, especially in writing. One that trips up a lot of students (in China as well as the U.S.) is when to use 的, 得 and 地 —all of which are pronounced *de*.

The first one, 的 *de,* indicates a possessive. It's like adding "apostrophe s" to a word. For example "Dave 的书" *Dave de shu* means "Dave's book."

The second one, 得, is used to make complements. These are constructions that "show the duration, quantity, degree, result, direction or possibility of an action," according to *A Practical Chinese Grammar for Foreigners.* So 走得慢 *zǒu de màn,* means "walks slowly."

Then there's 地, which also can help mark an adverb. So 慢慢地说, *màn màn de shuō,* means "talk slowly." To further confuse matters, it is also sometimes pronounced as *di.*

But unlike when I was studying Chinese, the teachers won't lecture about the use of 着 *zhe,* the "continuous dynamic event" in Chinese. Your child will simply know that when you put 着, *zhe,* after a verb it means that whatever's happening is still happening. It's kind of like adding –ing to an English verb.

Just because they can't translate doesn't mean they're not learning

The hard part for parents who don't speak Chinese is that our kids aren't taught how to translate between the two languages. That's a very separate skill from learning to speak, read and write, and it's not part of the immersion curriculum. If your child understands everything the teacher is saying, he or she is doing great. The problem comes when they can't translate what they know into English. Too often parents think this means they don't know anything at all, but they do. Here's an example of how that works in real life:

Scene: Mother and daughter on the couch on a Sunday afternoon.
Fourth grader: "I need to *fùxí* (review) for my test tomorrow."

Mom knows the drill. Her daughter has to make sure she can correctly write each of the characters the class was assigned this week. Students in China get exactly the same kind of homework. "Okay, where's your character list?" she asks.

Fourth grader: "Here it is. I need to know all of them."

Mom takes a deep breath, then tries her best to approximate the *pinyin* tones written next to each of the characters on the paper her daughter just handed her. Over long years of helping them study, her children have learned to understand which tone she means by the way she says a word, though it's highly unlikely an actual Mandarin speaker would hear anything but a cat being strangled. "*Piāo*," she says.

Fourth grader writes 飘, which is correct.

Mom: "What does that mean?"

Fourth grader ponders: "You know, like a leaf *piāo's* down from a tree?" She waves her hands in a fluttering motion.

Mom realizes her daughter knows exactly what the word means so she lets it go, but resolves to look it up later online. When she does, she finds it is translated as "flutter."

Ninety percent of what goes on is invisible to parents

Immersion teaching is "the hardest kind of teaching there is," says immersion expert Myriam Met. In fact, a major study currently underway in immersion schools in Portland, Oregon found "in most cases, principals perceive dual-language immersion teachers to be among the strongest teachers in their buildings."[12]

Unfortunately, much of that complexity is lost on parents who don't understand Mandarin, sometimes leading them to believe their kids aren't actually learning much. This is despite the fact that the students aren't just learning Mandarin and they aren't just learning math or science: they are learning both *at the same time*. But from the outside it can look as if nothing is happening when actually a great deal is being taught.

For example, one November the third graders at our school's Mandarin program learned a song about a mother frog looking for her tadpole. All the parents dutifully came to class for a presentation and watched the kids squirm around on the floor like tadpoles while the girl playing the mother frog croaked and sang. Each in turn came up and described themselves and then the mother frog said "You're not my tadpole." Finally she found her tadpole and they all lived happily ever after.

We left thinking, "That was lovely," but with no idea what we'd actually seen.

A few months later I attended a workshop led by master Chinese immersion teachers who demonstrated this exact same lesson. I realized the play the students performed was like an iceberg—90% of what they had learned was invisible to the watching parents. Here's what was actually happening:

Two weeks before the performance, the third grade Mandarin teachers began teaching the students about the life cycle of frogs, a general part of the third grade science curriculum. They learned vocabulary such as amphibian, life cycle, egg, tadpole, froglet and frog. They also learned environment words like swamp, pond, algae and habitat. They drew pictures of the life cycle and watched videos of tadpoles becoming frogs.

Grammar was also being taught, invisibly. They were learning to use sequence in narration, words like *first, then, after, finally*.

So the lesson might sound something like this, only in Chinese:

First, all frogs start as eggs. Then, these eggs become tadpoles. Next, the tadpoles grow two back legs. Later, they grow two front legs. The tail shrinks while the legs grow. When the tail is done shrinking, then they are young frogs. Finally, they grow more and become adult frogs. The life cycle of a frog takes approximately sixteen weeks.

Next the teachers read them the story about the mother frog searching for her tadpole. Now that they had the vocabulary, the students could integrate all the science they had learned into a Mandarin language story.

For the final part of the unit she had them write a play based on the story that was read to them. This allowed them to work on writing. She wrote the key words up on the board so they could refer to them, along with important phrases they might use. This is a technique in immersion education called "scaffolding," using phrases to help students build longer and more complicated sentences.

By the time the parents were sitting at the back of the room watching a play most of them couldn't understand, the students had had two full weeks of science, vocabulary, writing practice and speaking practice. All that was invisible to us. The only thing we understood were the words on the program, "Mother Frog Searches for her Tadpole."

I still have one of my daughter's assignments from that lesson. It is a paper plate divided into sections. On each wedge she drew what a frog looks like during a given part of its life cycle, and the word for that part of the life cycle in Chinese next to it. When it came home in her backpack I had no idea at all what it meant. All I knew is that she was very proud of the googly eyes she'd glued on the drawing of the froglet and liked to shake it so I could see that they moved.

Sheltered subject matter

The tadpoles are a good example of how most subjects are taught in school, in English and every other language. Lessons are integrated into the broader curriculum and made interesting and inviting, with lots of hands-on activities. There's very little sitting at your desk and memorizing in today's U.S. schools.

That said, immersion classes are taught somewhat differently in that teachers use what's called "sheltered subject matter." This is where programs use more carefully chosen language to teach a given topic than a regular textbook might. For example, a fourth grade English language textbook on social studies and the arrival of Christopher Columbus might presume a certain level of vocabulary on the part of students. But if you translate that textbook into Chinese, the vocabulary would be too advanced for students in immersion. For that reason, programs try to create "sheltered" readings and worksheets in Chinese that are easier for students to understand while still covering all the necessary information.

The material is not "Simple Math" or "Simple Science." It is math and science, just taught with a slightly more constrained vocabulary to make sure students understand the full lesson.

A whole new world for parents

Signing up for immersion means your child will quickly become an expert in something in which you (most likely) have no expertise. You'll find yourself having many conversations in which your child will say something you simply have to take on faith. For example, this morning my fifth grader was working on her homework. She looked up and asked, "What's a sentence with 'sail' in it?"

This is the kind of question you'll hear a lot. Most Chinese immersion students get weekly worksheets in which they have to practice writing a character or a word and then write a sentence using that word. My kids usually are fine at writing the sentence in Chinese, they just can't think of anything to say. So it's pretty common to have someone shout from the kitchen, "Mama! What's a sentence with "tie" in it?" Then you've got to ask, "Do you mean 'tie' like, 'Tie your shoe or you'll trip over the lace,' or 'tie' like, 'Daddy wears a tie to work some days'?"

In this instance, my exciting sentence suggestion was, "We couldn't get the sail up so the boat wouldn't go."

"Mama! In the Chinese language, 航行 is a 动词, not a 名词. 帆 is a 名词," she admonished me.

Translated, that means "Mama! In the Chinese language, *hángxíng* (to sail) is a *dòngcí* (a verb), not a *míngcí* (a noun.) *Fān* is the noun."

"Fine," I said. "When we were sailing, I fell in the water."

1. "Definition of Terms," Center for Advanced Research on Language Acquisition, University of Minnesota. 2004. http://www.carla.umn.edu/conferences/past/immersion/terms.html Accessed Feb. 23, 2014.

2. Kenji Hakuta, *Mirror of language: The debate on bilingualism.* (New York, Basic Books, 1987)

3. "Language Development in Children," *Child Development Institute.* http://childdevelopmentinfo.com/child-development/ language_development/ Accessed Jan. 14, 2014.

4. "Age-Appropriate Speech and Language Milestones," Lucile Packard Children's Hospital at Stanford. http://www.lpch.org/DiseaseHealthInfo/HealthLibrary/growth/aaslm.html Accessed Jan. 14, 2014.

5. Stephen Krashen and Douglas Biber, *On Course: Bilingual Education's Success in California.* (Ontario, California, California Association for Bilingual Education, 1988) 29.

6. Myriam Met and Chris Livaccari, "Basics of Program Design," *Chinese Language Learning in the Early Grades: A handbook of resources and best practices for Mandarin immersion* (New York, Asia Society, 2012) 16.

7. Stephen Krashen, *Foreign Language Education: The Easy Way*, (Culver City, Calif., Language Education Associates, 1997) 11.

8. Stephen Krashen, "Immersion: why it works and what it has taught us," *Language and Society.* 61–62.

9. We'll see in later chapters that there's a great deal parents can to do heighten that exposure to Chinese, which will turbocharge language acquisition.

10. L.I. Wei, Chao-Jung Wu, "Code-switching: Ideologies and Practices," in *Chinese as a Heritage Language: Fostering Rooted World Citizenry.* Agnes Weiyun He and Yun Xiao (eds) (University of Hawai'i at Manoa. National Foreign Language Resource Center, 2008) 235.

11. Stephen Krashen, "Immersion: Why it works and what it has taught us," *Language and Society,* 61.

12. Jennifer L. Steele, Jennifer, "The Effect of Dual-Language Immersion on Student Achievement in Math, Science, and English Language Arts." RAND Corporation, Society for Research on Educational Effectiveness, Fall 2013 Conference Abstract. http://www.sree.org/conferences/2013f/program/downloads/abstracts/984.pdf Accessed April 23, 2014

五
wǔ
5

How Immersion Programs Are Structured

Immersion programs are organized differently from the elementary schools most of us attended. As you begin considering a school, it's helpful to understand the various program structures and terminology you're likely to hear.

Program models

This sounds complicated but it's simple. "Program model" refers to how much class time students spend in Mandarin and how much in English. Most U.S. immersion programs were originally modeled after the Canadian immersion system, meant for students from English-speaking homes who were learning French. In those programs, students started out with 100% of their school day in French. English wasn't introduced until second or third grade, with the amount of class time in French slowly decreasing until it reached 50% by the end of elementary school.[1] This was possible because French immersion programs in Canada are only open to English speakers. They're meant for English speaking children who want to learn French, not French students who wanted to learn English.

The language-learning situation is a little different in the United States and here programs vary how much of each language they start with, though all programs end up at 50/50 by the end of grade school, with two classes in middle school and one or two high school.

In most U.S. elementary schools, students usually have a single teacher and stay in the same room all day, with the teacher switching from math to English to social studies and other topics over the course of a day. In immersion schools, students usually have two teachers, one who teaches only in Mandarin and one who teaches only in English. Often two classes in the same grade will swap classrooms, spending half the day in the Chinese classroom and then after lunch moving to their English classroom, or vice versa. That only works if the program is 50/50.

In schools that start out with 90 or 100% Chinese, their English time might be taught by a native English speaker or it might be taught by a different Mandarin-speaking teacher teaching in English. Most programs have a rule that no teacher who teaches Mandarin to students will ever be required to teach them in English as well—it's too easy for students to start using English with the teacher during Mandarin time.

There are some programs that call themselves immersion but are actually what is more appropriately called FLES (Foreign Language in Elementary School). These teach less than 50% of the day in Mandarin. That's the case in the Immersion in Mandarin Achieves Gains in Education (IMAGE) program in the Englewood Public Schools in New Jersey. Students in the program spend 90 minutes per day in a Mandarin language classroom, about 25% of their school day. In Detroit, at the Foreign Language Immersion and Cultural Studies School, students get about two hours taught in Mandarin (Spanish, French and Japanese are also options.) However teachers also use English in the classroom when students are having difficulty understanding the material in the target language. So while very ambitious FLES programs, neither are actually immersion.

Three program models

100% to start

Some programs begin with 100% of the academic day taught in Mandarin, though art, music and PE are generally taught in English. The Minnetonka public schools and the Denver Language School, both public programs, use this model. It works because all their incoming students are English speakers. Some educators call these programs "full immersion." You can read more about Minnetonka's program in *Chapter 21: School Profiles, Minnetonka.*

80/20

In 80/20 programs, kindergarten and first grade students spend 80% of their instructional day in Chinese and 20% in English. Most subjects are taught in Chinese. English time is devoted to reading and writing English. In second grade, students receive 70% of their instruction in Chinese and 30% in English; in third grade, 60% is in Chinese and 40% is in English. By fourth and fifth grades, the students' instructional time is balanced between English and Chinese, and students continue to receive formal language arts instruction in both languages.[2] Some educators also call these programs "full immersion."

Students in these programs tend to demonstrate higher levels of Chinese proficiency than students in 50/50 programs, but their English language arts scores lag behind a bit at first.

This model can require that students are taught English by Mandarin-speaking teachers. For example, in San Francisco's public immersion program, the hour a day of English work that students do in the lower grades is taught by a Mandarin-speaking teacher (but not *their* Mandarin teacher), while that teacher's class is doing its English time. Programs don't like teachers to switch languages with their own students because it becomes too easy for them to use English during Chinese time. So, for example, a first grade class might have Ms. Xie for Chinese time and then Ms. Fang for English time. They know that Ms. Xie will never answer them if they speak English to her, while Ms. Fang will.

That is often not ideal as it's a rare teacher who is fully comfortable in both languages, but can work well in some schools, depending on the teachers.

You can read about this approach in *Chapter 21: School Profiles, Pioneer Valley Chinese Immersion Charter School.*

50/50

In the 50/50 immersion model, students receive half of their instruction in Chinese and the other half in English throughout all of the elementary years. Mandarin and math are generally taught in Chinese. Students in these programs tend to have higher English proficiency in the early years than students in 80/20 programs, but their Mandarin is not as good then. Some educators call these programs "partial immersion," though most consider anything that offers 50% or more of the day in Chinese to be immersion.

You can read about this model in *Chapter 21: School Profiles, Utah State Immersion Schools* and also *Chapter 21: School Profiles, Washington Yu Ying.* A charter school in Washington D.C., Yu Ying is fascinating because while it is a 50/50 program, instead of doing half of each day in Chinese, students spend every other day in Chinese So on one day, students in a class will have all their subjects taught in Chinese and the next in English. This allows students to get *all* subjects in *both* languages.

Heritage schools

These are schools for children who speak Chinese at home but whose parents want them to learn to read and write the language. There are more than 750 in the United States, and it's estimated that over 150,000 students attend weekend classes. In some larger communities, these schools also have classes for students who don't speak Chinese at home.These schools tend to be organized through one of two Chinese heritage language school organizations.[3] The National Council of Associations of Chinese Language Schools is primarily organized by parents from Taiwan and Hong Kong. The

Chinese School Association in the United States is organized by parents from the People's Republic of China.

Language program types

These are all programs that teach languages the traditional way, usually an hour a day (or a week) resulting in little actual fluency. While these don't have much to do with immersion, it's useful to know the terminology so you understand what is immersion and what isn't. I've had schools tell me they had immersion programs because they had a teacher who gave an hour of instruction a week to each classroom and that teacher only used Mandarin with the students. That's actually FLES (Foreign Language in Elementary School). Don't be fooled by programs that use the word immersion, but aren't immersion programs.

Submersion

Submersion is the policy of putting students who don't speak any English into all-English classrooms with no support, leaving them to "sink or swim." This has technically been illegal since the 1971 Supreme Court case *Lau vs. Nichols*, which mandated language support for students learning English. That doesn't mean it doesn't happen, just that it is illegal.

FLEX

Foreign Language Exploration. These classes introduce students to other cultures and languages, but don't actually teach them to speak the language. They generally meet once or twice a week.

FLES

Foreign Language in the Elementary School. This is similar to the one-period-a-day language class you had in high school. In elementary school, the learning is much less formal than you might remember from high school, but the idea is still that students are learning the language during this period. Sometimes the teacher only speaks in the language the students are learning, sometimes the teacher also uses English.

Typically, students in elementary school generally don't learn much in language class, though they do develop some level of familiarity and comfort with the language they're being taught. In one private school I toured, they proudly talked about their Spanish program and how it began in first grade. When I asked what happened when students transferred in for middle school, the academic director told me "Oh, usually if you put your child in a summer Spanish program they can come in fine even if they haven't had

Spanish before." Clearly, in this case five years of daily Spanish lessons didn't actually teach all that much.

Immersion

These are language programs in elementary school in which students are taught *in* the language they're learning. They range from 100% of classes offered in the "target language" (in our case Mandarin) to 50%. Anything less than 50% isn't considered immersion.

Whole school versus strand

This describes whether the entire school consists only of immersion students or whether each grade has some immersion classrooms and some English-only classrooms. It's rare to have the chance to choose between a whole-school environment and a strand-within-a-school. Most cities have one Mandarin immersion program, if that, so you take what you can get. However, should you find yourself with a choice, here are some pros and cons.

Whole-school

A school that's entirely devoted to Mandarin immersion allows it to focus on Chinese without the concern that other strands at the school will feel left out. It also often allows for enough students to provide a critical mass to take the program through the upper grades. The minimum necessary is two classes per grade, and three or four is better. That's because students will move or transfer to other schools over time and it is rare to find new students with the necessary Chinese proficiency to replace them.

This is a problem because by fourth or fifth grade, a single class that was full with 22 to 30 students (what "full" is depends on the school district) can dwindle to 15 or fewer students. This can result in the school having to create split classes in which two grades are combined. These are difficult to teach, especially in immersion where vocabulary acquisition is important, and require much more work on the part of teachers. They also make differentiation harder as the range of ability is even greater.

Differentiation means matching students' abilities to what's taught them, rather than teaching to the middle. It's what schools increasingly do now, rather than having tracks for students at different abilities. So when a third grade class is learning about geology, more advanced students might get more advanced materials to read and more complex questions to answer, while struggling students would be given material better suited to them. It can work well when teachers are well trained in differentiation techniques and there are smaller class sizes. Without those in place it is difficult to have it work well.

In middle school, class sizes generally increase. This can mean too few students to fill a class, which makes scheduling difficult. Some programs don't continue into middle school for this reason.

Strand

Being a strand within a school often allows for a larger school body in general, which can make it possible to fund extras like music, art and activities. It also offers a wider range of students and the chance for immersion students to interact with children outside of the immersion program. It also makes it possible for school districts to offer immersion in multiple schools, because they don't have to take any neighborhood schools out of the system to create them.

Some programs tout the possibility of students moving between immersion and non-immersion strands if it turns out that immersion isn't working for a given student. However that can be problematic for two reasons. First, in some cases strand programs are placed in poor-performing schools. Middle class immersion students may not find their academic needs are well met in their school's non-immersion strand. You can read about why this is the case in *Chapter 19: Why Schools Choose Mandarin Immersion.*

It can also be difficult for students who started in immersion, but are no longer in the immersion strand, to be around their former classmates. It can feel to them as if they failed and went to the "lesser" program. This of course isn't true; it's only a different program. But that's not always how the students perceive it. In my experience, students who leave a strand program tend to transfer to another school and make a fresh start of it.

Teachers

Finding enough teachers is a bottleneck in Mandarin immersion. There aren't a lot of fluent, highly literate Mandarin speakers who are also credentialed elementary school teachers in the United States. There also aren't many education schools nationally that offer the necessary training. All good teachers are gold, but a good Mandarin immersion teacher is platinum—hard to find and extremely sought after.

In general, you're likely to find three types of teacher in immersion classrooms:

Guest teachers

These are teachers from China or Taiwan who come to the United States to teach for one to three years on guest teacher visas. They're often English teachers back home. They come through the Chinese Guest Teacher and

Trainee Program, which is a collaboration between the College Board and Hanban[4].

Heritage speakers

These are teachers who grew up in and attended school in China or Taiwan and then came to the United States as adults, where they went on to get an education degree.

Native English speakers

Generally American-born Chinese ("ABCs," as some call themselves) who grew up speaking Chinese at home and studied it in school, but also grew up speaking English because they went to American schools. Occasionally, you'll also run across a non-Chinese teacher who learned Mandarin in China, though these are pretty rare at this point.

Each type of teacher has pluses and minuses. Guest teachers are helpful because many school districts have trouble finding Mandarin-speaking educators with the necessary credentials to teach here. Using a guest teacher program allows districts to rapidly expand their Mandarin immersion program because they have access to a much larger pool of teachers. These teachers need strong support and professional development from the school or district simply because they're working in a very different environment than the one they trained for. U.S. schools, and U.S. students, are quite different from schools and students in China and Taiwan.

Heritage speakers usually have a deep and abiding love of the Chinese language and culture, which makes them excellent teachers of Chinese. In addition, because they have long lived in the United States, they are better able to work with American students and follow American educational norms. However, their English is often not as proficient as their Chinese, which can be a problem if they have to also teach English classes.

Native English speakers are very easy for parents and administrators to work with because they're American and their English is perfect. However, sometimes their Chinese isn't as good as that of people who were educated in China or Taiwan. While they might be fluent speakers of Chinese, their written Chinese is sometimes not as developed. This can be a problem, especially in the upper grades.

One-way and two-way immersion

Two terms you're likely to hear when you start looking into immersion are "one-way" and "two-way." These refer to whether the programs are meant primarily for English speakers, or for both English and Chinese speakers.

Both have positive points and which one a school program chooses to use depends in part on the needs of its students and the make-up of its student population.

In one-way programs, all the students come into the program speaking English and together they all learn Chinese. This is how the French immersion programs in Canada are constructed. In the United States, they're generally used when there isn't a large population of speakers of the "target" language in a school district. So, for example, Spanish immersion programs are frequently two-way, because most U.S. communities have at least some Spanish speakers. However, most Mandarin immersion programs (83%) are one-way because many communities don't have enough Mandarin speakers to make up half the students.

Two-way immersion programs are meant to include approximately equal numbers of native-Chinese-speaking and native-English-speaking students, so that each group is coming to one of the languages as a novice. In some communities, such as the San Francisco public schools, the ideal classroom configuration is one-third native Mandarin speakers, one-third native English speakers and one-third bilingual Mandarin-English speakers. The idea is that students can learn from each other, providing native speech models for the non-native speakers. All students are experts in at least one of the languages. These programs are more common in areas of the country where there are large Chinese-American communities. The model that a school chooses to adopt depends on its student population and how many Chinese-speaking students it has. It's not surprising that California has the most Mandarin immersion schools, given the population figures from the 2010 U.S. Census: 36.2% of Chinese immigrants lived in California. What's perhaps more surprising is that New York, Hawai'i and Texas have so few immersion schools compared with their Chinese population: 15.4% in New York, 5.0% in Hawai'i, 4.6% in Texas.[5]

1. Myriam Met and Chris Livaccari, "Basics of Program Design," *Chinese language learning in the early grades: A handbook of resources and best practices for Mandarin immersion.* (New York, Asia Society, 2012) 13.
2. Kathryn Lindholm-Leary, "Student Outcomes in Chinese Two-Way Immersion Programs: Language Proficiency, Academic Achievement, and Student Attitudes," *Immersion education: Practices, policies, possibilities.* (Avon, England, Multilingual Matters, 2011) 7.
3. Shuhan C. Wang, "Sustaining the rapidly expanding Chinese language field," *Journal of the Chinese Language Teachers Association.* 47:3 (October 2012) 26.
4. Hanban, 汉办, is the commonly used abbreviation for the Chinese National Office for Teaching Chinese as a Foreign Language. It is governed by the Office of Chinese Language Council International. Hanban is a non-profit affiliated with

the Chinese Ministry of Education. It works to provide Chinese language and cultural teaching resources and services worldwide. Hanban is the sponsor for Confucius Classroom programs and donates books to many Chinese programs. It also has an extensive program to bring Chinese teachers to the United States.

5. The Asian Population: 2010, *2010 Census Briefs.* March 2012.
    http://www.census.gov/prod/cen2010/briefs/c2010br-11.pdf p 18
    Accessed April 23, 2014.

Immersion and Your Child's Academic Career

六
liù
6

You never know when speaking some Chinese might come in handy. One of my first jobs in journalism was as a news clerk in the Seattle bureau of the Associated Press. I filed papers, fetched court documents, made coffee and, on good days, got to write the weather report. I was the lowest of the low and basically ignored by the real reporters. One day the phone rang. There was a woman on the line speaking in rapid Mandarin and she didn't speak any English. The bureau chief poked his head out of his office and yelled, "Hey, Beth! Don't you speak Chinese?"

I said I'd studied it but didn't really speak it well.

"It doesn't matter. Take the call," he said.

I got on the phone and was able to figure out the woman on the other end had met one of AP's correspondents in Beijing the year before. She was now in the U.S. and was trying to find him. I got his extension in the New York bureau, gave her the number and hung up.

Mind you none of this was very complex Chinese—a fourth grader in any immersion classroom could have had that conversation without any problem. But to the bureau chief it was nothing short of a miracle that this lowly news clerk had actually accomplished what none of the veteran reporters in the room could. That moment helped launch me into a career as a journalist in which I haven't really had much occasion to use Chinese at all. It didn't matter; it launched me.

It's this kind of serendipity, the possibilities opened by speaking the language of one-seventh of the world's people, that immersion can offer. Whether or not anything like this will happen to your child in some far-distant future we can't know. Your task today is to understand how the program at the school you're contemplating works, as well as understanding how it fits into a longer-term educational program beyond elementary school. Your children will take care of the future—or the future will take care of your children. Either way, it's all about creating possibilities for them.

After grade school

What happens when students get to middle school and beyond? In most Mandarin immersion programs, middle school students get two classes a day in Mandarin; Mandarin language arts and social studies. That's United States social studies, not Chinese social studies. Students in public school immersion programs must study the same exact curriculum they would have if they were in an English language classroom. Some parents feel that social studies, which is often about history, dates and specific American events, is an odd thing to learn in Mandarin. It is true that it can be jarring to have your child come home and tell you all about the 阿兹台人 [*Ā zī tái kè rén* — the Aztecs.]

However, notes Portland's Koji Hakam, who runs that city's middle school immersion program, social studies isn't just about dates and events. "What's far more critical are the analytical skills they learn, looking at primary source materials. Doing that in two languages actually enriches the experience," he says.

For example students might be asked to read an essay about the arrival of the *Conquistadors* in Mexico and their effect on the Aztec kingdom, then a history of the Spanish conquest, in either English or Chinese. Then they've got to be able to discuss—in Chinese—why the Aztecs fell to the Spanish, despite the small number of Spanish soldiers who were actually in Mexico. They're learning to take material from multiple sources, in both languages, decide how valid it is and then express it in Mandarin. This is a classic Common Core type of exercise, one that you'll see more of as states move towards this more in-depth and analytical type of lesson. Not bad for a day's lesson on the 阿兹台克人.

High school

There aren't that many immersion programs that go through high school yet. At this point, most are still in the elementary school years. However, the general trajectory appears to be that students in the ninth grade will take an advanced class in Mandarin language arts, taught in Mandarin. This is to prepare them to take the Chinese Advanced Placement test (i.e. AP Chinese) in the spring of ninth grade or the fall of ninth grade. Though I know of at least one fourth grader, a student at Bilingual Buds in Summit, New Jersey, who took and passed the AP exam with a 3. That score would qualify the student for college credit (although he hasn't started middle school yet). By the way, the student's family only spoke English.

In some school districts in which the International Baccalaureate program is offered, students take the IB Chinese exam. The IB program offers Standard Level exams and Higher Level exams. There are two possible series of courses students might be offered, Mandarin B or Mandarin A2. Mandarin

B is for students with two to five years of experience in Chinese. Mandarin 2A is for students who are close to bilingual and who have been taught subjects other than Chinese in Mandarin, i.e. immersion students. The 2A exam has a strong focus on Chinese literature.

Typically, students who pass either the AP or IB exam with a sufficiently high score are able to begin at third- or fourth-year Chinese classes in college. This will vary by school, of course.

In some school districts students go on to take college-level classes at local community colleges during high school, or appropriate level Chinese courses at their own high schools. Other systems presume they will study a third language for three years in high school, having reached as far as they can go in Chinese prior to university.

College

So what happens when your child graduates from high school? A common problem when immersion students get to college is that there's nothing left for them to study in Chinese. Most easily test into fourth-year Chinese, which gives them the option to study perhaps newspaper Chinese (which really requires specialized skill, unlike newspaper English), Classical Chinese and maybe Chinese literature. Beyond, that there isn't much for them to do in most college Chinese programs.

However, a program called the Chinese Flagship changes that. It's available at 11 universities in the United States. These programs serve both students who come in with no Chinese and students who come in already speaking some (or a lot) of Chinese. The aim is not to produce students with degrees in Chinese Language and Literature, but to produce students with degrees in Political Science or Engineering or Biology or Computer Science *who also* speak Chinese and know their area subject matter *in Chinese.* (Which, when you think about it, is really just immersion, at the college level.)

Two of the schools, Brigham Young and the University of Oregon, have a K–16 program that begins in kindergarten and continues all the way through college, linking up with Chinese immersion programs in the schools in both states—creating a seamless pipeline for the teaching and learning of Chinese.

Flagship colleges and universities as of 2013-2014:
Arizona State University
Brigham Young University and the Utah State Office of Education
Hunter College
Indiana University
San Francisco State University
University of Mississippi

University of North Georgia
University of Oregon and Portland Public Schools
University of Rhode Island
Western Kentucky University Pilot Program
Georgia Institute of Technology

Flagship students are expected to achieve at least superior level by the time they graduate, according to Der-lin Chao, who directs the Chinese Flagship Program at Hunter College, City University New York. See *Chapter 14: How much Chinese will they learn?* for exactly what those levels mean.

Students who arrive at college with no Chinese spend a huge amount of their time learning Chinese, which includes summer and winter break courses, until they get to an advanced level of Chinese by their third year. Only at that point can they begin professional classes in the language.

Students who arrive at college already speaking Chinese can focus on the professional training right off. Students coming from K–12 immersion programs arrive with Chinese good enough to immediately begin their professional training. Starting Chinese early gives them a huge advantage, says Robert E. Murowchick, with the Center for East Asian Archeology and Cultural History at Brown University. "It's really difficult to start a language when you're also trying to meet the department requirements for history or political science or archeology or any other field," he said at the National Chinese Languages Conference in Boston in 2013.

In the Flagship programs, students take subject matter classes in their area of study in Chinese. If they're studying sociology, they study sociology in Chinese. If they're studying history, they study history in Chinese. In addition, they get one-on-one tutoring in which they read articles in their professional domain in Chinese and discuss them. In their final year, called the Capstone Year, they go to China, where they take classes in their area of study at either Nanjing University or Tianjin Normal University.

Students also do internships in which they're matched with a company related to their major. In 2013, Chao said Hunter College had 33 students doing internships in China. She has an environmental science major at the Yunnan Ecology Conservation Association, a pre-med student at the Shanghai Institute of Neuroscience and a computer science student at Baidu, the largest search engine in China (their Google.) She has also had students placed at trading companies, accounting firms and law firms. Through this training, both in the classroom and their internships, the students develop professional language skills.

These students are in extremely high demand, Chao said at the conference. "A recruiter who works for a China-related company told me that they're desperate to find college graduates with high levels of language proficiency. He said that even if you have *no* work experience they'll hire you if you have a superior level of Chinese." It takes years to develop the necessary language proficiency, so students who began studying Chinese in college usually aren't fluent enough. The recruiter told her that sometimes companies simply can't find someone with the necessary language ability so they hire two people, one who speaks Chinese and some English and one who speaks English and some Chinese.

The recruiter was very excited to learn about the Flagship program. "Before, he looked for future employees at Ivy League schools. But now he says, 'Forget the Ivy League. I can come to Hunter because the Flagship students are exactly the kind of students I'm looking for.'"

Sigrid Berka, executive director of the International Engineering Program at the University of Rhode Island said she'd heard the same thing. Job recruiters aren't always worried about whether a graduate has a specific skill set. They've told her students: "If you have survived Chinese and China, we know we can send you anywhere in the world."

"It's much more than just learning a technical language, it is also problem solving and seeing the world from a different perspective, having stepped out of your bubble and seen yourself from a little more critical perspective as an American," Berka said "All of these are extremely powerful learning and growth opportunities for our students."

The ability to have access to multiple ways of looking at a topic is a huge advantage to students, says Berka. When you combine immersion with a passionate interest in a topic and another major, "this is when learning really kicks in." This ability to use advanced, technical Chinese gives immersion students a massive edge because they arrive ready to launch into learning the technical vocabulary. "If they're in a team of engineers and have to tackle a technical problem, they learn a different way of problem solving. The Chinese engineers might approach a technical problem differently than German engineers or French engineers. It's much different from simply learning the language."

A group at her university is looking at Utah, which has 60 or 70 immersion programs in K–12 in multiple languages, as a model for their state K–12 system. "We're working with legislators and companies in Rhode Island. We've received a grant from the Flagship Program to start immersion programs in the schools."

Other schools are beginning to partner with Chinese universities in ways that will work extremely well for students graduating from high school highly competent in Chinese. May Lee is the vice chancellor for strategic planning in Asia for New York University. Her university is launching NYU Shanghai (its motto is, "Make the world your major") with a goal of being accredited in both the United States and China. It's a program in which students will be expected to move between English and Chinese and graduate with credentials that will be equally highly regarded in both countries."That's the minimum baseline," she said at the Boston conference in 2013. "If you want your

Chinese students to come and be competitive with the *Beidas* or the *Fudans* or the *Tsinghuas* of the world, they have to get a degree that's recognized inside of China so they can get jobs inside of China.[1] And the same is true of U.S. kids who want to study in China, they want a diploma that's recognized in the United States so they can get a job."

What if my child has no interest in China?

Even if your child doesn't choose to study in China, most students who've done well in immersion should be able to test into third- or fourth-year college Chinese and thereby be allowed to forgo additional language classes in college.

Some students choose to do a gap year in a Chinese-speaking area between high school and college. Others might do a semester or year abroad in China, Taiwan, Hong Kong or Singapore once they enter college. The possibilities are ever-increasing. By the time a kindergartener today graduates from high school with good Mandarin skills, it's hard to even imagine what possibilities might be open to them.

It's also possible that they might not want to work in China at all. But in this interconnected world we live in, speaking Chinese will never be a useless skill. They might end up doing a job in which speaking Chinese is a plus, perhaps at a tech company or a store or merely helping out a tourist from Guilin trying to figure out the local bus routes.

Even if they never set foot in a Chinese-speaking country, they will have developed strong cognitive and academic skills "through learning Chinese characters and more generally, by the encounter with a language and culture as different from English as Chinese," says Chris Livaccari, Chinese program director and upper school principal at the International School of the Peninsula in Palo Alto, California. "So at the end of the day, it's not just about a connection to China, but about training the brain to be adaptable, flexible and good at recognizing patterns."

1. Beida is 北京大学, *Běijīng dàxué*, Beijing University. Fudan is 复旦大学, *Fùdàn dàxué* in Shanghai. Tsinghua is 清华大学, *Qīnghuá dàxué* in Beijing. They are collectively the Harvard, Yale and MIT of China.

Is Mandarin Immersion Right for Your Family?

七 qī 7

Note that I didn't say, "Is it right for your child?" but, "Is it right for your family?" That's because choosing whether or not to put your child into a Mandarin immersion program is a family decision. There are many variables that will go into the decision which have to do not with your child but with your family. Here are some questions you should consider before you sign up. They include some that Vivian Tam, the principal at Jing Mei Elementary School in Bellevue, Washington added. They are issues that often crop up for parents, she says.

Will you be in the same school for at least six to nine years?
Immersion programs are designed to begin in kindergarten or first grade and continue at least through the end of middle school in eighth grade. If you know you're likely to move from your school district in that time for work or other reasons, it's probably not a good fit. Just a taste of Mandarin doesn't really work. If your child leaves mid-way through the program, he or she most likely won't retain any Chinese (unless you speak it at home) and it's also possible his or her English won't have caught up with (and sur-passed, as we'll see in *Chapter 13: But will they learn English?*) students in other programs.

There are two caveats to this. There are getting to be enough Mandarin immersion schools in the nation (170 in the 2014–2015 school year) that you might be able to transfer your child into another program. But you'll want to look at where those programs are to see if there's one where you think you might be headed. You can find the full list on the Mandarin Immer-sion Parents Council website.

The other is if you are likely to move to a country where there are Chinese schools, which includes China, Taiwan, Singapore, Malaysia and Japan. If your company does a lot of business in any of those countries, then chances are you'll be able to find a program where you're posted that will work. See *Chapter 23: Going to School in China* and *Chapter 24: Going to School in Singapore* for more on this.

Are you able to be pretty involved in your child's education?

Mandarin immersion requires more involvement on the part of parents than regular English programs. You'll be reading a lot about that in this book. If that involvement seems unworkable (maybe you're busy curing cancer or advocating for battered women or simply earning enough money to pay the rent) then you should seriously contemplate whether entering such a program is right for your family. You can't just drop kids off at the school door in kindergarten and pick them up again at the end of eighth grade—or at least you can't if you want your child to really get all they can out of this education.

Is the school within a reasonable commute distance from your home or work?

This seems odd but it's a bigger deal than you might imagine. You could be driving back and forth between school and home for six or more years, two times a day. And that doesn't count evening PTA meetings, parent immersion workshops, fund-raisers and report card meetings. This is especially true if a family has more than one child and each child attends a different school.

So the distance has to be manageable for your family. I have a nephew whose wife really, really, really wants their children to be in immersion. However the nearest Mandarin immersion program is a 30 to 40 minute drive from their home during commute hours. They both work as teachers and start early, so as much as they'd love to, it simply isn't feasible for them to choose a school that far away.

That said, don't forget to factor in the possibility of car pools, which can take the sting out of a school that's far away. However you should make the drive to the school in morning and evening commute times before you commit to spending the next six or more years driving to it, even if it is only a few days a week.

Can you as a parent stop worrying about your child's English development?

You really have to be able to trust that in the end your child will learn both languages. See *Chapter 13: But will they learn English?* for more on this.

If the child has learning disabilities, should the family enroll the child in a Mandarin Immersion program?

For this one, talk to the school in advance to find out what sorts of support they have for students with learning disabilities. Another excellent resource is the book *Struggling Learners and Language Immersion Education: Research-based, Practitioner-Informed Responses to Educators' Top Questions* by Tara Fortune and Mandy Menke. It is available on Amazon.

***If you are monolingual, can you accept and support
the fact that your child will be on a very different path
from the one you grew up on?***

Your child will end up speaking and being involved in a language and culture
that's not yours. Our job as parents is to get our children to the point that
they can be independent and lead their own lives. That means letting them
follow different paths from us. For immersion parents, this starts to happen
earlier. Will you be comfortable with it?

***If it's a private school, can you really afford
the cost of tuition for the next eight or nine years?***

I know we're all supposed to be willing to sacrifice everything for our children, but do the math first. In San Francisco private schools run about
$23,000 or so a year. That's $180,000 for a K–8 education. You've also got
to factor in that private schools generally increase their tuition 3 to 4% per
year. So a school that begins at $20,000 might end up being $30,000 a year
by the time your child finishes. I know people who have taken money out of
their house's equity to pay for private school. In fact one school's financial
aid officer actually told me the school expected parents to use the equity in
their homes before they'd be considered for financial aid.

That's a *terrible* idea. A very wise father put it to me this way, "If paying
for a private school for your children means you're not saving for retirement,
are you willing to put the burden of supporting you in your old age on their
shoulders?"

Save for retirement first. If you can swing private school after you've
taken that money out of your paycheck each month, go for it. But don't short-
change your own future. In the end it's just putting your children in another
kind of debt.

八
bā
8

Being Bilingual is Better

It was once thought that speaking two languages as a child was a bad thing. Bilingual children were believed to be significantly disadvantaged linguistically and thought to end up with smaller vocabularies overall. In fact, it was common in the 1960s and 1970s for teachers and doctors to tell parents that having their children speak more than one language would confuse them and have negative consequences on their development and intelligence. It still happens today.

That advice was based on studies done in the United States, Ireland and Wales in the 1950s and 1960s. However, it turns out that what was really being studied was poverty. Children from wealthier families spoke only English while children from poorer families were either immigrants or spoke Irish or Welsh at home and English at school. More recent studies done in the United States, Canada and Europe that matched children with families of similar socio-economic status found that bilingual and monolingual children acquired language at about the same rate and ended up with similar vocabularies in the dominant language of their community. But truly the bilingual children actually ended up with double the vocabulary of the monolingual children, because they knew the words in *both* languages.[1]

Finnish linguist and education expert Annika Bourgogne, in her excellent book *Be Bilingual: Practical ideas for multilingual families*,[2] outlines the reasons these old assumptions were wrong.

In fact, there's quite a bit of evidence our ancestors were effortlessly multilingual and that it was the normal state for humans at least until the arrival of agriculture and large nation-states around 4,000 years ago. Hunter-gatherers typically live in small bands that over time evolve their own dialects and eventually languages. But they constantly interact with other nearby bands to share food and find marriage partners, so most people grow up speaking multiple languages. Jared Diamond in his book *The World Until Yesterday* describes spending time with New Guinea Highlanders around a campfire and realizing that of the 20 or so people there, all spoke at least five languages, most between eight and 12, and one person spoke 15![3] They learned them as children playing with other children who lived near the villages they grew up in, and then from marrying women who spoke other languages, and interacting with other adults who spoke still others. Traditionally Aborigines in Australia spoke on average five different languages or dialects.[4] In the Vaupés River area on the border of Columbia and Brazil, the local people typically speak four languages. They learn them from the people who live in their longhouse and from visitors. And that doesn't just mean being able to say, "Ni hao!" The Vaupés River Indians told the anthropologists who lived with them it took a year or two to learn a new language fluently. It was considered shameful to not speak correctly or to use words from other languages when speaking to someone in their own language.[5]

This happens worldwide. I was recently in Botswana and met Kane Motswana, a safari guide. He comes from the San tribe (what used to be called Bushmen) and grew up speaking a San dialect. He also learned Setswana, the language of about 70% of people in Botswana, because it was spoken around him. Then when he got to school he suddenly had to pick up Kalanga, a minority language in Botswana, because most of the kids in the school spoke that. Later on in school he started studying English, which really kicked into high gear when he began working, because that's what most tourists spoke. So he's fluent in four languages and doesn't really consider that he had to work at any of them; they were all around him so he learned them, and that was that.

Being bilingual builds the brain

Research shows that not only does being bilingual do no harm, it is *good* for the brain. According to Tara Fortune, coordinator of the Immersion Research and Professional Development Project at the Center for Advanced Research on Language Acquisition at the University of Minnesota:

> There's a well-established positive relationship between basic thinking skills and being a fully proficient bilingual who maintains regular use of both languages. Fully proficient bilinguals outperform monolinguals in the areas of divergent thinking, pattern recognition, and problem solving.
>
> Bilingual children develop the ability to solve problems that contain conflicting or misleading cues at an earlier age, and they can decipher them more quickly than monolinguals. When doing so, they demonstrate an advantage with selective attention and greater executive or inhibitory control. Fully proficient bilingual children have also been found to exhibit enhanced sensitivity to verbal and non-verbal cues and to show greater attention to their listeners' needs relative to monolingual children. Further, bilingual

students display greater facility in learning additional languages when compared with monolinguals.[6]

In fact, when you look at the studies, being a monoglot[7] begins to sound like the brain equivalent of being a couch potato:

> Numerous studies demonstrate a correlation between the study of languages and increases in higher-order critical thinking and problem solving. Cognitive processing, including perceptual discrimination and organization or spatial reasoning and more advanced verbal processing are demonstrably higher in bilingual students. One study of French immersion students in kindergarten through fourth grade found that the bilingual students had higher I.Q. measures over a five-year period when compared to their peers who had received instruction in one language only. Other benefits of bilingualism include decreased memory loss and problem solving skills, and increased brain function related to attention and inhibition.[8]

Bilingual people are not smarter or faster thinkers but their brains do appear to work differently. They are better at something cognitive scientists call "executive function" or "cognitive control." This is the ability to process all the information coming into us and pay selective attention to what is important. It's what keeps us from being distracted and allows us to concentrate on the problem at hand rather than wandering off into daydreams. Children are hard at work developing this ability from early childhood through kindergarten or first grade.

Being bilingual is excellent brain training for executive function because a person who speaks two (or more) languages must always be choosing which word, in which language, they need to use at any given time. "Bilingual or multilingual people have constant unconscious practice in using executive control. They are forced to practice it whenever they speak, think, or listen to other people talking, constantly throughout their waking hours,"[9] is how Diamond, who speaks English, Indonesian, German, Tok Pisin and Spanish, puts it.

People who are bilingual seem to be especially adept at dealing with tasks where the rules of the task change unpredictably or are somehow misleading, or when there are other things going on that confuse the issue.[10] Which, when you think about it, sounds a lot like modern life.

And while it's difficult to imagine as you watch your adorable four-year-old and ponder whether you want to put him or her in a Mandarin immersion program, there's excellent evidence that being bilingual is protective against the ravages of Alzheimer's disease. A study conducted among over 400 people with a probable diagnosis of Alzheimer's (you need an autopsy to confirm it) found that Toronto residents who were bilingual first showed symptoms four or five years later than monolingual patients. It's known that mental exercise helps slow Alzheimer's symptoms and using two language is excellent brain exercise. Because the patients were already in their 70s, those four or five years meant that almost half of them would die from other ailments before they begin to show symptoms of the disease. That is an outcome anyone who has lost a parent to that devastating disease knows is a huge blessing.

Bigger brains?

Learning more than one language may actually change how the brain looks. Johan Mårtensson, a researcher at Lund University in Sweden, compared[11] the brains of students at the Swedish Armed Forces Interpreter Academy with those of medicine and cognitive science students at Umeå University. Both groups study intensively. The medical students study science and the interpreter trainees study languages—they become fluent in Arabic, Russian or Chinese in 13 months.

Mårtensson and his team gave both groups of students MRI scans before and after three months of intense study in their respective subjects. The medical/science students' brains remained unchanged. But the brains of the language students grew, especially the hippocampus, a deep-lying brain structure that is involved in memory, learning new material and spatial navigation, as well as three areas in the cerebral cortex where higher-order reasoning is processed. Exactly which parts of their brain grew depended on how well they did in their classes and how much effort they put into their course work.

> Students with greater growth in the hippocampus and areas of the cerebral cortex related to language learning (the superior temporal gyrus) had better language skills than the other students. In students who had to put more effort into their learning, greater growth was seen in an area of the motor region of the cerebral cortex (middle frontal gyrus). The areas of the brain in which the changes take place are thus linked to how easy one finds it to learn a language and development varies according to performance.[12]

So learning a language intensively strengthened the part of their brain that is in charge of memory and learning, while studying hard increased the part of the brain involved in higher-order reasoning. That's excellent news for immersion students because they do both; they learn another language intensively and they work hard. And quite possibly end up with bigger brains.

Metalinguistic awareness

There's also evidence that bilingual children simply "get" the idea of language earlier on than monolingual children, because they think more abstractly about language in general. Katie Stern-Stillinger, a high school student who began in Mandarin immersion at the age of four, says one advantage of having learned to speak Chinese early and well is that it has made it easier for her to learn other languages. She began studying Spanish in middle school after eight years of Mandarin. "Part of learning a language is just accepting the fact that the way a language is, that's just how it is. Sometimes people can't get past that," she says. For her that wasn't a stumbling block.

This ability to accept how languages work in turn can aid students when they learn to read and write. As Finnish linguist Bourgogne puts it:

> ...scientists explain that bilingual children often have more knowledge about the symbolic nature of language (also called metalinguistic awareness) than monolinguals of the same age. Having two or more languages, the bilingual children often start to understand the nature of language and how it works earlier. They can also think of their languages abstractly, because they know that the same object or idea can be referred to with two (or more) different words. They might also realize, at a conscious level early on, how changes in phrasing, word order or verb tense can change the meaning of what is said.
>
> What does this mean in practice? Scientists claim that having this knowledge about language itself and its functions is the foundation of learning to read and write, and that bilingual children are often ready to do so earlier. Experts often link this ability to think abstractly to academic success and creativity.[13]

Better at multitasking

Being bilingual also appears to fine-tune the auditory nervous system and help the human brain juggle linguistic input in ways that enhance attention and working memory. A bilingualism expert at Northwestern University in Evanston, Illinois, Viorica Marian, worked with auditory neuroscientist Nina Kraus to look at how bilingualism affects the brain. It's already been shown that lifelong music training enhances language processing. They wondered if being bilingual had the same effect. When they studied bilingual teens, they found the answer was yes.[14]

"People do crossword puzzles and other activities to keep their minds sharp," Marian said in an interview with Northwestern's news center. "But the advantages we've discovered in dual language speakers come automatically, simply from knowing and using two languages. It seems that the benefits of bilingualism are particularly powerful and broad, and include attention, inhibition and encoding of sound."

The researchers recorded brain responses to complex sounds in 23 bilingual English-and-Spanish-speaking teenagers and 25 English-only–speaking teens. When the group listened to someone talking in quiet conditions they responded the same, but when they had to deal with background noise bilinguals were better at processing the sound.

"Bilinguals are natural jugglers," said Marian. "The bilingual juggles linguistic input and, it appears, automatically pays greater attention to relevant versus irrelevant sounds. Rather than promoting linguistic confusion, bilingualism promotes improved 'inhibitory control,' or the ability to pick out relevant speech sounds and ignore others."

It's a pattern several researchers have seen, says research psychologist Ellen Bialystok of Toronto's York University. "The loss of efficiency when we rotate among tasks is called the global switch cost. Everyone slows down some or makes more errors, but multilinguals in all age groups have less of a drop-off."[15]

Given the increasingly plugged-in world we inhabit, and especially the way teens seem to multitask as if their lives depended on it, being bilingual is true brain training for the future.

Is first grade too late?

Researchers used to talk about a "language window" in the brain that closed around adolescence. Learn a language before that and you'll have a native accent. Learn it later and you'll always sound like a foreigner. Now many language theorists think it's a whole lot simpler than the brain rewiring itself to lose the ability to learn a language perfectly. The real problem, they now believe, is that we just get self-conscious.

Self-conscious?

Yes. It's called the affective filter. Babies and toddlers and little kids just talk, they're not self-conscious about their babbling. By the time you start to hit adolescence you begin to be self-aware in ways children are not. You worry about what you sound like and *what people will think about how you sound.* You cease to be fearless in speaking. This, the affective filter theory says, is why we lose the ability to become fluent in languages after our teen years. It's our self-awareness that gets in the way of learning. Which could explain why it often gets easier for adults to speak a foreign language after a couple of drinks—because alcohol helps you forget to be embarrassed. My German, for example, improves greatly after a few beers.

Whatever the cause, while high school students can of course learn new languages, they tend to learn them with an accent. You can hear this when you speak with people who learned English at various points in their lives and compare their accents. Someone who came to the United States at 11 sounds very different than someone who came at 16.

Immersion is a long-term process

An important point to remember in all this is that the brain benefits we're talking about here don't appear until people are quite fluent. A year of college Spanish doesn't do it and neither will a year or two of immersion. The research shows that you've got to actually become someone who thinks in the second language—which should be what immersion students end up doing. Research by York University professor Ellen Bialystok in Canada found that students from English-speaking homes who were in a French immersion school in Canada began to attain the metalinguistic awareness of language gradually. By fifth grade the students were developing the same kinds of executive control (the ability to switch back and forth between ideas) that bilingual students had.[16] Researchers in Belgium found that the results were already apparent by third grade. They studied French-speaking students in an English immersion program. After just three years of immersion, the second-language immersion school students' "reaction times were significantly faster than those of the monolingual group on tasks assessing alerting, auditory selective attention, divided attention and mental flexibility, but not interference inhibition."[17]

Other benefits

Being bilingual isn't just better for your brain. There's also evidence it makes people more creative and more effective problem solvers.[18] They know that there are multiple ways to say something and they tend to come at problems with a broader range of possible solutions. Just as some people do crossword puzzles to keep their brain sharp, being bilingual means always thinking of what word or phrasing fits in a given situation.

People who can communicate in two languages have access to a broader range of possibilities in their lives. Some researchers have dubbed these resources "social capital" or "funds of knowledge."[19] It basically means they can draw on relationships and deeper interactions with a larger group than monoglots. And if that language is a world language such as Chinese, the social capital they can make use of is very large indeed.

A principal at a Mandarin immersion school notes these benefits that she sees in her students:

- Language is culture. Children who are in an immersion environment are simultaneously learning a different culture: the way the target culture thinks (culture perspectives), uses (culture products) and practices (culture practices). In turn, they will be able to understand their own culture(s) through a different lens.

- Being able to see other cultures through an insider's lens brings tolerance, teaches acceptance to differences and fosters cross-cultural competence.

- Studying a different language provides the learner different ways to look at his/her native language, thus enhancing understanding of his or her native language.

- Being bilingual and biliterate provides access for information gathering from more than one source. This enables one to look at the world with wider perspectives, to think critically, and to make better informed choices. Isn't this a required skill for 21st century learners?

It makes parents more mobile

This seems like an odd advantage but it's increasingly true. When offered a job or transfer to Asia, one of the biggest concerns for parents is what it will do to their child's education. I've known several parents who turned down job offers that would have been fascinating, or a great promotion, because it would have been too disruptive to their children's schooling.

Having your child in Chinese immersion turns that on its head. At one point at our elementary school we had five families who had moved to Beijing for jobs and one who had gone to Singapore. We joked that we should just set up a Starr King Elementary campus in China for all the families who move back and forth. In each case, having children in Chinese immersion made it possible for the parents to embrace job possibilities in Asia that otherwise would have been too disruptive. It also gives parents the possibility of putting their child in the local school rather than choosing expensive international schools. See *Chapter 23 Going to school in China* and *Chapter 24 Going to school in Singapore* for more information on this.

This phenomenon is not unique to San Francisco. When my friend Judy Shei was offered a promotion to the Singapore office of Autodesk, she was thrilled at the possibility of moving her family there and putting her two sons in a school with a Mandarin language strand. It seemed a little daunting but she and her husband were excited. She started putting out the word on various social networking sites and within a week she was connected up with a family who had three sons at Broadway Elementary School in Los Angeles, one of LAUSD's three Chinese immersion schools. That family was moving to Singapore for a job the same month Judy's family was and they've become friends.

The best news is that when they at some point do move back to the U.S., they can jump right back into one of the 170 or so immersion programs across the nation.

1. Jared Diamond, *The World Until Yesterday* (New York, Viking, 2012) 387.
2. Annika Bourgogne, *Be Bilingual: Practical ideas for multilingual families* (Amazon Digital Services, 2012)
3. Jared Diamond, *The World Until Yesterday* (New York, Viking, 2012) 369.
4. Jared Diamond, *The World Until Yesterday* (New York, Viking, 2012) 384.
5. Jared Diamond, *The World Until Yesterday* (New York, Viking, 2012) 385.
6. Anthony Jackson, "What the Research Tells us About Immersion," *Education Week*, Sept. 27, 2012.
   http://blogs.edweek.org/edweek/global_learning/2012/09/what_research_tells_us_about_immersion.html
   Accessed Jan. 14, 2014.
7. And isn't *that* an unlovely word?
8. Christina Burton Howe, "Marketing and Advocacy," *Chinese Language Learning in the Early Grades: A handbook of resources and best practices for Mandarin immersion* (New York, Asia Society, 2012) 49.
9. Jared Diamond, *The World Until Yesterday* (New York, Viking, 2012) 339–392.
10. Jared iDiamond, *The World Until Yesterday* (New York, Viking, 2012) 389–390.
11. Johan Mårtensson, "Growth of language-related brain areas after foreign language learning," *Neurolmage*, October 15, 2012.
    http://www.sciencedirect.com/science/article/pii/S1053811912006581
12. Lund University, Language learning makes the brain grow, October 8, 2012.
    http://www.lunduniversity.lu.se/o.o.i.s?news_item=5928&id=24890
    Accessed April 23, 2014.
13. Annika Bourgogne, *Be Bilingual: Practical ideas for multilingual families* (Amazon Digital Services. 2012) Chapter 2.
14. Jennifer Krizman, Viorica Marian, Anthony Shook, Erika Skoe, Nina Kraus, "Subcortical encoding of sound is enhanced in bilinguals and relates to executive function advantages," Proceedings of the National Academy of Sciences, 2012; published ahead of print April 30, 2012, doi:10.1073/pnas.1201575109 Accessed Jan. 14, 2014.
15. Jeffrey Kluger, "The Power of the Bilingual Brain," *Time Magazine*, July 29, 2013.
16. Ellen Bialystok, Kathleen Peets, Sylvain Moreno, "Producing bilinguals through immersion education: Development of metalinguistic awareness," *Applied Psycholinguistics*, Cambridge University Press, 2012.
17. Anne-Catherine Nicolay, Martine Poncelet, "Cognitive advantage in children enrolled in a second-language immersion elementary school program for three years," *Bilingualism: Language and Cognition*, Cambridge University Press, 2013 Volume 16, issue 3.

18. Ellen Bialystock, "Words as things: Development of word concept by bilingual children," *Studies in Second Language Acquisition, 9.* 133–140.
19. Lucy Tse, *"Why don't they learn English?" Separating Fact from Fallacy in the U.S. Language Debate* (New York, Teachers College Press 2001) 30.

Chinese 101 for Parents

Many parents who choose Mandarin immersion think having their child learn Chinese is a good idea, but know very little about the language itself. As their child moves up through the grades, they begin to realize learning Chinese is really, really different from learning Spanish or French. This chapter is meant to give families who don't know much about Chinese a basic understanding of the language and how it works. It won't teach you Chinese but should give you a framework to help you understand the new world your child has entered.

First off, Mandarin is the most commonly spoken native language on the planet, with at least 1.3 billion speakers. That's one in seven people alive today. The next language that's even close is Spanish, with about 390 million speakers, followed by English with an estimated 375 million native speakers. Mandarin is one of the six official languages of the United Nations. About 70% of people in China speak it as their first language.[1] The other 30% learn it in school beginning in kindergarten, because Mandarin is the main language of instruction in the People's Republic of China. Another 23 million people speak it in Taiwan.

It is also a national language in Hong Kong and Singapore and spoken internationally by the Chinese diaspora. It is considered an important "world language" by the United States State Department and the Department of Defense, both of which fund Chinese language programs at primary, secondary and graduate schools around the United States with the aim of increasing the number of Americans fully bilingual in Mandarin Chinese. In addition, China is a country of growing global importance, with rapidly increasing trade, manufacturing and cultural links to the rest of the world.

A little about Mandarin for the non–Chinese speaker

Mandarin and Chinese are not the same thing. Mandarin is one of many Chinese dialects. It has the largest number of speakers in China and is the national language of China and Taiwan. It is the national language because it is the dialect spoken in Beijing, China's capital.

Chinese is a language family within the larger Sino-Tibetan family of languages. Depending on who is counting, there are between eight and ten main Chinese dialects. All are considered "dialects" rather than separate languages for political reasons, though to linguists they're more like languages within a broader language family, as most are mutually unintelligible. Mandarin is spoken in the north, west and far northeast of the country. There's a nice map showing all the Chinese languages and where they're spoken at the web site listed in this footnote.[2]

All Chinese dialects are similar in that they have tones, ranging from two in Wu (spoken in Shanghai) to four[3] in Mandarin to six to ten in some southern dialects. They also all have similar, though not identical, grammatical structures. However the words are pronounced differently, often very differently. For example the word for "friend" is written 朋友. In Mandarin it is pronounced *péngyǒu,* in Cantonese *pang jau* and *bing yu* in Taiwanese. All Chinese dialects are written with the same characters for the most part, though some, such as Cantonese, have some of their own characters. These dialect-specific characters were often suppressed in the name of unifying the language but are enjoying a resurgence today.

In general, written Chinese serves as a way to connect the various dialects spoken across China. You can think of the country as a linguistic area much like Europe in the medieval era. In post-Latin Europe, the various vernaculars such as French, Provençal Italian, Spanish, Catalan and Romanish (a Latin-derived language spoken in a small part of Switzerland) developed into languages of their own. Everyone still wrote in Latin, even though there wasn't a word-for-word correspondence to the spoken language. Written Chinese serves something like that purpose today in a China that could easily fracture along regional lines.

Without getting into really deep linguistic territory, it is enough to know that an educated person from Hong Kong who picks up a newspaper from Beijing can read it aloud in Cantonese, making a rough character-for-character transliteration into Cantonese as they go along. Think of it as someone from Portugal reading a Spanish newspaper—the outlines of the grammar are the same but many words and structures would be different.

This is why one properly says, "I speak Mandarin," but "I read Chinese." The written language is always called Chinese, so one reads or writes Chinese no matter what the dialect. The spoken language has many variants, so it's appropriate to say, "I speak Cantonese" or "I can understand Shanghai dialect." It sounds very grating to the Chinese ear to be asked, "Do you read Mandarin?"

As Harvard-trained sinologist (and San Francisco Mandarin immersion parent) Dr. Alexander Akin puts it, "The written language has always been its own phenomenon and is different from the spoken language for most people. This only began to change a hundred years ago and is still changing fast, especially with electronic media."

Why Mandarin Chinese is called Mandarin

The English word mandarin comes from the Portuguese *mandarim*, which is from the Malay *menteri*. That in turn comes from the Sanskrit *mantrin*, which means "minister or counselor." It originally meant an official in the Chinese empire. Because these officials came from across China, they spoke different dialects, many of which were mutually unintelligible. To communicate they used a common language based on the northern dialect spoken in the capital, Beijing. When Father Matteo Ricci and other Jesuits came to China and learned this standard language in the 16th century, they called it "Mandarin," from its Chinese name 官话, *Guānhuà* which mean "language of the officials." In English that has come to be the name used for Standard Chinese.

Chinese speakers use different terms for official standard spoken Chinese, called Mandarin Chinese in English, depending on where they come from:

- 普通話 *Pǔtōnghuà* "common speech" in China
- 国语 *Guóyǔ* "national language" in Taiwan
- 华语 *Huáyǔ* "Chinese language" in Malaysia and Singapore

These terms, particularly "*Pǔtōnghuà*" and "*Guóyǔ*," represent more than regional differences. Until recent decades, whichever term was used for the official dialect strongly identified a Chinese speaker with either the mainland China Communist government or the Nationalist government on Taiwan. Those distinctions are not as strong today.

Chinese in America

For most of the 19th and 20th centuries, most Chinese in America spoke what in America is called Cantonese, because they came from Guangdong (Canton) province. Actually, most of these immigrants spoke one of several southern Chinese dialects in the *Yuè* language family (粤语, *yuèyǔ*), spoken in Guangdong region.[4] This first large Chinese immigration wave to the United States coincided with the 1849-era California gold rush. Emigration from China was actually forbidden at the time, which is why people from the southern coast (who were further away from Imperial control and had easier access to ships) were the ones most likely to leave.

The history of racism against Chinese immigrants in the United States is extreme. It wasn't until 1854 that Chinese were allowed to offer legal testimony in trials. The Transcontinental Railroad hired 50 Chinese immigrants to work as strike breakers in order to keep the railroad working in 1854. The final ten miles of rail were laid in one day, on April 22, 1869, by Chinese workers. However *none* of the photos of that event, widely reported nationally and internationally, include any Chinese.[5]

That wave of immigration was slowed and then stopped by the Chinese Exclusion Act of 1882, which prohibited the immigration of laborers from China and forbid Chinese in the United States from becoming citizens. In 1924 it was extended to bar all Asian immigrants from citizenship, naturalization, marrying Caucasians or owning land. It was not repealed until 1943, when the United States and China were allies against Japan. But even then it restricted the number of Chinese immigrants into the United States to 105 per year. It was only when the Immigration and Nationality Act of 1965 was passed that national origin quotas were lifted and the numbers of people from China, Taiwan and Hong Kong who immigrated to the United States began to rise substantially.

Until the 1980s, a large number of Chinese immigrants to the United States still spoke *Yuè* dialects. That began to change as people from other parts of China also began to emigrate. This has caused a shift in the balance of Chinese dialects spoken in the United States for two reasons. Some of these immigrants came from the north of China. Some came from Taiwan, where the majority mother tongue is Taiwanese Hokkien but education is in Mandarin. The other shift was that by the 1980s and 1990s anyone coming from China who had a good education also spoke Mandarin, the national language. Almost all schooling is now conducted in Mandarin and at universities Mandarin is often the only language used. Prior to the 1970s and 1980s this was not the case. Today in many parts of the United States it is becoming as common to hear Mandarin spoken in restaurants and shops as Cantonese, which represents an enormous shift in the language map of the Chinese American community.

Mandarin language

For people who don't speak a Chinese dialect, Mandarin can be linguistically surprising. Our children accept as natural that their second language doesn't have the same kind of subject/verb agreement or plurals or tenses as English, that it doesn't conjugate verbs and that measure words are required for all nouns. This actually makes Chinese a very easy language to learn to speak compared to English and other highly inflected languages, especially if you learn it as a child when the tones come naturally.

For adults who don't speak Chinese it can all be a little confusing. I've had people ask me how you conjugate verbs in Chinese, because that's what they did in high school French or German. When I tell them, "You don't!" they find it puzzling. Here are a few very basic points about Chinese that should help a bit. Remember that to your child all of this will seem natural and as it should be, just as it does to native speakers. We're the ones trying to keep up.

Tones

Chinese is a tonal language. Mandarin has four tones, Cantonese has between six and ten. Shanghainese has only two. Below are examples of the four Mandarin tones, or five if you include the "neutral" tone. Each of the first four have a specific mark used to designate which tone the word is pronounced with. The neutral tone doesn't get a mark.

- 妈 *mā* mother

- 麻 *má* numb

- 马 *mǎ* horse

- 骂 *mà* scold

- 吗 *ma* (indicates a question)

This gives the possibility of crazy sentences like, "*Māmā mà mǎ ma?*" which is something of a nonsense sentence meaning, "Did mother scold the horse?" One thing many non-native speakers have difficulty with—especially if they don't learn as kids—is that the tone fundamentally changes the meaning of the word. Unlike English, where a foreign learner can use slightly "off" pronunciation and still be understood, in Mandarin changing the tones can create complete incomprehensibility. Think of the difference in meaning between, "Ready?" and "Ready!" in English.

To hear some real tones, check out this website in the endnotes.[6] Or just ask your child to read something aloud to you.

To give you a sense of how much tones impact meaning, there's a famous joke poem by Zhao Yuanren (赵元任), a well-known writer in the early 20th century. It's called "The Lion-Eating Poet in the Stone Den." This is what it looks like in Chinese:

《施氏食獅史》

石室詩士施氏，嗜獅，誓食十獅。
氏時時適市視獅。十時，適十獅適市。
是時，適施氏適市。
氏視是十獅，恃矢勢，使是十獅逝世。
氏拾是十獅屍，適石室。
石室濕，氏使侍拭石室。
石室拭，氏始試食是十獅。
食時，始識是十獅屍，實十石獅屍。
試釋是事。

Which is translated as:

Lion-Eating Poet in the Stone Den

In a stone den was a poet called Shi, who was a lion addict, and had resolved to eat ten. He often went to the market to look for lions.
At ten o'clock, ten lions had just arrived at the market.
At that time, Shi had just arrived at the market.
He saw those ten lions, and using his trusty arrows, caused the ten lions to die.
He brought the corpses of the ten lions to the stone den.
The stone den was damp.
He asked his servants to wipe it.
After the stone den was wiped, he tried to eat those ten lions.
When he ate, he realized that these ten lions were in fact ten stone lion corpses.
Try to explain this matter.

But when you write it in *pinyin*, the Chinese Romanization system (more on this later,) it looks like this:

Shī Shì shí shī shǐ
Shíshì shīshì Shī Shì, shì shī, shì shí shí shī.
Shì shíshí shì shì shì shī.
Shí shí, shì shí shī shì shì.
Shì shí, shì Shī Shì shì shì.
Shì shì shì shí shī, shì shí shì, shǐ shì shí shī shìshì.
Shì shí shì shí shī shī, shì shíshì.
Shíshì shī, Shì shǐ shì shì shíshì.
Shíshì shì, Shì shǐ shì shì shí shì shí shī.
Shí shí, shǐ shí shì shí shī, shí shí shí shī shī.
Shì shì shì shì.

The best joke of all, of course, is to try to pronounce any Chinese word with the correct tones when your child says it to you. They will derive endless hours of enjoyment making fun of your pronunciation and especially your tones. There's really no way around it; let them enjoy their superiority. My usual response is "This is exactly why we put you in Mandarin immersion, so your tones *won't* sound like mine!"

Names

Chinese puts the family name (also called the last name or surname) first, the personal name (also called the first or given name) last. The family name is almost always a single character. The personal name is usually two characters, though sometimes it can be one.[7]

The former Chairman of the Central Advisory Commission of the Communist Party's name was named 邓小平, *Dèng Xiǎopíng* in Chinese. However in English his name would have been Xiaoping Deng. Chairman Mao's name was 毛泽东, *Máo Zédōng*. So in English his name could have been Zedong Mao, though he was never called that even in English.

If your child doesn't already have a Chinese name his or her teacher will give him one. In many Mandarin immersion programs this happens after the winter break of the first year (either kindergarten or first grade depending on when your program begins.) In some programs teachers make a little bit of a ceremony out of it. Names have meanings in Chinese so teachers wait to get a sense of the children in their class before they give them their Chinese names.

That name won't be a direct transliteration of their English name, as those sound odd in Chinese. Instead, the teacher takes the child's last name and finds one of the hundred or so most common Chinese last names that match it. They'll also try to make sure not every child in the class has the last name. For example, my last name is Weise (it rhymes with "geese") so the family name my Chinese professor in college gave me was 魏, *Wèi*

Chinese women don't traditionally change their names when they marry, so your child's teacher will likely have a different last name from her husband. Children take their father's last name.

Teachers are always addressed by their family name and the title 老师 *lǎoshī*, teacher. If your child's teacher is named Mrs. Wang, everyone in school will call her Wang Laoshi. Because the Mandarin spoken in Beijing tends to add an "r" sound to *shī*, her name might sound closer to Wang Laoshir if she is from northern China.

Asking questions in Chinese

Chinese sentences use a pretty straightforward Subject-Verb-Object construction that English speakers will immediately grasp.

我 是 中国人。
Wǒ shì Zhōngguórén.
I am [a] Chinese person.

But some things are different. One question many English speakers have is how you can ask a question in Chinese when there are tones in the language. In English we ask a question by going up at the end, "The TV is broken," sounds different from, "The TV is broken?"

You can't go up at the end of a sentence in Chinese because you'd be changing the tone of the final word, and thus possibly the word's meaning. To get around that, the most common way of making a question in Chinese is to add 吗 *ma* at the end. 吗 is what linguists call a "final interrogative particle" but what Chinese teachers simple call "a question word." When it's added at the end of a sentence it's like adding a question mark with sound, turning the sentence into a question.

这是一本书。
Zhè shì yī běn shū.
This is a book.

To turn that into a question, you just add 吗 at the end.

这是一本书吗?
Zhè shì yī běn shū ma?
This is a book?

Another way to ask a question is by adding the Chinese equivalent of "isn't it?" to the phrase. You'll hear this a lot because it's something they teach the first week of kindergarten. It's also the construction used to ask permission to do something, such as going to the bathroom or getting a piece of paper. The construction is properly called an "affirmative question tag" in Chinese grammar and it looks like this:

可不可以?
Ke bù keyi?
May I or may I not?
[Literally: May, may not?]

我可不可以去洗手間?
Wǒ kě bù kěyǐ qù xǐshǒujiān?
May I go to the bathroom?
[Literally: May I or may I not go to the washroom?]

You can use the same construction with other verbs as well.

听得懂 听不懂？
Tīng de dòng tīng bù dòng?
Do you understand?
[Literally: Hear and understand or hear and not understand?]

Tense

Anyone who struggled to memorize French or Spanish verb tenses will love Chinese—it doesn't have them. Verbs don't change; you just put another word after them to indicate you've done something or you're going to do something.

To make the past tense, you use 了, *le*.

了 = This thing has already happened; it's a finished action.

我吃。
Wǒ chī.
I eat.

我吃了
Wǒ chī le.
I ate.

For the future, you use 会, *huì*. It means something that is going to happen and also that something is possible.

我吃
Wǒ chī.
I eat.

我会吃
Wo huì chi.
I will eat.

Just as in English, Mandarin has a lot of ambiguities that are determined by context. This sentence could mean, "I will eat" at some point in the future or could also mean "I am able to eat." It sounds a little odd to the Chinese ear, but I wanted to come up with a simple sentence to explain how you do future tense.

Measure words

This is something that we do in English, but only sometimes. In Chinese you have to do it all the time. Here are some English measure words:

A *loaf* of bread
A *flock* of geese
A *flight* of stairs
A *gallon* of milk
A *bundle* of sticks

Chinese has a measure word for every noun. Any time you talk about a noun, you need to use its correct measure word. When in doubt, 个, *gè*, is the all-purpose measure word, and one kids try to get away with using when they can't remember the right one.[8]

一个人
Yī gè rén
One person (literally: A thing of person)

一本书
Yī běn shū
A book (literally: A binding of books)

一张桌子
Yī zhāng zhuōzi.
A table (literally: A flatness of table)

You can't leave them out. If you tried to say:

一书
Yī shū
A book

It would sound as bad in Chinese as saying "I have book" instead of "I have a book" sounds in English.

What is a word?

English speakers commonly think that one Chinese character equals one word. They're right, sort of. But they're also wrong, which can cause misunderstandings and tears at homework time when children and parents use the same word to mean very different things, so understanding the distinction is important.

When students start learning to write, they first learn single words:

大
dà
big

书
shū
book

But don't let that fool you into thinking that each syllable or character equals one *and only one* word. While it is true that each Chinese character is a stand-alone word in its own right, Chinese today consists of many words made up of two (or even three) characters/syllables.

Linguists call the smallest unit of a language that carries meaning a morpheme. In English, morphemes don't have to be words. "Un" is a morpheme because it means something. In the word "unforgettable," "un" means *not*, even though it isn't a stand-alone word. In Chinese, while it's true that each morpheme is a stand-alone word, a large percentage of actual words are composed of several characters/syllables.

Parents can get into trouble because they call something a "word" on homework as they point to a specific character, but what their child sees is a "word" is made up of several characters. It's easiest if you call a character a character but a word a word.

In Chinese that's:

character: 字 *zì*
word/phrase: 词 *cí*

(Okay, I'll admit that to those of us who don't speak Chinese the difference between *zì* and *cí* isn't all that easy to hear. Have your child drill you on it awhile until you get it down.) Here's a little background on how Chinese creates words, which might clarify how it works. Just as in Chinese, English creates words from morphemes:

geography
geo (Earth) + graphy (writings about)

rhinoceros
rhino (nose) + keras (horn)

thermometer
thermos (heat) + metron (measure)

While classical written Chinese (ca. 700 BC–200 AD) tended to prefer single-character words, modern Chinese has moved towards many more multisyllabic ones. That one-two beat sounds better to the modern ear. So you see a lot of word groups that build upon each other. This is one reason that as your child's vocabulary increases it becomes easier to learn new words, because they already know part of them. For example:

中国
Zhōngguó
middle + kingdom = China

That means that your child might have an easier time learning this word:

中文
Zhōng wén
middle + language = Chinese

Here are some others:

明白
míngbái
illuminate + white = understand

眼红
yǎnhóng
eye + red = jealous

天气

tiānqì

heaven + breath = weather

So you might point at 白 on a homework sheet and say, "What's that word?"

Your child would answer back, "明白 means "understand.""

You'd say, "No, this word, here: 白."

They say, "That's not the word, the word's 明白."

And then you'd both be confused. But not if you remember that one character does not always equal one word!

Another thing to keep in mind is that not all words are as transparent as these examples. There are many that just have to be learned as words; they don't really make sense as two characters together. As Kevin Chang, the Mandarin coordinator at the Chinese American International School in San Francisco, puts it, "students who can recognize individual characters sometimes struggle with finding the meanings of a phrase that is formed by two familiar characters." For example, let's take:

东

dōng

east

and

西

xī

west

Though you might think 东西, *dōngxi,* would mean east-west, it doesn't. It actually means "things" or "stuff."

My friend Liyao Zhu points out that there are often stories behind Chinese words, and learning the stories makes them much easier to learn. Your child's teacher will likely tell the class these stories when they're introducing new words. For example, for 东西, *dōngxi,* Liyao told me this story:

东西 means "things" or "stuff." A long time ago, there wasn't a word for "things" or "stuff" in general. In the Tang Dynasty (about 1,500 years ago), the first official markets were established. These markets were regulated by the government. In the capital of Xian, two markets were established for trading. They were the 东市 (*dōng shì*, East Market) and 西市 (*xi shì,* West Market). 东市 was at the eastern part of the city and 西市 was at the western of the city. Outside of these two markets, no one was allowed to sell or buy anything. In other words, when people wanted to buy or sell stuff, they had to go to either 东市 or 西市. Gradually, from the meaning of "going to 东市 /

西市 to buy/sell stuff/things", people implied 东西 to mean "stuff" or "things."

This is also an excellent example of the great depth of language knowledge that most Chinese people have. Liyao isn't a scholar of ancient Chinese, but like anyone educated in China, she was taught these stories from elementary school on. I don't mean to denigrate English speakers, but most Chinese speakers I know have a very deep understanding of the historical links between the language and history of China in ways most English speakers do not.

Homonyms

Chinese is full of homonyms, words that sound alike but mean different things. We've got them in English too, of course.

to, two, too
air, e'er, ere, err, heir
aisle, I'll, isle
bald, balled, bawled

But that's nothing compared to Chinese, which has thousands of 词 *cí* and 字 *zì* (see above) that are pronounced exactly the same but have very different meanings.

This is actually why Chinese developed tones. During the Classical period the language had more consonants at the beginning and end of words and a more complex sound system, making it easier to distinguish one word from the other. But as with all languages, it changed over time and speakers dropped some of the consonants. To clarify which word meant what, people started using tones to distinguish between them.

Still there are many that sound alike.

西, *xī,* west
吸, *xī,* to inhale
溪, *xī,* creek

If you're talking to someone and want to make clear which character you mean, you would say

东西的西
Dōngxī de x.
The "*xī*" in "things"

Or

吸烟的吸
Xīyān de xī
The "*xī*" in "smoking"

Or

溪流的溪

Xīliú de xī.

The *"xī"* in "creek"

As your child moves up through the grades and starts having more complicated homework in Chinese, you hear them saying things like, "I don't know if it's the 溪 in 溪流 or the 吸 in 吸烟."

When they really get fluent they'll start writing the character in the air or on the palm of their hand with their finger, to show the person they're talking to which character they mean.

Polyphones

Just to make things more interesting, there are some characters that have two different pronunciations, where each pronunciation means something different. In Chinese these are called 多音字 or *duō yīnzì* (many word sounds). They aren't a huge problem as there aren't all that many of them. But it's helpful for parents to know they exist. That way you don't insist, "No, 重 is pronounced *zhòng*, not *chóng!*" (Okay, highly unlikely you'd find yourself saying that, but you never know. Maybe you'll find you have a photographic memory for characters.) Some examples:

长

zhǎng, chief, to grow

cháng, length

行

xíng to walk

háng, a row

重

zhòng, heavy

chóng, to repeat

Fractions

This isn't something you'll need until second or third grade, but it will *really* confuse you and your child if you don't know it when the time comes. Chinese describes fractions exactly the opposite of English.[9] In English, we say two-thirds, meaning "two of three parts." In Chinese, you say "of three parts, two":

三分之二

San fenzhi er

"Of three parts, two"

So when you say one-third to your child and she writes 3/1, she's not making a mistake, she's just thinking in Chinese.

Simplified versus traditional characters

Chinese in China and Singapore is written using simplified characters. In Taiwan and Hong Kong it's written using traditional characters. Most older Chinese immigrant communities in the United States use traditional characters. However, the vast majority of Chinese speakers worldwide now use simplified characters, as do most Mandarin immersion programs.

What's the difference?

Simplified characters are simpler. They use fewer strokes and are easier to read, write and remember. Unless you learned traditional first, in which case you think traditional are easier to read, write and remember. Some examples:

學校 (traditional)
学校 (simplified)
xuéxiào
school

個 (traditional)
个 (simplified)
gè
a measure word for people, etc.

邊 (traditional)
边 (simplified)
biān
side

龜 (traditional)
龟 (simplified)
guī
turtle

The 個 / 个 pair is a great way to tell if something's written using simplified or traditional characters, even if you don't read Chinese. It's a pretty commonly used character, so you can look for 个's and if you find them, you that whatever you're looking at is written in simplified characters.

Most simplified characters are based on common handwriting simplifications that had existed for hundreds of years in China. Not all characters are simplified, only a subset are. All together it's about 2,200 characters. But it's not really that many, because in most cases it's just a part of the character that's been simplified.

For example, the radical (more on radicals below) for gate or door, *mén*, appears in many characters. In traditional script it is written 門, in simplified it is written 门. So words such as 问, 间, 阅 (*wèn, jiān, yuè;* ask, between, inspect) would look like 問, 間, 閱 in their traditional forms. Once you learn the rules for simplifying, it's easy to recognize them in either direction.

There aren't two completely different sets of characters, one simplified and one traditional. And once you learn the rules for simplifying, it's not too hard to go back and forth. So parents shouldn't worry that their children will need to memorize 2,000 or so characters to read in China and then another 2,000 to read in Taiwan.

History of simplification

Activists working to modernize China, such as Lufei Kui, began agitating to simplify written Chinese beginning in the early part of the 20th century, to make it easier for people to learn to read and write. Some even suggested that China switch to a phonetic alphabet. They were very adamant about it. Sinian Fu, a leader of the May Fourth Movement to modernize China, called Chinese traditional characters "the writing of ox-demons and snake-gods," 牛鬼蛇神的文字, *niúguǐ shéshén de wénzì.* (Try to get your child to work *that* phrase into an essay someday.)

However, simplified characters weren't codified and promulgated until the 1950s and 1960s, when the government of the People's Republic of China decided that they would make it easier for the Chinese masses to learn to read and write. They were first officially adopted in 1958 in China. Today 80% of Mandarin immersion programs teach simplified characters because they're used by the majority of the Chinese speakers on the planet.

It takes practice and some training to learn to read the other type of characters but it's not that difficult an undertaking, most people say. Many well-educated people can go back and forth, though it takes time to get used to reading in the other form. It's impossible to be literate in China without being able to read simplified, and it's impossible to be literate in Taiwan without being able to read traditional. Should your child end up in a country using a different system than the one he or she learned, he or she should be able to pick it up without too much difficulty.

Which form Mandarin immersion programs should use is a political (and emotional) minefield. People tend to choose whatever they learned as children. They will say that simplified are best because the characters are easier to learn and write, or that traditional are best because the characters contain more information about their origins and meaning. For people who learned traditional characters as children, simplified characters look ugly and wrong. People who learned simplified as children think traditional characters are fussy. Everyone has strong feelings in the matter.

Pinyin

Pinyin, 拼音 *pīnyīn*, is the official system used to transcribe Chinese characters into Latin script. It literally means "spelled sound." Officially it's called 汉语拼音 or *Hànyǔ Pīnyīn*, Chinese Pinyin. *Pīnyīn*, to be properly written, must also include the tone mark. So 龟 is correctly written *guī* in *pinyin*, not *gui*.

And please note that it's *not* pinG-yinG, as English-speakers sometimes pronounce it. That drives Chinese teachers crazy.

Pinyin was developed in the 1930s and became official in China in 1958. Pinyin pronunciation isn't always like English, so it's difficult for students to learn them both at the same time. For example *cai* and *ceng* sound very different in *pinyin* than they do if you try to pronounce them as an English speaker would pronounce those words. Ask your child to pronounce them (if they've learned *pinyin* already.) Then try to pronounce them yourself. They will laugh at you. There's a fun video on YouTube that features cartoon kids singing all the syllables in *pinyin* that's actually kind of helpful.[10]

In China, *pinyin* is introduced in kindergarten and first grade and used to aid in learning. Children's books often include it early on but you don't see it much past second grade.

In Taiwan a similar syllable system, called *Zhu-Yin-Fu-Hao,* is used.[11] Most people call it Bopomofo, after the first four syllables in the system. It was developed from the Japanese hiragana and katakana syllabaries.

Almost all Mandarin immersion programs in the United States use pinyin and it tends to be introduced around second or third grade, so students can first get clear on the English sound-to-letter system before learning the Chinese one. Many Chinese dictionaries are arranged by pinyin.

All on computers and phones, writing is done using pinyin. You type pinyin in and the program chooses the most logical characters and lets you choose which one you mean by typing in the number corresponding to the correct word or phrase and the program inserts it.

Pinyin hasn't always been used

There are other systems for transcribing Chinese into English, using Roman letters. Today pinyin is almost universally used, but you'll see remnants of others. The most common is Wade-Giles, developed by American Thomas Wade and British diplomat Herbert Giles in the 19th century. Most books about China prior to 1979 used this system. What's *quan* in pinyin is *ch'üan* in Wade-Giles.

You'll also sometimes see words in the Yale Romanization system, developed at Yale University in 1943 to help American soldiers communicate in China. In this system the word for knowledge, 知识, *zhīshì* in pinyin, is written *jr-shr* (which is really pretty close to what it should sound like to the American ear.)

An interesting note is that you can sometimes tell where someone comes from by how his or her name is written in English. The common Chinese surname 周, for instance, is written *Zhou* in pinyin (pronounced like Joe) but people who come from Taiwan tend to write it Chou, whereas families that speak Cantonese and came over awhile ago tend to write it Chow or Chao.

Written Chinese

Chinese characters first arose in approximately 1,200 BC as ideographs written on tortoise shells used for divination. Questions were scratched onto the tortoise shell, which were then exposed to heat. The resulting cracks were "read" by shamans as answers from the gods.

In China, the definition of literacy is recognizing more than 1,500 Chinese characters (for a farmer) or 2,000 characters (for an office worker or urban resident). It's pretty common to hear that one needs to know about 2,000 characters to read a newspaper and that someone in college can recognize between 3,000 to 5,000 characters, with graduate students perhaps being able to read 8,000. This, however, is subject to endless debate.

Stroke order

Stroke order will loom large in your child's life, starting in kindergarten. Each character has a specific order in which the strokes (the lines that make it up) should be written. Writing them in the wrong order is incorrect. Doing them in the right order makes writing easier, and faster, and the characters look better. It's important to do them correctly from the beginning so it becomes second nature. When your child first starts getting character worksheets, usually towards the middle of kindergarten, the stroke order will be written out for each character. Make sure they follow the correct order and direction as they do their homework.

The general order is this:

from top to bottom
left to right
horizontal before vertical
center before outside
enclosures before contents
dots last

After your child has been taught how to write 20 or 30 characters by their teacher they'll start to instinctively know which stroke should go first, which next. There's a nice English language tutorial, with animations, on About.com.[12] Most online dictionaries and many English-Chinese children's dictionaries also give the proper stroke order so it's easy to check.

Each individual stroke also has a name. You'll see posters with all of them listed and named in your child's classroom.[13] As they get more comfortable in Chinese, you'll hear your kids describe how to write a character by its strokes, things like "You know, it's a *wanggou* here and a *youdian* on this side."

No word breaks

One more thing about written Chinese, Chinese does not come with breaks between words the way English does.

Itsasifeverysentencewaswrittenlikethisandyouhadtofigureout-wherethewordbreakswere.

To be fair, Latin and Greek used to be written like that too (the fancy phrase for this is *scriptio continua*), as were earlier forms of English. But around 1,000 AD word breaks became common, to the great relief of readers. However in Chinese this never happened, in part because in Chinese the look of writing on a page is an art in and of itself. Think of all the beautiful Chinese calligraphy you've seen, the flow of characters wafting down or across the page (they can go either way). That would be destroyed if there were breaks between words, so they're not added.

Sometimes children's books use word breaks but they're never used in books for Chinese readers. Readers must figure out for themselves which characters go together. For experienced readers this isn't an issue but for students it can feel something like doing a crossword and trying to guess where a given word starts or ends.

Radicals and sound-elements

About 80% of Chinese characters contain two distinct parts, a meaning or semantic radical (部首, *bùshǒu*) and a sound element. Radicals (from the Latin word for "root") often, but not always, tell something about the meaning of the word. The sound portion tells something about how the character is pronounced. There are about 190 semantic radicals in use.[14] There are estimated to be about 800 phonetic elements, most of which are characters in their own right.[15]

Some examples of characters and their radicals:

水 *shuǐ*, water

河 *hé*, river

湖 *hú*, lake
海 *hǎi*, sea

The water radical is written 氵, and is based on 水, *shuǐ*, water. You can see it in the final characters shown above. Some radicals look different than the character they come from, in the same way a cursive Q can look different from a print Q in some fonts. Ask your child to show you what the 心, *xīn*, heart radical looks like. It's cool.

On the left-hand side of the character you can see the radical for water 水 *shuǐ*. If you see it in a character, you can make a pretty good guess that it's got something to do with water or liquids.

Here's another set of characters and their radicals:

金 *jīn*, gold

铁 *tiě*, iron
钢 *gāng*, steel
针 *zhēn*, needle

You can see the radical for gold on the left-hand side. If you see this radical, the word probably has something to do with metal.

Things aren't quite so simple for the sound portion of characters. Generally it's not a one-to-one correspondence but more along the lines of "it *kind of* sounds like this." For example, in 湖 *hú*, lake, the 胡 part of the character on the left means "recklessly" and is pronounced *hú*. So if you see the character 湖 but don't know how to read it, you might be able to work it out. "It's got something to do with water (did you find the water radical on the left?) and it's probably pronounced something like *hú*. Ah ha! That would be *hú*, meaning lake!"

Or take the word 词, *cí*, word or phrase. The radical on the left is 讠 (it looks like 言 when it's not a radical), which indicates it's about words or speech. The sound element is 司 *sī*, which means "to take charge of, to control." Put them together and you get something that's got to do with speech that sounds like *sī*: 词!

According to experts, "skilled [Chinese] readers are, in fact, capable of such parallel information extraction during character recognition." Meaning, they've got a fairly good chance of figuring out what a character means even if they've never seen it before, if they know how to pronounce the word the character represents. Having a strong spoken vocabulary is important. If you don't know how to say the word *hú*, lake, you wouldn't have much chance working out what 湖 is.

Some immersion programs are beginning to teach students these sound elements. In the Mandarin immersion program in the San Francisco Unified School District, Mandarin coordinator Angelica Chang has included them in all the flashcards for kindergarten through fifth grade, so students begin to get used to the idea that characters have a sound component as well.

How to use a Chinese dictionary[16]

Looking up a word in Chinese is slightly different than looking up an English word and requires a little training. Feel free to grab a Chinese-English dictionary and follow along. Your school should recommend one for students, so you want to get comfortable using it.

If you know how a word is pronounced, it's relatively easy. Almost all Chinese dictionaries today are arranged alphabetically by pinyin. So if you see the word 冷 and you know it's pronounced *lěng*, you simply look under **L** and find it alphabetically to see the meaning. And there it is, "cold!"

If the word you're looking up is composed of two characters, look up the first one first. So say you see a word, 饼干, *bǐnggān*, you first look up饼, *bǐng*. All the characters that are pronounced *bing* will be divided up by the four tones. First will come the characters pronounced *bīng*, then *bíng*, then *bǐng* and finally *bìng*. (*i.e.* first tone, second tone, third tone, fourth tone.) 饼, *bǐng*, is third tone, so it comes third. Go down the listed pinyin until you find *bǐng*.

You'll see several characters that are pronounced *bǐng*. They include 柄, an axe handle; 稟, a petition; 屏, to hold one's breath; and 秉 to grasp. And 饼. Underneath 饼 you'll see 饼干, *bǐnggān*, and the useful information that it means biscuit, cookie or cracker.

But what if you don't know how to pronounce the character? That's where using a Chinese dictionary becomes more an art than a science.

Say you find yourself looking at the word 汽车. You don't know what it means. You don't know how to pronounce it. What do you do?

First, you need to look up the character 汽. To do so, you first need to find its radical. When characters are taught, students also learn what radical they include, so a student of Chinese should easily be able to pick out 氵 in 汽. 氵 is the water radical, based on the character 水, *shuǐ*, water. As a radical, you can think of it as two drops of water and a third running down the page.

Now you know the character's radical. All Chinese dictionaries have in their front section what's called a Radical Index, a list of all Chinese radicals in order of how many strokes they contain. This is one reason why stroke order and knowing how to correctly write characters is important, because you have to know how many strokes there are in a character and in its component parts.

In the case of 汽, the water radical contains three strokes. So you look at the Radical Index in your dictionary and go to the list of three-stroke radicals. Sometimes these columns are numbered in Chinese, sometimes using Arabic numerals. In my dictionary, the columns are numbered 一, 二, 三, etc.

Look under 三 and run down the list until you come to the water radical, 氵. Next to it you'll see a number; in my dictionary it's 40.

Right after the Radical Index should come a list of all the characters in the dictionary, arranged by radical and then stroke order. Go to number 40 and you'll find a long list of characters all of which contain 氵, the water radical.

Here's another stroke-counting exercise. You have to look at the secondary component of the 汽 character and count how many strokes it has. In this case, it uses four strokes.

The list of characters that use radical number 40, 氵, is broken down by stroke order. So there are the characters whose secondary component uses two strokes, three strokes, four strokes and so on.

In the case of 汽, go to number 4, 四, and then run down the list until you see the 汽 character. In my dictionary it is number 13 on the list. Next to it is a number, 292. That tells you what page in the main dictionary the character is found on.

Turning to page 292, you see that one-third of it is comprised of words that contain the character 汽, and that 汽 is pronounced *qì* and means "steam."

You still don't know what 车 means or how it's pronounced. You could go through the same process of looking it up by radical and stroke order, but now that you know what the first character sounds like, it's easier just to run down the entire list of words that include the character 车 until you come to 汽车.

Which turns out to mean automobile, pronounced *qìchē*.

If you had looked up 车, you would have found out that it means vehicle or wagon. So the word for automobile is literally "steam wagon," because 汽油 *qìyóu*, steam (or vapor) oil, means gasoline. So a car is a gas-powered vehicle.

Now perhaps you understand why when you tell your child, "Go look it up!" for a Chinese word, it's a little more daunting than looking up an English word.

Another option is to use one of the many dictionaries available online. Two popular ones are YellowBridge.com and Pleco.com. Both also allow you to simply write the character and the computer will read what you've written and tell you how to pronounce it and what it means.

There are also several helpful smart phone apps that allow you to sketch a character with your finger on the screen to look it up. Ask your child's teacher which they prefer. Note that good handwriting makes these apps much easier to use, so handwriting remains important, even though more and more is done on computers.

This is also why having a classroom email list is so helpful, for those moments when despite heroic efforts your child can't figure out the meaning of a given character. That's when you take a picture of it on your phone and mail it to the list, asking for help.

Could Chinese characters
ever be replaced by pinyin?

If you think people get upset when you talk about shifting from traditional to simplified Chinese, that's just a light mist of rain compared to the typhoon this topic brings up. And yes, it's being discussed in China—though most often by those who are lamenting the increasing lack of literacy among Chinese youth.

First off, know that this is not a popular line of discussion among fluent readers of Chinese, who note, correctly, that to move from characters to pinyin would mean discarding several thousand years of rich cultural history. Second, Chinese has enough homonyms that it can be difficult to distinguish between different words. Chinese speakers often resort to drawing a character in the air as they say it, to distinguish between two words pronounced the same but with different meanings. It's kind of the way that an English speaker might say "Tail, a – i – l, not tale, a – l – e," to differentiate between the two.

But there are a few people inside and outside China[17] who at times suggest that pinyin, written with tone marks and broken up into separate words, is the way forward for Chinese. Even revered Chinese author Lu Xun made the suggestion in 1934.[18] It would certainly make Chinese a much easier language to learn and make it a more global language. Vietnamese and Korean both made the switch, for example.

People who support the idea note that today, when most Chinese people write, they actually write in pinyin, because that's how you type Chinese on a computer or phone keyboard. The computer then gives them options for which characters they want it to show. It's the frequency with which younger Chinese choose the *wrong* characters that is so horrifying to the older generation, who learned to write with a pen on paper and so can actually produce each character from memory. Some writers lament it may come to that eventually anyway because the younger generation is already forgetting how to write characters and only knows pinyin.

Others have noted that there might be pushback against a switch from pinyin by the Chinese government, in part because the government has worked so hard to make Mandarin the national language, requiring that it be used as the universal language of education. If people got used to writing and reading in an alphabetic form, it might be too easy for them to begin writing in their local language—which would destroy the linguistic unity China has created over the past thirty or so years.

Either way, this isn't going to be decided anytime soon, so your child needs to learn characters. Sorry, kids.

It could all be *much* harder

If your child complains about having to learn characters instead of pinyin, tell them they should be thankful they're learning Chinese now and not in the beginning of the 20th century. It was only then that China moved away from writing in classical or literary Chinese (called 文言, *wényán*) to colloquial writing based on spoken Mandarin called *baihua* (白话, *báihuà*, plain speech.)

Wenyan is now only taught in literature courses. It's based on Chinese as it was written in the Han dynasty (206 BC–220 AD) and feels as bit like reading Old English—it's that far removed from regular spoken Chinese today. So it could be worse. Much, much worse.

1. Ethnologue: Languages of the World, Mandarin.
   http://www.ethnologue.com/show_language.asp?code=cmn
   Accessed Jan. 14, 2014.
2. Wikipedia, The Sinitic Languages.
   http://upload.wikimedia.org/wikipedia/commons/6/6f/
   Map_of_sinitic_languages-en.svg
   Accessed Jan. 14, 2014.
3. Or five, if you include the neutral tone.
4. Place names can be complex. The word for Guangdong province is 广东, *Guǎngdōng*. Its capital is 广州, *Guǎngdōng*. In English we call both Canton. But the Chinese abbreviation for Canton is 粤, *Yuè*, because that's the name of the language spoken there.
5. Heidi Smith, *Chinese Immersion: A Study of Effective Elementary School Programs*. (Fielding Graduate School, Santa Barbara, Calif. 2007) 13.
6. Mandarin QuickStart Lesson 1: Tones, YouTube.
   http://www.youtube.com/watch?v=Tm37kO4lOJQ
   Accessed Jan. 14, 2014.
7. Though as my friend Liyao Zhu (who is Zhu Liyao in China) points out, there are some names that have two or more characters. They include what in the West would be a double last name (something like Smythe Weston) or names that originated in non- Chinese languages. Some names come from old official titles. For example, 司徒, *Sītú*, means "Minister over the Masses" and is from the Han dynasty. 司马, *Sīmǎ*, means Marshal. 爱新觉罗, *Àixīnjuéluó*, means gold and is from the Manchu language. The last emperor of the Qing Dynasty was named 爱新觉罗。浦仪, *Àixīnjuéluó Pǔyí*, Aisin-Gioro Puyi, because that dynasty was Manchurian.
8. Many Chinese dictionaries list the measure word for every noun. If you really want to get into it, get a copy of the *Cheng & Tsui Chinese Measure Word Dictionary: A Chinese-English English-Chinese Usage Guide* by Jiqing Fang and Michael Connelly. (Boston, Cheng & Tsui, 2008)

9. Here's a nice explanation. Chinese Language Blog, Fractions. http://blogs.transparent.com/chinese/decimals-fractions-and-percentages/ Accessed March 10, 2014.
10. Chinese *pinyin* in six minutes. www.youtube.com/watch?v=b9Ayvjy-Dgs Accessed June 19, 2014.
11. This literally means "symbols of phonetic pronunciation." It's made up of 37 created characters representing all the sounds of Mandarin.
12. About.com, Mandarin language, Stroke Order for Chinese Characters. http://mandarin.about.com/od/characters/ss/stroke_order.htm Accessed Jan. 14, 2013.
13. Here's a cheat sheet for you from Chico State University. Writing Chinese Characters. www.csuchico.edu/~cheinz/syllabi/asst001/spring98/chinese.htm Accessed Jan. 14, 2014.
14. Keiko Koda, Chan Lü, Yanhui Zhang, "Effects of print input on morphological awareness among Chinese heritage language learners," *Chinese as a heritage Language: Fostering Rooted World Citizenry.* (Manoa, Hawai'i, National Foreign Language Resource Center, 2008) 67–87.
15. Rumjahn Hoosian, Psycholinguistic Implications for Linguistic Relativity: A Case Study of Chinese (Hillsdale, N.J. Psychology Press, 1991
16. For this, I've used the dictionary I learned to use in college, because it's the one I'm most comfortable with. But all Chinese-English/English-Chinese dictionaries should work the same. Mine is *Times Chinese-English Dictionary* (Hong Kong, The Commercial Press, 1980).
17. This is a really fun site with a ton of information about pinyin. Pinyin.info, A guide to the writing of Mandarin Chinese in Romanization. www.pinyin.info Accessed Jan. 14, 2014.
18. Pinyin.info, A guide to the writing of Mandarin Chinese in Romanization. http://pinyin.info/readings/lu_xun/writing.html Accessed Jan. 14, 2014.

✝ shí 10 — Why Parents Choose Mandarin Immersion

As you contemplate whether Mandarin immersion is right for your child and your family, you'll find that you have many different hopes and desires. You're in good company. While all parents have expectations about their children's education, parents of children in immersion programs have specific linguistic, cultural and academic issues of their own.

After spending years as a parent in the Mandarin immersion world, I've seen parental motivations break down into six broad categories. Note that I don't say *families*, because often a single family may have one parent in one group, the other in another. Actually, even that's too simple. Many people have one, two, three or all six sets of desires and expectations within them. But let's start with what I've come to call the six types of Mandarin immersion parent:

Pioneer
Global
Academic
Adoptive
Heritage
Chinese

Of course, no one family, or person, can be encompassed by a single word. For example, I consider myself a Global/Academic/Pioneer parent. My wife's more Global/Academic. Our daughters' dad is definitely Heritage/Academic with a strong dash of Global while his husband is more Academic/Global. Thankfully our children, 周情, *Zhōu Qíng,* and 周忆, *Zhōu Yì,* are just good kids who do their homework without too much whining.

Understanding what motivates parents to have their children in these programs can go a long way toward calming the tensions that now and again rise up. That's why I offer up these archetypes. They offer generalizations that might help you understand why the parent sitting next to you at parent-teacher night has such different expectations from your own.

Pioneer families

These are the stalwart families who sign up for a new, untried program because they believe in the promise of immersion. They're willing to take a chance on something that's unknown to give their children a shot at becoming Mandarin speakers. While they're generally only at a school for the first six or nine years (depending on whether it's K–5 or K–8), the imprint they leave lingers for many more years because they create so many of the structures and institutions within a school.

The first few years of any program are always rough. These families go where few other families would, knowing that their child will always have teachers who have never taught immersion in this school, a curriculum that has never been taught in this school and often little in the way of resources in the beginning. They arrive filled with hope and determination, and often with the lingering doubts of their friends ringing in their ears. However, it's quite likely that in just a few short years those same doubting friends may be calling to ask if there isn't some way they can get their own child into the now thriving and fully enrolled program.

This initial shake down period can be eased in some cases. States that have state-wide immersion programs, such as Utah and Delaware, give schools enough support and backup that the initial years aren't nearly as bumpy as they are elsewhere. That's also true of schools that are part of the Flagship–Chinese Acquisition Pipeline consortium, which has created a model Mandarin immersion education program that is easy to implement and offers support to teachers and staff at schools that join. Read more about F-CAP and other consortia in *Chapter 22: Immersion Consortia, The Support Schools Need.*

In schools going it alone, especially in urban school districts, not only is the program new but the school itself often is under-enrolled and has poor test scores. The school district will have chosen the new program for exactly that reason—because it has space and needs an influx of energetic parents. Read more about this in *Chapter 19: Why Schools Choose Mandarin Immersion.* It's a second hurdle the pioneer families must clear, both because of their own concerns over the academics in what can be a struggling school and because of the doubts of family and friends. These early families are committed in a way few others are.

For families in immersion programs placed in low-performing schools, the road is long and hard indeed. They generally have just one or two immersion classes per grade and are typically one strand (one or two classrooms per grade level, alongside one or more regular English language classrooms) in a larger school. Because school districts choose under-enrolled schools that have the space for a new program, they often have to build not only the Mandarin program but also many of the institutions that other schools take for granted, such as a robust Parent-Teacher Association. In the early years these associations are often looked on as both saviors to the school and (it can sometimes feel) a cash register that only has to be asked to miraculously raise money for necessary items. The teachers arrive with nothing and there's often no money for the extras that a language program needs, such as Chinese books for the library or Chinese dictionaries for the classrooms.

Because Mandarin immersion families are also often middle class, they can find that many of the programs in place at a low-income school aren't set up for students in different circumstances. Before-school and after-school programs, for example, may preferentially give space to low-income families, leaving the new families to scramble to create aftercare programs for families who can afford to pay.

Our own school, Starr King Elementary, was a case in point. The parents in the first few years banded together and dug in. An example: When our immersion program began, the hard-working and wonderful staff at our school didn't have a system in place for students to pay for school lunch. Prior to the arrival of the Mandarin program, almost all the students who ate school lunch were on the free lunch plan, so the issue had simply never come up. It took multiple calls to the district and a whole year before it became possible to pay for lunch.

While I hesitate to call these pioneering families a true "type" among parents, it's true that without these stalwart and dig-in-and-get-it-done families in the first years, a new program won't thrive.

These families are different from the ones that come after them, first because they're so willing to make a flying leap of faith, and also because they're so strongly motivated by the desire to teach their children Chinese. "Mandarin or die" is how one mom put it. "Anywhere they put our program, that's where we're going to school." For these families, Mandarin is the single most important reason they choose a school. They're willing to take a perceived educational risk if it means getting Chinese-speaking children out of the deal. They tend to be made up of more white, Asian-American and mixed families because, as discussed below, many Chinese families aren't comfortable in the kind of urban and often low-test-score schools where these programs often are placed. (Or at least until the program really gets going, when test scores rocket up and the school suddenly becomes sought after.)

This can lead to some interesting divisions among parents as the program matures. These pioneer families put blood, sweat and tears into building the new program from the ground up. "And then you've got new parents coming in who think that everything that was done was wrong," says Renée Tan, the mother of two Mandarin immersion middle school students and a pioneer parent at both Starr King Elementary and Aptos Middle School in San Francisco.

Thankfully that attitude is rare. Most families support and honor the work of those who went before them. Frank Han, a parent at the Broadway Mandarin Immersion Program in Venice, California, says that in its third year, their program,

> ...has largely settled into a routine. As is often the case, the pioneering class, now second graders, were the ones blazing the trail, wading into the unknown, trying and failing, trying and succeeding, setting the stage for classes to come and hopefully improve upon the program. And for that, this year's kindergarten class is grateful and indebted to these pioneers. Now, an established Mandarin Immersion Program in its own right, we are happy to see our child blossom under the guidance of Principal Wang and the tutelage of both the English and Mandarin teachers, who have crafted a wonderful and academically challenging program to mold our children into better citizens of the world.

The picture is a little different in programs placed in schools that are already thriving academically. There pioneer families *only* have to deal with new teachers, a new curriculum that's never been taught in Chinese in their district, and staff and administration who are figuring out how to make it all work. They can sometimes face anger on the part of other parents who feel that the new Mandarin program is taking away classroom space from the existing school, which already was doing quite well, thank you very much. They face questions from friends and family who wonder why they would take a chance on a new program when the existing school is already excellent.

The final type of pioneer parents are the ones who help found charter schools. This is a not-uncommon route for families who want Mandarin immersion and can't get their school district to create it. They undertake an enormous amount of effort, often over the course of several years, without knowing whether they'll succeed. The saving grace is that when their school is finally launched, they're almost always a one-school environment in which the entire student body is in Mandarin immersion, and the staff, families and administration are all dedicated to the idea. Still, these parents pay a huge price in sweat equity to create their school, in addition to the ongoing work necessary once the school is up and running.

Global

These are the families who get written about and marveled over in the media. "WOW! White and Black Kids Speak Chinese!" is how one mom described the seemingly unending series of articles about her son's class, which always seemed to feature photos of her blond son and an African-American classmate.

They do make for enticing headlines and there's a reason for it. It's just not that common—yet—for non-Chinese kids in the United States to speak Chinese. But that's changing rapidly. Non-Chinese kids today make up the largest proportion of participants in Mandarin immersion programs nationally. These Mandarin immersion students come from every race and socioeconomic group but have no specific connection to China. For their families, Chinese is about opportunity. They have seen China's extraordinary rise to power over the past 20 years, realize that Chinese is the most commonly spoken language on the planet, and figure having their children grow up with near-native fluency can't be a bad thing.

A deciding factor for my wife and me was recognizing that this window of cognitive development closes after a certain age. It's just easier for kids to learn another language at an early age. For us, the decision centered around learning a language other than English. Both our kids are fluent in English and Spanish. We placed the highest value on learning a third vastly different and more challenging language.

That's how Matt Cahill, who calls himself a Global/Academic parent, puts it. His children attend José Ortega Elementary School in San Francisco, one of three schools in the city's Mandarin immersion program.

With the growth of Mandarin immersion programs, especially through the F-CAP consortium, it's not uncommon to find Mandarin immersion in school districts with very low numbers of Asian-American students.

Once parents figure out that their child is going to graduate from high school with the same skills as the kids in immersion, but that those immersion kids are also going to be fluent in a different language and maybe able to get a better job, they want that for their children as well," says Ann Tollefson, a world language consultant who has worked extensively evaluating immersion programs nationwide. "These programs are going to be more common around the country. Parents drive the engine in any school district anywhere in the country. When they want these programs, the districts will make them happen.

For some of these families, Mandarin can be "value-added" to their child's education. They realize their children may never set foot in China, but also know that speaking it will still be useful because Chinese is an important world language that will only become more important. And although it's a long way off, some will admit they hope it might give their kid a leg up when it comes time to apply to college. "I mean, come on, how many Irish-American boys are they going to get who speak fluent Mandarin in high school?" one dad said to me at a fundraiser, after we'd all had a few glasses of wine. For some, but not all, their expectations for how fluent their children will be in Chinese are often lower than the expectations of parents who speak Mandarin or who have connections to the language, and this can lead to tensions.

"You have the non-Chinese speaking parents who complain that there's too much work and the Chinese-speaking families who complain that it's not enough and they're not learning enough," says Tan, the San Francisco mom.

These global parents also tend to be very involved in their children's education and treasure time spent with their kids as they discover and learn. They can sometimes feel disconnected when the child is learning in a language they can't understand. Not being able to measure their child's academic progress (because they literally can't read and help with the homework coming home) can make them anxious, and having little or no control over their schools is also difficult for them. Especially if the child struggles academically, these parents become very concerned because they can't help. They're prone to what some call the "First Grade Freak-Out," when there comes a point in first grade at which they realize their child's English reading ability isn't quite as high as that of kids who aren't in immersion. This eventually evens out but takes a little talking down to get them to believe it. There's another freak-out that hits around second or third grade, where parents realize they have no understanding of much of what their child is learning, and homework is an impenetrable brick wall of Chinese. This is cured by making sure that your teacher and room parent do a great job of communicating with parents, see *Chapter 25: Tips From Parents*.

At a certain point, some of these parents also realize that having chosen Mandarin immersion entails more of an academic commitment than they might have first realized. When students' work in Mandarin kicks into high gear in fourth and fifth grades, they see just how much old-fashioned sweat it takes to master hundreds of characters as they learn to read and write Chinese. One mom, whose family decided to stick with it despite the extra homework, said, "Learning characters requires a lot of rote repetition, which is anathema to more liberal styles of learning."

Another mom who chose a Chinese immersion school for her children put it this way:

> Both my kids really learned grit and perseverance. They learned how to work hard and not to give up. When we started looking at private high schools, they weren't worried at all [about the workload]. They knew they could do it. Though I have to admit it wasn't always easy as a parent when they were little and crying over their homework. It was hard for us sometimes.

A fascinating trend we've seen in San Francisco is the establishment of multiple Mandarin immersion preschools. Families who want their children to learn Chinese see no reason to wait until grade school to start. Today they can choose one of several Mandarin immersion preschools that enroll students as young as three years old. This is creating an interesting situation given that our program in San Francisco reserves one-third of its seats for bilingual students who speak both Mandarin and English, one-third for Mandarin speakers and one-third for English speakers. The aim is to have a classroom of students who come from both Chinese-speaking and English-speaking homes so that students will learn from each other. The system is meant to give priority to newly-immigrated students who are learning English.

However, when the system was set up, no one at the school district ever imagined there would be a flood of students from English-speaking homes who had spent two to three years in a Mandarin-immersion preschool and were functionally fluent. These students easily pass the Mandarin test required of incoming kindergarteners. That test consists of the child going into a room with a Mandarin-speaking tester, who first reads a story to them and then asks questions about the story. The school district employee also points to pictures and asks the child to say what he or she sees.

In 2013–2014, the Starr King program for the first time filled its quota of Mandarin-speakers because of this new influx of students. However, few of them actually came from Mandarin-speaking families. The school district hasn't quite figured out how to react to this latest example of the hunger of parents to offer their children a second language as early as possible.

Academic

This is the group that surprises many school administrators and sometimes confounds parents in the other groups. In most programs there exists a substantial minority of parents who couldn't care less about Chinese. They choose Mandarin immersion simply because they expect it to be a strong, rigorous academic program full of students from families who prize education. Their child could be learning "Latin or German or Hebrew," as one dad put it. As a mom said, "Nobody puts their kid in Mandarin immersion by mistake."

For them, Mandarin immersion is a proxy for other things they want in a school. It is a way of ensuring that their children are in an educationally demanding and rigorous school. Mandarin is not an easy language to learn and because it requires memorizing several thousand characters, it takes lots of work to become literate. It is a way to ensure their children are in school with students whose families are committed to education, no matter what their socioeconomic status. None of this would come as a surprise to parents in Canada, where French immersion is often called "the poor man's private school."[1] A report by Statistics Canada found that students in French immersion "tend to come from higher socio-economic backgrounds and are more likely to have parents with a post-secondary education." While we don't have figures for that in U.S.-based Chinese programs, anecdotally, the picture looks very similar to French immersion.

In fact, this book really was launched with an essay I started writing back in 2011. It was called "Is Mandarin the new Latin?" I was trying to understand the families in our school for whom Mandarin wasn't important. They reminded me of kids I'd known growing up in Seattle whose parents sent them to Nathan Hale High School. It was one of the better public high schools in Seattle and also happened to be the only one that still taught Latin. I knew a couple of girls whose parents signed them up for Latin so they'd get assigned to Nathan Hale. Not that they cared about Latin, they just wanted all the constellation of attributes that tended to also exist in a school where there were enough students who wanted to study Latin. That essay morphed into this chapter, and the realization that I needed to write a whole book.

Mandarin immersion can also be a proxy for gifted and talented education (called GATE in many districts). Especially in public school systems where there are few academically high-achieving schools or where GATE classes no longer are funded, Mandarin immersion programs are a substitute for rigor and difficulty. Many of these districts say that teachers will provide a differentiated learning experience in each conventional class, providing for the needs of students at every level. However, many parents of gifted kids find that's not always possible, so they turn to Mandarin immersion.

The gifted/immersion link has been made explicit in a few districts. In Australia in the 1980s, French immersion schools were first proposed as a way to provide a challenge for gifted students. In San Francisco, the San Francisco Unified School District's GATE coordinator specifically told parents at a 2011 meeting that with almost no funding for GATE programs in elementary schools, they should consider putting their kids in immersion programs instead because they would provide a challenging academic environment. She singled out Mandarin as especially difficult.

In San Mateo, California, Mandarin classes were first offered in the school district's GATE magnet school in 2004. In 2007–2008, it launched a Mandarin immersion program for kindergarteners. The school's website states: "Mandarin Immersion and GATE are natural, complementary programs at College Park Elementary. Students apply critical thinking, problem solving and advanced vocabulary development in both languages and across all disciplines."

Of course, this isn't the case everywhere. Minnetonka, Minnesota, has a Mandarin immersion program and a very strong GATE strand, called the Navigator Program, which is separate from immersion. Navigator is for exceptionally gifted students and requires that they test in with an IQ of at least 145.

What is different about Academic parents is they don't have the attachment to Chinese that the other five groups can have. One father said he was "happy if his kid was exposed to Mandarin." That's heresy to Mandarin-language families, whose only reason for choosing the program was to teach their children to read and write Chinese fluently.

According to some school administrators, this is also the group most likely to drop out of Mandarin immersion programs "due to concerns about the quantity and quality of the English provided in the Mandarin immersion program." The fact that their kids are also learning Mandarin isn't enough of a motivator that they're willing to accept lower English standards, as one administrator put it.

Adoptive

This group consists of parents who have adopted children from China. For many immersion programs this was a large cohort early on, although it's been shrinking more recently. In 1991 China loosened laws regarding international adoptions to address the problem of abandoned children—most often girls—because of the national one-child policy. Between that year and 2010, 66,630 Chinese children were adopted by U.S. families, 90% of them girls, according to the U.S. Department of State. Many of these families have sought out Mandarin immersion schools to give their children the opportunity to maintain a strong connection with their birth country and culture.

In Portland, Oregon, the creation of one of the nation's oldest Mandarin immersion programs was championed in part by a strong group of families formed through adoptions, says Gary Rydout, a former chair of ShuRen, the non-profit that supports the program. He is the father of two daughters who were born in China. In his oldest daughter's class, "one-third of the students were adopted," he says.

Program-wide, in the early years between 40% and 60% of ethnically Chinese students in Portland's Mandarin immersion program were adopted. "When you walk into the classroom people think they're all Chinese heritage language students," but many actually come from English-speaking, non-Chinese households, says Michael Bacon, Portland Public School's Immersion Achievement Coordinator.

Other programs also have come into being in part because of efforts by adoptive families who wanted to give their children access to Chinese. Yinghua Academy, a Chinese immersion public charter school in Minneapolis, opened in September 2006 with 77 students and was the first Chinese immersion school in the Midwest. It was founded "largely by (mainly white) adoptive parents of Chinese-born children. Initially these kids comprised the vast majority of our students. Today it's more balanced, but there are still a significant number of Chinese adoptees among Yinghua's student population," says Michele St. Martin. Her two daughters, both adopted from China, attend the school.

This used to mean it could be easier to get a spot in a Mandarin immersion school if you had a boy, because schools were trying to maintain a rough gender balance in their incoming classes. But as adoptions from China have diminished, and more boys are adopted from there as well, it's not as much of an issue.

None of this is to say that families formed through adoption are looking for their children to be "made Chinese" by attending Mandarin immersion, says Eileen Drapiza, whose daughter was adopted from China and attends Yu Ming Charter School in Oakland, California. She feels that her family brings a very different set of factors to the Mandarin immersion table. "While I want a language immersion program for my child, we are not necessarily attempting to raise her with hopes of plugging her into a Chinese educational system, or to imbue values we don't agree with," she says. Instead, her goal is to support her daughter now so that one day she can gain access to her birth culture and country of origin in a way that will be more meaningful than as a mere tourist with a language barrier. Giving her daughter the opportunity to develop a sense of ethnic pride is a joy because it is the foundation for a healthy sense of identity, says Drapiza. She continues:

> Adopted children from China are not made global citizens by virtue of speaking Chinese. They are already global citizens by virtue of being who they are, and what they have experienced. They were very young immigrants, and made a huge transition, often at a pre-verbal stage. People are mistaken if they think that just because a child cannot talk about the difficulty of adjusting to such a big move that there is no memory or feeling about it. Quite the contrary. It is likely to be a very frightening experience—everything that might have been familiar in the first months or years of their life, the sights, the smells, the sounds—it all suddenly changes, and that's on top of the loss that led to their availability for adoption in the first place.
>
> Our original vague plan, perhaps similar to other adoptive families, was to one day, in the distant future, enroll our daughter in a Mandarin class so that she could reconnect with her heritage. Then we realized we had the chance to provide an almost continuous exposure to Mandarin, which meant that when she was an infant, at least we were able to provide continuity with the sounds and the language of her native land. Over the years, our daughter has benefitted from attending Mandarin-speaking day care, and a Chinese playgroup, and then immersion school starting in kindergarten. Early continuous exposure has been key; we're told our child's Mandarin is very good, especially given that we are not native Mandarin speakers (my husband studies and speaks a little Mandarin). Put-

ting the effort toward creating this continuity made better sense as an option over waiting until she'd completely forgotten the sounds of her infancy in China, and then somehow expecting that she might have an interest in learning Mandarin as a foreign language as an older child. Our daughter is being raised bilingual, so she's not had to give up one language for another. She has both, and she would be a different child today had we not found our way to a Mandarin immersion school.

Being in an immersion school also means that she is surrounded and has contact with many more Chinese people than she would have in the school she would have normally attended, including Chinese teachers, Chinese parents, Chinese American parents, and other children born in China. At her school it is the norm to be Chinese, look Chinese, or to come from an Asian-mixed family. The environment promotes a development of positive self-image for her. While there is a welcome drive for greater diversity at the school, nonetheless, there is also a self-selected dominant culture based on the language choice, and our daughter benefits from that.

It is Drapiza's hope that the school will embrace all that her daughter is and that "her loss (which is great for someone so young) is never intensified at her school because of insensitive lessons or thoughtless assignments."

Thankfully, most Mandarin immersion programs do a good job of supporting all students, adopted or not. But at times teachers can inadvertently fail to honor the ways these families have come into being, for example by asking, "Where are you from?" That can be a complex question for a 5- or 6-year-old born in China but raised in America to answer. Having students create family trees is a common way to teach Chinese words for various family members but it has to be approached thoughtfully so adopted children are equally included.

Appropriate inclusive vocabulary can be incorporated into lessons. Terms for bio-mom, bio-dad and adoptive parents can help provide a positive spin and normalize the different ways in which families come together.

Because Mandarin immersion classrooms can have such a high percentage of students who are adopted, education for the entire school about adoption is also important. Some families have reported that classmates have told their girls: "You're lucky. If you had stayed in China, you would have died." Other children demand, "Where's your real mom?" when they see a student with Chinese features being picked up at school by a non-Chinese parent. Several parents I've spoken with have said their school showed the film "That's a Family!"[2] and that it was helpful in getting students to understand and talk about how different families are formed. The documentary is about children who grow up in many different kinds of families, including adoptive, with grandparents, with single parents or in divorced families.

Heritage

Heritage parents are American-born Chinese and, increasingly, biracial families who may or may not still speak Chinese but who would like their children to be able to. This is a large and expanding group. The United States has a relatively small Chinese population, though on the West Coast it's relatively large. In 2010, 3.34 million people identified themselves as Chinese and another 334,144 identified as part-Chinese, for a grand total of 4 million out of a total U.S. population of 314 million.[3] However, Chinese-Americans are a fast-growing group, up 58% since 2000.[4] And many of them are not recent immigrants. About one-third of the U.S. Chinese-American community is second-generation or beyond.[5] Because of that, a relatively large percentage of Chinese-American families don't speak Chinese at home or at all.

Immersion appeals to these heritage parents for several reasons. First, it's a way to get their kids speaking, reading and writing Chinese without having to send them to Saturday school. A fairly large percentage of these parents were subjected to Saturday Chinese school as children, which, in the words of one parent, "taught me to hate China and all things Chinese." Also called Heritage schools, these privately organized weekend schools tend to be taught in a very traditional format by parent volunteers, usually taking up much of a child's Saturday. While more modern and professional Saturday schools are beginning to emerge, that's not the experience many parents had as children.

They remember Chinese school with dislike and in some cases outright hatred. "We never got to do sports or anything fun on the weekends because we had to go to Chinese school," one father told me. "We were the weirdos in our neighborhood." While he wants his kids to learn Chinese, he's not willing to put them through that, so he chose a Mandarin immersion school. Now his kids not only get to learn Chinese, but they're in a school where everyone does, so it seems normal and not weird—and they have their weekends free to play soccer and baseball.

Another reason Mandarin immersion is popular among these families is the regret many second and third generation Chinese parents have about not retaining more of their family's language. They often feel more comfortable speaking in English than in Chinese, and wish they'd paid more attention in Saturday school and not stopped speaking Chinese with their relatives. They want to ensure that their own children can speak to older family members and thus connect to their family's culture and history.

Heritage families also choose immersion because it's a way to push back against the social pressure that causes so many children to give up their home language in favor of English, says Kathleen Wang, principal at Pioneer Valley Chinese Immersion Charter School in Hadley, Massachusetts. Immersion gives them "a peer group of other people who speak and study Chinese. Kids don't like to be different. In immersion they're not."

However, these families generally don't have the same expectation of rigor as parents educated in China. Said one mom, "In general, heritage speakers have high expectations that their child's Chinese will be 'better than theirs,' but given their first-hand knowledge of how difficult it is to maintain a second language, even with fluent parents, they tend to be a bit more forgiving" than Chinese-born parents. This group also includes families in which one parent is Chinese and one is from another race. At Starr King, being bi-racial (which is what my own kids are) is so normal that it's not even anything the kids think about. That's a nice added attraction for many families.

Chinese

You might think that if you sign up for Mandarin immersion, most of the families sitting next to you on Welcome to Kindergarten night would be Mandarin speakers. Surprisingly, you'd be wrong. There are about 3.4 million Chinese-Americans in the United States, and 76% of them are foreign born.[6] But you won't find many of them in Mandarin immersion classrooms—yet. That's because for many of these families, their educational focus is making sure their children gain a strong command of English. A high percentage of Chinese immigrants speak a Chinese dialect as their primary home language—83% according to the 2012 U.S. Census. They expect their children to learn to speak Chinese, because they speak it at home. School is a place to learn English. If they want their children to read and write Chinese, they send them to a Saturday or Heritage school.

These recent immigrants are only slowly warming to the idea of bilingual classrooms that offer both languages, although it is beginning to happen. It's a bit of a chicken-and-egg problem. Immersion schools quickly fill up with English-speaking families who want their kids to learn Chinese. As a result, the schools don't develop support mechanisms, such as bilingual office staff, Chinese-language outreach materials etc. That makes it harder to recruit families that speak only Chinese.

Some Chinese-speaking families do send their children to immersion schools. It appears to me, based on anecdotal evidence, that many tend to be families confident of their English, so they worry less that their children won't become fluent. Others are from families in which only one parent speaks Mandarin and the other is an English speaker, so they feel they've got English covered. Of course, the decisions Chinese-speaking families make vary tremendously by school and city.

Chinese-speakers

When Chinese-speaking families enroll their children in immersion schools, they tend to be very academically minded and push hard for high standards and high levels of accomplishment, both for their children and the school. Nationally, Chinese American adults have very high levels of education, with almost double the number of bachelor's degrees (51%) compared with college graduates over 25 in the nation as a whole (28%). These parents worked extremely hard in school back home. It's difficult for Americans to even understand the level of study and commitment required to secure a coveted place in a Chinese university. In our family, we have a tradition called "Family Movie Night." Most Fridays, one family member gets to choose a movie that we all watch together. When our older daughter went to China for three weeks with her middle school class, she stayed with a family in Beijing. There she was introduced to a different tradition, "Friday Homework Night."

It was a stark example of day-to-day reality there. Students in China routinely study six and seven hours a night and the entire weekend, from elementary school onward. The focus is on passing the National Higher Education Entrance Examination, or 高考, *gāokǎo* (high test). This single, grueling, nine-hour test determines whether applicants win a spot at a Chinese university. About 30% fail.

Parents who succeeded in that system tend to have high hopes, and expectations, for their children. Because the children already are fluent speakers of Chinese from speaking it at home, their parents frequently expect them to learn to read and write Mandarin at a level close to what they might have attained had they attended school in a Chinese-speaking country.

This expectation creates tension because Mandarin immersion students in the United States tend to read and write several grade levels below their counterparts in China. (*See Chapter 16: Chinese Literacy Issues.*) By fifth grade students might only be reading at the level of a second or third grade student in China. A third grader from my daughters' school who moved to Beijing tested in at halfway through first grade reading abilities in a Chinese school, for example.

The desire for greater literacy runs very deep. In China, perhaps more so than in many countries, written language is directly connected to culture. China retains strong links to literature and poetry from its classical period. Well-educated adults and children are presumed to know by heart multiple poems, telling a story and making a point that is etched on the heart of those who memorized them. These parents want to ensure that their children share those emotions, which only exists for them in Chinese and cannot truly be translated into English.

As one mother put it,

Imagine moving to and raising your children in China. As they matured you would want them to read classic American literature that you loved growing up, literature that shaped you. But then you discover that their English vocabulary is too limited to be able to read it, and you find a gulf between you and your child you hadn't expected.

To overcome this, parents in programs that have been around awhile tend to reach a point at which they begin to want to move the needle a bit. In San Francisco, Cupertino and Portland, Chinese-speaking parents have pushed hard on school districts to add more rigor to the Chinese curriculum. They are more comfortable with demanding harder schoolwork, including more homework, a longer school day and more repetition, than many American parents and school districts seem to be.

Another difference is one of class. Many Mandarin-speaking families who come to the United States are college-educated professionals. They haven't necessarily moved due to financial need or political persecution, but out of a desire for a more global sense of belonging. These parents have no reason to accept just what is given to them—if a program is not up to their standards, they demand that it be improved.

As one mother (who speaks three languages fluently) said of her daughters:

I don't feel [my daughters'] Chinese language achievement is where it should and could be after six years in the program. It is no secret that the way to get the kids to read and enjoy reading Chinese more is to build up their vocabularies so they can read more. I feel the curriculum is not rigorous enough. For example, I feel the kids can handle more than one word a day starting from kindergarten. If we can up the requirement by 20% each year, the accumulative effect in six years will be quite substantial.

In addition if the requirement for reading and writing is also upped by 10 to 20%, our kids are more likely to be able to read, write, speak more fluently. I know it won't be easy for some kids and families. But we have to believe that our kids can do better, with a lot of our support, of course. They do live up to our expectations— (especially) if those expectations come from the teachers and not from their nagging moms.

One Taiwanese mom had her kids in an immersion school in the United States and then the family moved to Beijing. She was able to enroll her children in a Chinese school that followed the national curriculum and has seen close-up and personal the differences between an immersion school here and a regular Chinese school—and how hard Chinese students have to work to read at the levels they do.

I've witnessed my kids' Chinese grow exponentially since coming to China. I also realized not every American would feel comfortable subjecting their kids to such a volume of memorization. In order for this to work, you have to sign on to the whole package. There's no shortcut; your kids just have to study a lot harder and memorize a lot of Chinese phrases and characters. Chinese education also tends to emphasize achievement and competitiveness.

That's not always palatable in an American setting, some programs find. And it's not only an American phenomenon, says Jianqui Wang, one of the founding parents of the *Deutsch-Chinesische Grundschule*, a public school launched in 2011 at Planetarium Elementary School in Berlin, Germany. They hope to add a full Mandarin immersion program once the German authorities figure out how to allow Chinese as a language of instruction. Currently it offers a Mandarin preschool, language classes and extra cultural activities for its students.

Wang says there's been tension between the German and Chinese educational styles among parents. Chinese families want higher levels of Chinese because the language is part of their culture. Although American parents might imagine German parents are academically demanding of their children, in reality she says they're against pushing kids too hard. "They say, 'It should be fun; we don't need too much pressure.' But we'll find a way to balance both," she says.

At the same time, not all Western parents reject the Chinese emphasis on rigor and hard work. I know one mother in San Francisco who, when she was touring elementary schools to choose one for her daughter, had a 30% rule. She didn't want immersion for her kids but she did want a strong focus on academics. To get it, she decided she wouldn't even consider a school that didn't have at least 30% Chinese families. "I know they're going to demand a lot from their kids and I want my kids in school with peers for whom that's the norm."

Non-Chinese Chinese speakers

There is also a small, outlier group in this cohort: non-Chinese parents who learned Mandarin in college or from working in China and who want their children to speak it. Their issues tend to be similar in some ways to the Mandarin-speaking Chinese parents. They want their children to attain a high level of spoken and written Chinese. Depending on how good their own Mandarin is, they can be pleased or disappointed with the level achieved by their children.

An interesting counterpoint to these families is provided by the numerous American parents in China who say that it's almost impossible to find truly bilingual schools there that teach both Chinese and English well. Most international schools only provide an hour of Chinese a day and those students don't learn much. Chinese public schools don't do well teaching English. So I've heard from several families that their children learned more Chinese attending an immersion school in the United States than they did when they lived in China. Immersion schools are beginning to emerge in China but they're still rare and, not surprisingly, very expensive.

A mixing pot with some big shoes to fill

So there you have the six types of Mandarin immersion families. You might have seen yourself in some of those descriptions or recognized other parents you know. Whether all or only some are present will depend on where you live and what kind of school your child is in. But even if not all six are side-by-side in your school, realizing that other parents might have different motivations from your own can help when there's conflict in a classroom, a PTA or a school. Only with understanding is true communication possible.

I'm using a deliberately mixed metaphor above because as you can see, it's a mixed bag in Mandarin immersion. Here are some of the issues that various parents have described to me over the years as having come up at their schools. Acknowledging them can help school communities work together to get past them.

The energy and determination of **Pioneer** parents, who fill the first few years of classes in any Mandarin immersion program, is crucial to getting them off the ground. But they can feel protective of the program as it grows and feel that any criticism demeans the blood, sweat and tears they put into making it work.

Chinese-speaking parents can sometimes feel the Mandarin portion of the education isn't rigorous enough and that the students aren't expected to become nearly fluent enough.

Some non-Chinese parents can be culturally insensitive about the expectations and desires many **Chinese** parents have for their children, which they dismiss as "tiger-parenting."

On the other hand, **Adoptive** and **Global** parents can feel excluded from decision-making because they're not considered "culturally competent" to make any comments about their children's schooling because they're not culturally or linguistically connected to the language.

Some **Heritage** parents feel that the history of injustices against Chinese and Asian-Americans in the United States is ignored in their schools. Especially in urban school districts where the problems faced by African-Americans and Latinos are championed, the very real history of discrimination and violence against Chinese in the U.S. is almost never taught.

Parents whose families were formed through **adoption** from China often can feel that teachers don't take into account the feelings of their children, especially when it comes to heritage and family tree issues.

Academic parents can feel that there's too much time and emphasis on Chinese (which freaks out the other five groups).

None of these tensions and strains should scare you away from Mandarin immersion in the least. Talk to any parent who has been through five or six years at almost any (non-immersion) school in the United States and they'll tell you all sorts of stories about power struggles in the PTA, homework battles (too much versus not enough) with principals, stellar teachers who make you swoon, and teachers who probably should consider another profession. Immersion programs aren't immune to any of this, but they also have their own specific idiosyncrasies. By reading about some of the motivations you're likely to encounter in other parents and yourself, hopefully you'll be able to better understand where everyone is coming from—and that's the first step to building the bridges. And those bridges are one reason Mandarin immersion is such a wonderful thing.

1. Tim Johnson, "A look at French immersion," *Canadian Family.*
    http://www.canadianfamily.ca/parents/look-french-immersion/
    Accessed Jan. 14, 2014.
2. *That's a Family.* A documentary film available through Groundspark.org. Check your local library or
    http://groundspark.org/our-films-and-campaigns/thatfamily
3. "The Rise of Asian Americans: Chapter 1: Portrait of Asian Americans."
    Pew Research Social & Demographic Trends, p. 14.
    http://www.pewsocialtrends.org/2012/06/19/the-rise-of-asian-
    americans/2/#chapter-1-portrait-of-asian-americans
    Accessed March 14, 2014.
4. "The Rise of Asian Americans: Chapter 1: Portrait of Asian Americans."
    Pew Research Social & Demographic Trends. p. 15.
    http://www.pewsocialtrends.org/2012/06/19/the-rise-of-asian-
    americans/2/#chapter-1-portrait-of-asian-americans
    Accessed March 14, 2014.
5. "The Rise of Asian Americans: Chapter 1: Portrait of Asian Americans,"
    Pew Research Social & Demographic Trends.
    http://www.pewsocialtrends.org/2012/06/19/the-rise-of-asian-
    americans/2/#chapter-1-portrait-of-asian-americans
    Accessed March 14, 2014.
6. "The Rise of Asian Americans: Chapter 1: Portrait of Asian Americans,"
    Pew Research Social & Demographic Trends.
    http://www.pewsocialtrends.org/2012/06/19/the-rise-of-asian-
    americans/2/#chapter-1-portrait-of-asian-americans
    Accessed March 14, 2014.

Parent Profiles

shí yī 11

A Chinese-speaking family in Los Angeles

The Hans are a Mandarin-speaking couple who live in Southern California. Their experiences offer insight into the difficulties Chinese-speaking families face in retaining the language in an English-speaking country and show how hard they are willing to work to make it happen.

Frank and Mindy Han live in Calabasas, a town in the San Fernando Valley that's an hour away from Los Angeles' West Side. And yet, twice each day, they make that drive so that their daughter can attend Broadway Elementary School. In doing so, they've chosen a school that until recently had so few students that the Los Angeles Unified School District wanted its principal to take on the leadership of another small school in addition to Broadway.

What brought them to Broadway, an underperforming school in a neighborhood that 15 years ago was considered sketchy at best, was Mandarin immersion. In Frank's words, "We are both second-generation, American-born Chinese from families whose parents put an incredible amount of effort into having us learn Chinese. We spoke only Mandarin at home; our parents taught us Chinese lessons daily; and we had private Chinese teachers weekly. When we grew up and went to college, our Mandarin fluency was a lot better than most ABCs (American-born Chinese) who had been 'subjected' to the usual Saturday morning Chinese school routine, and we saw how difficult it was for them to learn Chinese so late in life."

Even so, the Hans felt their proficiency levels are still far from a native speaker's level, so having their children learn Mandarin from day one has always been a priority. They've invested a tremendous amount into ensuring that happens, even when it wasn't the easiest thing for them to do. "We speak Chinese at home, we hire Chinese-speaking nannies and those things all help." Still, they realized that to keep up with fluency, "especially learning to read and write, an immersion environment at school is the only real alternative, short of moving to Asia."

A less conventional but no less important reason they chose Mandarin immersion was because of the other families in the program. "We seek people who come from different backgrounds, have traveled and studied extensively around the world, and have a more global perspective and life experience," says Mindy. Frank grew up in Germany, spoke Mandarin and Shanghainese at home, and learned German, English, French and Latin. He came to the United States as a high school exchange student and stayed for college. Later, he studied in Taiwan, and worked in New York, San Francisco, Houston and Los Angeles.

Mindy grew up in New Mexico, in a primarily Spanish-speaking environment, but chose to study German in high school. She, too, traveled and studied all over the United States, Europe and Asia. "In fact, we met in Taiwan at a language-intensive university program when Mindy went looking for someone to practice speaking German with," Frank says.

When the time came to decide which school was right for their children, they visited "many highly-rated schools, public and private, that are fantastic academically but had a very uniform student body. For us, because of our 'melting pot' background, it was hard to find a place where we fit in completely. Do we choose a school where mostly hedge fund managers or investment bankers send their children? Do we send them to a German immersion program? A math-and-science magnet program? Our neighborhood public school in an affluent community where the dominant second language is Hebrew? A private Christian school?"

After two years at Broadway, they've found that the program has parents who share their priorities and who care about education and about seeing the world through different cultural lenses. It's a place where their children aren't in a bubble but spend their day with people of different races, ethnicities, socio-economic levels and overall walks of life.

As their daughter begins her second year in the program, the Hans are pleased with the education she's received. Their daughter has "blossomed under the guidance of Principal Susan Wang and the tutelage of both the English and Mandarin teachers, who together have crafted a wonderful and academically challenging program to mold our children into better citizens of the world."

More Chinese

How much Chinese students in immersion programs learn is one issue the Hans have grappled with, as have many Chinese-speaking families. Ideally they would like their children to be fully bilingual and biliterate, but they realize that balancing the needs and levels of all children in a U.S.-based program makes that impossible.

"We were initially frustrated with the level of Chinese fluency with many of the children in kindergarten," says Mindy. Most of the children in the program came from homes where the families spoke little or no Chinese. This was very different from their daughter, whose first language was Mandarin. That had been a deliberate choice on their part, and one which required a great deal of work and planning.

"Keep in mind, we are second-generation Chinese, so it wasn't natural for us to speak it at home. We really had to work at it. We kept our children home until three with a Chinese nanny before they went to preschool; we sent them to Saturday Chinese schools; we watch all kinds of movies and TV shows in Chinese; and listen to children's nursery songs in Chinese. Their grandparents only speak Chinese to them, and my husband and I speak Chinese to them, even though we speak English to each other because it's so much easier," says Mindy.

When their daughter began kindergarten, she came in speaking both English and Mandarin, which didn't make for a very engaging program for her, Mindy says.

"We spoke with our principal about this exact concern. While other children in the class certainly benefited from the few fluent children in the class, the fluent children were getting very little out of the Chinese class, especially in the beginning when they spent weeks on numbers and colors. For a good three months, our daughter was bored out of her mind."

"The principal and my husband and I met with our Chinese teacher, and they decided to supplement our daughter's homework. Every week, she got additional words to learn and practice on top of what everyone else got. In class, the Mandarin teacher used the two or three fluent speakers as 'helpers.'

That level of differentiation helped make school interesting and fun for their daughter. They've also begun to focus on other learning opportunities for her that aren't necessarily Chinese-related. For example, "We have a Chinese tutor during the summer but not during the year," Mindy says. "I guess it's an option, but we choose not to. There are so many other things they can be learning and experiencing. Mandarin half the day at school is sufficient. If there was an after-school enrichment program like Lego (using Lego Robotics building blocks to learn to program computers), cooking or hip hop dance taught in Chinese, we'd definitely consider that, but our school doesn't have that all set up yet."

In the end, the Hans have come to terms with the fact that while they'd love for their daughter to be in a school that exactly fits her level of Mandarin fluency, and the Mandarin and English academic levels they hope for her, they realize that no such school exists in the United States.

"Really, if you care about learning the language, what is your alternative?" Mindy asks. "Any other option (your local public or private school) is less Chinese, not more, so we stuck it out. For those who want 100% immersion, perhaps they should start a different school, or better yet, move to China or Taiwan."

The irony of this is that all the Hans' friends and relatives in Taiwan and China "spend a ton of money and energy sending their kids to the American or British school to learn English," says Mindy.

Some Chinese-speaking parents feel that Saturday Chinese schools provide the same level of Chinese instruction as an immersion program, so they choose to place their children in English-only programs in school and then enroll them in Chinese school on the weekends. For the Hans, that wasn't the experience they've seen among their friends. "After we enrolled in Mandarin immersion, we stopped going to Saturday schools, because who are we kidding here? Those classes, while well intentioned, are often mind-numbing and boring, taught by volunteers and a huge waste of time."

"Once in a while, if you are lucky, you get an amazing teacher, and the kids love it," but that isn't generally the case, at least among the people they know. "Over the course of twelve years, ask any of your friends in college who were 'forced' by their parents to go to Saturday Chinese school. Most detested it and saw it as a necessary evil. And few of them speak or write Chinese fluently."

That wasn't how they wanted their daughter to feel about the language. "We want her to love learning the language and the culture—not resent it and roll her eyes that her entire Saturday morning was gone," says Mindy.

If immersion weren't available they'd be putting their educational efforts into Saturday school "because something is better than nothing," Mindy says. But for their family, a public Mandarin immersion program—even one that requires an hour's drive each way—is what works.

"In the end, the Mandarin immersion program looks more like the vibrant city of Los Angeles, indeed the world, that we live in today," says Mindy. "So, in addition to our cultural heritage, the desire to stay connected to our family, and for future business and work opportunities, the Mandarin immersion program is the best fit for us."

Being black and bilingual

Jamila Nightingale is the founder of Parents of African-American Students Studying Chinese, which can be found at PAASSC.com. She and her family live in Berkeley, California. Her children attend the Chinese American International School in San Francisco. Here she describes her experience and that of other African American parents who have chosen Mandarin immersion for their children.

My family's road to Chinese immersion began just days after my husband and I walked down the aisle. While we were honeymooning overseas, we came across a short magazine article on raising bilingual children. The article posed a question: Which language would you choose, Spanish or Chinese? This sparked a five-minute conversation, during which we briefly discussed the benefits of raising bilingual children, quickly agreed that we saw the benefits and decided on Chinese, specifically Mandarin.

Nine years later, both of our young daughters are enrolled in a full-time Chinese immersion school and I have started a parents' association to support other African-American families who have selected this route for their children. Following this nontraditional path hasn't always been smooth, but like the Ashford-and-Simpson song that played when we took our first steps from the altar, "We built it up and built it up and now it's solid—solid as a rock!" We are happily committed to Chinese immersion education.

In this essay I'll elaborate on our experiences with Chinese immersion and connect it with those of several other African-American families I have met through Parents of African-American Students Studying Chinese (PAASSC). I hope I can give a sense of what motivates African-Americans to pursue Chinese immersion education and how some of us have experienced it. I emphasize "some of us" due to both the small sample size—nine families—and the specific demographic that we represent: married, middle-class, San Francisco Bay area couples (several are interracial), all college educated (several have earned advanced degrees) and internationally traveled. Many of the parents mentioned in this article are themselves fluent in at least one language other than English; some speak two or three. As Chinese immersion takes off in communities throughout America, African-American families from diverse geographic, economic, educational backgrounds and family structures will likely echo some of our experiences while adding other perspectives.

Why immersion?

At the heart of the interest in language immersion is, of course, a family's desire to raise a bilingual child. This desire is often rooted in the parents' high aspirations for their child's education and in their own values and exposure to other languages and cultures. As I mentioned above, our interest in bilingual education began with international travel and a magazine article. We agreed that our job as parents is to give our children better opportunities. In considering the opportunities we had as children, one that didn't come until later was learning another language.

Other parents were drawn to the many benefits that being bilingual offers their children. "Being a teacher, I know that language learning enhances cognition," says Dawn Williams Ferreira. "We wholeheartedly support language learning and have always thought that our children would be multilingual." Giving her son a global perspective attracted Tracey Helen to multilingual education. "We live in a big world," she says. "The more languages you speak, the more you can learn and the more people you can have relationships with. I think Americans isolate themselves; the rest of the world, they speak multiple languages." For Andie Acuna, language immersion was a way to help her son "understand how differences in culture are a strength instead of a barrier to understanding and appreciating."

Once we decide to give our children the gift of a second language, the next decision is which format works best for them. Whether the parents speak one or multiple languages themselves, they have to weigh the pros and cons of language immersion versus traditional language education for their child. Heneliaka Jones chose immersion over a typical foreign language class because she wanted her daughter to understand another country's culture, as well as its language. "We want her to know how to tell and receive jokes in the language," she notes. "That's when you know that you understand the culture—when you understand the nuances and idiosyncrasies of the culture." Jones' emphasis on the cultural aspect of language learning is based in her own international travel, which began when she was still a student. "As much as I appreciated the cultures, the barrier was the language," she says.

Like Jones, most African-American parents weren't raised by bilingual parents or in a bilingual home. So while articles and experts may inform us that dual language immersion programs are a great educational opportunity, those of us without direct experience of being bilingual are walking by faith. We can't truly understand how those benefits will manifest until we see it happening in our own child. For example, I had to explain to my grandfather that my daughter might actually dream in Chinese to help him understand what this process may mean for her.

I wish I had had the benefit of my friend and fellow immersion parent Lia Barrow's advice back then. She encourages parents to examine their own motivations for language immersion. "If you want it so that your child can access better jobs and for that reason alone, you will be undoubtedly be in for more work than you expect," she cautions. That's exactly what I discovered.

In my family's case, we put our eldest daughter in a Saturday Chinese language class when she was three years old. By the end of the 12-week course, I had decided that the lure of raising a bilingual child was more time intensive than we could manage, especially since she had only learned about three words and there was no way to support her language learning at home. Because of that, my husband and I decided to discontinue our pursuit to raise a bilingual child until a fortunate set of coincidences—not the least of which was our daughter's insistence on returning to Chinese—drew us back.

Why Chinese?

In surveying PAASSC-affiliated parents, I learned that while bilingual education was a high priority for each couple, my husband and I were one of the few that specifically sought out Chinese as the language of choice. For instance, Helen actually started her daughter off in a French-language day care before enrolling her in Chinese preschool, and plans to reintroduce French at a later date.

Several factors influenced our family's preference. Our early research indicated that once a child has a second language, additional languages are easier to pick up. Spanish is Latin-based and therefore easier to learn. Also, my husband understands and speaks enough Spanish to hold a conversation, or at least to understand one. By contrast, its unique script and syntax make Chinese the most inaccessible language to us, so it seemed to make sense to start with the most difficult language. And when you look at the globalization of the world, there are a billion Chinese who our daughters would be able to talk with.

The Barrows didn't specifically decide to enroll in Chinese immersion. "We decided that our son needed more of a challenge in school. We were open to Spanish, French, Japanese, anything." Jones also sought general bilingual education first and foremost. She says that, "over time we began to see the benefits and necessity of learning Chinese." In each case, it was the atmosphere and promise of the specific school, rather than the language itself, that appealed to these families.

As Barrow's earlier advice implies, earning potential is another motivator for parents who select Chinese over other languages, even if it does require more work. "We looked at what we could do to prepare him for the future," says Acuna, "and decided that based on the economic movement of the country, a brown boy with Mandarin language skills would be able to write his own ticket in various industries and be able to work anywhere in the world." The age of the language and its character-based script attracted Ferreira. "The characters communicate language in a way similar to Egyptian hieroglyphics, so thinking in terms of characters versus phonetics is also interesting," she notes.

Some parents were not looking for immersion at all, but found it by happenstance. Tony Hines, a mother of four and a fierce community advocate, was recruited to enroll in the Mandarin immersion option by the principal at her daughter's school, Starr King Elementary. Bernadette Jackson was attempting to enroll her daughter in the same school that her older children attended, but the general education program was full. She chose the Chinese immersion education option so that children could go to the same school.

However they come to it, most African-American parents who pursue a Mandarin immersion education for their children come to realize that Chinese immersion programs provide their child with a strong math and science curriculum, teachers who have high expectations for their students regardless of ethnicity, and challenging, stimulating curricula and lesson plans.

Overcoming resistance

When we first reached out to friends and parents for their advice, many were curious about our interest in a Chinese immersion program, but very few supported the idea. In fact, there were only two friends in our corner. Luckily, these two parents were the ones whose opinions we most valued. I also found an ally in our daughters' godmother, who had enrolled her own children in an independent school. After I shared the doubt and dismissiveness of our family and friends with her, she encouraged me by saying, "If I had a chance to do it again I would choose a language immersion school for my children. You are a trailblazer and should not let this opportunity pass you by."

Regardless of the source of resistance, the issues raised fall into two categories: academic and cultural. In the first category, our friends questioned how our children would learn to read and write English in an immersion classroom. How would I correct their homework? How would I support their Chinese language learning? These are valid concerns facing every monolingual parent of a bilingual learner. Helen addresses the reality of language acquisition in 100% immersion settings, especially at an early age: "My daughter's program is all Mandarin until she gets to a certain grade, so it's not surprising that English skills will be delayed. They catch up by the second or third grade."

African-American families are faced with additional hurdles based in historical and current stereotypes that some Blacks and Chinese hold about one another. These range from how Blacks are portrayed in the entertainment and news media to perceptions that Chinese (and Asian-Americans in general) own all the stores in predominately black neighborhoods and mistreat black customers. "My mother was very concerned with how 'they' were going to treat her granddaughter," says Jones. "We told family and friends, 'You have to trust our judgment.'"

I had reservations as well, mostly about whether Chinese teachers would be able to provide a culturally supportive learning environment for my children. Both my husband and I had attended primarily white schools growing up. Unlike him, however, I had a lot of resentment about it. I didn't want my daughters to be isolated in their schooling or disconnected from a rich African-American cultural experience. In today's predominately white schools, especially in the Bay Area, diverse cultural heritages and traditions are celebrated. Chinese immersion schools, by their very definition, focus on Chinese heritage and culture.

Chinese heritage and culture

As a social worker, I recognized the value of providing my daughters with a progressive education, which a number of Bay Area schools offer. Such schools are built around a curriculum that teaches students the benefits of using non-oppressive language and engaging with diverse communities in a manner that honors and respects their community structures. It is important for me that my children understand that there are diverse family structures and diverse family values. This is often conveyed in the classroom and through service learning projects.

I am a strong supporter of the learning opportunities that come through community service, but I find that, too often, such projects are unidirectional; that is, they involve affluent students donating resources to underserved schools or communities. A non-Mandarin immersion school that ranked high on our list developed an innovative project that involved eighth graders in mentoring and tutoring students at a local underserved school, and fifth graders from that school providing reading and mentoring to the first school's primary students. This creates a reciprocity of service that helps students see that an "underserved" community has valuable gifts and talents to share, as well as needs that must be met.

I felt discouraged by the lack of these progressive education elements in the local Mandarin immersion schools we were considering. However, I had the benefit of a husband without my concerns, fears and need to advocate for diversity. He consistently emphasized the benefits of the language immersion experience. When I wanted to back out he stayed firm and pointed out that it would be our job as parents to compensate in those areas where the school lacked culturally and progressively.

So far, my daughters don't show any signs of feeling culturally isolated in their immersion programs, but they are still very young. Forming PAASSC was, in part, a way to prevent feelings of isolation. It allows them to regularly interact with up to a dozen other African-American children who speak Chinese. PAASSC also gives us a vehicle to develop relationships with students from different cultural and socio-economic communities and create opportunities for reciprocal service learning outside of the classroom.

"Do" diligence: Finding the right immersion program

While the presence of a few immersion-friendly allies helped overcome my resistance, Acuna recommends, "acknowledging your fears and facing them head on by asking questions." She offers interested parents four ways to soothe concerns with actual information:

- Go to the school and spend time on campus to observe how the staff engages the students, peer-to-peer relationships, etc.

- Talk to administrators, teachers and other parents to assess whether the school will be a good match for your child and your family
- Be patient
- Actively participate

It's also a good idea to identify what's most important to you and find a school that most closely fits your goals and values, whether you opt for a public, private or parochial school. These proactive measures are a recurring theme in each of our families' stories of how they fell in love with their particular school. My family's case involved a good bit of trial and error, and serendipity as well.

Every new parent has many hopes, dreams and expectations for their first child. Education was one of my primary interests when my oldest daughter was born but I was shocked to learn that I was behind the curve when it came time to put her in day care. The best centers had waiting lists of parents who had signed up shortly after conception, while I had waited until my daughter was four months old—two months before I had to go back to work. After struggling to find day care, I was determined not to let a lack of awareness cause us to miss opportunities for a top-quality kindergarten. The search for kindergarten just happened to coincide with my daughter's requests to return to "Chinese school."

You see, after that 12-week introduction to Chinese in the Saturday program, my daughter was captivated. At the wise age of 3, she repeatedly informed me that she didn't want to go to dance class on Saturday and wanted to return to Chinese class instead. While we were weighing the decision to pursue a Chinese immersion experience, Alameda County was in the process of confirming Yu Ming Charter School as the first Chinese immersion charter school in Oakland, California. The other public Chinese immersion programs on the eastern side of San Francisco Bay are in Fremont, Hayward and San Ramon, all relatively far away.

At the time, I was teaching at California State University, East Bay, so I used the university's research resources to educate myself on language and cultural immersion. I was dismayed to find that there wasn't much literature on the benefits of bilingual education for African-American youth. What little there was came primarily from doctoral students, covered a variety of immersion programs in the United States, Canada and Latin America, and focused on several languages, including French, Spanish, German and even English.

As I mentioned earlier, diversity was important to me. My direct experiences with African-American parents pursuing Chinese immersion schools for their children confirmed what the girls' godmother said: We were on the cusp of a new trend that should not be denied to our children. In working with Yu Ming to confirm their charter, I was impressed with the number of other African-American families that had stepped into leadership positions to ensure that Yu Ming's charter was approved.

Dawn Williams Ferreira and her husband were among them. They weren't new to language immersion—their oldest child was already enrolled in a Spanish immersion school and taking Chinese lessons. So when they heard that Yu Ming was opening in their neighborhood, they enrolled their middle son and became part of the first group of parents to get the school off the ground. "Being a founding family meant that we were very involved in making sure that other Black children attended the school," she says. "We did not want our child to feel isolated and we understood that we had a responsibility to make it the school that we wanted for our child."

The presence or lack of diversity helped Helen decide between schools that weren't very different in their academic structure. "I realize that's a conscious choice to have diversity or not. And from my perspective, that didn't seem important to them," she says of one school that she crossed off the list.

Barrow and her husband were committed to the public school system and preferred one close to home. So while language immersion had been a latent interest for them, they didn't actively pursue it until they were accepted in the lottery at the first full-time immersion school in their district, where Chinese happened to be the target language. Acuna's priorities included, "identifying a school where the teachers were kind and loving to students" because it matches her belief that, "kids who feel supported in learning learn better." Barrow and Acuna are both the parents of children with special physiological and learning needs so it was extra important that they felt comfortable with the school's capacity and willingness to be both responsive and sensitive, especially given the language difference.

The cultural aspect of immersion, teaching style and parent community helped Jones' family fall in love with their daughter's school: "When you walk into the school, it's like walking into China. The landscape of the school, the classroom design, the learning tools, etc. It's also a Montessori curriculum in the pre-K, and our daughter is a hands-on learner." She cautions against basing your total impression of the school on open houses and similar recruitment activities, "Admission tours can be scripted. We attended events prior to enrollment." Those activities helped her family get a "backstage" view of the parents, teachers and students, so to speak. "When we went to events outside of admission events, we were well embraced by the community and felt connected," she notes. "If we didn't feel comfortable, we would not send our child."

Where the rubber meets the 道路*

However thorough one's research process may be, the real "fitness" of immersion education—and a particular school or program—can only be

---

* *dàolù*, road.

gauged once your child is enrolled. We were amazed to witness that our oldest daughter's natural talent for language and learning exceeded our expectations. A few parents have told us that she is "the best Chinese speaker in the classroom."

Unfortunately, her report card did not reflect that level of proficiency at first. Her teacher initially stated that my daughter wasn't interested in reading Chinese books, even though her English class marks were higher than those for math and social skills. Because she had been so persistently enthusiastic about Chinese, we signed her up for a more intensive Chinese language class. She actually looked forward to the extra work. When I asked her about the class, she said she really enjoyed it because "the homework is more challenging than homework at school."

Our youngest daughter's affinity for Mandarin has been even more surprising. She looks to her older sister for guidance but displays much more confidence, grasps the language more naturally and earns higher marks on her report card. We believe this is the result of her exposure to Chinese for almost as long as she has been speaking English. When we enrolled her in the program, she already knew many of the songs and was able to initiate fluent sentences.

All of the parents we interviewed found similar success in both their children's classroom performance and enjoyment of the experience. Ferreira says that her 6-year-old son's teacher "joked that he speaks so well that he is beginning to argue with her in Chinese." Helen's daughter is doing well in her second year of pre-school. "She can't really read the books, but she'll pretend read it," she says. "She likes to speak Chinese at home, she likes to sing in Chinese. Sometimes she'll try to teach momma Chinese." Jones is thrilled to watch her normally shy three-year-old become more enthusiastic and participatory in classroom activities, though she admits that this blossoming could be due to normal development or the school's teaching style, or perhaps both.

Likewise, Acuna has watched her six-year-old son improve in both Mandarin fluency and self-confidence in the three years that he has been enrolled. "Initially his proficiency in understanding was growing but not his willingness to speak it. Now he is so confident and gets great feedback from his teacher while we are out in the community." She credits the teacher's style with this improvement, along with the school's willingness to support her son's Individualized Education Plan and his specific needs. Her son has Attention Deficit Hyperactivity Disorder, Inattentive—one of three subtypes of ADHD, which specifies the low attention span, versus hyperactive-impulsive behavior. She explains how his teacher worked within his limits by agreeing that he would only be required to speak in Mandarin until lunchtime. "The teacher has stated that he continues past lunch, although the other children don't speak primarily in Mandarin," she says. "The experience has been an excellent challenge for him."

It almost goes without saying that whether traditional or immersion, not all schools or teachers are created equal. Add each child's unique needs and personalities to the mix and challenges will inevitably arise. Teachers spend so much time influencing our children that a problematic relationship between them can be a deal breaker for the entire immersion experiment. It is easier to walk away than to remain committed, particularly with so many other educational options available.

In one instance, an African-American mother consulted the classroom teacher, the teacher's aide, and even another parent about a problem her child was having, but she was unsatisfied with their responses. She was ready to give up, but gave it one last try and approached the principal, who was so responsive that she was encouraged to persevere. The lesson here is that it may take multiple attempts to find an administrator or teacher who "gets it" and it may not be the person who is directly responsible for your child.

Barrow faced a situation that highlights the specific cross-cultural differences and expectations that can arise in an immersion setting. She has raised an eyebrow more than once at the dominant instructional style of her son's teachers, all of whom are native Mandarin speakers from China or Taiwan. "California is advanced in looking at what classroom environments are good and healthy for encouraging student growth," she notes, "but most of his teachers have very little fluency in English and very little understanding of the American cultures and customs. They seem used to students being docile and obedient and are open to calling students 'bad' if they don't seem to conform. On my son's report card, the teacher actually wrote that he 'is very often bad in class.'"

Helen had a similar experience during her daughter's first year in Chinese immersion. Recognizing that the school's administration did not have an effective structure for communicating with the parents, she says, "the onus was on me to really get out there in the second year to do the work and make the relationship."

These families' approach to resolving their issues demonstrates how active parental involvement can create a solution-oriented climate. Neither of them removed their child from the school; in the Barrows' case, they met with the teacher to explain why "bad" was insufficient to explain what their son was doing, to obtain clearer descriptions of the undesired behavior, and to express their disappointment at the school's lack of response to their requests for feedback prior to the report card distribution, especially given his medical history. "We have to provide the staff with space for a learning curve," Barrow explains.

She's been pleased they did. Despite their concerns, her son is flourishing in both his language facility and in his mastery of other subjects. "He was recently diagnosed with epilepsy and it has become increasingly difficult for him to read and write in English, but it doesn't seem to affect his Mandarin. So development of his math skills have not been impacted (math is taught in Mandarin), and the continued development of his Mandarin language seems to have helped his English reading and writing." The fact that he's thriving is the most crucial part for her. Even if he were in a school that was more culturally competent, if her son wasn't thriving she wouldn't keep him there, she says.

And speaking of cultural competency...

Black History Month or Chinese New Year?

I've said that one of my reservations involved an immersion school's ability to provide my daughters with a rich understanding of their own African-American heritage. As much as Chinese immersion programs promote their focus on the whole child, it's also clear that they offer a heritage-based education that is often devoid of the African-American experience. Several of my fellow parents shared my husband's view that we would have to assume primary responsibility for this at home.

The Ferreiras accomplished this by enrolling their son in an Afrocentric homeschool before he began attending Yu Ming. "Parents should reinforce home culture first," says Dawn, who credits that experience with strengthening his sense of self, confidence and pride in his own heritage. "Children need to really love themselves before they can appreciate other cultures."

I also came to realize that "cultural competency" means different things to different people, even within my own race. Barrow applies this term to explain the school's understanding of California's educational expectations, as well as broad American social customs. Jones, on the other hand, uses the phrase to describe the school's ability to impart the subtle rules of Chinese culture. "Black History Month would be nice," she says, "but for families who want a child to learn Chinese that's not a deal breaker. We read the mission statement right away. They were very clear on what their focus is." She went on to state that as her daughter's first role model, it was her job as a mother to instill a sense of self-esteem and cultural pride. At the same time, she monitors her daughter for "any signs of disrespect or feeling inferior, use of pejorative terms on the playground, feelings of a child being targeted because of color or differences."

Barrow echoes Jones' emphasis on the family's role in balancing Chinese culture with African-American heritage, "I don't expect the school to reach the level of what I am able to provide for my son as it relates to his cultural identity and history." Because the staff at her son's school is so new to

America and our culture, she finds that they are learning about this nation's history, including the history of African-Americans, Latinos, women and gay and lesbian people, along with the students. Ferreira adds that "the responsibility is on us as parents of children of African descent to make our presence known. We, as parents, have come together for Kwanzaa celebrations at the school and Black History Month presentations. We organize this on behalf of our children."

For my part, I did not want my children to feel like they were "the only" Black students learning Chinese. This was a big factor in my decision to start PAASSC. Our earliest events were simple play dates, where children could come together and practice their Mandarin skills. As our network of parents continues to grow, we will expand our efforts to educate families that may be interested in Mandarin immersion, assist administrators and teachers in building their capacity to deliver culturally competent and anti-oppressive education, and connect our mostly monolingual parents with resources that empower them to support their children's academic development, even though they don't speak the target language.

The need is especially great in the third area. Of the parents I interviewed, only three were actively supplementing their children's Mandarin education with extra-curricular activities. Many do not have access to age-appropriate Mandarin resources beyond a few tapes and movies they find in Chinatown. I had the great fortune of traveling to Beijing at the end of 2012, where I was exposed to a wealth of educational materials that I have been sharing in the Bay Area and, as Chinese immersion schools become more popular, throughout the United States.

Parent recommendations

In polling my fellow PAASSC parents for recommendations to families, specifically African-Americans considering immersion, several emphasized that cultural sensitivity is a two-way street. Jones puts it bluntly, "If you can't embrace another culture, you are doomed before you start," adding that she has actually found that there are more similarities than differences between the Chinese and African-American cultures, including the importance of family and cultural history, reverence and respect for elders, and focus on community instead of the individual.

Barrow adds that parents must seriously consider their own expectations for both the school and their children. For example, she says that no matter what race your family is, "If you expect your child to attend a Mandarin immersion school because they will be the 'only' child with specific qualifications or to ensure that your child is 'super' or 'special,' you are going to be in for an awakening. This is a booming trend and very competitive. Through this process you will find that there are numerous children who are just as focused, skilled and bright as your child."

I would add that both parents need to be on board, willing and able to support and encourage their child's language development—in both the native and target languages. Language immersion cannot take place in a vacuum. Early childhood exposure is essential for success, from museum trips, music and movement, to various sports, and interactions with other children. As Jones points out, "Your child has to be school-ready before even considering a program like this—eager, ready and excited to learn."

Helen emphasizes financial preparedness because a public school option for language immersion may not be available or practical for every family. At the same time, she recommends not stressing over the prospect of immersion itself: "It doesn't have to be rocket science. The rest of the world teaches their kids language in their school systems."

These first three years of our quest to raise bilingual children has taught us a lot about ourselves individually, and as parents. We have learned that it is important to find ways to continue to discuss our goals and expectations of our children. We have discovered that nearly every parent—regardless of race, school type or other specific traits—shares a common, primary goal for their children: that they are able to be successful and content.

On a personal level, I have realized that my knowledge of the Chinese language and my ability to support my children's learning are stronger than I anticipated. I am capable of helping them with their homework, providing a supportive home environment that encourages Chinese language learning and creating a community that allows my children to feel supported and encouraged to speak Chinese outside of the classroom setting.

It has been a thrilling and often humbling journey, as my husband can attest. "If you choose to pursue a Chinese immersion education, accept that it is going to be something that you have no experience with—something that is going to be foreign to you—and you must get comfortable with not knowing," he says. "If you have multiple children in Chinese immersion, the day will come when your children will have conversations with one another that you will have no ability to understand."

His advice for surviving the uncertainty is simple: "Enjoy the ride."

A Cantonese immersion experience

Mandarin immersion public school programs are relatively young in the United States. The first was founded in 1996 in Maryland. However, another kind of Chinese immersion program has existed on the West coast since 1984. That's when the first Cantonese immersion program was founded at West Portal Elementary in San Francisco. Today San Francisco's four Cantonese immersion elementary schools are among the top-scoring programs in the city's public school system. Sarah Beth Chionsini, a former English as a Second Language teacher, describes her family's experience in one of these much sought-after schools. You can read her son's thoughts on Chinese immersion in Chapter 12: Student Profiles.

At 9:30 p.m., Fernando and Don Miguel, both day laborers taking night classes in English, came up to my desk.

"Teacher, question. Look," said Fernando pointing to the traffic sign we'd used that night. "I say 'Eh-stóp'. Is it correct?"

"No," Don Miguel was shaking his head. "'Éh-stop.' Say 'Éh-stop.' I know."

"Estoy seguro (I'm sure), 'Eh-stóp'", said Fernando turning to his friend.

"'Éh-stop' correct, Teacher?' Don Miguel asked.

Both gentlemen thought that his reading of "Stop" was the correct choice. I was confounded, though. To me their readings of "Eh-stóp'" and "Éh-stop" sounded the same!

I said, "Thank you for your question. You say 'Stop.' 'Stop' is correct. 'Stop.'"

Don Miguel turned and gave his friend a playful smack on the arm, "Ya te dije! (I told you!) 'Éh-stop' es correcto!" he declared with mock triumph. We all cracked up laughing.

"Oh, sí. 'Eh-stóp'. Ok," said Fernando, nodding his head, smiling. "'Eh-stóp.' S-T-O-P. Thank you, Teacher."

"I'm happy to help you. Have a good night," I said, self-consciously modeling comprehensible input.

For years, stop signs have triggered that memory. I contemplate the complexities of learning a language and the bravery it can take to ask one question. Any of us who has studied another language in adulthood has hit on Fernando and Don Miguel's pronunciation issue: What's in our heads is different from what comes out of our mouths. What we hear ourselves say may not be what the listener hears. Adult learners have to come to terms with this process and their sometimes faulty pronunciation. But, young children are famously adept at learning languages, pronunciation and all.

When I started the kindergarten search process I toured 10 impressive schools in the San Francisco Unified School District. I was intrigued by the district's language-immersion programs, but they were unfamiliar. I also thought about the need to support and strengthen the city's general education schools, which at the time were not as popular as our alternative and immersion schools. Paused at a stop sign one day, I remembered the two gentlemen from the English class I'd been teaching so long ago and the courage they had to do something unfamiliar and difficult. It occurred to me that public schools would be getting my support no matter which one I chose for my family. And so I decided I'd only list language immersion schools on the kindergarten lottery application.

I knew no one program could resolve the economic inequality and structural racism present in American schools. However, I was hopeful that the city-wide lottery system used to put kids in language programs would at least promote economic and ethnic integration. I thought that, in conjunction with positive additions to school life (for example, quality tutoring and mentoring, mental and physical healthcare, and effective professional development), language programs might have the potential to innovate classroom practices and strengthen time-tested strategies.

It was amazing to my family and everyone we knew that we "won the lottery" and got into our first choice—a K–8 immersion school that started the day at 9:30 AM! It was Alice Fong Yu Alternative School (AFY), which consistently has the highest test scores of any elementary school in the city. AFY principal Liana Szeto had been the first kindergarten teacher at West Portal Elementary School's Cantonese Chinese-immersion strand back in 1984. After nine years she left West Portal's program to head up an entire public school dedicated to Cantonese immersion. It opened in 1995 as the first public school of its kind in the United States. Starting in kindergarten, AFY students learn Cantonese and traditional characters. In middle school, students add an extra class period to their day to study Mandarin, simplified characters and pinyin.

At kindergarten orientation Principal Szeto explicitly told us that the next nine years would be hard. Success would require serious commitment from the entire family. On top of the school's daunting requirements, friends and family expressed concerns:

"You won't be able to help him with homework."

"But Mandarin is the official language of China, not Cantonese."

"I heard Chinese school is tough on kids."

I wondered if I'd made the right choice. Today I know I did. My son is in seventh grade and my daughter is in second grade. I admit, there have been times when we've wanted to quit. In the end we always change our minds. Our children like their school. They can speak Cantonese to our neighbors, write Chinese letters to their teachers, and explain the mechanics of making a polite request in both English and Chinese. I will always be proud of my son and my daughter for the hard work they do at Alice Fong Yu Alternative School.

I'm grateful to our friends and family for voicing their concerns back when this all started. Now, I have some experience that may help assuage the worries of anyone thinking about Chinese-immersion for their family.

Homework?

You must do it. Here's the table, pencil, paper. Here's an apple. If you get stuck, call a classmate, or ask a neighbor. Take a break on the mini trampoline.

Yes, you can watch a movie. Here are Chinese DVDs from the library.

Cantonese?

Cantonese is spoken all over the San Francisco Bay area. In the Bayview-Hunter's Point neighborhood where we live, we talk with Cantonese-speaking neighbors at the library, bus stop, condo complex, everywhere.

Whatever language children learn (and whatever amount they learn), the foundation for future language learning is being laid biologically, emotionally and socially.

Tough?

The things that are tough (sitting still, resisting giggles, paying attention, organizing paperwork, taking turns) are ubiquitous to all schools.

Like any public school, the majority of teachers have the professional skills that make frequent yelling and shaming unnecessary.

There is homework, a lot, including during the summer (see "Homework" above).

What do my kids say?

Don't ask us to "show off" to your friends or total strangers!

We prefer classrooms without yelling.

We like that we have a "secret power" to whip out at the store or on the playground. We often get dramatic responses from Chinese speakers!

Since the stop sign conversation with Fernando and Don Miguel, I've studied and taught adults English as a Second or Other Language here and abroad, tried to learn some Cantonese, Korean, American Sign Language and Spanish, and watched my children learn to read in two languages. I've had input about language acquisition from all kinds of sources. But that moment with the stop sign sticks with me. Because of those two students, an ordinary stop sign became a signal to reflect on the processes involved in learning languages. I've been able to discover that Chinese immersion school is the right choice for our family.

Una familia trilingüe: Español, Inglés y 中文*

Carmen Cordovez is a native Spanish speaker from Ecuador, married to an American from New England. She lives in San Francisco with her husband and two children, ages 10 and 6. Both go to a Mandarin immersion school. She writes about why a mother who embraces her Spanish heritage also wants her children to be fluent in Chinese.

---

* A trilingual family: Spanish, English and Chinese.

As my daughter and I wait for our school's drum and dance troupe to begin marching at the Lunar New Year parade, I'm amazed that I'm here at all. While growing up in Quito, Ecuador, I would have never dreamed of marching in this parade.

It was important to me for my kids to speak Spanish and to be acquainted with my culture. Therefore I only spoke Spanish with them, beginning when they were babies. Each year I take them to Ecuador for two months in the summer. Their experience visiting and interacting with the Latin side of their family wouldn't have been the same if they didn't speak Spanish.

With so many Spanish immersion public schools in San Francisco, some of my friends wondered why we didn't choose one of them. But because our children were already fluent in Spanish when it was time for them to start elementary school, and because my husband had studied Asian history and was interested in exposing them to a third language and culture, we decided to send them to a Mandarin immersion program instead.

Initially, I had reservations about sending my kids to a Chinese language program (either Mandarin or Cantonese). I was afraid I would not be able to help them with their homework or participate in school activities. I was also afraid that Asian instructors' ways of teaching would be too strict and less creative.

Despite my initial skepticism, I've been able to participate fully in my children's school activities, in both English and Mandarin. I've gone on field trips to Chinatown, cooked Chinese noodles for festivals, helped organize the Lunar New Year Parade, and more. In terms of Mandarin homework, though we have used a tutor at times, I have discovered that helping my children is more an issue of offering them the tools and space to work rather than instructing. Assisting children in learning to write Chinese characters is more about patterns and stroke order (clearly conveyed in the homework), or using a dictionary, than in understanding the meaning of the words.

At least for the first five years, being in Mandarin immersion has been an experience that has expanded my son's and daughter's world and creativity. During the initial years, when the Chinese was simpler and they only wrote single characters in school, they would write the word from a depiction of its meaning, much like drawing the object. My daughter loved learning to write the characters with brush and black ink on a blank piece of paper.

Later they learned different words to call each object. For them, everything in the world has three names, one in English, one in Spanish and now one in Chinese. They have expanded their understanding to the concept that things can be seen from different perspectives. Now my son and daughter love to find words in Chinese that come from the meaning of other words: For example, they see words they know in other contexts in their Chinese names—hers meaning happy and big, his big and serene.

Since I have exposed them as much as possible to my Latin culture and my husband as much as possible to his American one, it has been amazing to have been able to expose them to a third culture. Their babysitter (who is from Central America) had not been exposed so much to Chinese culture and it has been really interesting to observe how my daughter has been able to correct our sitter's prejudices, which stem from that lack of exposure.

I do have to admit though that as my daughter gets older (she is in fourth grade now,) the constant memorization of hundreds of written Chinese characters becomes tedious. But something must be working well because she continues to be as happy and creative today as she was in the play-based preschool she loved years ago.

I was also concerned I would not be able to connect personally with the Asian-American parents at our school as well as I thought I might have in a Spanish immersion school. I have to say, I have been pleasantly surprised. As a lot of the Asian-American parents come from bicultural, and in many cases bilingual, families they are open to the idiosyncrasies that I bring as a foreigner and so have been open to who I am, more than non-bicultural families might have been.

In regards to maintaining my own culture and language with the kids, I just have to make the extra effort to keep exposing them to it, speaking to them only in Spanish and travelling to Spanish-speaking countries as often as possible.

But for now, while we are in San Francisco, we shall enjoy our march in the Lunar New Year Parade.

Student Profiles

+二
shí èr
12

Madeleine Adams lives in Portland, Oregon. She is the daughter of a second-generation Chinese-American mother and a Caucasian father. She began studying Chinese as a toddler. Now in high school, she writes about how she has benefited from her years in Mandarin immersion.

When I started at age 2 in the Mandarin immersion program at The International School in Portland, my parents had no idea just how well it would prepare me for my future endeavors.

There were several reasons my family decided to try language immersion. Both of my parents worked—my father at Intel and my mother at Hewlett Packard. After investing in two years of day care, they wanted to try something that was more educational and would also keep me occupied while they were at their respective jobs. They saw an advertisement for The International School in a parenting magazine, and my dad began researching it. Through his research he found that knowledge of a second language is not only highly useful but also helpful in learning other subjects as well.

On a more personal level, this was a way for me to get in touch with my heritage. My mother's parents emigrated from China to the U.S. after World War II and Chinese became a way for me to keep in touch with my family and culture. And so my Chinese-American mother and Caucasian father decided to "give it a shot" and enrolled me in the school's only Mandarin immersion class, which at the time was only in its second year.

In the eight years that followed, I learned not only the language from native-speaking Chinese teachers, but also the culture. In my earliest years, the customs, traditions and Chinese classroom environment were the only school experience I knew, and it was normal to me. My teachers taught us early on how to handle a large workload. By the time I got to middle school the amount of homework I was given there was actually a relief! My classmates and I who came from The International School were two years ahead of most other students in math. When we got to middle school we discovered that if we wanted to learn a third language, it would be much easier for us. Chinese immersion has truly been present in every decision I've made, and everything I've accomplished. I expect it to remain so for the rest of my life.

I've had several chances to use and practice my Chinese. The first big opportunity I had was our Capstone trip in fifth grade. That's a program at the school when the graduating fifth graders in the Mandarin program go to China together with their families and teacher. That was when all the pieces of the puzzle seemed to come together. I was seeing the country I'd learned about my whole life. I got to stay in a boarding school with kids the same age as me. I became a part of China, a part of that school.

The opportunity to learn, firsthand, what it's like in other countries is so enriching because you can create ties, relationships you'll never forget with the people you meet. I still feel that bond, that connection I shared with my roommate and with the kids in the class who helped me that entire week. I could relate to them, and at the age of 10, this was something I was sure I wouldn't be able to do. Because of my immersion education I knew the songs they sang, the stories they read, even some of the games they played! I learned how they were just like me, how even though they lived on the opposite side of the world. They were still just kids like me. This experience shaped the way I see the world and has allowed me to be more open-minded as a young adult.

In addition to helping open my eyes to other cultures and customs, my Chinese language skills have helped me academically. It's something that has helped set me apart in school. Now that I'm applying for internships and summer programs, as well as preparing to apply for colleges, I'm seeing that it will set me apart even more on my résumé.

Because I experienced Chinese culture and because it means so much to me, I jumped at the first chance I had to share my experience with my current school, The International School of Beaverton. In my freshman and sophomore years of high school, I co-founded our school's chapter of the National Chinese Honor Society. We are currently working to open up a new side of Chinese culture to our fellow students. We plan events to help celebrate the Moon Festival and Chinese New Year, and show the modern side of such a rich and ancient culture. We are also hoping to reach out to younger students to get them started on a path to learning the language. We're also working to establish an exchange program so that our classmates not only improve their Chinese, but learn what I learned, that kids in China are not so different from us.

Having started so early in a Mandarin immersion program, my language skills and study habits have helped me become a better-rounded student. In the summer of 2013 I was selected to be a part of the ASE (Apprenticeships in Science and Engineering) program, which was run through Saturday

Academy in Portland. My Chinese language skills were an interesting talking point during the interview process and my ability to speak Chinese allowed me to have an incredible experience during the course of my internship.

A big highlight of that summer was when a group of Chinese college students came from Nanjing Agricultural University to visit the Food Innovation Center at Oregon State University in Portland. I was at the FIC as part of my ASE internship. The project I was working on involved researching the effects of heating and caramelization on the texture of freeze-dried pear puffs, a product we were experimenting with. I was measuring success based on water activity level, firmness (using a machine called the Instron), and color (using a spectrophotometer).

I got to talk to them about my project and was able to use my Chinese to speak to them personally. Because we had broken the language barrier, we could talk freely about what we enjoy doing and why we were studying what we are studying. It allowed me to relate to them on a whole new level. This was a wonderful experience for me because I have always imagined a career in which my language skills would coincide with my love of science and innovation. That day, if only for a few minutes, I got to experience the crossing of cultural boundaries with science.

I don't think there is any way to describe just how lucky I was to experience Chinese immersion as a child. My teachers instilled in me a love of learning and a desire to always push myself academically. My parents were supportive and embraced the learning environment that was so different from the one they had experienced as children. I've learned just how applicable my second language skills are to a variety of situations.

Most importantly, I feel that this experience has made me more mature and independent. Ultimately it has prepared me for anything the world might throw at me after I graduate from high school.

Day Chionsini is a middle school student at Alice Fong Yu School in San Francisco. AFY is the nation's second-oldest Cantonese immersion program and is considered one of the best schools in the San Francisco Unified School District. Many families with no connection to China or Cantonese choose it because of its stellar academics. It is a K–8 whole-school program. Day's mom, Sarah Beth Chionsini, interviewed him about his feelings about immersion. You can read her thoughts about Chinese immersion in Chapter 11: Parent Profiles.

There's a lot to learn about Chinese immersion education. It may be unfamiliar, but it's still school. The pathways to success in Chinese and traditional schools are similar: Do your homework, try to pay attention and don't punch out your friends. Families can help keep up with homework and follow up with teachers about any concerns. These are all cooperative practices that promote success in any school.

Chinese immersion school communities can nurture children's growth. High academic expectations can be supported by hiring trained tutors; community-building events can foster inclusion; and an engaged principal can provide crucial guidance. Teacher excellence can be encouraged by offering compensation for extra work hours and requiring high-quality professional development. As in every public school, money is a big issue.

The students in Chinese immersion programs don't know any different way to be in school if they started in kindergarten. They go every day to learn reading and math and play with their friends. As they get older, though, students compare their experiences with friends from other schools. Chinese immersion students may realize that they have more homework, especially if they have summer homework, and may think that "English school" would be easier.

But no matter what kind of public school it is, they all have to sit in a classroom and they all have to do homework. Talking to students about their experiences can be enlightening. In this interview, my middle-school son reflects on learning Chinese. However, his primary concern is that teachers are fair and kind. Just like any kid in any school.

Sarah: Tell about a time you were glad that you speak Cantonese.

Day: When I first moved into my new apartment complex. There was this lady who wanted to know if I could speak Chinese, and then I just started talking to her. She was one of the first people I met in the apartment complex and she's really nice. I can talk to my friends' parents in Chinese; they like that. I get invited to eat dinner a lot, so that's really good.

Sarah: When you are out and about (in San Francisco), what is the most frustrating thing?

Day: Sometimes I don't have the nerve to talk to people because you can't really tell by the way they look if they speak Cantonese; you just have to assume. And then, if you get it wrong, then you're kind of embarrassed and you just have to walk away.

Sarah: What are some things that you can't read in Chinese?

Day: Sometimes the Chinese menus are hard to figure out. But I can read signs in the stores and on the buildings.

Sarah: Could you give an example of how you use Chinese to navigate in San Francisco?

Day: Sometimes when I'm taking the bus, I see some of the people that I met, that I spoke Cantonese to before. And it's kind of good, like if I need help with where I'm going. For example, one time I was going to my tutor's house on the bus. I saw a lady I recognized from when we went on a field trip to Angel Island. I talked to her in Chinese on that field trip. She helped me get to my tutor's house.

Sarah: How do you think studying Cantonese or Chinese culture now will help you when you are a teenager or going to college?

Day: That will probably help me when I go to college because we'll probably owe China so much money, and way more and more Chinese people will start coming to the U.S., immigrating. And if there are more people in the United States to talk Chinese with, that will probably test my skill.

Sarah: If you could change one thing about learning Chinese, what would that be?

Day: I would choose that all the teachers would treat everybody equal. Even if they don't get good grades or if they have trouble listening in class, that they would accept them. They might have a learning disability and the teachers might not know that. I would like it to be that the teachers would still help them and not just expect them to do everything on their own.

Sarah: What advice would you give to a younger kid who is having trouble learning Chinese?

Day: What I would say to a little kid is that if you procrastinate, issues will get bigger and bigger, and you'll never be able to deal with them once they're the biggest they can be. If you procrastinate in Chinese, you probably won't know some of the words and it might be difficult to catch up. There are some teachers who you would probably really like. And some teachers might be rude, but that's just how they are and you can't do anything to change it.

Sarah: What do you do when you need help with Chinese?

Day: When I'm in school, I usually just go up and ask the teacher. But if the teacher is in a really sour mood, then I don't do that. I grab a dictionary or ask a friend. And when I'm at home, I have a lot of neighbors who speak Chinese, so I ask them. Or I call a friend. Or take a small break and have a snack to help my brain focus. Then I go back to work.

Sarah: If you could go back in time knowing what you know now, would you want to go to the same school?

Day: Well, if I was already at the end of eighth grade and they sent me back to preschool, then I would probably tell my parents to send me to a different school. That way, I would have two school experiences in my whole life! And so when I went to high school, I would know Chinese plus whatever language they speak there, like French or Russian. If I went back to Chinese school again, I'd get a second chance on my grades!

Sarah: Do you think it's worth it to learn Chinese?

Day: The teachers are strict and I have a lot of homework, but if you ask me, I say it's still worth it, because I got a whole language out of it. And I made friends there. Most teachers are really good; they know what they're doing, they're nice. But a few, they yell if you get something wrong that they think you should know. Or they act condescending, talking to us like we're babies.

Or it feels like they want to intimidate you and don't really like you. I wish they wouldn't do that.

Most teachers give lots of advice. They want to help you when it's hard. Like when I first learned to write an essay in Chinese, I remember my teacher said, "Don't give up at all, don't even think about giving up." She told us, "If you never learn to write essays in Chinese and English now, you'll never do it because...once you pass up into the higher grades those teachers are going to teach you harder stuff. So you better do it now."

The way she said it to me helped a lot. Because, well, listen to this: (in a bored mumble) "Yeah, yeah. Just do it now. Go ahead." And now listen to this: (in an enthusiastic voice), "Yeah, you can do it! You can just keep on pushing! You can do it!"

Which one do you think is more encouraging? Well, that kind of sums it up for you.

Anya Hauptmann lives in Portland, Oregon. She attended Portland's International School, where she was in the Mandarin immersion program through the fifth grade. She then continued in Mandarin immersion at Gilkey International Middle School, which offers immersion for students in French, German, Spanish and Mandarin. She now attends St. Mary's Academy, a Catholic girls high school in Portland.

I was adopted from China at the age of 12 months by a single woman. I was enrolled at The International School at age two. My mom decided to put me in an immersion school because I am Chinese, and she wanted me to have that culture incorporated into my life. My mom is from the Midwest and I have a sister who is also adopted from China.

I enjoyed going to an immersion school because you are in a completely different environment than you would be at any other school. Because The International School is an elementary school, you begin studying the language at a young age, so you quickly learn and develop skills that other students may not have acquired yet.

Being in immersion didn't feel different. While I knew other kids normally took classes in English, I was okay with it because I was surrounded by kids taking classes in another language. There were times when I thought I'd understand what we were being taught better if it were in English, but I figured it would work out—and it did.

One thing about being in an immersion school that had just started offering Mandarin was that our class was really small. We started out with maybe 20 kids but by fifth grade there were only three students in my class, including me.

In middle school I transferred to Gilkey International Middle School, which is part of Portland's French American International School. There were 50 people in my grade, but in the Chinese class there were only two, including me. We combined grades so we had 10 in our class.

I speak a lot of Chinese because I went to an immersion elementary school, took Chinese at my middle school, took a class at my high school and am tutored in it. I also recently attended a camp outside of Los Angeles at Pomona College where we took a pledge to only speak your target language. The language pledge is exactly like being in immersion; it challenges you to speak with others in your everyday life all in Chinese.

My sister and I both attended immersion and we both speak Chinese. So now, if we don't want my mom to know something, we just discuss it in Chinese and it works out perfectly. That is a good benefit!

For my first year of high school, I went to Lincoln High, which is where Portland's public Mandarin immersion program students go. They offer a Mandarin International Baccalaureate program. However the school wasn't a good fit for me overall. My next year I moved to St. Mary's Academy. They don't teach Chinese at all so I now have a tutor. We watch a lot of Chinese videos and I'm studying to take the HSK test.[1]

I have found many opportunities to use my language skills. I have gone to China several times and am able to communicate with people there. When we have foreign exchange students, I am able to speak comfortably with them. Even at camps, I am able to chat confidently with the counselors.

I am so thankful I was given the chance to learn Chinese. It opens so many doors and possibilities. If it is your passion, you can pursue it as a career or simply bond over it with other people. As China's economy is growing, you can develop relationships and connections that can be helpful. Learning another language is important to see the various cultures and customs of the world.

I am a rising junior, but I am still undecided on my major for college. Something in the medical field though, because of family influence. I have definitely considered minoring in Asian studies but I'm still deciding.

Overall, I hope Chinese will be a part of my future. Being fluent in a language is a very valuable skill that will make you a unique candidate in whatever you are applying for. I was so inspired from learning Chinese that I decided to learn Spanish starting in middle school. Being trilingual in some of the world's most-used languages is really helpful when traveling, finding job opportunities, applying for colleges, or simply meeting new people.

This spring I will go on a medical mission to a South American country, where I will be able to utilize my language skills. I can also go back to my orphanage in China and speak with my caretakers.

If you are a parent debating whether to put your children into an immersion school, I would say go for it. Because they are starting young, it will be easier to learn and they will have a different experience than other kids. I am so glad I was enrolled in an immersion school, because now I see how much it has benefitted me.

Katie Stern-Stillinger began her studies at a private Mandarin immersion school and later continued on in public school. She talks about what it was like to be in a somewhat new program and how not all her classmates ended up being as interested in Chinese as their parents were.

Katie was adopted from China as an infant. At age 4, her parents enrolled her in one of the first Mandarin immersion classes at The International School in Portland, Oregon. The private school started as a French immersion school in 1990 and later expanded its program to include Japanese and Chinese. As a pioneer student in a new program, Katie experienced many of the same issues that families in new programs encounter—a tiny student body, changing curriculum and new teachers. "It was pretty small and it got smaller and smaller, and by the time I got to fifth grade I had 13 kids in my class," she says.

The school launched in full Mandarin mode. "We had the entire day in Mandarin except for music class, PE (physical education) and art classes," she says. English wasn't taught as a subject until she was in the third grade.

"It was a little weird. But it helped that we spoke English at home," she says. Her mother taught her to read in English. "For a few of the kids who dropped out, it was because their parents were worried that their English wasn't good enough."

The school presumed a high level of parental involvement in a student's education, especially in the early years, says Katie. "If you wanted to learn cursive writing, your parents had to teach it to you at home."

Since those early days, the school has strengthened its curriculum into a very solid program, but in the beginning it was a work in progress. Katie remembers that the strong emphasis on Chinese meant she often only knew terms in Chinese. "The teachers used a lot of visuals to teach. Sometimes if we *really* didn't get it, they'd try to describe it to us in Chinese and then when someone did get it, they'd say it in English and they'd tell us and we'd all go 'Ohhh!'," she remembers. "My math textbook was written in Chinese so I had to translate it into English so I could ask my parents for help."

While it didn't make for a smooth and easy school time, Katie is very grateful for the education she received. "The International School gave me such a great basis. I became fluent pretty fast."

When it came time to choose a middle school, she opted to go to Portland's public Mandarin immersion program at Hosford Middle school, mostly because she wanted to experience a larger school. "I didn't really like the small classroom size. I wanted more diversity of friends."

At Hosford, students in the program had two classes in Mandarin a day, Chinese language arts and social studies. Socially, she really liked the transition. "I made good friends." But she did feel that going from a more Chinese-intensive program to one that only had two classes per day in Chinese was detrimental to her language ability.

In eighth grade she took part in Portland's Chinese Research Residency in Suzhou, China. The two-week program sent almost the entire class to China. It was made possible by fundraising done by Portland's Mandarin immersion parent support organization, Shu Ren, together with parent contributions.

"It was a lot of fun," says Katie. The students stayed with host families and were accompanied by teachers and parents who didn't speak Chinese. They were broken into groups and given tasks to accomplish in Suzhou—from bargaining for something, to taking a bus, to visiting local sites. The students had to use their Chinese to navigate the activities. "They called them 'field studies.' Every day we had things we had to accomplish. We had to ask local people where things were or how to get somewhere; we had to purchase tickets; we had to bargain; and we had to buy food."

"I was with a family that had a kid who was a year younger than me and she took me to all these cool places in Suzhou. It helped that I was comfortable speaking in Mandarin," she says.

For high school, only about 15 students continued on with the Mandarin program at Portland's Cleveland High School. By Katie's sophomore year there were only eight students. By that point, says Katie, many of her peers were no longer willing to put in effort at the level required.

Some continued studying the language because was is required for Cleveland's International Baccalaureate program, designed to prepare students for the demands of college-level work. To complete the full IB program, students need four years of a foreign language. Because they had begun with Chinese, the students had to continue it all the way through high school.

To a certain extent, Katie felt her teachers had run out of things to teach the students, though she acknowledges that teaching was difficult because there were so few students and many of them were not engaged. "It's hard to teach students who don't care," she says.

The class spent their junior year preparing to take the Advanced Placement Chinese test, which allows high school students to get college credit for higher level work. In many colleges, a score of 3 or more on the AP language tests fulfills the school's foreign language requirement. "I got a 5 on the AP test. I was pretty happy," Katie says.

In her senior year, she prepared to take the IB Chinese test.

"There's only one other kid in my class who wants to study Chinese in college," she says. Katie and that other girl struck out on their own to find more opportunities to deepen their Chinese. They took an online class about

Chinese films, taught in Chinese, at another high school. It was mostly meant for heritage students who spoke Chinese at home. They also took an online course in sustainability. "It talked about China and the environment. It was all in Chinese. All the assignments were online. We met with the Chinese teacher once a month to talk about what we had learned," says Katie.

While many of her classmates dropped out, Katie believes they won't have lost their Chinese. "You'd just have to take a class in college or go back to China. You remember more than you think you do."

As she began her college search, Katie e-mailed Asian studies departments to ask about their Chinese programs. She plans to do a dual major in Chinese and international business and asked departments if their Chinese program would be a good fit for her. Just as Chinese has only recently become popular in K-12 schools, many colleges have relatively new Chinese programs and she found that many didn't have courses available at a level appropriate for her. That information helped hone her college search as she didn't want "to be stuck taking the same class over and over again," she says. The response was good, with some schools saying they would create another class if she needed it.

Katie was accepted at her top college choice, the University of Hawaii at Manoa, which offers both Chinese and international business majors. She also got into Florida International University.

One advantage of having learned to speak Chinese early and well is that it was easier for her to learn other languages. She began studying Spanish in middle school. "Part of learning a language is just accepting the fact that the way a language is, that's just how it is. Sometimes people can't get past that." For Katie, that wasn't a stumbling block.

"I like Chinese. I like being able to speak the language of where I was born. People in China, they know I'm Chinese. When I speak to them, they say, 'That's so great that you can speak Chinese, it's great that America teaches the kids who are adopted Chinese.'"

She's grateful for the path her parents started her on as a 4-year-old. "I'm glad that my mom had me learn Chinese. It's great to be able to speak such an important language."

1. 汉语水平考试, *Hànyǔ Shuǐpíng Kǎoshì,* the Chinese Proficiency Test, a standardized test used in China for non-native speakers. It's akin to the TOEFL (Test of English as a Foreign Language) for English.

shí sān

13

But Will They Learn English?

Once you've chosen Mandarin immersion, the first question people will ask is, "Aren't you afraid your kids won't learn English?"

Rest easy. It's virtually impossible for a child growing up in an English-speaking home, in an English-speaking nation, not to learn English. Your children already speak English, don't they? Even kids who speak another language at home learn English because they're immersed in it. (If you're a Chinese-speaker, please read *Chapter 18 For Chinese-Speaking Parents* for more on this.)

The research is pretty clear that students in immersion programs for all languages do *better* than other students in all areas of their education—English included. Still, programs are very aware of this concern, so much so that the often-repeated mantra of language immersion programs is, "First, do no harm."[1] The programs are designed to *add* to what children learn, not take away. They do not harm their English acquisition (though they can slow it down a tad). Instead they *add* abilities in a second language.

No less an expert than Myriam Met, who has run immersion programs in French and Spanish and now consults widely on the creation of Mandarin immersion programs, says this, "Immersion students gain proficiency in a new language without any detriment to progress in their native language or subject matter achievement."[2]

There are really three questions to be answered here:

- Will students in immersion learn to speak English?
- Will students in immersion learn to read and write English?
- Will students learn math, science and social studies well enough to pass English-language tests on those topics?

The answers are yes, yes and yes. But perhaps you'd like a little more detail?

First, and this gets asked a lot, students in public Mandarin immersion programs study an *American* curriculum. They learn the same subjects and the same material as their counterparts in the English-language classroom down the hall or across town. They simply learn it in Mandarin. They *do not* learn the curriculum taught in the People's Republic of China or in Taiwan. When they learn history, it's American history. When they learn social studies, it's American civics, not Chinese civics.

The research shows they learn these topics well, better, in fact, than students in English-only classrooms. In Palo Alto, California, a group of education researchers from Stanford University followed students in the Mandarin immersion program at Ohlone Elementary school from when it opened to when the first class of fifth graders moved on to middle school. They had been tasked by the school board with researching whether Mandarin immersion was good or bad for students. In their final report to the Palo Alto School Board, the researchers said,

> Students who are taught in Mandarin for much of the school day generally achieve at levels on California mandated tests in English language arts, writing, math and science that are as high as, or sometimes higher than, their non-immersion peers who attend the same school. These results are reassuring because they demonstrate that, when students receive instruction in two languages, they are not only developing as bilinguals, but also do not fall behind their peers on the essential core content.[3]

Research released in September 2013[4] from immersion programs in St. Cloud, Minnesota, found that in 2012, students in Mandarin and Spanish immersion had math and reading scores on Minnesota's Comprehensive Assessment tests that were higher than both the district and the state average. There's some data that suggests students in Chinese immersion do even better than students in Spanish immersion (probably because of the types of parents who tend to choose Chinese immersion, see *Chapter 10: Why Parents Choose Mandarin Immersion*).

Eighty-three percent of fourth-grade immersion (both Spanish and Mandarin) students in St. Cloud met or exceeded proficiency in math, when just 68% of students did district-wide. In English reading, 88% of third-grade immersion students in St. Cloud were proficient, whereas 74% of third-graders district-wide met or reached the standard.

To be honest, it's likely that some of that advancement stems from the type of parent who chooses immersion for their child—a committed and engaged parent who is involved in their child's education, which research also shows is more likely to produce a child who does well in school. But if you're reading this book, you're clearly one of those parents, and all the data we have shows that children like yours will do very well in immersion.

The educational research is abundant and clear. Students who arrive in kindergarten speaking English do fine in English in school. This applies to students from all socioeconomic and ethnic backgrounds. According to immersion expert Tara Fortune,

> "Academic achievement on tests administered in English occurs regardless of the second language being learned. ... English-proficient students will keep pace academically with peers in English-medium programs.[5]

How is this possible, when they don't spend the entire school day learning about and in English? The research shows that as long as students are exposed to age-appropriate academic English (exactly what they hear from their teacher) they'll absorb it and learn it. When you think about it, *all* school is really immersion. Our kindergarteners don't show up the first day of school talking about this rhombus and that polygon, or using the kind of descriptive language they'll be taught to write in later on. Instead, they're immersed in academic English during class time.

The academic concepts cross over very easily, though it is true that some of the actual vocabulary can require some support at home. That's where the committed, engaged parenting comes in. If you're reading to and with your child, helping out with math homework etc., they'll get a lot of it from you. They know what addition and subtraction are, they just call it 加法 and 减法 (*jiāfǎ* and *jiǎnfǎ*) in class. When you sit down at the dining room table to check that they've done their homework and say, "Oh, look, you're getting double digit subtraction now!" they get the English words for it. And in many districts, the teachers also make sure children learn necessary vocabulary in English as well, so students can take tests that are only offered in English.

What's remarkable, and really the true power of immersion, is that you don't have to have six or eight or ten hours of this a day for it to stick. Even schools that start out with 100% of the day in Mandarin see that their students do well in English by the time they finish fifth grade.

The first grade freak-out

But—and this is a very important point—it doesn't happen immediately and it doesn't happen as fast as for students in an all-English environment. Students in immersion classrooms do lag somewhat in their English proficiency. I'm not saying they don't learn it and I'm not saying they don't catch up. They do. But, especially in the first few years of grade school, they can be a little behind students in all-English classrooms.

This can cause what's commonly called "The First Grade Freak-Out" in immersion schools, though it can occur in first, second or even third grade.

Let's be honest here: Immersion parents are a special breed. We're more involved in our kids' education, more intense and, truth be told, a little more controlling than most parents. If we weren't, we wouldn't be signing up for what anyone who's done it will tell you is one of the most rigorous and demanding educational experiences you can get in a school. Mandarin immersion isn't a walk in the park. It's a steep climb up a mountain trail. The views when you get to the end are breathtaking, but not everyone's up for the hike.

So, we're a pretty education-minded bunch. Which also means that we're paying *a lot* of attention to how well our kids do in school. The problem is that sometime in first or second grade, something like this is bound to happen, if not to you then to a friend.

You go to a birthday party at another child's house. You're chatting away with the parents, hanging out, watching the kids run around like maniacs. The birthday boy doesn't go to your child's school. He is at the local public school that has an all-English program. Suddenly you notice the homework posted on the fridge, the spelling words he's studying on the dining room table. Then you leaf through the stack of *Magic Tree House* or *Geronimo Stilton* books next to their couch. And it hits you: That's more advanced than my kid is doing in English! You begin to breathe faster. Your daughter isn't keeping up. She's falling behind! She's not learning English! You start to hyperventilate. She won't be able to pass the SATs! She'll never get into college. Oh My God. Your daughter will never go to MIT and won't found a startup that will make her rich enough to buy the *New York Times*! All because you were stupid enough to choose Mandarin immersion. After a sleepless night berating yourself, the next morning you march into school, withdraw your daughter and transfer her to an English-only school so that she'll be a success in life. You've saved her from a Fate Worse Than Death and a life in the gutter.

Okay, I've exaggerated a bit here. The freak-out is usually more of a slow build. But at some point in every parent's Mandarin immersion journey, it really hits home that students in all-English classrooms *spend more time learning English*. And it shows in their work. The question you need to ask yourself is: How much of a problem is this? And the answer, *all* the research shows, is not much. But *only* if you look at how students do over time.

Immersion is a little like the miracle of Mark Bittman's No-Knead Bread.[6] This was a recipe that spread like wildfire in 2008 and beyond. It instructed cooks to take flour, water, salt and a tiny bit of yeast and mix it for less than a minute, then to let the resulting shaggy mess sit out in a bowl on a counter for 12 to 18 hours. When they finally plopped the bubbly dough into a pan and then into a hot oven, they were rewarded with an amazing, crusty, artisan-quality loaf.

All with no muss, no fuss and no kneading.

Our children are that dough. If we leave them be, and trust the process of immersion and the ability of our teachers, they'll come out six to eight years later doing as well or better academically as students in English-only programs *and* they'll be proficient in Mandarin at the level of a second- or third-year college student.

Let me repeat:

Students who complete Mandarin immersion through eighth grade

- Keep pace academically with peers in English-medium programs
- Frequently perform better than those peers
- Are proficient in Mandarin Chinese at the level of second- or third-year college students.

Just as with Bittman's bread recipe, you've got to trust the process. If you look at it after two or three hours, when any normal dough would be nicely puffy and ready for the oven, you'll find a ragged, barely-risen mess. At this point the instinct of almost any baker is to quickly add some yeast to *get that dough working*! But as I found out myself, if you do that you end up with a foul-smelling, over-proofed, un-bakable bowl of gunk you just have to throw away. Wait 12 or 16 hours though, and through the miracle of time and autolysis it is totally transformed[7] and bakes into a loaf you'd think only a professional could produce.

Part of the problem is that an immersion classroom is a total black box if you don't speak Chinese. What goes on inside is invisible. It's hard for a parent on the outside to get any sense of what's actually happening. Re-read *Chapter 4: How Mandarin Immersion Works* for a refresher on some of the stuff that's going on "behind the Chinese curtain."

In the end, it comes down to trust. First, of course, do your due diligence. Does your school have trained teachers? Does it have a Mandarin coordinator who oversees the overall program? Do students in higher grades do well on standardized tests? Check out the work they're doing in English in fourth and fifth grades. If your program goes through middle school, visit the middle school to see the quality of work the students from your program are doing. But once you've answered those questions, you've got to trust the professionalism and ability of the teachers in your school and the construction of the program as a whole.

Kids with learning difficulties

Here's another area that often comes up and with which many parents grapple: What if my child has learning differences? Will immersion make it that much harder for them to learn? In general, students with learning difficulties often do very well in immersion. In fact, for some children with language processing problems, learning a character-based language can be easier than a language like English, which requires decoding each individual word. Still, if you suspect your child has a learning problem, you should consult your school's staff.

I also encourage you to buy a copy of an excellent book on the topic: *Struggling Learners and Language Immersion Education: Research-based, Practitioner-informed Responses to Educators' Top Questions.*[8] It's by Tara Fortune and Mandy Menke of the Center for Advanced Research on Language Acquisition in Minneapolis and is available on Amazon and in an ebook format from the University of Minnesota bookstore.[9] It addresses the important topic of whether there are students for whom immersion is not appropriate and covers most of the topics that are of concern to parents. It includes stories about struggling learners from a range of educational specialists, background information and research summaries.

Have faith

In general, the vast majority of students in Mandarin immersion programs are going to do fine. In fact, they do better than fine. By the end of middle school they'll be doing as well as, if not better than kids from English-only programs. Plus they'll know Chinese on top of it.

And in another 20 or so years they may even thank you for being so foresighted as to have signed them up in the first place.

1. Ann Tollefson, Michael Bacon, Kyle Ennis, Carl Falsgraf, Nancy Rhodes, "Student Assessment and Program Evaluation," *Chinese Language Learning in the Early Grades: A handbook of resources and best practices for Mandarin immersion* (New York: Asia Society, 2012) 42.
2. Myriam Met, "Chinese Language Immersion: The State of the Field," *Chinese language learning in the early grades: A handbook of resources and best practices for Mandarin immersion* (New York: Asia Society, 2012) 5.
3. Amado Padilla, Lorraine Fan, Xiaoqiu Xu, Duarte Silva, "Ohlone Mandarin/English Two-way Immersion Program: Language Proficiency and Academic Achievement," an evaluation report presented to the Palo Alto School Board, November 2013.
   http://pausd.org/community/board/Weekly/112213_weekly.pdf
   Accessed Jan. 25, 2014.
4. Danielle Cintron, "Immersion programs see interest skyrocket in St. Cloud schools," *Saint Cloud Times.* September 13, 2013.
5. Tara Williams Fortune, "What the Research Says about Immersion," *Chinese language learning in the early grades: A handbook of resources and best practices for Mandarin immersion,* (New York: Asia Society, 2012) 5

6. Bittman, Mark, "The Secret of Great Bread: Let Time Do the Work," *New York Times*, November 8, 2008.
   http://www.nytimes.com/2006/11/08/dining/08mini.html?pagewanted=all
   Accessed March 14, 2014.
7. J. Kenji López-Alt, "The Science of No-Knead Dough," *The Food Lab*, June 17, 2011.
   http://www.seriouseats.com/2011/06/the-food-lab-the-science-of-no-knead-dough.html
   Accessed March 14, 2014.
8. Center for Advanced Research on Language Acquisition. "Resources for Struggling Immersion Learners."
   http://www.carla.umn.edu/immersion/learners.html
   Accessed March 14, 2014.
9. Center for Advanced Research on Language Acquisition, CARLA Working Paper Series. "Struggling Learners and Language Immersion Education." http://www.carla.umn.edu/resources/working-papers
   Accessed March 14, 2014.

十四
shí sì
14

How Much Chinese Will They Learn?

Mandarin immersion is like one of those Ginzu knife ads on late-night TV, the kind that could do a dozen different things and which always came with a ton of extras "thrown in for free!" And just when you thought the pitchman had finished with all its wonders, he always added "But wait, there's more!

Stick with the program through the end of high school and your child will come out a proficient, though not fluent, speaker of Mandarin. He or she will *also* have completed the same course work as students in English-only programs. But wait, there's more! We'll also throw in scores as good as or higher than students in regular, English-only programs—in both English and other subjects.[1]

If that's not enough to sell you on the idea, here are some more data points:

- Students in immersion typically will know as much Chinese by the end of third grade as they would if they'd taken three years of high school Chinese.

- By the end of eighth grade they will be at least at the level of a student with more than a year of college Chinese.

- They will have little or no accent compared to people who begin learning Chinese as adults.

- In many programs, they are set to pass the Advanced Placement Chinese test in ninth or tenth grade, giving them several *years* of college language credit.

- In some districts they will take college-level Chinese courses in high school and will be able to test into third- or fourth-year Chinese courses when they enter college.

- If they attend one of the 11 U.S. universities that have Language Flagship programs, they can study *in Chinese* at Chinese universities.

This hit home with me just this week. We recently hired a young man from Shanghai to shuttle our daughters around on their most complex day of after-school activities. He doesn't tutor them but we did ask that he speak only Mandarin with them. At first they were shy and he thought we were kidding when we said they spoke Chinese. But after a couple of days they got comfortable and started chattering away with him. He told them he was going to a ballet and that he'd never been to one before. When they heard it was *The Nutcracker* (which they've seen multiple times) our oldest daughter spent the entire car ride telling him the plot—in excruciating detail. When they arrived at our house he stopped me in the hallway out of earshot. "They really speak Chinese well," he said. "They sound like they come from China."

Chinese speakers are liable to say that of any child who gets beyond a rudimentary "*Nǐ jiào shénme míngzì?*" (What's your name?) But he got a sense of what other children their age learn the next week, when we added another girl the carpool. She goes to a well-regarded private school in San Francisco where Mandarin is taught as a separate subject. She'd been studying it for two years. Our daughters told him that she was studying Chinese too, so when they all got into the car he asked, "你今天唱得开心吗. *Nǐ jīntiān chàng de kāixīn ma.* [Did you have fun singing today?] It was clear she didn't understand this or any of the other things he said. By the end of the conversation all they'd been able to get through was *Ni hao?* (How are you?), to which she answered *Ni hao ma?* (How are you?)

This is a smart kid in a good school. But what was offered in her elementary school is what's called a FLEX class, for "Foreign Language Exploration." That means that they don't actually teach the kids to *speak* the language in question, they're just getting them *acquainted* with it. That's pretty common at the elementary school level in the United States when foreign languages are taught. But it's also a school that costs $20,000 or so a year and they've clearly added Mandarin because it's a 'must have' language these days. And yet after two years there wasn't much she could say beyond counting to 10, some colors and "*Ni hao.*"

Students in immersion do very well

As of early 2014 there was little published data on the performance of Mandarin immersion students in elementary school. Many studies are underway, including broad studies in Portland, Oregon and Utah. A flood of information will become available in the next several years. But the data that are available look good. One of the first is a study[2] of the Palo Alto Unified School District's Mandarin immersion program at Ohlone[3] Elementary. There, immersion students did as well as—or better than—their peers with respect to English and academic content and did very well in Mandarin.

Ohlone's Mandarin immersion program was launched in the 2008–2009 school year. A group of Stanford University researchers followed it from its inception through to the promotion of its first class of fifth graders to middle school in 2012–2013. Located at the beating heart of Silicon Valley, next to Stanford, the school draws from mostly middle- and upper-middle class families. Just 3% of its students are eligible for the free or reduced-price lunch program. The student body is 58% white, 31% Asian, 8% Hispanic and 2% Black. Just 8% of the students are English Language Learners.[4]

The program begins with 80% of class time spent in Mandarin and 20% in English in kindergarten and first grade. Second- and third-graders get 60% of their class time in Mandarin. For fourth- and fifth-graders it is 50%. So during their elementary school career the students spend the majority of their time learning in Mandarin.

Let's look how they did.

Mandarin ability

Listening and speaking

Towards the end of their first year, most kindergartners were only able to follow instructions or engage in very basic conversations in Mandarin. By fifth grade, most students were **intermediate** speakers on the ACTFL scale.[5] They "demonstrated control of the language, added their own details to regular expressions and attempted higher-level skills."[6]

Reading

By the close of their first year in Mandarin immersion, most kindergarteners were able to read a medium to high number of a selection of 100 high-frequency words. By fourth and fifth grade, students were able to read stories approximately 300 characters long, on their own, and answer questions about the central ideas and details of the story.

Writing

Most fifth graders were writing at an **intermediate** level. They showed accuracy when adding details to regular sentences and made efforts to try out higher-level skills.

Heritage speakers

Students who came from Mandarin or Chinese-speaking families outperformed non-heritage speakers slightly to moderately. However the gap became smaller by fourth and fifth grade.

Academic achievement at Ohlone

By the time the immersion students were into their third year of Mandarin, in second grade, they were performing slightly less well in English and math than their non-immersion peers in the same school, as measured by the California Standardized Testing and Reporting (STAR) test. The number of second graders in both groups who were proficient in English language arts was about the same (39% and 37%) but there were more non-immersion students scoring as advanced (45%) than immersion students (36%).

Fast-forward to fourth grade. After five years in Mandarin, the immersion students had pulled ahead of the non-immersion students in English language arts. Remember that it was only in fourth grade that students started spending half their day in English-using classrooms. And yet 86% of the immersion students scored advanced while only 72% of the non-immersion students did.

The numbers for fifth grade aren't quite as dramatic, 77% of immersion students scored advanced while 73% of the non-immersion students did. But that was also the pioneer class of the program and appreciably smaller, just 13 students.

In the English writing portion of the STAR test, 59% of the fourth graders in immersion scored advanced while 43% of the non-immersion students did.

Math was even more dramatic. Immersion students scored in the advanced range at higher rates than did their non-immersion peers. By fifth grade, 92% of the immersion students were getting advanced scores in math while 47% of the non-immersion students were.

In their final report to the Palo Alto School Board, the researchers said:

> Students who are taught in Mandarin for much of the school day generally achieve at levels on California mandated tests in English language arts, writing, math and science that are as high as, or sometimes higher than, their non-immersion peers who attend the same school. These results are reassuring because they demonstrate that, when students receive instruction in two languages, they are not only developing as bilinguals, but also do not fall behind their peers on the essential core content.

Note that Palo Alto public schools draw from a highly educated and achievement-oriented community. This isn't a case of more academically able students coming to a Mandarin program in a low-performing school. The entire school district is high performing. Ohlone Elementary gets an Academic Performance Index score of 949 out of a possible 1,000—a result many schools in California would swoon over.

It is possible that the families who choose to enter the Mandarin immersion program are more academically inclined than your typical Palo Alto parent. But even given that, it's pretty amazing that by fifth grade the immersion students were using Mandarin at the level of college Chinese majors *and* scoring higher than many of their peers in English.

Perhaps even more amazing is that the program in Palo Alto was bitterly fought against by parents in the district. It was first proposed in 2005 by a group of parents with young children, but was opposed by families who felt language instruction should be made available to all elementary school students or none, and that immersion would break up community schools.[7] All school board members but one voted against it the first time it was proposed. Only after several attempts and two years did the program begin.

Other schools have reported similar positive results for immersion students. Another study looked at two well-established Chinese immersion programs in the San Francisco Bay area. The research was conducted by Kathryn Lindholm-Leary of San Jose State University. She has conducted multiple studies of Spanish immersion schools. In this work, she looked at two Chinese immersion schools in northern California. They were different from most Mandarin immersion programs today in that a high proportion of their students came from Chinese families, many of whom spoke Chinese at home. The schools also used their own, home-grown tests to assess students' Chinese levels.

Her study found that students at each school developed listening/speaking and reading/writing skills in Chinese and also scored above grade level on the California Achievement Test, which measured their skills in English reading and math. By seventh grade, achievement was "well above average to very high"[8] in reading and in math. As Lindholm-Leary writes:

...immersion students meet the goal of academic achievement at or above grade level while learning content through two languages. These data also provide further impetus for parents who might be concerned that students will not be able to learn content through a language as difficult as Chinese and be able to compete with their English-speaking monolingual peers.[9]

What was that you said a while ago about "proficient"?

Ah, caught that, did you?

"Proficient" is the word many programs are using to describe the outcome they're expecting by the end of middle or high school. More and more they're acknowledging that students will *not* be fully bilingual and biliterate in Mandarin. Bilingual means that you speak two languages close to equally well, while biliterate means that you read two languages close to equally well. Students in Mandarin immersion programs who are not from Mandarin-speaking households speak, understand, read and write English much better than they do Mandarin.

"Wait just a minute!" I hear you cry. "Our principal says our students will be fully bilingual and biliterate. Doesn't that mean they'll finish eighth-grade at the same level an eighth grade student in Taiwan or China would in Chinese reading and writing?"

Well, no, they won't.

There are several reasons for this. Let's take them in order.

Chinese is a difficult language to learn because it's not a cognate language with English, meaning that there aren't words in both languages that share similar meaning, spelling and pronunciation. The United States Foreign Services Institute, which teaches foreign languages to U.S. government workers, classifies Chinese as a Category III language. That is in the same class as Arabic, Japanese and Korean. It is estimated that a native English speaker requires on average 88 weeks of full-time effort to achieve general professional proficiency. Compare that with Category I languages like French and Spanish, which take only 24 weeks.

U.S. students don't spend as much time in school as do students in Asia. In the United States, students typically spend 900 hours a year in school. In China the number is 1,560 and in Taiwan it's 1,640.[10] There's a reason they're ahead of us in international math and science rankings.

In addition, most children in China and Taiwan do substantially more homework than do students in the United States. Especially in cities, many students spend between five and 20 additional hours at tutoring schools (补习班, bǔxíbān) after school and on weekends.

Most students in Mandarin immersion programs come from non-Chinese speaking families. So they get at best three to four hours of Chinese a day. Compare that with students from Chinese-speaking households, who get Chinese while they're at home as well. Or to students in China, Taiwan and Hong Kong, who are surrounded by Chinese every waking hour.

This is well-known among immersion experts. Tara Williams Fortune coordinates the immersion research and professional development project at the Center for Advanced Research on Language Acquisition at the University of Minnesota. Immersion students, especially the ones who come in speaking English, do not achieve native-like levels of speaking and writing skills, she says:

> Studies consistently find that English-speaking immersion students' oral language lacks grammatical accuracy, lexical specificity, native pronunciation, and is less complex and socio-linguistically

appropriate when compared with the language native speakers of the second language produce. ... Even in high-performing immersion programs, advancing students' second language proficiency beyond the intermediate levels remains a sought-after goal.[11]

The Minnetonka, Minnesota public schools system, which has an *extremely* rigorous and demanding Mandarin immersion program, is very clear about this with parents. Immersion students' comprehension skills are comparable to those of native speakers at the same age after two or three years. However the district goes on to tell parents:

> Research, however, has found that immersion students' second language lacks the same grammatical accuracy, variety and complexity produced by native speakers. To attain that skill level is a long-term process. Native-like proficiency in every skill area is unlikely.[12]

What is fluent, anyway?

Here's where we get into the nitty-gritty of immersion. Remember that there's a big difference between "receptive" language and "productive" language. Think of the toddler I wrote about in *Chapter 4: How Mandarin Immersion Works*, the one who couldn't say much more than "Mama" and "Dada." But remember if you told her "Go get the red ball in the living room, the one that's on the couch," she could do it right away? That's receptive language, the ability to hear and understand.

Productive language is the ability to say things, to produce speech. Just like our toddler, students in immersion classrooms can understand a lot more than they can say. That's true for most of us. I can follow scientists on NPR discussing physics, but I couldn't explain it myself. I don't have the productive vocabulary.

It's the same with reading and writing. Reading is receptive language, and we're all able to read at a much higher level than we can write. You might be able to read *Scientific American* and understand the articles, but you might not be able to write them yourself. It's the same for kids in immersion. They can read at a higher level than they're capable of writing. That's even more true if they're writing by hand rather than on a computer, because writing in Chinese requires a muscle memory of how characters are written, in what stroke order and how their component parts are balanced. Students writing on the computer just have to type in the pinyin and choose the right characters. This turns writing from 100% productive language to something that's about 50% receptive (seeing and choosing the right character.)

So it's very possible that you could have a fifth grader in Chinese immersion with a broad a range of abilities (ranked on the scale created by the American Council on the Teaching of Foreign Languages) depending on what was being measured. (I'll explain exactly what these terms mean later in the chapter.)

Listening	**Advanced Low**
Speaking	**Intermediate High**
Reading	**Intermediate Low**
Writing	**Novice High** (by hand)
	Intermediate Low (on a computer)

There's also the issue of academic versus social language. This is where kids in Chinese-speaking families really leap ahead. Students who live with Chinese at home hear a much broader range of the language, in many more contexts, than do students who only hear it in the classroom. When Judy Shei's son was in second grade in San Francisco's Starr King Elementary School, she wrote,

> I see non-native speakers failing to learn things like reading a menu, calling a taxi, giving directions, everyday usage type of Chinese. For example, I have met second graders who can say "greater than" for math, but don't know how to say "last night."

Students can also get bogged down worrying about how to say things "right" versus just figuring out how to get their meaning across. When my daughters were in third and fifth grade our whole family went to China. We got into a cab in Yangshuo and I said, "Ask the driver when we'll arrive in Guilin."

"We don't know how to say that!" they wailed.

"Do you know to say Guilin?" I asked.

"Yeah," they said, "We heard it in the train station."

"Okay," I said. "Do you know how to say 'when'?"

"Sure," my third-grader offered.

"Okay, so you just say, 'Guilin, when?' and he'll tell you when we'll get there."

"But that's not how you say it!" they whined.

"If you don't ask him, then I will, and you know my Chinese will sound 100 times worse than yours," I said.

With the possibility of me embarrassing them horribly with my mangled, American-sounding Mandarin (with all the tones wrong, as they so gleefully point out), they figured it would be less embarrassing for them to say it wrong than to have to listen to me.

They said, "Guilin? When?" to the taxi driver.

He understood them perfectly. They understood him when he said it was an hour and 20 minutes but it depended on how bad the traffic was. And they easily translated what he'd said into English.

So there's an example of two girls, ages 9 and 11, who were able to have a conversation with a taxi driver in China (whose Mandarin accent was a little hard to follow because he spoke another dialect of Chinese as his native language) and they were able to communicate, get the necessary information, and transmit it an English speaker.

The take-home message here is that fluent can mean different things to different people in different contexts.

But Spanish immersion students are fluent, right?

Actually, no. Spanish immersion students from English-speaking homes are not totally fluent in Spanish. There really is a difference between hearing a language at home with your parents from the day you were born and learning it in school, no matter how many hours you spend using it at school. The first gives an innate, native-level comfort and command of social language. The second may result in less fluency but can also give more academic and formal speech. Both types of understanding are necessary to use the second language professionally.

Think about it. There are millions of Americans who speak Spanish or Korean or Tagalog or Chinese with perfect ease at home. However they couldn't run a meeting or make a presentation or talk someone through fixing a computer problem in that language. To be fully functional in a language, functional in the way Chinese immersion parents want their kids to be, you need both social and academic language.

Which isn't to say that Spanish immersion students don't attain fluency. They do. In fact they're much more fluent speakers of Spanish than Chinese immersion students are speakers of Chinese. That's because Spanish is a cognate language to English and Chinese isn't. By some measures 70% of Spanish words have English cognates. If you study Spanish, French or even German, you get literally thousands of words 'free' because they're similar in English and the other language, so your receptive ability (the words you can understand when they're spoken to you or you read them) is pretty high right from the start.

Even if you don't speak any Spanish at all, you can probably pick up a Spanish language newspaper and understand from a story that the president of Mexico is going to Guatemala, or that So-and-So had just divorced his third wife and they are fighting over custody of their son.

Él se está divorciando de su esposa. Ella quiere la custodia del hijo.
He is divorcing his wife. She wants custody of their son.

But try that in Chinese:

他是办理离婚手续的妻子。她希望儿子的监护权。

Tā shì bànlǐ líhūn shǒuxù de qīzi. Tā xīwàng érzi de jiānhù quán.

In Spanish you won't understand everything, but you'd probably get enough to make a good guess at what's going on. The Chinese words aren't free at all; they come at the cost of many hours of reading and study.[13]

To see this in action, Google "Father Guido Sarducci." He's played by bilingual comedian Don Novello. In one skit, he manages to give an entire lecture about similarities between the presidencies of Jimmy Carter and Calvin Coolidge, *in Italian,* while being fully understandable to an English-speaking audience. You could not do that in Chinese.

French immersion students don't reach perfection either

Even French immersion students don't become totally fluent, and it's the oldest, best-studied and best-funded type of language immersion in North America because it's been a cornerstone of the Canadian national education system since the 1980s. And it's a cognate language.

Years of Canadian research shows that English-speaking immersion students don't achieve full native competence in French by the time they finish school. They continue to make grammatical errors. Students in Canadian French immersion programs don't reach grade-level French until sixth grade. Research shows that even in 10th grade French immersion students in Canada score in the 20th to 35th percentile in reading and grammar in French. By 11th grade they're in the 40th and 50th percentiles. And these students have not only had over 6,000 hours of exposure to French, they've had at least 50% of their school day in French through eighth grade, and between two and four (of eight) classes in high school were in French.[14] And they live in a country where all the packaging and much of the signage is bilingual, so they see French all the time.

And it's okay...

Here's the important part: This is *not* a bad outcome. French immersion students in Canada are extremely competent and fully functional in French. More importantly, they're able to work in bilingual jobs and pass exams used to prove that a person is bilingual, required for many government jobs in Canada. Not only that, but they're like a flower waiting to bloom. Stick them in the "water" of a fully French environment (say they move to Montreal) and they blossom into near-native French speakers, becoming "indistinguishable from native speakers of French in their verbal expression."[15]

Anecdotally, it's looking like Chinese immersion students "flower" in the same way the French immersion students do. I've talked to several college students who were in immersion programs through eighth and sometimes twelfth grade who went on to spend time in China. Each said that they immediately felt at home in the language, even though they didn't understand everything that was going on. At a deep level the language "clicked" with them and they were able to communicate. They found things they'd learned years before bubbled to the surface and their speaking ability quickly ramped up as if it had been sleeping inside them. So start thinking about the gap year in China now.[16]

So will my child speak Mandarin?

Yes. Though just how proficient your son or daughter will be depends on several things, some of which are under your control and some of which aren't. These fall into five main categories:

- Do you speak Chinese at home?
- What are the expectations of your school's Mandarin program?
- Does your child do all of his or her homework?
- If you don't use Chinese at home, how much Mandarin is your child exposed to when he or she is not in school?
- How much Mandarin does your child read each day, compared to reading English. See *Chapter 16: Chinese Literacy Issues*, for why this is so critical.

If you're just getting into Chinese immersion, feel free to stop here. The take-home message for you is that if you keep your child in Chinese immersion until the end of eighth grade, he or she should enter high school with the same command of Mandarin that a U.S. college student would have after two or three years of classes. *And* they'll get all the subjects that would have been covered if they'd been in an English-only program. They lose nothing and gain proficiency in a major world language, all by the time they're 13. If your district has a high school program they could go even further.

If you want to go deeper, keep reading. It's all quite fascinating, though I'll warn you we're going to get into a lot of detail about language levels and testing. Here's what I'll cover:

- Where Chinese immersion programs have been
- Why they realized they needed to do better
- Why they need testing to do that
- How language ability is measured
- How children's Mandarin levels are tested
- Why parents should care

The Wild West days of Chinese immersion

For a long time, we simply didn't know how well kids in immersion spoke Chinese. From the beginning of these programs in the 1980s until quite recently, the general answer to, "How much Mandarin will my kid learn?" in most programs seems to have been, "They'll do fine—you worry too much." Students were most often compared to heritage learners in Saturday Chinese schools, and against those students they measured fairly well.[17]

"One of the challenges is even knowing what level kids can achieve," says Kathleen Wang, principal of the Pioneer Valley Chinese Immersion Charter School in Hadley, Massachusetts. It's a K–12 charter school that's entirely devoted to Chinese immersion. "Because there aren't national tests for kids, it is very difficult to even know where kids are and where schools are. As schools mature, there will be more data available and we'll know more."

When Michael Bacon, the Immersion Achievement Coordinator for Portland Public Schools in Oregon, started working in immersion education 17 years ago, "there wasn't a lot of talk about language proficiency outcomes." Teachers used Mandarin in the classroom, the kids learned to understand them, and that was the end of it. There's also been a certain "feel-good" aspect to immersion that tended to cloud the picture. "People get so excited when a kid says, 'Good morning,' in Chinese, but really we want them to be able to discuss refraction in physics and be able to order confidently in a restaurant," says Bacon.

The best proxy Portland had for determining how well students were doing was math scores, because math, taught in Mandarin, is a subject for which there were clear outcomes that could easily be compared with the performance of students who studied the same material in English. Portland's since started using other metrics, which I'll go into later.

But if you use math as a proxy, students in Mandarin immersion programs in Portland and nationally did quite well—scoring by and large as well or better than students in English-only programs.

"Our kids' math scores are through the roof and their English Language Arts performance and reading is meeting or exceeding expectations for almost every single kid, even though they're getting only half of a day in English," says Bacon.

To be fair, the inability of programs to tell parents how well their child is doing wasn't just a Mandarin problem, or even an immersion problem. "Even in general education we're bad at telling parents, 'This is where your fifth grader should be in mathematics,'" for example, says Elizabeth Hardage, the former assistant principal of Washington Yu Ying, a K–8 Mandarin immersion charter school in Washington D.C. She is now a Chinese curriculum consultant for several Mandarin immersion schools, including Yu Ying.

That said, there really wasn't any meaningful testing being done to measure students' Mandarin abilities until relatively recently. Students are learning math, social studies, science and a host of other crucial educational content in Mandarin but no one knew if their Mandarin was up to the task. For students who are supposedly learning in a rigorous academic environment, "if they don't have the language, it's a problem," says Bacon.

This is beginning to change, as you can see by the two studies at the beginning of this chapter. However, a gold standard for testing the Mandarin proficiency of an elementary school or middle school student hasn't yet emerged. So let's look at why it's difficult, and where things are heading.

It's no easy task to measure language ability

Here's where we're going to get deep into the weeds on all this. Stick with me; it's a fascinating hike that will take us from the State Department just after World War II all the way through to cutting-edge online testing today. And I promise we'll end up in a Chinese immersion classroom.

To start with, it is no easy thing to measure how well students understand, speak, read and write Mandarin. Remember these are children who, especially in the early years, aren't so good at sitting down and taking a huge test. In addition, what's being measured—language proficiency—is hard to grasp. To begin, let's talk about general language proficiency.

So here's a question: How good is *your* English? If you're like most people, you probably don't spend a lot of time thinking about your overall language ability. If you can make it through the day and everyone understands you, you're doing pretty well, right?

It depends. Are you a clerk at a 7-Eleven, a police officer, an engineer, a vice president at a large, multi-national firm or a professor of political science who writes books about the Russian land tenure system during the medieval era? Each position requires a different level of language ability and complexity. Measuring that level isn't easy. But it can be done, and the United States government has spent a lot of time and money figuring out how.

Back in the 1950s, the U.S. realized it had a language problem. There were people working in the diplomatic corps and the military who *said* their French was fluent or their Russian conversational, but was it really? At times the fate of the world could hang on a missed nuance or a bad translation, so the government formed the Interagency Language Roundtable,[18] a group that came up with criteria to determine whether employees or job applicants had enough language ability to do their job. For example, did they speak enough German to work in the Bonn embassy or enough Korean to do linguistic analysis for the Department of Defense? This group created a five-point ILR scale, with 1 being "very little ability" and 5 being "fluent." It became clear how useful this scale was in 1955, when all Foreign Service officers were surveyed. The results? Fewer than half had language levels "useful to the service."

In the 1980s, foreign language teachers realized this scale could also be used for their students. The American Council on the Teaching of Foreign Languages used the IRL scale as a template to create the ACTFL Scale, which explicitly describes what people can do at various levels of language proficiency. The scale starts at absolutely no knowledge of a language and goes all the way up to the level of a highly-educated adult native speaker. There are four levels.[19] As you read them, think about how well *you* speak English or any other language you know:

Novice: May be difficult to understand even for speakers accustomed to dealing with non-native speakers.

Intermediate: Understood, with some repetition, by speakers accustomed to dealing with non-native speakers.

Advanced: Understood without difficulty by speakers unaccustomed to dealing with non-native speakers

Superior: No patterns of errors in basic structures. Errors virtually never interfere with communication or distract the native speaker from the message.

Proficiency guidelines

In the classroom, you'll most often see more specific guidelines broken down into sub-groups and also by whether speaking, listening, reading or writing are being measured. These are broadly described below, based on a 24-page ACTFL document that goes through them in very specific detail.[20]

- **Novice low:** No ability whatsoever in the language

- **Novice mid:** When responding to direct questions, may say only two or three words at a time or give an occasional stock answer.

- **Novice high:** Conversation is restricted to a few of the predictable topics necessary for survival in the target language culture, such as basic personal information, basic objects, and a limited number of activities, preferences, and immediate needs.

- **Intermediate low:** Conversation is restricted to some of the concrete exchanges and predictable topics necessary for survival in the target-language culture. These topics relate to basic personal information; for example, self and family, some daily activities and personal preferences, and some immediate needs, such as ordering food and making simple purchases.

- **Intermediate mid:** Able to handle successfully a variety of uncomplicated communicative tasks in straightforward social situations. Tend to function reactively, for example, by responding to direct questions or requests for information. Capable of asking a variety of questions when necessary to obtain simple information to satisfy basic needs,

- **Intermediate high:** Able to handle successfully uncomplicated tasks and social situations requiring an exchange of basic information related to work, school, recreation, particular interests, and areas of competence.

- **Advanced low:** Able to participate in most informal and some formal conversations on topics related to school, home, and leisure activities. Demonstrate the ability to narrate and describe in the major time frames of past, present, and future in paragraph-length discourse.

- **Advanced mid:** Able to handle with ease and confidence a large number of communicative tasks. Participate actively in most informal and some formal exchanges on a variety of concrete topics relating to work, school, home, and leisure activities.

- **Advanced high:** Consistently able to explain in detail and narrate fully and accurately in all time frames. May provide a structured argument to support opinions, and may construct hypotheses, but patterns of error appear. May demonstrate a well-developed ability to compensate for an imperfect grasp of some forms or for limitations in vocabulary by the confident use of communicative strategies, such as paraphrasing, circumlocution, and illustration.

- **Superior:** Able to communicate with accuracy and fluency in order to participate fully and effectively in conversations on a variety of topics in formal and informal settings from both concrete and abstract perspectives.

What kind of work can you do at various levels?

To make it more interesting, here are the employment possibilities[21] at each level. As you read them, think about your child's English abilities right now, or your own abilities in any language you yourself might have studied.

Novice
Corresponding professions: None
Who functions at this level: Second language learners after two years of high school language study

Intermediate low
Corresponding professions: Receptionist, housekeeping staff
Who functions at this level: Second language learners after three-year high school sequences of study (AP, etc.) or one semester of college

Intermediate mid

Corresponding professions: Cashier, sales clerk (highly predictable contexts)

Who functions at this level: Students with four to six semesters of college study of the language.

Intermediate high

Corresponding professions: Auto inspector, aviation personnel, missionary, tour guide

Who functions at this level: Undergraduate language majors without year-long study-abroad experience.

Advanced low

Corresponding professions: Customer service agent, social worker, claims processor, K–12 language teacher, police officer, maintenance administrator, billing clerk, legal secretary, legal receptionist

Who functions at this level: Undergraduate language majors with year-long study-abroad experience

Advanced mid

Corresponding professions: Fraud specialist, account executive, court stenographer/interpreter, benefits specialist, technical service agent, collection representative, estimating coordinator

Who functions at this level: Heritage speakers, non-academic learners who have had significant contact with the language

Advanced high

Corresponding professions: Physician, military linguist, senior consultant, human resources personnel, financial broker, translation officer, marketing manager, communications consultant

Who functions at this level: Second language learners with graduate degrees in language-related area and extended educational experience in target environment

Superior

Corresponding professions: University foreign language professor, business executive, lawyer, judge, financial advisor

Who functions at this level: Well-educated native speakers and educated second-language learners with extended professional and/or educational experience in the target language environment

Benchmarking: Why the ACTFL scale matters in immersion

Okay, so perhaps you don't spend your day thinking about the language attainments of foreign-service staff. But these scales affect your child because they are used to understand language levels attained by students, and by immersion programs, to set expectations.

It's only been recently that immersion programs started to get serious about measuring achievement. Prior to that, the few programs there were nationwide tended to come up with their own testing methods or just presume everything was working fine. However, with a flood of new programs coming on line, schools need to know what's working and what isn't. To do that they need tests that can accurately measure language abilities in young children.

It's important to know what students understand because if they don't understand the language, they can't learn content (math, social studies, science) taught in that language. "Let's remember that in immersion programs, students are educated in Mandarin. This is a great responsibility—you have to make sure students are developing the level of language," to be able to access the academic curriculum, says Myriam Met, an education and language consultant who works with many of the larger Mandarin immersion programs nationwide.

Immersion program administrators are also realizing that there must be a goal set for achievement by the end of high school. As Met puts it, "You can't hit a target if you don't have one." Programs must know the language demands of the curriculum that students will be required to master by the end of fifth or eighth or twelfth grade as it's built up year by year, so that what they learn in second grade lays the foundation for what they need to know in fifth grade and then seventh and onwards.

It's not that they need to master a specific list of words in first grade to be able to get to second grade. It's that there needs to be coordination between the grades so that it all builds upon itself. If middle school students are learning in science class about tectonic plates, earthquakes and The Ring of Fire, they'll remember learning about the continents in grade school. If being able to write a clear, well-organized essay in Chinese is necessary for eighth grade, learning to write good, solid, linguistically complex sentences in Chinese is something they need to learn in elementary school. "Fourth grade sentences, not second grade sentences!" as my daughters' teachers tended to write on their homework.

On the ground, different programs are setting different targets as everyone tries to figure out what's possible. This is an enormous topic of conversation in Chinese language teaching circles, with many meetings, workshops and summits devoted to the topic.

For example, in Utah, which had 28 Chinese immersion schools statewide in 2013[22], the curriculum is being built so that it flows all the way to high school. The plan is that in ninth grade, Chinese immersion students will take the College Board's Advanced Placement Chinese exam. If the students pass, and they're expected to be able to, they will go on to take college level

Chinese courses in high school. When they graduate from high school, they'll be two courses short of a college minor in Chinese and able to immediately take classes in Chinese at a Chinese university.

"We don't just want kids who can wow a visitor," says Met, who consults with Utah and other districts on their Chinese immersion programs. "Our students have to be able to explain the relationship between fractions and decimals in Chinese, or explain what causes a shadow and what causes the length of a shadow to change. It's not just singing songs; that's not enough."

So all schools have to do is give kids the ACTFL test?

Sadly it's not that easy. This is all very new to elementary school language education and especially to Chinese immersion. When immersion schools first started to think about testing their students, there weren't many tests for them to choose from. Most tests of Chinese ability were meant for high school or college-level students. The most commonly used was the College Board Advanced Placement (AP) exam,[23] and that only became available in 2007. The other common test, especially in Asia, was the HSK[24] (汉语水平考 试 *Hànyǔ shuǐpíng kǎoshì*) Chinese Proficiency Test, a national standardized test to assess the Chinese proficiency of non-native speakers applying to university. It was first offered in 1984 and wasn't even available outside of China until 1991. It was originally designed by the Beijing Language Institute. The Youth version of the HSK test was only introduced in 2011.

Neither of these were very good at measuring how much Chinese a squirmy first grader knows or the language ability of a third grader who speaks well but doesn't read much. "If you ask a third grader to make a hotel reservation [as a test for adults might], it doesn't work. You have to have prompts that are within that kid's life experience," says Ann Tollefson, an immersion and world language consultant who assists in evaluating immersion programs.

For that reason, researchers have created several tests of Chinese (and other languages) ability, all based on the ACTFL scale and its underlying IRL scale. The current tests are by no means perfect, but they are getting closer to what is needed. Thus far there simply aren't that many great "assessment mechanisms" (as educators like to call tests) that are good, relevant, appropriately priced and easy to use for Chinese immersion students, especially in elementary school. Each year the tests get a little better. Don't expect that this is a fully built-out, perfect system that will easily and clearly tell you, your child and his or her teacher exactly how he or she is doing. That simply doesn't exist yet. But it's coming.

Currently available tests

Schools have an alphabet of tests to choose from. Your program might use several, for students at different ages. [25]

- AAPPL: The ACTFL Assessment of Performance towards Proficiency in Languages
- ACTFL/ILR Oral Proficiency Interview
- CAL Oral Proficiency Exam
- Middle School Assessment for Intensive Language Programs
- ELLOPA: Early Language Listening and Oral Proficiency Assessment
- SOPA: Student Oral Proficiency Assessment
- STAMP: Standards-based Measurement of Proficiency
- Youth Chinese Test, 中小学生汉语考试 *Zhōng xiǎoxuésheng hànyǔ kǎoshì*

Probably the two most commonly used tests right now are the AAPPL, created by the American Council on the Teaching of Foreign Languages, and the CAL tests created by the Center for Applied Linguistics, a language learning non-profit in Washington D.C.

AAPPL is an online test that's affordable and doesn't require extensive training for teachers and staff to use. It uses virtual video chats, emails and podcasts to assess students' abilities. An intermediate student would be expected to compose an email about school and interests and be able to read an article promoting their school. An advanced learner might listen to a video chat about technology, write a wiki article about their community and read a passage about social problems and then answer questions about it.

This test is what the 50 or so schools in the Flagship–Chinese Acquisition Pipeline, or F-CAP consortium,[26] are using to measure their students' progress. It has the advantage of being inexpensive and assessing listening, speaking, reading and writing.

The **CAL** tests can be used with many languages to assess oral fluency, grammar, vocabulary and listening comprehension at the appropriate grade level. However they don't cover writing. The tests are:

- ELLOPA: Early Language Listening and Oral Proficiency Assessment (pre-K through second grade)
- SOPA: Student Oral Proficiency Assessment (third through fifth grade)
- COPE: CAL Oral Proficiency Exam (middle school)

These tests are conducted using pairs of students who talk together. Two adults, an Interviewer and a Rater, observe. The Interviewer asks the students a series of leading questions to get them to talk about a desired subject while the Rater rates their speaking levels on a very precise scale. All three tests are entirely oral; they don't include written language.

Here's a sample conversation from the ELLOPA:

Q: How old are you?

A: Six

Q: Do you know when your birthday is?

A: No

Q: What do you like to do on your birthday?

A: Play

Q: Do you eat any special foods on your birthday?

A: Sandwiches

Q: Can you think of any presents you got on your birthday one time?

A: Ball

Here's what SOPA might look like for a fifth grade student in a Spanish immersion program. (I couldn't find an example in Mandarin.) This is an English translation of the student's answers as they were given in Spanish, complete with errors.

Q: What do you see in this picture?

A: The food chain. The plant produces photosynthesis. It makes it own food in the leaves and solar energy. How do you say '*lobo*?' Wolf needs rabbit to eat. Rabbit need plants to eat. The plants need sun to grow.

And finally here's what COPE might look like in middle school, with two students participating:

Objective: The students introduce themselves and chat informally on topics of personal interest in Chinese.

Time allowed for the conversation: Two minutes

Today is the first day of the school year. A Chinese student who has just arrived in the United States is entering the Chinese immersion program in your school. An American student notices that the Chinese student seems a bit lost and wants to help. Imagine that you are these two students. Introduce yourselves and then continue your conversation for a few minutes before classes begin.

[To the American student] Welcome your Chinese classmate. Tell him/her your name, age, and grade in school, and then ask him/her the same.

[To the Chinese student] Continue the conversation, telling your classmate about your favorite hobbies, sports and family, and ask your classmate the same.

As you can see, the tests aren't the typical foreign language test you might have taken in high school. They're meant to measure how well the students can function in the language, said Lynn Thompson, who works with the Center for Applied Linguistics.

"It goes along with the evolution we've seen with foreign language teaching in United States. In the beginning the focus was on grammar. Now it's more being able to use the language."

So what *do* we know?

Let's first look at Met's assessment of how much Chinese is learned by students who start studying the language in high school or college. On the ACTFL scale, "students who begin studying a language in high school are at a **Novice** level and when they finish it three years later, they were still a **Novice Mid** or a few might get to **Novice High**. It's kind of discouraging after three full years of study." Remember that there aren't any jobs for which **Novice** language abilities are sufficient. University students "who major in a foreign language and are not native speakers struggle to be above an **Intermediate**."

To put this in context, it's not easy to reach the Intermediate level, even for highly motivated adults. The U.S. Defense Language Institute in Monterey, California, specializes in educating military and state department personnel in languages as quickly and efficiently as possible. To get to the **Intermediate** stage in Chinese at the DLI, adult students (who have been specifically selected for the course and are highly motivated) study for four months, five hours a day, for a total of 480 hours of instruction. "And," notes Met, "they do *all* their homework."

So what about Chinese immersion students?

First, please remember that what's expected of a fully fluent child is different than what's expected of a fully fluent adult. "Parents need to understand the way kids develop. To become a fluent speaker takes years in English and proficiency in any grade level is going to be in that grade level," says Kathleen Wang, principal of the Pioneer Valley Chinese Immersion Charter School in Hadley, Massachusetts. "For example, we have kids in the elementary grades who are at intermediate level [in Chinese] but an intermediate fourth grader is not the same as an intermediate adult."

Here's an example: One of the tasks in the COPE test is for a student to express an opinion, support that opinion and then persuade the interviewer, who's playing the part of the principal. Perhaps they're supposed to make a cogent argument for why the school uniform should be changed or that they should be allowed to bring candy in their lunches.

"In general, I don't see fifth graders who can do that well even in *English*. It's developmental," says Thompson. "From my experience, eighth graders can do a pretty good job of defending their opinions. Younger kids can't, whether it's in their first or their second language."

That said, here are some programs for which I have been able to find proficiency targets for Mandarin immersion students. Note that these are draft targets—no one yet has hard data to know how large numbers of students will do as they move up through the grades. These are best guesses based on limited information and projections. Schools that make their benchmarks publically available should be commended. Far too many schools merely hope for the best, with no real sense of the outcomes they hope for their students—and keep parents in the dark about it. These districts are beginning to shine a light, so we know the heights our children can achieve.

Portland Public Schools

Grade	Listening level
3	Intermediate low
5	Intermediate mid
8	Intermediate high
10	Intermediate high/Advanced low
12	Advanced low/Advanced mid

San Francisco Unified School District

Grade	Listening level
Kindergarten	Novice low
1	Novice mid
2	Intermediate low
3	Intermediate mid
4	Intermediate mid
5	Intermediate high
8	Advanced low
12	Advanced mid

Pioneer Valley Chinese Immersion Charter School in Hadley, Mass

Grade	Listening	Speaking	Reading
Kindergarten	Novice high	Novice mid	
1	Intermediate low,	Novice high	
2	Intermediate mid	Intermediate low	
3	Intermediate high	Intermediate low	Novice mid

4	Intermediate high	Intermediate mid	Novice high
5	Advanced low	Intermediate mid	Intermediate low
6	Advanced low	Intermediate high	Intermediate low
7	Advanced mid	Intermediate high	Intermediate mid
8	Advanced mid	Advanced low	Intermediate high
9	Advanced high	Advanced low	Intermediate high
10	Advanced high	Advanced mid	Advanced low
11	Superior	Advanced mid	Advanced low
12	Superior	Advanced high	Advanced mid

Utah State Mandarin Immersion

Grade	Listening	Speaking	Reading
1	Novice low	Novice low	Novice low
2	Novice mid	Novice mid	Novice mid
3	Novice high	Novice mid	Novice mid
4	Novice high	Novice high	Novice high
5	Intermediate low	Novice high	Novice high
6	Intermediate,	Low intermediate	Low Intermediate
7	Intermediate mid	Intermediate low	Intermediate low
8	Intermediate mid	Intermediate mid	Intermediate mid
9	Intermediate high	Intermediate mid	Intermediate mid
10	Intermediate high	Intermediate high	Intermediate high
11	Advanced low	Intermediate high	Intermediate high
12	Advanced low	Advanced low	Advanced low

Here, for comparison, is the number of hours the U.S. government assumes it would take a motivated adult to reach those same levels.[27]

Classroom hours	Minimum aptitude	Average aptitude	Superior aptitude
480 hours	Novice high	Intermediate low	Intermediate low/mid
720 hours	Intermediate low/mid	Intermediate mid/high	Intermediate high
1,320 hours	Intermediate high	Advanced low	Advanced mid/high
2,400–2,760 hours	Advanced high	Superior	Superior

What this all looks like in the classroom

A big part of proficiency-setting is sitting down with teachers and going over exactly what **Advanced mid** or **Intermediate low** look like, says David Kojo Hakam, a curriculum specialist for the Portland Public Schools Chinese Flagship Program. He says the game-changer for Portland was when they introduced the OPI [Oral Proficiency Interview] training, which measures how well students speak and understand spoken Mandarin.

"Now even when I talk to someone in English I think 'Is that **Intermediate high** or **Advanced low**?' It totally changes how you look at teaching," Hakam says. Portland teachers do a one-week workshop every June just on assessment.

It's not just for teachers. In Portland, they teach the ACTFL scale to the students in the first weeks of middle school. This has dramatically changed how students look at their own work, he says. "Now, in eighth grade after a student gives a presentation, they don't come up to me and say, 'Did I get an A?,' they say 'Was I **Intermediate high**?'" says Hakam.

These tests also help parents. Portland teaches parents what to expect from their immersion program and posts the information on its website.[28] "We have a big meeting in the fall explaining the proficiency guidelines, giving samples of work, showing them exactly what an **Intermediate mid** or **Intermediate high** speaker is able to do," he says. "We also talk to them about what those levels look like in English so they can compare."

This helps parents get a handle on what's reasonable. For example, they can listen to their children's English and think, "Hmm, do they speak in paragraphs when they're speaking English? Maybe it's *not* reasonable to expect them to do it in Chinese if they're not doing it in English."

Getting from good to better

Here's an area where immersion teachers tend not to want to be quoted, because it sounds like they're being harsh. But a common criticism of immersion students, not just in Chinese but all languages, is that they can easily develop bad habits. They get to a certain comfort level with the language and can express what they need to say so don't move up to more sophisticated constructions.

It's the ke-bu-keyi problem. Here's a phrase you'll hear a lot from your child beginning in kindergarten:

我可不可以⋯
Wǒ kě bù kěyǐ ...
May I...

Students learn to ask to do things using this basic construction in kindergarten and it works. You'll hear this a lot in the classroom:

我可不可以去厕所？
Wǒ kěbu kěyǐ qù cèsuǒ?
May I go to the bathroom?

The problem is that students don't always move on from here; they don't advance to more complex and age-appropriate ways of saying things.

Fourth and fifth grades are when teachers really start to push students to use more complex constructions. This is especially true as the Common Core Standards—education standards adopted by most states—come into effect and they focus on teaching students good, solid expository writing skills.[29] (And I must say, as a reporter who gets emails from college students who want to go into journalism but who can't seem to compose a clear sentence in English, thank God for it!)

A lot of homework in the upper grade involves prompts and sentence pattern work, teaching methods also used extensively in China. These are usually worksheets in which the teacher provides more sophisticated phrases the students are expected to use in their written homework. For example instead of using "if...than," they might be asked to use "because of this...therefore" or other similarly more complex wordings (but in Chinese of course.)

Remember that this is only partly a Chinese problem. All students, as they move upwards through the grades, begin with simple statements and move to more complex thinking. "We expressed this to the YuYing teachers as 'higher level thinking questions/answers,'" says Elizabeth Hardage. All schools teach this, whatever language they use. You'll hear educators speak of Bloom's Taxonomy, which notes that children move from simply remembering to understanding, applying, analyzing and evaluating. The goal is to give students the language to be able to express ever more complex ideas as they grow older.

Students can also develop what's called "fossilized errors," in which they learn to say something the wrong way early on and don't hear it or read it in the correct form often enough to begin saying it correctly.[30] This is common to many second-language learners and you hear it all the time in English speakers who learned Spanish as adults. (I do it myself, making simple mistakes that I haven't learned how to fix because I don't spend enough time speaking or reading Spanish to cement the correct form in my head.) It makes us sound a little odd, and clearly not someone who's an **Advanced** speaker, but we get by.

The problem is, we don't want our kids to just get by in Chinese.

Varied reading for pleasure in Chinese makes a big difference here, as it constantly reinforces higher levels of language as students read gradually more difficult (but still fun) books. You can read about this more in *Chapter 16: Chinese Literacy Issues.*

The task of immersion teachers—actually all teachers in all languages—is to get students to stretch and refine their language so it becomes more sophisticated as they move up through the grades. So while a third grader might say:

There was this guy named Lincoln and he was president. Then there was a war, a long time ago, and we won. But he died.

A sixth grader needs to put it more formally:

In 1861 Abraham Lincoln was elected President of the United States. Southern states began leaving the Union because they wanted to keep slavery. He fought against slavery and the Confederacy. He was assassinated in 1865.

And by senior year of high school, if they hope to do well in college, they should be writing something along these lines:

Multiple economic factors were behind the dissolution of the United States during the Civil War. The agrarian South and the industrial North were at odds. The South felt it had no choice but to maintain slavery as slave labor was the basis for its economy. In the North, industrialization that began in New England around 1815 meant slavery could be a purely moral issue.

It's not only Chinese immersion students, or immersion students in general, who have trouble achieving this level of sophistication in their language. Portland's Bacon points out that most adult English speakers in the United States spend much of their day speaking at an **Intermediate** level. A fairly high percentage of Americans would have difficulty writing the high school level paragraph above without a lot of prompting. It's just not the kind of language they're exposed to and they haven't used it since leaving school. As one teacher put it, "People don't speak in paragraphs when everyone understands them just fine when they speak in sentences."

However, it's exactly the level of language that Chinese immersion parents expect of their students in English, and hope for in Chinese. And programs are working hard to make sure they get there, in both languages.

The answer? Celebrate teacher training days!

There are so many moving parts to creating a successful Chinese immersion program that sometimes I feel that it's amazing they function at all—and a miracle that they work as well as they do, given the funding constraints most schools face today. Bravo to our teachers and principals who labor far more than the 40 hours a week they're paid to make them happen.

Tests are helpful and good textbooks are helpful. Getting your child to read at home in Chinese will pay enormous benefits. But the real challenge is what happens day-to-day in the classroom. "That's the roll up your sleeves work," says Portland's Bacon.

For that, what schools need more than anything are great teachers. And great teachers are made, not born. They need training in how to do immersion; they need to work with master teachers to hone what they know; they need to keep up with current knowledge and new curriculum; and they need to know how to give and create tests that tell them how their students are doing. On top of that, they need to know how to track and analyze the data they get and create school-wide assessments to track progress based on their school's curriculum.

For example, in the spring of 2014 the 金山中文教育协会 – Jinshan Mandarin Education Council raised $5,000 to send five teachers from the San Francisco Unified School District's Mandarin immersion program to the Chinese Education Conference in Salt Lake City, Utah. The topic was "Practical Literacy, Making it Work in the Classroom." The teachers wanted to go and the district wanted them to, but there was no money to send them. So the parent-led non-profit that supports Mandarin immersion in the San Francisco public schools put out a call for donations. In the end we were able to send teachers from each of the program's three schools. They in turn came back and shared what they'd learned with their colleagues.

So the next time you hear that your child's teacher is out of the classroom for a teacher-training day, celebrate the fact. Far from being a day lost to movies and worksheets, it's what will make your school a great school, and a great Mandarin immersion program.

1. Kathryn Lindholm-Leary, "Student Outcomes in Chinese Two-Way Immersion Programs: Language, Academic Achievement, and Student Attitudes," *Immersion education: Practices, policies, possibilities* (Avon, England, Multilingual Matters, 2011).
2. Amado Padilla, Lorraine Fan, Xiaoqiu Xu, Duarte Silva, "A Mandarin/English two-way immersion program: Language proficiency and academic achievement," *Foreign Language Annals*, December 2013. Vol. 46, Issue 4, 661–675.
3. It is pronounced 'Oh-loan-ee.' The Ohlone were the Indian tribe that lived between San Francisco and Monterey Bay.
4. Great Schools, Ohlone Elementary School, Students and Teachers. http://www.greatschools.org/california/palo-alto/5616-Ohlone-Elementary-School/?tab=demographics Accessed Jan. 25, 2014.
5. Only the fifth graders were tested because the STAMP 4Se test is an online assessment measure developed for older learners and thus wasn't appropriate for younger students.

6. Amado Padilla, Lorraine Fan, Xiaoqiu Xu, Duarte Silva. "Ohlone Mandarin/English Two-way Immersion Program: Language Proficiency and Academic Achievement," an evaluation report presented to the Palo Alto School Board, Nov. 2013. http://pausd.org/community/board/Weekly/112213_weekly.pdf Accessed Jan. 25, 2014.

7. "Mandarin immersion proposal sparks controversy among Palo Alto community," *The PalyVoice*, January 11, 2007. http://palyvoice.com/2007/01/11/node-17973/ Accessed Jan. 25, 2014.

8. Kathryn Lindholm-Leary, "Student Outcomes in Chinese Two-Way Immersion Programs: Language Proficiency, Academic Achievement, and Student Attitudes," *Immersion education: Practices, policies, possibilities*, (Avon, England, Multilingual Matters, 2011) 17.

9. Kathryn Lindholm-Leary, "Student Outcomes in Chinese Two-Way Immersion Programs: Language Proficiency, Academic Achievement, and Student Attitudes," *Immersion education: Practices, policies, possibilities*, (Avon, England, Multilingual Matters, 2011) 18.

10. United States: K–12, 36 weeks of school a year, 180 instructional days per year × 5 hours per day = 900 instructional hours.
China: K–12, 39 weeks of school per year, 195 instructional days × 8 hours per day = 1,560 instructional hours.
Taiwan: K–12, 41 weeks of school a year, 205 instructional days × 8 hours per day = 1,640 instructional hours.

11. Tara Williams Fortune, "What the research says about immersion," *Chinese language learning in the early grades: A handbook of resources and best practices for Mandarin immersion*, (New York, Asia Society, 2012) 13.

12. World Language Goal Report, May 17, 2012, Minnetonka School Board. 4 http://www.minnetonka.k12.mn.us/administration/Board/Meetings/Study%20Session%20Summaries/2012_05_17_summary.pdf Accessed Jan. 15, 2014.

13. There's a classic essay on this that is read by every college student trying to learn Chinese who's ever sobbed over their dictionary. It's called "Why Chinese is So Damn Hard" and is by David Moser, now at the University of Michigan Center for Chinese Studies. It's a little depressing and you probably shouldn't let your kids read it just yet, but you can, so you'll know what they're up against. http://pinyin.info/readings/texts/moser.html/

14. Stephen Krashen and Douglas Biber, *On Course: Bilingual Education's Success in California* (Ontario, Calif., California Association for Bilingual Education, 1988) 30.

15. Wallace E. Lambert. and G. Richard Tucker, *Bilingual Education of Children: The St. Lambert Experiment* (Rowley, Mass., Newbury House, 1972) 152.

16. A gap year is when a student takes a year off between high school and college to travel, do volunteer work or spend time abroad learning another language. It got its start in the 1960s in the United Kingdom and has since spread. Colleges like it when kids apply, get accepted and then defer for a year so they can go do something worthwhile—like perfect their Mandarin.

17. Keiko Koda, Chan Lü, Yanhui Zhang, "Effects of print input on morphological awareness among Chinese heritage language learners," in Agnes Weiyun He and Yun Xiao (eds) *Chinese as a Heritage Language: Fostering Rooted World Citizenry* (National Foreign Language Resource Center, University of Hawai'i at Manoa, 2008).

18. Martha Herzog, Interagency Language Roundtable. An overview of the history of the ILR language proficiency skill level descriptions and scale: How did the language proficiency scale get started? http://www.govtilr.org/skills/irl%20scale%20history.htm Accessed Jan. 14, 2014.

19. American Council on the Teaching of Foreign Languages. Alexandria, VA. ACTFL Proficiency Guidelines 2013. http://www.actfl.org/sites/default/files/pdfs/public/ ACTFLProficiencyGuidelines2012_FINAL.pdf Accessed April 25, 2014.

20. American Council on the Teaching of Foreign Languages, Alexandria, Va., ACTFL Proficiency Guidelines 2013. http://www.actfl.org/sites/default/files/pdfs/public/ ACTFLProficiencyGuidelines2012_FINAL.pdf Accessed April 25, 2014.

21. Elvira Swender, "ACTFL Proficiency Levels in the Work World. A talk presented at the CIBER 2012 Conference, March 21, 2012," Chapel Hill, NC. http://nble.org/wp-content/uploads/2012/03/ ACTFLWorkplaceProficiencyAssess.pdf Accessed Jan. 14, 2014.

22. For the 2013–2014 school year.

23. You can read about the test here: http://www.collegeboard.com/student/testing/ap/sub_chineselang.html

24. You can read about this test, more frequently given in China, here http://www.hsk.org.cn/english/Intro_summ.aspx

25. The wonderful folks at the Center for Applied Linguistics keep a searchable list of this kind of test at http://www.cal.org/calwebdb/flad/ You can also read more about such testing in: Ann Tollefson, Michael Bacon, Kyle Ennis, Carl Falsgraf, and Nancy Rhodes, "Student Assessment and Program Evaluation," in *Chinese Language Learning in the Early Grades: A handbook of resources and best practices for Mandarin immersion* (New York, Asia Society, 2012) 42–45.

26. See *Chapter 22: Immersion Consortia: The Support Schools Need* for more information on F-CAP.

27. Elvira Swender, "ACTFL Proficiency Levels in the Work World. A talk presented at the CIBER 2012 Conference, March 21, 2012," Chapel Hill, NC. http://nble.org/wp-content/uploads/2012/03/ ACTFLWorkplaceProficiencyAssess.pdf Accessed Jan. 14, 2014.

28. Portland Public Schools, "Assessments: The Role of Assessment in Our Program." http://www.pps.k12.or.us/departments/immersion/4383.htm Accessed Jan. 15, 2014.

29. Let me say here that I'm a *huge* fan of the Common Core standards. I've already seen them in San Francisco and they're great. The focus on reading for information and writing clearly to convey information is wonderful. The difference between how and what my older daughter and younger daughter were taught to write really brought it home. It's a hassle for districts to switch and yes, the test scores go down (because they weren't learning so much or so deeply before!) but it's really much better overall. If you want to get into it even deeper, read the

book below and then get ready to debate with lots of your friends.
Robert Rothman, *Something in Common: The Common Core Standards and the Next Chapter in American Education* (Cambridge, Mass. Harvard University Press, 2011).

30. Stephen Krashen, *Comprehensible Output*, 1998.
    http://www.sdkrashen.com/content/articles/comprehensible_output.pdf
    Accessed Jan. 14, 2014.

十五
shí wǔ
15

How to Get More Chinese in Your Child's Life

Families with children in Mandarin immersion programs in the United States have a problem—we live in an English-speaking environment. Even families who seak Chinese at home face an uphill battle ensuring that Chinese is a living language for their children outside the home.

No matter what percentage of their academic day takes place in Mandarin, students still spend no more than four hours daily immersed in Chinese. In programs that are 50% Chinese from the beginning, it's often fewer than three hours. Getting more Chinese in your child's life is something like getting more vegetables in their diet—you've got to think strategically about how to slip it in where and when you can. The good news is that it's not impossible and Mandarin immersion families have been figuring out how to get more Mandarin in for years now.

One caveat. There are a flood of books, CDs, computer games and apps out these days that claim they'll teach your child Chinese. Mostly they're just ways for non-Chinese-speaking kids to pick up a few simple words—words most immersion students learn their first month in school. So don't waste your money on "teach your child Mandarin" products (and warn grandparents away or you'll get a ton of them as soon as you say you're signing up). Instead, you want to offer opportunities to have what language teachers call "authentic" language experiences. Here are some ideas, gathered from parents at immersion programs across the country.

One thing you might notice is a somewhat girl-centric tilt to many of the products for teaching kids Chinese that started to come out in the 1990s and 2000s. That's in part because the first wave of "learn Chinese" products in the U.S. were geared towards families who had adopted children from China and wanted them to continue to have exposure to the language, because the vast majority of those children were girls. Thanks to mom and Mandarin speaker Lelan Miller in San Antonio for pointing this out to me. She had a hard time finding things that worked for her three boys, though it's starting to even out.

Seek out Chinese speakers in your community

Don't let your discomfort with interacting with families who speak a different language keep your kids from playing with their kids. Kids want to play with their friends, but at times parents go the route of least resistance, which can result in only having play dates with kids whose parents they can easily email and talk to on the phone. Go outside of your comfort zone. Have your son or daughter call to ask for a play date. By first grade they should have learned enough Mandarin to do it. Don't be shy. You'll make friends, they'll get to play with their friends, and your program will be strengthened because there will be social connections that didn't exist before!

Look for local businesses with Mandarin-speaking staff. When you go in for a haircut or for dinner, ask the staff to only speak to your child in Mandarin. Note that this *isn't* the same as asking your child to speak Mandarin with the waiters at a restaurant, where they're supposed to spout out a stream of Chinese and impress everyone. This is simply a chance for them to experience navigating in the world in Chinese. The waiter might ask them questions about what they'd like to eat, asking yes or no questions your child can easily answer.

Share with families at your school. In San Francisco there's a hairdresser who now has as clients multiple students from the Mandarin immersion program. She knows when they come in to speak only in Mandarin with them. And our students have learned how to say things like "I want bangs" and "Not too short!"

Parent tip: "We keep an eye out for Chinese businesses and try to figure out what the characters on the signs are. Sometimes I chat with the shopkeepers and shoppers too, because many can speak basic Mandarin even if they are Cantonese speakers. Menus in Chinese are also always fun to try to decipher. The kids don't know most of the characters (menus use lots of flowery language) but they're able to pick some out."

Look for the Asian supermarkets in your area

Most cities of any size in the United States have an Asian supermarket or mall someplace. Ask your child's teachers where the nearest one is. Going shopping in one is like a short trip to China. They also often have great lunch box snack-type foods that will make your kid the hit of the playground. Spicy Korean seaweed packs are big lunch trading items at our schools.

Attend Chinese cultural events

There are many cultural events across the country, especially around the Autumn Festival and Chinese New Year. Keep your eyes open and share with other families in your school.

Babysitters

Planning a date night or weekend getaway? Consider hiring a Mandarin-speaking babysitter who will help reinforce vocabulary and might even be able to help with homework. Often local community colleges have English as a Second Language programs where you can post notices looking for babysitters.

Chinese children's songs

For younger children, get CDs of Chinese songs and put them in your car's CD player. Ask your child's teacher for recommendations. Ask families with older kids in your school what they listen to. You can find lots of these CDs at local Chinese stores. Ask a clerk which are good for kids.

Chinese Children's Classics v 1.0, music for kids.
http://alittlemandarin.com/

Some suggestions from parent from Jackie Chou Lem:

DVD: Dance and Learn Chinese with Mei Mei, Vol. 4
You can preview on YouTube:
http://www.youtube.com/watch?v=8_T1r-FE7OM on Amazon:
http://www.amazon.com/Dance-Learn-Chinese-With-Vol/dp/B0002J4ZR8
"This is the first DVD my daughter ever watched, when she turned two. She still loves watching it now that she is three. The songs are sung and performed by girls in China. Each song is also spoken slowly, with pinyin, characters, and English running across the screen. This makes it easy for parents to learn the songs too. This DVD is the fourth in a series by Mei Mei. We bought some others in the series, but ended up returning them because they were boring, but they might be more interesting to a family with no previous Chinese exposure."

CD: Speak and Sing Chinese with Mei Mei
Available on Amazon:
"We've listened to this CD in the car probably a 1,000 times! There is English on this CD, which some parents might not like if they are going for 100% Mandarin. But Sophie loves the songs and has practically memorized them all."

Other CDs:

Little Dragon Tales
http://littledragontales.com/
"These songs have a good beat; a welcome break from the standard children's CDs."

Two Little Tigers Songs

http://www.chinasprout.com/shop/BSR033

"This comes with a book that has illustrations and characters; it has many of the standard Chinese kids songs: *Da Xiang, Hou Che Kuai Fei, Ba Luo Po, Liang Zhi Lao Hu, San Lun Che.*"

Teach Me More and More Chinese

http://www.amazon.com/gp/product/1599726092/ref=oh_details_o05_s00_i01)

"This has English and Chinese songs and spoken words; it comes with a coloring book. The songs and book are all about a girl named Mai Rei. Sophie loves listening to the CD and following along with the book. However, some of the songs are English songs that have been awkwardly translated into Chinese."

Radio

Find the local Mandarin language radio stations and set your car radio to them. Ask families or teachers in your program what stations are good. Pop music is pretty universal.

For those who don't speak Mandarin, there's a nice site from 2012 that lists ten popular Mandarin songs and includes the characters and pinyin, as well as the embedded video. If you click on the English Translation link up towards the top of the page (it's right after Home, Wats Up and Charts) you can read what they're singing about.

http://top10pinyinlyrics.blogspot.com

Online streaming radio stations

C-Pop

There's a whole world of Mandarin language popular music out there. Just as K-pop (Korean pop music) is huge (think "Gangnam Style") there's a similar wave in Chinese called C-pop, or sometimes MandoPop.

Some online links to get you started:

Mandopop videos and a streaming site
http://www.last.fm/tag/mandopop
(search on "C-pop")

Best Mandopop Groups/Artists
http://www.ranker.com/list/mandopop-bands-and-musicians/reference

TuneIn
http://tunein.com

Poke around on this one, there are some interesting stations. Search Chinese or Mandarin.

Chinamerica Hit Radio
http://tunein.com/radio/Chinamerica-Hit-Radio-s118155/

Mandarin Radio
http://tunein.com/radio/Mandarin-Radio-p494243/

All Chinese Hits
http://www.live365.com/index.live

Television

Find out if you get any Mandarin language programs on television where you live. Again, ask families who speak Mandarin what shows are good. For example, there's a Taiwanese kids' show called 水果冰淇淋 [*Fruity Pie* in English] that airs in some areas. There are also lots of kung-fu movies, historical dramas and even old-fashioned variety shows.

Sesame Street

In 2013 Sesame Street's Children's Television Workshop launched a Mandarin language version of the iconic children's show. In Chinese it's called "Fun Fun Elmo." It's not a translation of the American show but an entirely new program designed specifically for Chinese-speaking children. It's really fun and a must-watch for anyone with kids. It's especially cool to see how they teach characters, in a different and yet totally Sesame Street kind of way that you recognize instantly from watching the English version. It's available on YouTube. Mandarin immersion students well beyond preschool enjoy it.

http://www.youtube.com/
playlist?list=PL8TioFHubWFvJ3ijWovmCYes-jKfgPqnn

Cable

Many cable TV companies have various "ethnic" packages available. Call your cable company to ask if they have an Asian or Chinese package. It will probably come with Mandarin, Cantonese, Vietnamese and Korean programming.

Streaming TV from China and Taiwan

Many of these sites are only available in Chinese. But it's amazing what you can do with Google Translate. Copy a block of text, paste it into Google Translate and you'll have some sense of where you are. Or ask your kids for help.

If you find something you like, bookmark it! It can be very hard to find them again if you don't know the name in Chinese (or if you can't write it in

Chinese.) Also, you'll be able to send the URL around to the other families in your school.

Don't let your kids wander online by themselves. You need to be there to edit, quickly. It's easy to click on things in Chinese and end up someplace you didn't expect. As I was doing copy editing on this chapter I clicked a link by mistake and ended up on the "Pretty Lady Asian Dating Service," which featured some very R-rated photos.

KyLinTV
http://www.kylintv.com
English version:
http://www.kylintv.com/kylintv/us/eng/home/home
KyLinTV is a large Chinese internet TV station aimed at Chinese all over the world. It's got a great children's section.

Parent tip: "You can get a cable box from them for your TV, but the PC/iPad internet access is cheaper. I picked the Taiwan TV package because I like the kids' channel that it comes with–YOYO TV. However, the part that my kids really like is "Kids VOD" (Video On Demand). I added that for $10 more per month and they can watch a huge selection of kids' shows, such as *Pleasant Goat & Big Wolf*, which has 470 episodes. It's expensive, but there's no contract for the Internet subscription, so you could get it for some extra Chinese over the summer and cancel when school starts up again."

http://www.pptv.com
This is one of the more popular Internet streaming video software programs in China. You download a player to your computer, iPad or iPhone and then can chose from a large variety of TV shows and movies from China, Taiwan and Korea. You can either find a friend who reads Chinese to talk you through the process or just click on things and see what happens. You'll get a message saying you need to download the app, which I did. Then it gets fun. For example, when I was writing this I clicked on a few things and ended up with a TV news report about an international computer game playoff that features players from China, Korea and Japan. The report featured footage from the games they were playing, including dwarfs in chain mail firing spells and exploding trees.

http://Tv.sohu.com
Another Internet streaming site from China. Not all the shows require use of its downloaded player, but some do. It had lots of programs, including a fair number of popular U.S. TV shows dubbed into Mandarin.

http://Tudou.com
Popular streaming site. All in Chinese but poke around and see what you find. I started watching a program called Vieworld, about some Chinese

students studying in Australia. It was partly in Chinese, partly in English. Kind of funny.

Movies

Make it a rule that one day a week the kids can watch TV or movies *if* they're in Mandarin. Though beware: In some of the dubbed Disney movies the sound is so muddy that it's difficult to understand.

Players for Chinese DVDs

All commercial players should be able to play Chinese DVDs. The problem is that players sold in the U.S. are set to view just Western DVDs. To get around this you have two options:

1. Unlock your player. You can go to this website, type in your model number, and follow the simple directions; www.videohelp.com/dvd-hacks

2. If you'd rather not mess with your DVD player, another option is go to your local Chinatown and buy a cheap travel DVD player there. Confirm that it can play Chinese DVDs, preferably before you leave the shop.

Note that if you go to China there are lots of very cheap DVDs sold there but most will only work on a player set for China's region code.

Netflix

If you get movies from Netflix, you can click on Foreign and then Foreign Languages and then Mandarin to see the offerings. Though sadly, Netflix doesn't have many children's movies in Mandarin yet.

One popular title with middle school students is "Lost in Thailand," a comedy caper. It's a sequel to "Lost on Journey" (人在囧途). It's something like "Planes, Trains and Automobiles," only set during Chinese New Year. But it doesn't look like Netflix offers the first one, though it does have "Lost in Thailand." It's worth trying your library to see if they have "Lost on Journey."

Your local library

Check with the librarian to see if they have movies in Chinese. They might be in a different branch, or shelved elsewhere, so ask. And ask for help choosing appropriate ones for your kids. Sometimes the images on the DVD package make it seem a movie might be appropriate for children when it's actually not. Librarians are always eager to assist you.

Mom Lelan Miller in Texas says don't forget about interlibrary loan programs. "I've done that here in San Antonio where Spanish (materials) outnumber Chinese at the library."

Read

Reading is key to broadening vocabulary, deepening understanding and strengthening your child's grasp of grammar, in all languages. For parents who don't read Chinese, there are a few possibilities:

Books with CDs

Lots of Chinese storybooks come with attached CDs in which the story is read aloud. Look for them online and in your local bookstores. Some books also come with links to the story read aloud online.

Parent tip: "We have a Chinese tutor who comes over once a week to spend time working with our son in Chinese. She's a student from Shanghai at the local community college. She has been reading my son books that she helped me buy from ChinaSprout. Last week my husband had the idea of recording her reading one of the books on his iPhone, using the Voice Memo app. The next time we were in the car I brought that book and I handed my son the phone and he listened to her reading it, following along in the book. We're going to have her record more next week."

Mandarin-speaking mom Vickie Tsui was frustrated enough at the lack of good bilingual books that she sat down and wrote one herself. It's available here

http://mandarin-tiger-mom.blogspot.com

She also has a website where she reviews books in Chinese and explains what they're about. She also links to some files where she reads them aloud. She hasn't updated recently but the reviews are still very useful when you are looking for books to get at the library.

http://vickietsui96.blogspot.com.

Online stories

5QChannel.com
A stellar site out of Taiwan that has apps and stories online, in both simplified and traditional characters. Kids love it and they have nice animation. Definitely worth signing up for. The site lists a very high yearly fee of $140, but that is really aimed at schools. 5QChannel offers a special rate for U.S. parents here:

http://www.5qchannel.com/order/grouprate2011.htm

ChildRoad

http://www.childroad.com

This is a digital library of over 1,000 books read aloud in Mandarin. Children can see the story and hear it read to them. There are stories for kids age 4–12, including fairy tales, idiom and famous novels, all narrated by professional Chinese narrators including TV and radio hosts.

Idiom or proverb stories (成语, *chéngyǔ*) are the stories behind traditional Chinese idiomatic sayings. They're sometimes called Four Character Stories. They're used a lot in everyday speech, something like "A bird in the hand is worth two in the bush," only much more literary. You have to know the story to understand the meaning of the idiom.

Pearson Singapore

Pearson is a large international producer of educational materials. Their Singapore office has created multiple iPad Mandarin books. They can be read simply as books, be read aloud in Mandarin or the reader can touch individuals phrases to hear how they're pronounced. There are over 50 titles available, each at $5.99. They range from relatively simple to stories appropriate for students in fourth grade and beyond.

http://www.pearson.sg/chinesereaders

eGlobalReader

This site offers books in Chinese that can toggle between characters, pinyin and English. They only had eight books in 2014 but plan to expand.

http://www.eglobalreader.com

Children's Cultural Center

This website from the Taiwanese Ministry of Culture features fun Chinese videos and information for kids. It's kind of like PBS for kids in Chinese. It's all in traditional Chinese. There are no worries about stumbling upon something inappropriate. Most of the stories have Bopomofo transliteration system (Taiwan's version of *pinyin*) next to the characters. It doesn't matter if your child doesn't know traditional characters, the stories are fun to watch.

http://children.moc.gov.tw

Online bookstores

NanHai

This is a good Chinese bookstore with lots of children's books in simplified characters and lots of books with CDs for kids.

http://www.nanhaibooks.com/

Little Monkey and Mouse

This is an online bookstore with a nice blog about new books, CDs and games that might be of interest to parents. The owner works with several

Mandarin immersion schools, so she has a good sense of students' reading levels.

http://blog.littlemonkeyandmouse.com/

ChinaSprout
This site has a very broad selection, with lots of storybooks, graded readers and an excellent video section.

http://chinasprout.com

Chinese Child Book
It's got books, CDs and DVDs

http://www.childbook.com

Oznoz.com
Lots of U.S. *Sesame Street* videos dubbed into Mandarin. Their motto is "Stuff for bilingual kids."

https://shop.oznoz.com/index.php/language-culture/chinese/dvds.html

Chinese comic books

As researchers at San Francisco State University found in a multi-year project, it's a lot easier to get kids to read Chinese comic books (often called *manga*, from the Japanese) than regular books. See *Chapter 16: Chinese Literacy Issues* for more on this. Comics are equally effective at increasing vocabulary and Chinese ability. Here are some sites where you can find manga in Chinese. Be aware that topics vary in how age-appropriate they are. Also check to see if the comics are in traditional or simplified characters and buy the kind your school uses. Be aware that manga are something of a rabbit hole; kids get addicted to the things. But that's not really a bad thing as long as it's all in Chinese, right?

Some reviews are posted at the site below. You can then look for Chinese language versions of these manga.

The Spectrum
http://www.thespectrum.net/manga/

Yes Asia
http://www.yesasia.com/us/en/chinese-comics.html

If your child really gets into comics, there are several online forums devoted to Manga, including Mangahelpers.com and mangashare.com. According to them, there are databases of Chinese language manga available at these sites:

http://comic.sky-fire.com/
http://comic.kukudm.com/
http://dm.99770.com/

http://www.finaleden.com/
http://www.zxmh.net/

Monthly storybook/DVDs from Taiwan

There's a monthly Taiwanese magazine that comes with storybook, workbook, CD and sometimes DVDs or toys, based on a similar product from Japan. It's very popular there, something like *Highlights For Children* here. The materials are age-specific and go all the way up through elementary school. One mom said, "my kids absolutely love the materials. My 2.5 year old can 'read' the books and listen to the CDs by himself and sing along in Chinese." Unfortunately, the website is all in Chinese and the magazine only comes in traditional characters. But it might be appropriate for someone in a program that uses traditional, and a teacher could help with ordering.

http://www.benesse.com.tw/

Resources with online texts in Chinese

These come courtesy of the Asia Society's Heather Clydesdale. Her article, "To Grow Good Writers, Feed Them Great Literature," is worth reading:

http://asiasociety.org/education/chinese-language-initiatives/grow-good-writers-feed-them-great-literature

The sites below are in traditional characters. They could be navigated with the help of an older child, a Chinese-speaking friend or a teacher.

信宜基全會
http://hsin-yi.org.tw (Taiwan)

和英文化
Heying Wenhua
A publisher with more than 200 books and poems.
http://heryin.com (Taiwan)

親親文化
Has nature and science books, videos, and demo units.
http://www.kissnature.com.tw/ (Taiwan).

新雅文化
Focuses on moral learning and emotional development.
http://www.sunya.com.hk/default.asp (Hong Kong)

儿童文化
Online story telling, animated with lesson plans and discussions tiered to different levels.
http://children.moc.gov.tw/home.php (Taiwan)

教育部生命教育学习网
Biology and other subject areas.
http://life.edu.tw/homepage/new_page_2.php (Taiwan)

Cartoons

Animation is hugely popular in Asia and there are multiple programs that many adults will wax poetic about from their childhood, going all the way back to Speed Racer (which was originally a Japanese series called Mach GoGoGo.) There are lots of programs from China, Japan, Taiwan and Korean that are translated into multiple languages, just find the Mandarin version and you're good to go. It shouldn't be hard to find a series that your kids like. Once they're hooked you can have them listening to Chinese for as many hours a day as you want.

Popular shows include *Pororo, Thumb Bear, Martin Morning* and *Big Head Son*. To preview these series online, go to http://www.tudou.com/ and search for:

"大头儿子小头爸爸" (*Big Head Son*)
"马丁的早晨" (*Martin Morning*)
"小企鹅 pororo" (*Pororo the Korean Penguin*)
"拇指熊" (*Thumb Bear*)

There's a great China Central Television site where you can find cartoons:
http://space.tv.cctv.com/podcast/xxh2

Cartoons on Chinese YouTube (called Tuduo.com)
http://cartoon.tudou.com/

FruityPie
This is the Taiwanese equivalent of Captain Kangaroo with some Mr. Rogers thrown in. The main character is Granny Fruity Pie (played by a man in drag). You can Google 水果冰淇淋 and find lots of episodes posted. Kids up to third grade like this one. Search on FruityPie and lots of videos will pop up on YouTube

YouTube
You can have endless fun wandering YouTube searching on the word "Mandarin." It's a nice chance for the kids to be the experts. They can tell you about what you're hearing or seeing or, if they can't, you can have lots of fun guessing together.

For example, here's American claw hammer banjo player Abigail Washburn singing the classic folksong Little Birdie in Chinese with kids in China.
http://www.youtube.com/watch?v=fA1lVEWl1Tw&feature=relmfu

Or here are some kids in Hong Kong singing about how they hate veggies
http://www.youtube.com/watch?v=i8VZGcVGcrM
And here's one about how everyone's learning Chinese these days
http://www.youtube.com/watch?v=uy8PktMIBuI

Binbin's Magical Bubble Adventure.
For kindergarten and first graders mostly, but all in Mandarin.
    http://www.kakekids.com

Smart Tiger/*Quiahu* 巧虎
This is based on a Japanese anime show for preschoolers called *Shima Shima
Tora no Shimajirō* in Japanese. It launched in 1993 and has been translated
into Chinese, where it is very popular. The cartoons help foster good habits
and character, kind of like Sesame Street.
    http://www.youtube.com/watch?v=RMPcEHoOMqY

iPhones and iPads

iPads and iPhones are great all-purpose, "I've always got Chinese for you to
play with" items to have to hand. Here are some places to start.

http://5QChannel.com
Great story apps for iPads. The perfect car-ride solution. You can toggle back
and forth between traditional and simplified characters. The stories are
nicely animated and very popular among elementary school kids in immersion programs.

DragonDian
http://www.innovativelanguage.com/products/DragonDian
    A Chinese dictionary app that allows you to practice Chinese characters
by drawing them on the screen.

Skritter
A character-practice app in which you draw on the screen.
    http://www.skritter.com/

Doodle Chinese
A games app for learning characters and more. Available in the iTunes app
store.

Pleco
http://www.pleco.com
    For iPhone, iPad and Android devices. It has an optical character recog-
nition feature that allows you to take a picture of hard-copy text and automatically see the *pinyin* and English definition. This is a huge time-saver
compared to looking up words in a dictionary by radical and stroke count.

Final thoughts

Chinese is spoken by over one billion humans, so it's not hard to find people speaking, singing and acting in Chinese online or in the real world. Look around and you'll probably find lots of opportunities for your child to engage with Chinese. When you find something that works well for your child, be sure to share it with the rest of your class or school. It's one thing if your kid listens to Chinese radio in the car. It's amplified when five kids in the class listen to the same station and talk about the cool song they heard that morning on the way to school. Suddenly Chinese is something that exists *outside* the classroom and they're singing along on the playground.

So here's your mission: Find. Enjoy. Share.

shí liù

16

Chinese Literacy Issues

Reading is the Achilles' heel of Mandarin immersion. I know of no program in the United States, public or private, that produces students who read at grade level in Chinese. They reach and frequently *exceed* grade level reading in English, but not in Chinese. Immersion students do learn to read Chinese, but not at the same level as would a child of the same age in China or Taiwan. There are many excellent reasons for this, which I'll cover below. However, parents need to enter into immersion with reasonable expectations—and realize how much of a part they play in the process. Schools create a baseline literacy level, but only by encouraging children to read *for pleasure* in Chinese at home will they exceed that baseline.

Reading in Chinese is an issue all programs struggle with and are working on. Thus far no one has found a clear path to getting American students reading at higher levels in Chinese. In a Mandarin immersion handbook they co-authored, experts Myriam Met and Chris Livaccari agree:

> Developing literacy in Chinese simply takes longer than in any other language, and the difficulty of learning to read and write Chinese is not confined to non-native speakers. It is also true of native speakers.[1]

It's such a known problem that in 2014 the entire focus of the Chinese Education Conference held by the Utah State Office of Education, the Mandarin Center and the Confucius Institute was on literacy.

The reality seems to be that most programs are to be able to get children reading between two and five years below their grade compared to students in Taiwan and China. But that *doesn't* mean immersion doesn't work. Let me reiterate:

Immersion students learn to read and write Chinese!

They just don't read at the levels they would if they were Chinese children growing up in Chinese-speaking homes in a Chinese-speaking country attending a Chinese-speaking school. As Michael Bacon, the Chinese Flagship director and immersion achievement coordinator with Portland Public Schools in Oregon says, "If they want to have kids reading at grade level, they need to move to China." See *Chapter 23: Going to School in China* to get a sense of the amount of work it takes even for students there. Attaining literacy in Chinese simply requires more work that it does for students learning languages written with alphabets.

If an international move isn't in the cards, don't fret. There are *many* things you as a parent can do to make your child a better reader in Chinese. These also have the lovely effect of significantly boosting their Chinese ability overall. See *Chapter 15: How To Get More Chinese in Your Child's Life* and *Chapter 17: Getting Your Child Reading in Chinese.*

Your job, if you want higher literacy levels than your program sets, is to create as much of a Chinese linguistic and literary environment for your child as you can. As Bacon says:

> Step One is setting appropriate expectations with families that they're not going to be like native speakers. That doesn't happen in any language, except perhaps for Spanish to a certain degree. The thing with Chinese is, unless the kid is doing something outside of the school that's significant, they're not getting the environmental input that kids get in English. Therefore high levels of exposure are required.

Families have often been told that their children will be "bilingual and biliterate" in Mandarin, but administrators are beginning to be more frank. Parents come in expecting that their children will read at grade level in both English and in Chinese, says David Kojo Hakam, a curriculum specialist for the Portland Public School's Chinese Flagship program. "They won't," he says flatly. While immersion students will gain a fairly high level of spoken proficiency in Mandarin (see *Chapter 14: How Much Chinese Will They Learn?*), their reading levels will be well below that of kids their age in China.

Mandarin is different than Spanish or French

Schools aren't trying to deceive parents about the benefits and outcomes of immersion, says Elizabeth Hardage, a consultant to Mandarin immersion schools and former vice principal at Washington Yu Ying in Washington, D.C. Chinese literacy and language arts are her main focus, and literacy is a topic she grapples with daily in the schools she works with. Until recently, Mandarin immersion schools had been "taking what research says about Spanish or French and then thinking it will apply to Chinese." It's becoming clear it doesn't, she says.

Chris Livaccari, former director of Education and Chinese Language Initiatives at the Asia Society in New York City, and now a principal at the

International School of the Peninsula in Palo Alto, California, says immersion programs across the world are working on this very problem. The literacy issue is not being ignored, far from it. But while that work is on-going, Livaccari says educators may need to do a better job of helping parents understand the literacy challenge. "Your kids are not going to be able to pick up a Chinese newspaper[2] and read it," he says.

There are four reasons students from non-Chinese speaking homes have lower literacy levels in Chinese than in English. First it takes a tremendous amount of time, effort and repetition (through both reading and memorization) to learn to recognize the characters necessary to become a grade-level reader of Chinese. U.S. programs typically shy away from requiring the level of work expected of students in China and Taiwan, in part because of time constraints in the school day and year. In those countries, students typically are familiar with 4,000 characters by the beginning of sixth grade. In American immersion programs that number is typically 1,000 to 1,500.

Second, American students live in an English-speaking country and are surrounded by English, spoken and written, for all but the 10 to 20 hours a week they're in Mandarin language classes. Students in China and Taiwan are immersed in Chinese their entire waking day, except for perhaps four or five hours of English class a week.

Third, American students almost never read Chinese for pleasure and so never enter into the virtuous cycle of reading: The more you read, the more words you learn, the easier it is to read so the more you read. Students in Mandarin immersion typically don't read more than 15 minutes a day in Chinese, if that, in school or for pleasure. Most of those children will read two to four times that in English each day, just for fun.

Finally, the biggest barrier to getting kids to read in Chinese is they don't have access to fun, age-appropriate books in Chinese. These are now beginning to come on the market, though we have a ways to go, especially for upper grade students.

Why learning to read Chinese takes more time

Learning to speak Chinese, if you're a child, isn't harder than learning any other language. Reading is a different matter. "That's one of the general challenges of Chinese in general. The oral skills really do progress at a much faster rate than reading and writing," says Livaccari.

Chinese simply requires more time to learn to read because it is not written phonetically. Rather than learning to recognize 26 letters, student must learn to recognize upwards of 3,000 characters. While it's true English speakers learn to sight-read words just as Chinese speakers do, in English it's a lot easier to make an educated guess about how an unknown word is pronounced than it is in Chinese. As we'll see later, to a certain extent it is possible to guess the sounds of many Chinese characters. But it is nowhere near as straightforward as the basic phonics that work for many English words.

Let's go over several issues students face in learning to read in Chinese.

Learning characters

When students first see the word 学校, there's no way for them to know it's pronounced *xué xiào* until someone says it out loud. Because they're in an immersion classroom, they very likely know exactly what a *xuéxiào* is ("school" for those of us who aren't in an immersion kindergarten) because they've heard their teacher use it and they say it themselves all the time. However, in Chinese, the connection between the written form and the spoken isn't explicit[3] in the way it is in alphabetic languages.

Sometimes students can know the English meaning of a given character or word even if they don't know how to pronounce it. Here in San Francisco you see enough bilingual signs and vans emblazoned with company names in both English and Chinese that eventually even I figured out 公司 must mean "company." But there was no way for me to know that it is pronounced *gōngsī*. Students who live in China or Taiwan have this happen all the time and learn tons of words that way, just by seeing them on TV or signs or hearing their parents read aloud. Or by seeing the Chinese *Sesame Street*,[4] which teaches characters just the way the English version teaches words. Unfortunately for kids in Mandarin immersion whose parents don't read Chinese, that only happens in school during Mandarin time. So they're immediately facing a huge deficit compared to children in Chinese-speaking households.

And just to add another twist, when students start reading more complex material in middle and high school, the sheer amount of literary and historical knowledge necessary to read at that level adds a layer of difficulty that doesn't exist in English. Chinese has a literary history reaching back millennia and educated writers routinely make use of it. It's as if English authors constantly dropped lines and allusions from the Bible, Shakespeare, Chaucer and all the way back to Beowulf into everything they wrote. As Met and Livaccari note:

> ...written Chinese (particularly that used for newspapers or other formal communications) combines classical forms of the language with more familiar, colloquial expressions. While written languages tend to be more formal than their spoken counterparts, in Chinese the difference is far more extreme than in most European languages.[5]

Then there's the issue of what characters should be taught and when. Many parents ask about this in immersion programs. An example that sticks in my memory is the frustration of some parents in my daughter's classroom when in second grade one of the vocabulary words was 孔雀 *kǒngquè* (peacock). It was in a story the students read in class and they were expected to learn to write it as well. The parents asked, "Can't they learn more *useful* words? When are they ever going to need to be able to read the word 'peacock'?"

The teacher asked, pretty reasonably, if the parents would have been equally frustrated if the class had to read the word "peacock" in a story during English class. And she had a point—in English by second grade most of the kids would not only have heard the word "peacock" but could also easily sound it out. None of the parents felt it was inappropriate for them to learn peacock in English. But in second grade Mandarin immersion the students had never seen either of the characters in this word, so their parents were hoping they'd somehow learn "the most important characters" first, just to save time and hassle.

However, those "important" words can be difficult to identify. There is no one list of the Chinese words all elementary school immersion students should learn, and in what order. Another point the teacher made was that all but the most obscure characters end up coming in handy once a child is reading more advanced material. By learning the word 孔雀, students were learning characters that they'd be able to use later. The 孔 in 孔雀 is also used in 孔丘, *Kǒngqiū*, a gentleman whose English name is Confucius. And 雀 means "small bird or sparrow" and often comes up in other bird names. For unclear reasons it's also the first character in the transliteration of Nestlé, 雀巢, *Quècháo*. So they'll be able to find Nesquik in China.

The other issue is that of difficult-to-read words versus easy-to-read words. Just as in English, students will know many words that aren't easy to read. Your five-year-old knows the word "supermarket," but you wouldn't expect her to be able to read or write it. The same is true in Chinese.

Chinese immersion students begin learning to read with simple characters. You'll recognize them from the writing practice sheets that come home with your kindergartener.

水 = *shuǐ* = water
山 = *shān* = mountain
大 = *dà* = big

But soon they need to learn the words they're using in class. Those can be made up of complex characters that aren't quite so simple:

地毯 = *dìtǎn* = rug
餐厅 = *cāntīng* = lunchroom

Teachers are faced with deciding between teaching easy characters that aren't always so useful and common words that can be very complex. "Do you teach the characters that go with the oral language or characters that are easy to read?" says immersion consultant Met. The emerging consensus among educators seems to be that frequency and usage, not ease of reading or writing, should define what characters students learn.

Thankfully easy-to-read books are beginning to become available in Chinese. You can find a list in *Chapter 17: Getting Your Child Reading in Chinese.* These books won't be translations of *I Can Read* books in English, because easy-to-read characters are different from easy-to-read English words. After all, *The Cat in the Hat Comes Back* is 戴帽子的猫回来了 (*Dàimàozi de māo huílai le*) in Chinese.

Going deeper: How do kids learn languages?

There's an ongoing argument in education circles right now about how children learn language. On the one side are the skill-building advocates, who say that you need to teach children the building blocks of language (phonics, grammar, vocabulary). This method uses drill and memorization, among other tools.

On the other side are the comprehension advocates, who say if you simply expose children to language at their level of understanding, they'll naturally get all the grammar, phonics and vocabulary they need. This method focuses on lots of listening and, even more crucially when it comes to literacy, *reading for pleasure* to make sure children are naturally exposed to as much language as possible.

According to the skill-builders, for children to develop both speaking and reading skills, they need to memorize lots of words and spelling rules. According to the comprehension folks, all you really need to do is make sure that they hear lots of people speaking the language at a level they can understand, and that they are surrounded by readable, captivating books that make them *want* to read, and they'll pick it all up naturally. This is called comprehensible input.

Both sides agree you've got to start out with some skill building, which in English includes the alphabet and basic phonetics. Where the two groups diverge is how much of the drill and memorization kids need.

This same debate exists in Mandarin immersion, somewhat among teachers and a great deal among parents. Parents educated in China and Taiwan, where educational systems tend toward the skill-building mindset, often feel more memorization and drill is needed. Others want to see programs work more on the comprehension input side of the equation. Thus far, programs are doing a little bit of both, which isn't getting kids as far as many parents, whichever philosophy they follow, would like.

One teacher said anonymously, "Personally, I think the divergence appears when the parents and administrators making the decisions don't speak or read Chinese. Any Chinese learner knows that there has to be a drill-and-kill aspect to memorizing the characters, but the parents and non-Chinese speaking administrators seem to be the ones who feel most uncomfortable with it."

Another parent, who reads Chinese but was educated in the United States, said

> We just need to get them reading, reading, reading in Chinese! If they read more, it would become easier for them and they wouldn't feel so afraid of it. But our school doesn't really focus on reading in Chinese at home at all. I don't think my son has read one book in Chinese yet, that I know of. He's read hundreds in English.

Another mom says this is why she only texts her sons in Chinese, as well as doing a Chinese Book of the Month Club with them, "because otherwise they won't read in Chinese."

This is beginning to change in many programs, both as the need to focus on literacy in Chinese becomes clear and as books that are appropriate for immersion students become available. In the early years of San Francisco's Mandarin immersion program, students read few books outside of class. By 2012–2013 the fourth and fifth grade teachers were assigning students a book a week to read and report on.

The first time my daughter brought home a book, I was convinced she'd never be able to read it. But she picked it up and read it right through to the end. She didn't know all the characters but she knew enough of them to understand the meaning and enough that she could answer questions in the book report. Later I realized this is exactly the same as English—when she reads a book in English there are many words she may not know. However, she's able to grasp the overall idea even if she skips over them, or she gets the meaning from context or pictures.

In 2013, the Utah Dual Language Immersion statewide program got a grant to create a free online summer reading program that's accessible to any immersion student. It's available at http://utahchineseimmersion.org/startalk/startalk-2013/.

They posted stories that were designed for students who have between one and four years of experience in Chinese immersion. Each week a new story was posted for each grade level. The program was created through STARTALK, a program of the National Security Language Initiative, which is working to expand and improve teaching of strategically important world languages. Mandarin is one of those languages.

How many characters should they learn?

This is a frequently asked question that has no good answer. No one asks how many words you need to know to be literate in English. Because characters have to be learned individually (though not always, as we'll see later), the question frequently comes up. Most college-level Chinese courses introduce students to about 500 in the first year and another 500 in the second year. You'll frequently see references saying between 2,500 and 4,000 characters are required to read a Chinese newspaper. However it should be noted that newspapers in Chinese use a rather specific vocabulary which includes a lot of classical Chinese words and contractions not found much elsewhere. So newspaper-reading ability is not a good marker of general literacy, especially not in children.

Overall, teachers and programs will tell you character counts are *not* a good metric for how well or how much kids read. "I don't think it's appropriate to just count characters. Nobody says to an English speaking kid, 'How many words did you learn today?'" says Kathleen Wang, principal at Pioneer Valley Chinese Immersion Charter School in Hadley, Massachusetts. "When they're emerging English readers, we learn the 100 sight words every first grader should know. But in third and fourth grade we don't say how many words they should know," she says. Character counts are "a component of language acquisition, but it can't be the only measure of proficiency. A truly fluent native speaker won't be able to tell you the number of characters they know," Wang continues.

The good news is that research by Shih-Kun Huang and C.H. Tsai[6] has found that the top 1,000 characters are used 91.1% of the time, the top 1,500 characters 95.7% of the time, the top 2,000 characters 97.9% of the time, and the top 3,000 99.4% of the time. So by the time a student knows between 1,000 to 1,500 characters they will be able to read a lot and by the time you get over 2,000 characters they should be doing pretty well. As near as I can tell, students in Mandarin immersion programs typically learn somewhere between 1,000 and 1,500 characters by middle school, depending on their program, their teachers and how hard they work.

However, memorizing a bunch of individual characters doesn't necessarily mean a student will be able to use them in reading. Almost all Chinese words are made up of two or more characters. Once a student learns 100 characters, they know hundreds of words, but only if they're learned them as words and not individual characters. An example: Your child could memorize the character 回, *huí*, to return and 收, *shōu*, to receive or collect. But unless their class has talked about how important recycling is, they won't know that 回收, *huíshōu* is the word for "recycle".

Some teachers report that they've had students whose parents quiz them using flash cards and the students know hundreds of characters—but they don't know how to read them in context. "It's like kids who know how to win spelling bees by memorizing words, but they don't know what they mean and wouldn't be able to read a passage that uses the words and understand it," one teacher told me. Just memorizing a bunch of characters doesn't automatically mean a child is literate.

This is where reading is crucial, because it turns those memorized characters into useful words that tell a story. "Just knowing 500 characters may not give you the richness of the language. For that you need to read, or be read to," says Wang.

Given the paucity of tests available for measuring children's reading ability in Chinese, parents can feel there's nothing to do *but* count characters. Before you start counting, please take into account several important points:

- The number of characters in the students' Chinese textbook isn't the sum total of all the characters they know.

- One character does not equal one word.

- Students' listening and speaking vocabulary is much larger than their reading vocabulary.

The confusion arises because almost all immersion schools have a textbook for Chinese language arts, just as in English class students have an English language arts textbook and in math they have a math textbook. The Chinese textbooks generally come with a list of characters they teach, so parents might think students learn *only* the characters in their textbooks. That's not the case. Immersion, by definition, means that subjects are taught in Mandarin. Students are taught math, science, social studies and other subjects in Mandarin, and each subject has its own vocabulary. Teachers use material from other textbooks, worksheets, poems, songs and books the kids are reading as well as topical information like pumpkins at Halloween and turkey at Thanksgiving or national observances like Martin Luther King Jr. Day.[7]

In the San Francisco Unified School District's Mandarin program, the *Mastering Chinese Language and Culture* textbook series known as Shuang Shuang is the Mandarin language arts text. (It's called 双双, Shuang Shuang, because the author's name is Wang Shuang Shuang.) The book states on the back that at the end of the series students will have been introduced to 970 characters. However, those 970 characters are only a portion of the characters students will have learned. In fourth grade social studies students study the Spanish in America, Hernán Cortés and his conquest of the Aztec empire, Francis Drake and the founding of New Spain. While words like *Tenochtitlan* and *Cortes* are taught in their English forms, there's a huge amount of written vocabulary being taught in these lessons as well: empire, capital city, conquest, defeat, discovery, sailing ships, wind patterns—none of it in the program's Chinese textbook.

More is needed

It's probably impossible to get students in an English-speaking country who only get Chinese for 50% to 80% of their school day to the same level as students in China or Taiwan in terms of reading. However many programs and parents are asking what it would take to get them closer. The issues are still being sorted out. The outlines are beginning to emerge, but the best methods aren't yet clear. As a parent, you have a big role to play in increasing your child's reading level, no matter what point in this process your school has reached (and no one's gotten there yet so we're all in it together).

Support your school, your teachers and your program so they can focus on the work of building out curriculum.

- Make sure your child does all his or her homework.

- Reinforce what they learn in Mandarin by having dedicated Chinese Time in your house: 30 minutes a day when they only watch Chinese TV, read Chinese books or comics, or play Chinese games.

- Read to them in Chinese if you can. If you can't, use web sites or apps that can.

- Play flashcard and other learning games using their vocabulary words. Drill if it's your style.

- Help financially so your school can purchase more books in Chinese. Take a look at your school library and see how many books there are in English and how many are in Chinese.

- Organize a Chinese book fair, along the lines of the Scholastic Book Fairs many schools offer. Often local Chinese bookstores will organize a book fair for you, though make sure they have inventory in the type of characters your program uses (simplified or traditional). If you can't find a local bookstore, check with the larger online stores. See *Chapter 15 How To Get More Chinese into Your Child's Life* for suggestions.

How reading (and being read to) builds vocabulary

If you really want to build your child's vocabulary, you'll make sure they spend time reading in Chinese every day and have stacks of fun books. This cannot be stressed enough. Reading, reading and more reading is the key to becoming literate in Chinese, just as it's the key to becoming literate in English. Reading isn't just an end in itself. It also helps speaking by building vocabulary[8] and allowing students to acquire more sophisticated and formal language. The more you read, the more you *can* read. The data supporting this is very strong, for English, Chinese and every other language.

Being read to is also important. Clearly parents who don't read Chinese can't do this at home, but your child's teachers will do a great deal of reading aloud in class, probably more than they might do in English. This reading aloud, especially while students see the characters in front of them, aids in the acquisition of literary vocabulary. Spoken Chinese uses different words and constructions from written Chinese, just as spoken English is different from written English. Being exposed to that through reading aloud will make it easier for your child to read when they get there. Some parents have expressed concern their child's teacher is "still" reading to the class in second or third grade. Actually, you'll see the same thing in good English classes as well. It's a crucial part of getting students literate, so don't fret that it's somehow something that should only happen in kindergarten.

Chinese reading strategies

As Mandarin immersion programs mature, they're able to incorporate teaching methods that have been shown to work well in English. Immersion consultant Elizabeth Hardage explains some of the methods many schools use when teaching reading in Chinese.

Picture walks. This is just what it says, flipping through a story and looking at the pictures first, to get a sense of what the story's about. This way the student can make better guesses about what unfamiliar words are.[9] If there's a cow on the cover, chances are the 牛 character they keep seeing in the book means cow.

Predicting words. If you predict what's happening in the story, you can make a better guess of what the word might be. If the girl in the story went to see her grandmother, and then she got tired, could that word 睡觉 possibly be *shuìjiào*, sleep?

Radicals. Look at the character to see what the radical is. Does it tell you what the word might have to do with? 说 has the speech radical in it. Hm, maybe it's about talking. Right! There's the word *shuō*, to say. Maybe that's it. Does it make sense? The sentence is 他 说, *Tā shuō*. "He says" would make sense there. You nailed it!

What's near it? Look at the surrounding words or characters to help you decide what a given word is. If you see 期 and you don't know what it means or how to say it, look at the word next to it. You might see 星. That one you recognize, it's *xīng*, star. And suddenly you remember that 星期 *xīngqī*, means week. So 期 is probably *qī*, and the word is week. And you can read it! (期 means "a period of time." Together with 星, star, it means "week." But your child doesn't have to know any of that, they just have to remember what their teacher says when she says "We'll have a test next week.")

Sound elements. Is there a sound element in the word you recognize? Can it give you a clue as to how the word is pronounced? Think about some words you know how to say that sound like that and see if they make sense in the context. (More on this below.)

Use the "Five Finger" rule. Count out Who, What, Where, When and Why on your fingers. Look at the sentence or the paragraph. Do you know who did it, what they did, where it was, when it was, or why it was? If you answer some of those questions, you might be able to figure out what's missing— maybe it's the when or the where. Then you at least know that a given word might be a when or where word. That narrows it down. Do you see 星期? Is it this week? Or how about 这里 *zhèlǐ*, "here," or 那里 *nàli*, "there?"

Ask: Find out if a classmate knows how to pronounce it.

Circle: Mark the word so you can ask your teacher during guided reading time and keep going.

Look it up: For students in third grade and up, go to the dictionary and look it up.

Giving students these strategies helps students a lot in Chinese says Hardage. She learned to read and write Mandarin as an adult, so she understands the challenge it presents. "Instead of looking at a character, getting frustrated because they don't know it and just stopping, these are ways to keep reading and get more out of the story, even if they don't know every single character." The idea isn't that they'll simply skip the words they don't know and never learn them, but instead that these reading strategies help them learn. No adult feels they're a failure at reading if they don't know every single word used in the latest John Grisham novel. The idea is to teach students that they learn as they go.

"As adults we think, 'Of course you would do that, how else would you figure that out?' But if you take a step back, you remember that you've either been taught that along the way or you figured it out. That's what you have to do to be a good reader. We're teaching students these steps explicitly, in Chinese," says Hardage. The goal is to turn students into self-learners, she says. "So when they run into a character they don't know, they feel comfortable that they can tackle it without just quitting."

In general, reading in Chinese or English isn't taught in the old reading circles many of us remember from grade school. Today, teachers use a variety of methods to let students work with new material in multiple ways. This helps different kinds of learners and also provides reinforcement. One that's very common in elementary school is called The Daily 5. It's made up of five components; Read to self, Work on writing, Read to someone, Listen to reading, and Word work.

At Yu Ying, the teachers use multiple strategies for teaching how to read new material in Chinese, says Hardage. In Chinese language arts class the focus is on a single topic in the day's lesson but there can be five work centers around the room. During the class, small groups of students shift from one to the other, allowing them to come at the new material in multiple ways.

Read to self: At one table students would find printed-out paragraphs they read to themselves.

Work on writing: At another table there might be a writing prompt. That's the beginning of a sentence that the students have to finish. If the lesson is on cells, it might be "The outside of the cell is ...."

Read to someone else: At another table the students might find paragraphs to read aloud to each other.

Listen to reading: At the sound station they find books about this week's study topic, and headphones that allow them to listen to those books being read. Or the teacher or a teacher's aide might be sitting at this center, reading to the groups as they come through.

Word work: At the word work table there might be the new vocabulary words for the lesson on large pieces of paper, with the meaning and sound radical on separate sheets so the students can see the different parts and put them together, and other games.

Read first, write later

This is an intriguing idea that's being explored by several programs in Asia and a few U.S. schools. It's based on a fundamental shift in the idea of what it means to know a character. Does it mean being able to pronounce it? Use it in a sentence? Read it in a story? Recognize it on a computer screen? Write it by hand? It's a question Chinese-speaking countries grapple with and in some places that discussion has resulted in a new approach to Chinese literacy.

Schools have begun to experiment with what's called the "read first, write later" approach. In these programs, students are expected to read and recognize many more characters than they are able to write.[10] This allows them to read more complex material earlier on, which aids their overall vocabulary. That in turn enables them to read more complex and interesting material, which at the same time increases their vocabulary. It's that wonderful virtuous circle of reading again. All without forcing students to memorize every character they encounter and be able to reproduce it from memory by writing it by hand.

Singapore, educationally at the top of most lists worldwide, uses this system. The national Mandarin language track makes a distinction between characters that students must be able to read versus characters they must "master," i.e. be able to read *and* write. According to Dr. Chin Chee Kuen, executive director of the Singapore Centre for Chinese Language at Nanyang Technological University, by the end of second grade students will have learned between 600 and 650 characters, 300 to 350 of which they must be able to write. By the end of fourth grade they must know between 1,200 to 1,300 characters, 700 to 750 which they must 'master.' By the end of grade six they know between 1,600 and 1,700 characters, of which they must have mastered between 1,000 and 1,100. By the time they take their O Level (Ordinary) tests when they're 15 or 16, they will have mastered about 3,000 characters.

This all is possible because of computers. Today in China many young people pretty much stop writing by hand once they leave school. Instead they write on their phones or their computers, entering words or phrases using pinyin and then choosing the proper characters from a list the computer predicts based on the input pinyin. Speeds of up to 34 words per minute are possible with this method.[11] Because of this shift in how people create written Chinese, being able to pronounce a word and then recognize its written form is crucial, while being able to write it from memory is less important.[12]

The Chinese American International School in San Francisco began to work with this concept in 2008. Andrew Corcoran, who was head of school at the time, wrote:

> Traditionally, students learn to write characters at the same time they learn to read them. As a result, reading and writing levels advance together. The problem rests in the fact that learning to write characters takes much longer than learning to recognize them and much longer than to learn to write with an alphabet.
>
> Learning to properly form all the strokes, in their specific stroke order, without missing any of the strokes that are present in each character takes much longer than being able to recognize the same character when reading. This slows a student's progress in reading to the same pace as her progress in writing. If there were some way to disconnect reading from 'replicating' characters, it would seem that reading levels could advance at a much faster rate."[13]

That's what the "read first, write later" strategy does—allow students to quickly advance their reading level, getting them to more interesting reading material faster. It has the added advantage that it easily allows for differentiation. More advanced students can be asked not just to recognize the characters, but "master" them, as the Singapore educational system calls it.[14]

Learning from context

Just as in English, the more you read the easier it is for you to guess the meaning of new words from context. Researchers from Beijing Normal University and the University of Illinois at Urbana-Champaign studied vocabulary acquisition and reading in students in China. They found that to broaden vocabulary, students needed to see new words repeatedly, in context and presented in as many ways as possible. Children who read a lot were three times better at learning new words from context than children who did some reading and over *seven times* as great for children who did little or no reading.[15]

How does that work in real life? Well, say you're reading *The Wind in the Willows* in Chinese. You come across the character 獾. You have no idea what it means or how to pronounce it. From context, you figure it's probably a noun. Then you look at it and see that it's got the 犭 radical in it, which you know is used for dogs and other mammals. So now when you see the character 獾, you think *dog-animal*. You keep reading and every time you run into 獾 you think "dog-like animal" and the story flows on.

The next time you run into 獾, you're reading *Bread and Jam for Frances*. You remember the dog-animal word and that you didn't know what a 獾/dog-animal was. But now, because of the pictures (see Hardage's Picture Walk reading strategy above) you realize that 獾 must mean badger. Actually, if you're like a lot of elementary school kids you probably have no idea what a badger is in English. But now you know that Frances and her family are all 獾. At this point you ask your teacher to pronounce it for you or you look it up. Now *huān* is stuck in your head. Later that year you go to the zoo with your family. Your parents' hearts swell with pride when you point to a cage of badgers and say "Hey, look, those are 獾!"

Fine, you say. So my kid learns what a badger is. That's not going to get them a job at Alibaba.com[16] when he or she graduates from college. But literacy is a numbers game and the numbers are on your child's side. According to language researchers Y.M. Ku and R. Anderson,

> An average American fifth-grade child reads about 1,000,000 words every year, among which he or she might encounter about 16,000–20,000 new words. If a child learns 10% of these new words, then 1,600–2,000 new words would be learned during normal reading each year simply from reading.[17]

Have them read that much in Chinese every year for four or five years and you'll be hiding 哈利 · 波特[18] from your children until they finish their homework.

Lest you imagine this is something only super-smart kids can do, the research shows it works for everyone. All students do this, each at their own level. "High ability children might have more knowledge of words and learn mainly harder words in the text, and low ability children might have less knowledge and learn mostly easier words in the text. But all of the children have the chance to acquire some new words," write Ku and Anderson."[19]

Today in China there isn't the strong focus on reading for pleasure outside of school that there is in U.S. schools. But Chinese kids do read. Go into any bookstore in China and you'll find children draped everywhere, reading. Those children, the research shows, have bigger vocabularies and do better in school than their non-reading counterparts. Yet most immersion students do little or no reading in Chinese for pleasure. Is it any wonder their Chinese literacy isn't so great?

Learning to "sound-out" in Chinese

This is another of those linguistic asides you should feel free to skip, but learning how to sound-out words in Chinese can be a valuable tool in learning to read.

About 80% of Chinese characters contain two distinct parts: a meaning or semantic radical (部首; *bùshǒu*) and a sound element. Radicals (from the Latin for "root") often, but not always, tell something about the meaning of the word. The sound element tells something about how the character is pronounced. There are about 190 semantic radicals.[20] There are estimated to be about 800 sound elements, most of which are characters in their own right.[21]

Some examples of radicals used in characters:

水 *shuǐ*, water
河 *hé*, river
湖 *hú*, lake
海 *hǎi*, sea

On the left-hand side of the characters above you can see the radical for water 水 *shuǐ*, written as 氵 .[22] If you see it in a character, you can made a pretty good guess that it's got something to do with water or liquids.

Here's another one:

金 *jīn*, gold
铁 *tiě*, iron
钢 *gāng*, steel
针 *zhēn*, needle

In this set, you see the character for gold first and in the rest you see the radical for gold or metal (in simplified characters it looks different from 金) on the left-hand side. If you see that radical in a word you know it probably has something to do with metal.

This also works for sound-elements, to a certain extent. It's not the one-to-one correspondence you get in alphabetic languages, where "c-a-t spells cat" and "*c-a-n-t-a* spells *canta*" (in Spanish). It's more like a rhyme, along the lines of "long *kind of* sounds like song."

For example, the character for star, 星, is made up of two parts. There's 日, *rì*, which means sun and 生, *shēng*, which means life. The 日 gives you a sense it might have something to do with astronomical things in the sky. The 生 *shēng* sounds a little bit like *xīng*, which is how 星 is pronounced.

Or take the character 词, *cí*, which means word. The radical on the left is 讠, which indicates it's about words or speech. The sound element is 司 *sī*, which means "to take charge of, to control." Put them together and you get something that's got to do with speech that sounds like *sī* — 词!

According to experts, "skilled [Chinese] readers are, in fact, capable of such parallel information extraction during character recognition." They've got a fairly good chance of figuring out what a character means even if they've never seen it before, if they know how to say the word.

This can be taught, though it's not so common in programs right now. "I think there's a tendency to say it doesn't work for every character, so people don't use it. But I think it should be included as a reading strategy," says Hardage.

In San Francisco's Mandarin immersion program, Mandarin Content Coordinator Angelica Chang incorporated both the meaning radical and the sound element into flashcards created for each grade. Teachers include both when they're introducing new characters in class. Over time, this gives students the ability to sound out at least some unfamiliar characters.

It works. Judy Shei's second-grade son Emmett Shei-House was a student at Starr King in San Francisco. He was reading a book in which a frog eats a mosquito. "He wasn't familiar with the character for mosquito, 蚊子, but between the context of the story, the sound element 文 *wén* and meaning radical 虫 for insect, and because he knows that a mosquito is *wénzi* from just everyday conversation, he could put it all together and see that this unfamiliar character is 蚊子 *wénzi* (mosquito)," his mom says.

If programs don't teach the sound elements, students will begin to pick them up on their own, usually once they know about 2,000 or so characters, says Dr. Keiko Koda, a professor of second language acquisition at Carnegie Mellon University in Pittsburgh. She does research on both Japanese and Chinese heritage language schools in the United States. When that threshold of characters is reached, students are able to find the patterns in characters.

However, Koda worries that if they're not actively taught to look for the sound element, many heritage and immersion students will never develop this ability because they don't learn the necessary baseline number of characters. It's something students in China and Taiwan begin to do at around third grade, which really helps turbocharge their reading vocabulary. As U.S. programs increase the number of characters taught, and explicitly make students aware of the sound radicals, learning to read starts to go from a "hopelessly unmanageable task" to something that builds on itself, making reading easier as more words are learned, says Koda. Immersion programs and immersion educators are working to create Chinese teaching methods that make use of these building blocks, so students can begin to ramp up their ability to read. And then we get to that lovely cycle: The more they read, the easier it will become. The easier it becomes, the more words they will learn, and the easier it will be to read.

"If we do it right, children would work harder for good results. That would motivate them to work even harder, so we don't have to push them. That's the ideal cycle," says Koda.

Chinese versus English language arts

One question parents who read both languages bring up is the differences they see between how Chinese language arts and English language arts are taught. Says Shei, whose son figured out the meaning of 蚊子 from context,

> The Chinese work I've seen has more to do with just basic comprehension, and doesn't go into the same nuances as English language arts. For example, in second grade, their English homework is writing short summaries of what they have read, writing down main ideas, and supporting arguments. Chinese homework is just fill-in-the-blank and copying characters and writing sentences.

Another mom said this:

> For reading comprehension, I keep on comparing the English homework to the Chinese homework. Chinese homework is all about vocab, vocab, vocab, and writing characters with very little on comprehension, grammar, reading skills. ... Why is that? In English there is a difference between written and oral language, and English Language Arts explicitly teaches that difference. I don't see that in the Chinese language arts. Would love to have some focus on Chinese reading comprehension skills in addition to vocab, vocab, vocab. What are the thoughts about best practices around that? I think some attention to it will go a long way to giving kids the skills to read and retain better.

This does happen when students begin to hit fourth and fifth grade, and certainly in middle school, but it happens later in Chinese than in English. One reason is most Mandarin teachers are still scrambling simply to create a curriculum for their students. Without strong support and a solid curriculum in place, they don't have time to develop the kind of creative work that's being done in English classrooms—built on decades of teaching experience in English. It's beginning to come, but it takes a while for it to filter out to all classrooms.

Having Mandarin coordinators on staff within a school district can go a long way towards creating this kind of curriculum, but it generally doesn't happen at the same time that a school is being established. You've got to have kindergarten through fifth grade going for a few years before anyone's got much bandwidth to focus on nuance. These are the kind of teaching tricks and tips teachers learn from each other and at conferences and from reading books about teaching methodologies in their spare time. Those tips, conferences and books are starting to appear for Chinese but it's still pretty early. The Mandarin immersion consortia that are beginning to emerge are also helping with this, as they can share in the cost of creating this sort of curricular depth. You can read more about them in *Chapter 21: Immersion Consortia: The Support Schools Need.*

This is why parent support is so necessary for immersion schools. It's our job to do as much of the work unrelated to teaching (everything from laminating to making copies to stuffing newsletters to helping in the school yard) so staff can focus on the thing we can't do—teach our kids.

Some schools also make use of parents who can read Chinese, says Kathleen Ting, who has a child in Pasadena, California's Mandarin immersion program at Field Elementary.

An incredible parent set up reading groups in my daughter's class. A Chinese-reading parent guides a small group as they take turns reading aloud, able to prompt and explain as necessary. This is the first, and only, way most have conquered a chapter book in Chinese. Kids are grouped by ability, so we need multiple interesting reading selections, and the top group(s) have been given the extra challenge to read in traditional instead of simplified.

The reading circles focused first on upper grade classes. However it became clear that waiting was a mistake, because students didn't get into the habit of reading in Chinese. Now they're working "more aggressively on reading," says Ting. Starting early makes a huge different. By reading books "when they are younger and just starting out in Chinese, the easy books are not so babyish to them. That builds a foundation that gives students a comfort level for tackling reading in Chinese books."

Ting reads traditional characters and says there are more fun books coming out in Taiwan these days, which offers a richer variety of options to children who can read them. From her shopping forays, it appears there are fewer enticing books available in simplified characters from China.

How well should they be able to read?

No one has worked out what sort of "reasonable targets" for student literacy are achievable within the amount of time in the school day allocated to Chinese.[23] That's a line by Myriam Met from an important chapter in the first book on how to construct a Mandarin immersion program. The fact that the book, *Chinese Language Learning in the Early Grades: A Handbook of Resources and Best Practices for Mandarin Immersion*, was only published in 2012 tells you these are indeed very early days in Mandarin immersion education.

Currently there's no one right answer at this time to how many characters American students should or can learn. Different schools are coming up with different answers they feel are appropriate for their students and their program. One thing that's aiding this discussion is that programs are beginning to do "backward design," as we saw in the last chapter. They are figuring out what students need to be able to do when they graduate from high school then working backward to what they have to know at each grade level to get them there. Still, clear standards have not yet emerged.

Reading is fundamental

All programs recognize reading is important. It's not enough to learn to speak and understand spoken Chinese, says Met. "Reading is crucial for immersion students because it involves two of the program's most important goals: content learning and language learning."[24]

In U.S. schools, third-grade students move from "learning to read" to "reading to learn." Instead of teachers talking them through everything, students focus more on reading written material to acquire knowledge on their own. They begin to research topics using written material and writing reports. Reading also affects vocabulary development. Most of us acquire a great deal of vocabulary from reading, as well as from exposure to more sophisticated constructions. But this doesn't happen in Chinese as much as it does in English.

Why is getting to this level such a problem for Chinese? In a nutshell, many educators feel that asking American students to learn enough characters to become fluent, grade-level readers is too difficult for students in Mandarin immersion programs, given the amount of time that can be allotted for Mandarin. Advocates of literacy development through reading say there aren't enough appropriate books for students to do it on their own by reading for pleasure.

Are both true?

As to the characters, it depends on who you talk with. There are several schools of thought when it comes to how much students reasonably can learn to speak, read and write. The most common one today among immersion educators is that non-Chinese speaking students can easily learn to speak with Intermediate high level ability on the ACTFL scale by the end of fifth grade. (For more on this see *Chapter 14: How Much Chinese Will They Learn?*) That's the functional equivalent of finishing two years of college Chinese. However, students' reading and writing ability will be much lower because it is not felt they can learn the number of characters necessary to build up an equivalent reading vocabulary. The feeling seems to be that students who are motivated will learn to read more fluently in high school or college.

There is another group, mostly made up of Chinese-speaking parents and some teachers, who feel immersion schools should be able to produce fluent readers, writers and speakers of Chinese. Having learned to read and write Chinese themselves, they don't feel the number of characters that must be learned is unreasonable and they are comfortable with the added work required. They believe students in Mandarin immersion programs should memorize more characters and write more essays, so their ability to read and write Mandarin is at least somewhere near that of their cousins and friends in China and Taiwan.

A middle school teacher who has taught in two Mandarin immersion schools is emphatic about this. "Writing takes a lot, I mean *a lot*, of time to practice, even for me, a native Chinese speaker. We had to write 100 times, 200 times for one character in order to memorize it. Students here write 5–10 times, that's it."

American educators say that kind of forced memorization doesn't work well here. "The traditional rote approach is you write the character X number of times. In China you might have to do a whole sheet, 100 times. Here the push-back is there are other competing demands after school or the parent thinks this is boring, repetitive work," says Pioneer Valley's Wang.

Students do need to memorize and write characters dozens of times, though. There's ample research showing the physical act of writing is important for memorizing how to write properly balanced and formed Chinese characters, Wang says. "It's no different than pushing your child to practice piano. After time your fingers learn the visual motor connection. Writing characters is the same."

The key is finding the balance between the two so everyone feels students are getting what they need and in a way that works for a typical American student. "I think we have to adjust some of our approaches and strategies to teaching because we're in the United States," says Wang. "We don't want to be a school in China or Taiwan. We want to be a public school in the United States. More kids need the opportunity to learn Mandarin, not fewer."

This brings us back to the notion that it's still early days in Mandarin immersion. Part of this disagreement among parents will be solved "if or when schools get a better sense of what specifically they are going to require from the students *and* the parents in a Chinese immersion program," says Hardage. Only then will everyone be clear on the expectations; and hopefully there will be less push-back about requiring students to do what it takes to become fully fluent. If a principal tells you that students will become bilingual and biliterate in Chinese, ask him or her exactly what is meant by that. And make it clear that an honest answer is going to go farther than a pie-in-the-sky presumption that doesn't end up happening. Once administrators realize parents can cope with the truth, we can all begin to work to raise literacy levels.

The thicket problem

Written language uses a larger and more precise vocabulary than spoken language and the only way to acquire it is to read, notes Met. At a talk for parents in San Francisco on Chinese immersion she told a story about reading a book in English to her three-year-old granddaughter. It was about a bunny who went to hide in a thicket.

"Thicket," she told the parents, "is not a word you hear every day in English. In fact, it's the kind of word you only run into in books. But you *do* run into it there, along with a lot of other words and phrases that most people never say out loud." The only way to expand vocabulary beyond ordinary social language is through reading, she told them. "Oral language is more informal than print, even when we look at print written for a young listener or reader. To gain a large, well-developed vocabulary that allows you to speak or write with precision, you need to read and encounter 'thickets' often," says Met.

How to make that happen still confounds programs. "How do we get our kids literate, given the amount of time we have, given the fact that they're not native speakers, given the fact that the instructional language materials we have are not written for second language learners being educated in the United States?" she asks.

This isn't just a challenge for Chinese immersion programs. Spanish has one of the most straightforward and rationally spelled written forms in the world, second only to Italian and Finnish. But students in Spanish immersion whose home language is English tend to read preferentially in English because it's easier for them. They can read in Spanish, parents say, but it takes longer. And when they just want to get through the story and find out what happens to Harry and Hermione next, they want to go *fast*.

One strategy Wang of Pioneer Valley has found successful is to have teachers read aloud to students. "In the classroom the teacher needs to read *The Magic Treehouse* books to the kids" in Chinese, she says. The school uses lots of teacher-directed reading through the grades. "Kids love being read to. And that's a way to develop reading proficiency." The challenge, she acknowledges, is for English-speaking parents to do this at home. Thankfully there are more and more websites and apps becoming available which show a book while the story is being read aloud. 5QChannel.com out of Taiwan and ChildRoad.com out of California are two. In some school districts, such as Vancouver, Washington, teachers record themselves reading books so students can watch them being read on the computer at home.[25]

The more you read, the better you read

One literacy-enhancing tool most American parents would probably feel comfortable with is the Voluntary Free Reading approach espoused by Stephen Krashen, a professor emeritus of education at the University of Southern California. He has spent decades studying how students learn to read. He and others have done extensive research showing that students need "compelling and comprehensible texts" to boost reading comprehension.

Students need *extensive*[26] rather than *intensive* reading. The focus is on getting students to read a lot, without a lot of hard work and fuss, so they enjoy it and are encouraged to do more. The books don't have to be hard. In fact they *shouldn't* be. Reading things that are slightly below or just at their level helps students cement language structures in their brains and also take in new vocabulary—and have fun, a necessary ingredient. This may seem counterintuitive. In fact one Chinese person who read a draft of this chapter flagged that phrase as a typo—clearly I couldn't have meant students should read below their actual reading level. Reading is meant to be work, a hard slog that requires looking up words and constant struggle!

But that's not at all what the research shows. The more children read, the more vocabulary and grammar they learn *without having to be taught it*.[27] If you read one book in a week and have to look up every 20th word (and hate every minute of it) you won't learn that much. But read seven books, all fun and quick, and you'll see a lot of new words and learn more of them.

This approach is widely used in U.S. schools, in English, because it is a powerful means of developing a stronger vocabulary and ability to use and understand academic language. There's no "You must read this" or "You must now write a report on that." Instead, kids spend 15 or 20 minutes a day simply reading. This is enough to really significantly boost students' scores in English. Even if they don't know all the words, they subconsciously absorb them as they go along.[28] For example, in many schools in the San Francisco Unified School District, the first 30 minutes of each day are devoted to RED time, for Read Every Day.

We need better books!

One reason it's hard to get students reading is there isn't much for them to read, and programs know it. Portland's Bacon:

> What also impacts kids' ability to read is doing lots of it. What promotes lots of reading is when they've got compelling, comprehensible text. And to have that you've got to have something that's really engaging.

If you can get a child reading in English, chances are you can find *something* they'll be entranced by. That's harder to do, right now, in Chinese, but not impossible. In *Chapter 17: Getting Your Child Reading in Chinese*, I'll talk about "leveled" or "graded" readers, the Chinese version of *I Can Read* books, and how you can use them at home to boost your child's Chinese reading ability. They're starting to appear in Chinese, often in Singapore and Malaysia, where there are significant numbers of students studying in Chinese who may not speak Chinese at home.

While these readers are at a good level for younger students, so far no one's come up with a must-read series like *The Magic Tree House* books or *Geronimo Stilton* that Mandarin immersion students can easily read for pleasure in fourth or fifth grade and above. "We really need some entrepreneurial group in China to start writing these," says Hardage.

Unfortunately they haven't appeared yet. When popular American books are translated into Chinese they're too difficult for students in the appropriate grade level in immersion. When you give a fifth grader *Mummies in the Morning: The Magic Tree House* in Chinese they just roll their eyes because it is too hard for them to read. Says Jeff Bissell, head of school at the San Francisco's Chinese American International School, "in English they're reading *The Hunger Games*, in Chinese it's inane content. Students get frustrated. They say: 'I can't read half the words, this is baby stuff. I hate Chinese!'"

While not quite in the Percy Jackson realm of must-read fiction, some easy-to-read books for slightly older audiences are beginning to appear. They're based on similar easy-to-read books that have been available in French and Spanish for a decade or more. These can be so simple that they're easily read by third graders. While the content isn't thrilling, students are often quite proud to be able to read a real chapter book by themselves in Chinese. You can find some of them listed in *Chapter 17: Getting Your Child Reading in Chinese*.

One really important innovation these books use is that names are written in English rather than in Chinese transliteration. This makes them much easier for immersion students to read. Foreign personal names and place names are often transliterated using uncommon characters that few students know. These can be an enormous impediment to reading. Another problem is that because Chinese can't use capitalization to alert readers to a proper noun, it can be difficult for beginners to even know they're looking at a name rather than some combination of words they've never seen. In some books proper names are underlined, which helps a lot. Still, it's unlikely most fourth graders would see 赫敏格兰杰 and automatically think, "Oh, of course, that's the Chinese transliteration for Hermione Granger!" (It's pronounced *Hèmǐn Gélánjié*.)[29]

As students rise through the grades, finding books they want to read becomes harder. "Nobody's developed a reading program for middle school and high school, so we're always looking for appropriate reading," says Portland's Bacon.

It's only fair to note that reading in Chinese is harder for students in Chinese-speaking countries than it is for speakers of alphabet-based languages. It takes longer, even for them, to learn enough words to be able to read at an advanced level. This is documented in the research, says Met. Studies in China found students there "are not reading the same types of text at the same type of complexity as their counterparts are in the U.S. Not because they're not as smart, but because they're not able to get to the same level of complexity." As I said early on, Chinese simply takes longer to master.

A good example are the Harry Potter books. They're commonly devoured by students in fourth and fifth grade in the United States. But when Bissell, a fluent speaker and reader of Mandarin, read them when he was living in Beijing, he quickly realized, "you'd have to be at an eighth or ninth grade level in Chinese to read this."

Some other ideas, including comic books

One solution to the What To Read? dilemma is giving kids comic books. Comics never got much respect in English, though having been rebranded as "graphic novels," they're now considered a little less disreputable. However they've always been popular in China and Japan, where they are considered an art form of their own. They're called *manga* in Japanese, 漫画书, *mànhuà shū* in Chinese—and they get kids reading.

In the 2010s, Dr. Christy Lao, a professor of education at San Francisco State University, created a phenomenal summer program to get kids reading in Chinese. The children were students at either Chinese immersion programs or heritage language schools. Their spoken Chinese was excellent but they read at much lower levels. Lao worked with a group of students in San Francisco for several years running, in which they spent much of their summer in a big, friendly room at San Francisco State that is lined with bookcases filled with Chinese-language graphic novels.

They *loved* them.

"Some of these students were reading 10 books a week," Lao says. "We had one boy who read 644 books over the summer and wanted to take more home in his suitcase." The group of students who took the month-long summer workshop read from 96 to 644 (the aforementioned boy) Chinese graphic novels. Kids who had never before read a full book in Chinese were devouring them. One mother even called Lao to complain: "You said this was just a summer program, but you're making my child read five hours a night!" Lao had to explain to the mom that there was no homework—her daughter just wanted to read that much.

Picture books didn't work. Lao had a shelf full of them but they were ignored by the children. It was the comic books they couldn't keep them away from. And after becoming addicted readers of Chinese comic books, some of the students started reading chapter books in Chinese, without any prompting.

Lao has these suggestions for parents and schools. First, don't worry about your kid understanding all the words. The pictures will help them. Ideally they shouldn't ever touch a dictionary while they're reading. This isn't supposed to be hard, it's supposed to be *fun*—don't turn it into homework. You don't have to know all the words on a page to be able to follow the story.[30]

Let your child find books that they like. There are many genres of comic books and graphic novels—kung fu, romance, science fiction and adventure. *Tintin*[31] and *Astrix* and *Oblix* exist in Chinese. As do the *Smurfs*. Let your kid explore. They'll only read if they find a story that pulls them in. Think beach reading.

Don't feel you have to buy something that was originally written in Chinese. Translations are fine. Some of the most popular graphic novels Lao's staff found are translations from Japanese *manga*.

Many comic series have cartoon series as well. You can also by DVDs or watch them online to get your children interested in the series. After watching an afternoon of cartoons they'll know the characters and the kind of story and will have an easier time reading the comic. You can also do this with stories your children already know. Have them read the Smurfs or Tintin in English and then take away the English books and replace them with the Chinese ones.

Most of these won't look like the comic books we grew up with; they're graphic novels and as thick as any book. Both kinds are fine, as long as your child wants to read them.

Make sure you find materials in the right type of characters. Some programs use traditional, some simplified. There are many more comics available in traditional out of Taiwan but you can also find them in simplified if you look.

In this vein, I can't resist telling you about a study done with Korean immigrants in Los Angeles because it's such a great example of the power of reading and how it can turbocharge language learning. The participants in the study were all adult Korean women in their thirties. They had been living in the United States for years but had made little progress in their spoken English and didn't read English much at all. They had signed up for an English as a Second Language class but things were not going well.

Then the teacher hit upon the idea of having them read the *Sweet Valley High* series for girls. This was a series popular in the 1980s that comes in three levels, *Sweet Valley High*, for kids 12 and older, *Sweet Valley Twins* for ages 8–12 and *Sweet Valley Kids* for ages 5–8. The women started reading at whatever level they felt most comfortable (generally *Sweet Valley Kids*). Here's what happened to one woman:

> After one year, this subject, who had never read for pleasure in English prior to this study, had read all 34 Sweet Valley Kids books, had read many books from the Sweet Valley Twins and Sweet Valley High series, and had started to read Danielle Steele and other authors of romances in English.[32]

No one's suggesting every student in immersion start reading the *Sweet Valley High* books in Chinese, or that Danielle Steele is the literary end point you want your child to reach. But it shows that if you give people books with stories they enjoy, they'll read more. And besides, they read all sorts of fun books in English. It's our job as parents to make sure they've got fun books to read in Chinese as well.

Write it yourself

Another solution that's been found successful in Spanish and French immersion schools is having older students write books for younger students. The students aren't allowed to use the dictionary (or if they do, only sparingly) on the theory that if they don't know the words, their classmates probably won't either. The older students get the educational benefit of writing the stories. These are then printed out with a few photos from around school and *voilà*, books in Chinese ready for reading! Some schools simply make them on a copier, some use programs like Blurb and Shutterfly, which allow you to create books online. These are then available for their peers and younger students to read, creating interesting material the older students are proud of and the younger ones can understand.[33] I can especially see this being popular if the stories are about school-specific topics, and kids and locations all the students already know.

Imagine the possibilities:

- The Time Mason Snorted Milk Out Of His Nose in the Lunchroom
- The Secret Swimming Pool on the Roof the Fourth Graders Found
- The Great Parent Versus Teacher Kickball Tournament
- My Favorite Lunch and How to Make It
- Stories from Life in Middle School

How it works in real life

I cannot in good conscience publish the above without admitting that my own daughters now try to hide from me when I come at them with yet another newly-arrived Chinese book. "Just try it, I just want to know if a fifth grader can read it," I beg. "You don't have to read the whole thing. Just a bit," I plead.

Let's just say the copy of 玛蒂尔达 (*Matilda*, by Roald Dahl) Santa brought as a Christmas present was *not* a hit. However, I did find *Zhou Yi* curled up on her bed reading a Tintin in Chinese the other day, so perhaps some of it stuck.

In general, I console myself by looking at what they're reading in class now that they're in the higher grades and imagine it's easier for them because of the reading I made them do when they were younger.

1. Myriam Met and Chris Livaccari, "Basics of Program Design," Chinese Language Learning in the Early Grades: A handbook of resources and best practices for Mandarin immersion (New York: Asia Society, 2012) 20.
2. Newspaper Chinese has its own set of writing conventions and tons of abbreviations that make it especially difficult to read if you're not taught how. When I was in college we had an entire semester class on it and it was still slow going.
3. Well, let's be honest, semi-explicit in the case of English, with its rather eclectic spelling system. I remember when I helped my fourth grader try to sound out the word 'conscientious.' She was actually looking up the English meaning of 认真 *rènzhēn*, and after she stumbled over saying conscientious a few times, 认真 didn't seem so hard.
4. Sesame Street in Chinese is great for younger students and will really boost their speaking and reading. I highly recommend having them watch it online. You can find episodes here:
   https://www.youtube.com/results?search_query=sesame%20street%20 mandarin&sm=3
5. Myriam Met and Chris Livaccari, "Basics of Program Design," Chinese Language Learning in the Early Grades: A handbook of resources and best practices for Mandarin immersion (New York: Asia Society, 2012) 20.

6. Frequency and Stroke Counts of Chinese Characters, Chih-Hao Tsai's Technology Page, Aug. 3, 2005.
http://technology.chtsai.org/charfreq/
Accessed Jan. 15, 2014.

7. Every child in the San Francisco Unified School District's Mandarin immersion program learns about 马丁 · 路德 · 金 *Mǎdīng lùdé jīn* (Martin Luther King Jr.) during Black History Month, for example.

8. Y. M. Ku and R. Anderson, "Chinese children's incidental learning of word meanings," Contemporary Educational Psychology 2001, 26: 249–266. Thanks to Dr. Krashen for bringing the article to my attention.

9. This can backfire if you're a non-Chinese reading parent. In third grade I was looking through my daughter's homework one day and found a story with a picture of a princess lying in a bed. I got upset about it, ranting about how by third grade they should be reading something a little harder than Sleeping Beauty. "Aren't they teaching you anything in this school?" I finished with a flourish. My third-grader looked at me condescendingly. "Mama, it's from our science class. It's an article about how important sleep is and how if you don't get enough sleep you can't learn well. Remember the graphing project we did in math about how much everyone in our class sleeps each night?"
Clearly I needed to employ some better reading strategies.

10. The AP Chinese test requires no writing, only typing on the computer.

11. "Predicting Chinese Text Entry Speeds on Mobile Phones," CHI 2010: HCI in China. April 10, 2010.
http://dmrussell.net/CHI2010/docs/p2183.pdf
Accessed Jan. 15, 2014.

12. Mind you, there's also a lot of hand wringing about the lack of education of today's Chinese youth. It's even got a name, "character amnesia." In Chinese it's called 提笔忘字, *Tí bǐ wàng zì,* 'Take pen, forget character.'

13. Andrew Corcoran, " 'Read First, Write Later' for Chinese programs, immersion and beyond," The Mandarin Institute.
http://mandarininstitute.org/articles/read_first
Accessed Sept. 24, 2013.

14. He went on to say, "It is also important to note that the approach discussed here will not prevent accelerated learners from being able to write Chinese by hand. In fact, this approach may provide an effective way of differentiating in a classroom that includes students with different proficiency levels in Chinese. Those with higher levels of proficiency can spend time focusing on handwriting, formation of characters, using more traditional dictionaries, etc. that will enhance their experience. Simultaneously, those with lower levels of proficiency can focus on reading and writing/composing at higher levels and concentrate on learning practical and more commonly used vocabularies."
Andrew Corcoran, "'Read First, Write Later' for Chinese programs, immersion and beyond," The Mandarin Institute.
http://mandarininstitute.org/articles/read_first
Accessed Sept. 24, 2013.

15. Y. M. Ku. and R. Anderson, "Chinese children's incidental learning of word meanings," Contemporary Educational Psychology 2001 26: 249–266. 14. Emphasis added.

16. The eBay, Yahoo! and Amazon of China, all rolled into one.
17. Y. M. Ku. and R. Anderson, "Chinese children's incidental learning of word meanings," Contemporary Educational Psychology 2001 26: 249–266. 14. 17.
18. Hālì Bōtè, Harry Potter.
19. Y. M. Ku. and R. Anderson, "Chinese children's incidental learning of word meanings," Contemporary Educational Psychology 2001 26: 249–266. 14. 15
20. Keiko Koda, Chan Lü, Yanhui Zhang ,"Effects of print input on morphological awareness among Chinese heritage language learners," in Agnes Weiyun He and Yun Xiao (eds) Chinese as a Heritage Language: Fostering Rooted World Citizenry (National Foreign Language Resource Center, University of Hawai'i at Manoa, 2008) 196.
21. R. Hoosian, Psycholinguistic Implications for Linguistic Relativity: A Case Study of Chinese (Hillsdale, N.J. Erlbaum, 1991).
22. Yes, I know the radical doesn't look like the character 水. Some radicals look different than the character they come from. Ask your child to show you what the 忄, xīn, heart radical looks like. It's cool.
23. Myriam Met, "Curriculum and Literacy," Chinese Language Learning in the Early Grades: A Handbook of Resources and Best Practices for Mandarin Immersion (New York, The Asia Society, 2012) 37.
Available online at
http://asiasociety.org/files/chinese-earlylanguage.pdf
24. Myriam Met, "Curriculum and Literacy," Chinese Language Learning in the Early Grades: A Handbook of Resources and Best Practices for Mandarin Immersion (New York, The Asia Society, 2012) 37.
Available online at
http://asiasociety.org/files/chinese-earlylanguage.pdf
25. Vancouver Public Schools, Chinese immersion program, books read aloud by teachers.
http://welearntv.vansd.org/chinese-immersion-program
26. You can read more about this here:
http://en.wikipedia.org/wiki/Free_voluntary_reading
27. Stephen Krashen, "Fundamentals of Language Education," Chapter 2, The Development of Literacy: The Reading Hypothesis, (Laredo Publishing 1992).
28. I've been experimenting with this on myself and it works. My Spanish is conversational but not all that good. I'd never read a book in Spanish before 2012. But after reading several of Krashen's books I decided I should put my money where my mouth was. I've now read four books in Spanish, all meant for intermediate college students. Before I would have felt I needed to sit at my desk and look up every word I didn't know—which is why I never did it. Now I try to read in Spanish book for 10 or 20 minutes every day and either figure it out from context or don't. It works. The more I read, the easier it gets. Words that I didn't know at the beginning (aldea, village; escudero, squire) made sense from context by the end. And it flows so much faster now. But that first book was the hardest and I think that's the mental push we've got to get the kids past.
29. To get a sense of this, check out this website: Bathrobe's Harry Potter in Chinese, Japanese & Vietnamese Translation, "Names of Harry's schoolmates in the Chinese translations of Harry Potter."
http://www.cjvlang.com/Hpotter/names/matesct.html
Accessed March 21, 2014.

30. Jim Trelease, The Read-Aloud Handbook (New York Penguin Books, 2006) 102.
31. It works especially well if they already know the story in English. My daughters are huge Tintin fans in English. A friend bought us a stack of Tintin's in Beijing. One day when my sixth-grader was reading one during her "Chinese reading time" I asked her to translate one of the panels to me. She got to a part where Captain Haddock said, "Great blistering barnacles!" and I asked her how you said that in Chinese. She said "I have no idea, but that must be what he's saying, it's what he says in English and it's got an ! after it."
32. K.S. Cho and Stephen Krashen, "Acquisition of vocabulary from the Sweet Valley High Kids series: Adult ESL acquisition." Journal of Reading 37:662–667 1993.
33. B. Dupuy and J. McQuillan, "Handcrafted books: Two for the price of one," G. Jacobs, C. Davis, and W. Renandya (Eds.) Successful Strategies for Extensive Reading (Singapore, SEAMEO Regional Language Centre, 1997) 171–180.

Getting Your Child Reading in Chinese

Imagine you go to visit the home of a new friend of your child's. The mom gives you a quick tour of the house while the kids go off to play. It's a lovely home, warm and inviting. You really like the parents and you're looking forward to getting to know them better. But as you walk through the house, something seems wrong. You can't quite put your finger on it until it hits you—there are no books in this house. In fact there's really nothing printed here at all.

There are no books on the bookshelves, no magazines on the coffee table, no newspapers piled on the dining room table. There are no printed notes stuck to the refrigerator with magnets, no comic books stuffed under the beds, no word games stacked in the corner. The lone bit of print you see is a dictionary sitting forlornly on a shelf and some pages of homework sticking out of a backpack. This family is clearly totally illiterate.

"How," you think to yourself, "can this child succeed in school when no one in the family reads and there's absolutely no reinforcement for literacy at home?" You feel sorry for those children, knowing they are going to face an uphill battle as they go through school.

This is your house in Chinese

Think about it: How many Chinese language books do you have in your house, beyond a dictionary? A few picture books people gave you when you first said you were thinking of Mandarin immersion? A book in (insert either 'simplified' or 'traditional' here) characters, which your school doesn't use and which your child can't read, but which they were giving away free at the Chinese New Year's Parade if you listened to a talk about opening an AT&T account? A copy of *Harry Potter and the Deathly Hallows* in Chinese that a co-worker grabbed at the airport in Hong Kong as a gift, but which is about ten years beyond where your child can read? And maybe, if you're lucky, a few Chinese storybooks with pinyin that you bought at the annual book fair your PTA puts on?

Educators call your kind of home a "print desert" and that's exactly what it is, for Chinese. It's as if your family were illiterate—and you are, in Chinese. Now count up the number of English language books you have in your home. Dozens? Hundreds? When you go to the library, how many books do you bring home in English and how many in Chinese? Is it any wonder your child prefers to read in English? Is there anything *for* them to read in Chinese at home?

This matters, and more than you know. There's a huge amount of evidence that how well students read is based in large part on how much exposure they have to print and how much opportunity they have to interact with print outside of school. It's even got a name: The Matthew Effect.[1] In the International Association for the Evaluation of Education Achievement study of reading achievement, *the number of books at home was the single most powerful predictor of reading achievement* in most countries. So when teachers tell you to get library books in Chinese, buy books in Chinese and make sure that your children don't only see Chinese at school, listen to them.

The arrival of graded readers, finally!

Mandarin immersion teachers have talked for years about the need for "graded readers." Only now are grade level readers beginning to become easily available to U.S. parents of Chinese immersion students. They're meant to be fun, interesting books that are matched pretty closely to the student's reading ability so they don't get frustrated. The idea is that the story, not a parent or a teacher standing over them, will pull them through and make them keep reading to the end. Students shouldn't have to stop and look up words. If they can't get the gist of the story without looking up a ton of words, the book is too hard.

Leveled readers are the Chinese equivalent of graded readers like the I Can Read series in the United States. I Can Read books tell you the grade a child should be in to be able to read it; the leveled readers often give the number of characters used in the books.

Many of these readers are from Singapore and Malaysia, where there are significant numbers of students studying in Chinese who may not speak Chinese at home.

In addition, the Brigham Young University Chinese Flagship Center has begun producing books that go along with the Mandarin immersion curriculum used by the Flagship–Chinese Acquisition Pipeline, a consortium of over 50 Mandarin immersion schools nationwide. These books are written specifically for the Mandarin immersion market, thank goodness. They come in simplified and traditional versions. The series launched in 2012 and they're adding to it over time.

It's unlikely your child will be able to read their favorite English books in Chinese translations because the Chinese will be beyond them. Better to buy books in Chinese at the appropriate level so they won't get frustrated and give up.

Most of the easiest books will be appropriate for Mandarin immersion students who've finished two or three years of school, so they are suited for first or second graders, depending on whether your program began in kindergarten or first grade. Don't push your child to read books that are too hard. If you do, they'll just stop. You want them to see reading in Chinese as something that isn't too much of a chore.

For younger students who aren't yet ready to read but who have had enough immersion to understand spoken Mandarin, have someone else do the reading. Two websites that make that easy are 5QChannel.com in Taiwan and Childroad.com in the United States. Both offer dozens of books and stories in both simplified and traditional characters. On 5QChannel they are read aloud with animation, on Childroad they're simply read, with a series of still pictures that help tell the story. Both have relatively simple interfaces with enough English to get you going. If you run into trouble, staff at both sites usually reply within 24 hours via email, so don't give up. 5QChannel offers a special rate for U.S. parents here:

http://www.5qchannel.com/order/grouprate2011.htm

Finding leveled readers

Many Chinese bookstore sites have leveled readers available. However, they don't make it easy for parents who can't read Chinese to figure out which ones are appropriate for students in immersion, or even which books are part of a series. I've come up with a list of the books below that I've either seen myself or have been told about by other parents.

I've tried to give enough information so that parents who don't read Chinese can easily order these books. Multiple sites sell them. If I have a specific link to a given series, I've included it. I don't mean to slight the other stores, but if one website has made it especially easy to find a given series, I list the link.

Of course, there are many other possibilities and more are becoming available every day. These just happen to be the ones I was able to get enough information about to pass along. Ask teachers at your school and fellow parents for other recommendations. If you have a Chinese bookstore near you, take your child and to browse. When you find books that your child can easily read for pleasure, share the wealth. Pass them around to other families in your grade. You want it to be a cool thing to read in Chinese, and having kids talk about the books on the playground will help, especially if several students in a class have read the same book. Consider buying an extra set for your teachers' reading corner or the school library (check with your child's teacher first, of course).

Online bookstores to browse include:

- http://Cheng-tsui.com
- http://Chinasprout.com
- http://Littlemonkeyandmouse.com
- http://Nanhaibooks.com

Some leveled readers to start with

Step by Step Chinese Readers, 一步一步

These readers are being produced by the Brigham Young University Chinese Flagship Center. As they say in their promotional materials, "Most American parents do not speak Chinese—this challenges programs and teachers to find new ways to help parents and guardians support their young learners during the study of Chinese. Step by Step provides a variety of resources to meet this challenge, including full English translations, new word lists with *pīnyīn*, as well as a robust companion website complete with mp3 audio, flashcards, word lists and more."

http://www.cheng-tsui.com/store/products/step_step

The Mandarin Matrix

This is a series of graded readers created by the Hong Kong-based publisher P3 in conjunction with Cambridge University Press. They feature six color-coded levels of 40 readers each. They include fun and simple stories to introduce new vocabulary, Chinese characters, character recognition and key grammar. The easiest, Orange, level provides very basic vocabulary (often just one noun per page), while the most difficult Red level presents complex historical and mythological Chinese tales. Each level consists of 40 titles with "fresh, exciting and new stories," according to the website.

The Mandarin Matrix site in Hong Kong is available at:
http://mandarinmatrix.org/parent/chinese-readers/
They are available for sale at China Sprout:
http://www.chinasprout.com/shop/BSG029

I Can Read Rainbow Series, 我自己會讀!

These books come from the Greenfield Education Centre in Hong Kong. They feature four levels of books that gradually become harder. They include audio CDs with the stories read in both Mandarin and Cantonese. They also come in

simplified and traditional characters. The simplified editions include pinyin.
They've been used in immersion schools in Singapore and San Francisco.

http://www.cheng-tsui.com/store/products/i_can_read#Level+4

http://www.littlemonkeyandmouse.com (Search on "I can read rainbow")

Magic Story Box Mandarin Readers, 神奇的故事盒普通話讀者

These books come from New Zealand and have six levels: Purple, Blue, Red,
Orange, Green and Brown. Each introduces about 100 words and phrases.
There are six books in each level, each of which contains a story in Chinese
with an English translation and vocabulary list at the back of each book.
Pinyin is gradually removed to encourage character recognition skills as the
reader progresses through the story.

http://www.chinasprout.com/shop/BSG100

Reading Program 100 Words 学前阅读计划100字读本

These books come in a set of eight books. Each story is written using the
most commonly used Chinese words, starting with a set that only uses the
first 100 characters. They are only available in simplified Chinese. The sets
are:

- Reading Program 100 words
- Reading Program 200 words
- Reading Program 300 & 400 words
- Reading Program 500–800 words
- Reading Program 900–1,200 words

http://www.chinasprout.com/shop/BSE274

Learning Chinese Characters through Literacy 学前儿童分级阅读能力培养用书

These are from East China Normal University Press. They're meant
for preschoolers in China but work very well for grades two on up in
U.S. Mandarin immersion schools. They come in several levels. The
first level contains 10 books. It is worth buying the whole set of Level
1 for the second book alone. It's called "Whose Poop? 谁拉的便便?"
It never fails to make any child you give it to burst out laughing.

http://www.chinasprout.com

Disney New Concept Reading Series, Golden Seed Series
迪士尼新概念阅读 金种子系列

These easy-to-read books are from the People's Post Press in China. There are four series, each of which includes ten books based on Disney characters. Level 1 is for students who have learned 50 characters, level 2 for 100, level 3 for 200 and level 4 for 500. They are in simplified characters. I haven't seen the books myself, but they seem like they'd be fun.

http://www.littlemonkeyandmouse.com (search on "Disney")

Easy-to-read novels in Chinese

There exists an entire universe of easy-to-read novels in Spanish and French for new learners. These sometimes go under the moniker TPRS (for Teaching Proficiency through Reading and Storytelling.)[2] It's a method of teaching foreign languages in which teachers focus on stories with comprehensible input rather than a textbook. That's exactly what happens in an immersion classroom—teachers use language the students can understand, limiting vocabulary, constantly asking easy comprehension question and short grammar explanations to help broaden and deepen students' understanding of the language.

The TPRS method has its origins in the theories of James Asher, a professor of psychology at San Jose State University, and Stephen Krashen, a professor of second-language acquisition, bilingual education and reading at the University of Southern California. Their research has heavily influenced immersion education in this country. A Spanish teacher named Blaine Ray in California took their ideas and created written materials from them. Ray began writing very easy-to-read stories in Spanish for his students. There are now dozens of these novels, in Spanish, French and other languages. Some are set entirely in the present tense, some also use the past tense. Each lists the number of words used. Here's an example of a Level 1 Spanish novel on the TRPS website. You can see how they try to make an exciting story even though they're using no more than 150 different words in Spanish.

> *Felipe Alou: Desde los valles a las montañas:* Under ordinary circumstances, the odds of being struck by lightning are greater than the odds of becoming a Major League Baseball player, but Felipe Alou's circumstances in 1955 were anything but 'ordinary' ... He was a black athlete living in the Dominican Republic and he spoke no English—not exactly a recipe for success in the U.S., especially during the height of the civil rights movement.

Some of these stories have been rewritten for beginning Chinese students. My fourth-grader read *"Anna Mei Banfa* /Anna 没办法" over the course of two summer days without having to look up a single word. Her review:

> This was kind of boring but I read it and it wasn't hard, and I didn't even know there was a glossary in the back. Anna lives in America but she goes to China. Her friends have expensive stuff. She's a teenager.

Well, boring or not, it was the first novel without pictures that she'd sat down to read, so I say, "Hurray!" The books in the series are nicely done. The stories are set in easy-to-understand situations, often in the United States. In a touch I especially liked, English words such as names like Anna and Los Angeles were written in English, not Chinese. That's helpful because often the characters used to transliterate from Chinese are complex and rarely seen, making them difficult for beginning readers to comprehend. The book is in both characters and pinyin (on facing pages) and features a full glossary in the back. They've got another book for first and second grade students called 马丽在上海 "Mary in Shanghai." I expect more will be added.

At the absolutely simplest level, there's *Sheí hǎokàn* 谁好看 ("Who's Good-Looking?"), a very easy-to-read book. It's got characters, pinyin and English on each page and goes through many of the same questions students would use in a beginning class: Where are you from? What's your name? Who's good-looking?

It was much too simple for my fifth grader, but she actually read the whole thing because it was funny to read lines like "George Clooney 好看?" (Is George Clooney good-looking?) Of course, it made me feel old because she didn't know who George Clooney was...

This book is available from Command Performance Language Institute, which you can find online. Just click the "Chinese" button and then Easy Readers.

The Squidforbrains.com site has six easy-to-read novels listed, which you can find here:

http://squidforbrains.com/store/27-chinese-readers

Susan You Mafan: Susan 有麻烦 ("Susan's troubles")

Susan is caught on the treadmill of life in her boring town—dealing with an obsolete computer, a nagging mother, and that nice guy at the ValuMart who just doesn't know she exists. Until one day, that is—when a chance errand brings her family something that will change their lives—well, not forever, but at least for a few months!

Susan You Mafan is a true first-year Chinese reader. The first chapter can be read in the first month of Chinese study, and each chapter builds on the language that has been used in earlier in the book. The story is 9,871 words long, uses 207 unique Chinese characters and contains 431 Chinese words.

Anna Mei Banfa! Anna 没麻烦 *("Anna's Okay")*

This is a short, simple novel in Chinese characters and pinyin that emphasizes and repeats the highest-frequency words and phrases of the language while telling a story. First in a series for Chinese learners, *Anna Mei Banfa* tells the story of Anna, a high school freshman living in upstate New York, who is frustrated with her family and her problems.

An unexpected opportunity presents itself when her high school announces a chance for a student to travel to Taiwan for a summer. While living in southern Taiwan, Anna experiences the local culture and makes new friends.

Learners of Chinese may choose to read the Chinese characters or turn the page to see the pinyin. A full glossary of the words as they appear in the text makes this reader accessible to anyone with a basic knowledge of Chinese.

The Three Pandas

Based on the Three Bears, this story is about three pandas who dart out of their suburban Beijing home for just a few minutes to do a little shopping, but when they get back...they discover an unexpected visitor!

This 700+ character story is told in simple Chinese, using only 114 unique words and 89 Chinese characters in all. The text systematically repeats the highest-frequency vocabulary while still telling a coherent story, complete with unexpected twists and turns.

A great little read for a classroom library or for someone learning Chinese on his own. A full glossary is provided at the end of the story. Color-coding, word spacing and turn-the-page Pinyin support (not visible, but accessible) ensure that the text is made comprehensible to every reader.

Pandarella

The nearly-classic tale of the hardworking girl who just wants to go to the biggest party of the year...and might get to, with some help from a celebrity's little brother!

Pandarella draws on the familiar, but inserts twists and turns to keep readers engaged. Words are repeated in novel ways. The 1,072-word text of the story contains only 88 unique words and 87 unique Chinese characters.

A full glossary is provided at the end of the story. Color-coding, word spacing and turn-the-page Pinyin support (not visible, but accessible) ensure that the text is made comprehensible to every reader.

Herbert's Birthday

It's Herbert's birthday ... but life is a drag when your friends don't give you what you really want. This easy-to-read story helps new readers of Chinese become confident and fluent. Told in just 46 different words and 50 Chinese characters, the book is over 300 words long. Repetition helps the reader become familiar with and instantly recognize the most important, most frequently used characters in the language. A full glossary is provided at the end of the story.

Josh

Between helping with the milking on his family's dairy farm and getting picked on at school, Josh's days in high school are full. He's making progress to catch the attention of Julia, the beautiful, exotic, and—for ordinary, unremarkable Josh—unreachable new girl at school. But then Christian, a hunky but inarticulate boy Josh's older brother asks to keep the school bully off Josh's case, asks Josh for help with another girl problem. Josh soon finds out that his promise to help out comes with a price—one he may not be willing to pay. *Josh* is a late first-year or early second-year Chinese reader. In Chinese the title is 独一无二 (*Dúyīwú'èr*, Unique.) The story is 18,260 characters long, and uses 417 unique Chinese characters.

Middle School

So far, there isn't much out there for kids in middle school and up. Pretty much the only two series available right now are *Chinese Breeze* and *Chinese Biographies*. Both are used by several Mandarin immersion middle schools as reading material. They skew a little old, and are probably better suited to high school and college students. None of them are real page-turners, but at least they're not picture books or the same old Chinese legends students have been hearing since kindergarten. Both mark foreign names so students don't stumble over unfamiliar transliterations.

Chinese Breeze

This series is from Peking University Press. There are books at the 300-, 500- and 750 word levels. The stories are a little dull and don't necessarily capture the interest of younger children. They're more meant for high school and college students. Still, they come with websites where the story is read aloud, which is really helpful as the student can read along. They're not too difficult for upper grade immersion students to read.

http://www.cheng-tsui.com/store/products/chinese_breeze

Chinese Biographies

The *Chinese Biographies* series features five books about modern Chinese cultural icons that can be read by students who've mastered between 350 and 700 characters. The titles include biographies of:

- Yao Ming, basketball player
- Lang Lang, pianist
- Vera Wang, clothing designer
- Jay Chou, pop star
- Jeremy Lin, basketball player
- Ang Lee, director

The summer before sixth grade my daughter struggled with the Jay Chou book. But then halfway through seventh grade I gave her the book about Yao Ming and she said, "Hey, this is interesting about basketball in China." So their reading ability actually does get better over time when they do more of it!

http://www.chinesebiographies.com

1. This comes from the saying, "The rich get richer but the poor get poorer." That in turn comes from a verse in the Book of Matthew 24:29: "For to all those who have, more will be given, and they will have an abundance; but from those who have nothing, even what they have will be taken away." Paraphrased, that becomes "The (book) rich get richer and the (book) poor get poorer." The term was coined by education researcher Keith Stanovish in 1990.
2. TPRStories. Teaching proficiency through reading & storytelling. http://www.tprstories.com/what-is-tprs
   Accessed May 26, 2014.

十八
shí bā
18

For Chinese-Speaking Parents: Raising "Tigers with Wings"

This book is written primarily for families who don't speak Chinese. However, in researching immersion I've learned some things that might be useful for Chinese-speaking families. I'm neither Chinese nor a Chinese speaker, although my children are *hapa*[1] and their father, aunt, uncle and grandparents are all Mandarin speakers. So it is neither my culture nor my heritage. Here I offer what I've gathered with all humility, with the hope it might be of some use.

The news for Chinese-speaking families is good and bad when it comes to immersion programs. The good news is that students in these programs find a community outside their families in which speaking Chinese is normal, encouraged and rewarded. All the research shows that children of immigrants in the United States very easily lose their home language and switch to English. That's because they get little outside motivation to use their parents' language, and lots of motivation to drop it—children don't like to be different from their peers. In immersion, your child will be surrounded by peers learning Chinese.

As one Taiwanese mom with two children in a Mandarin immersion program put it:

> I could have sent my kids to a General Education program and supplemented them with Mandarin at after-school or Saturday school. But I know from my own experience that this kind of setup is not effective to induce my kids to learn Mandarin.

For her family, the school "created an environment to let the kids know that it is okay to speak Mandarin in this English-dominated society, an important starting point." She especially wanted this because her husband doesn't speak Chinese, so the children only heard it from her.

Another mom said that although she always speaks to her daughter in Mandarin, until her daughter began attending a Mandarin immersion kindergarten "she would only ever answer me in English. Now she speaks Mandarin with me at home."

The other good news is that students in Mandarin immersion programs reach and frequently exceed the levels of English attained by Chinese-speaking students in English-only programs.

The bad news is that Mandarin immersion programs expect a much lower level of Chinese literacy than Chinese-speaking parents typically expect and want. Programs don't teach children enough characters and don't ramp up quickly enough, or ever, to make them fluent readers. One mom, who launched into a program of teaching her son more characters at home, said that if she'd waited for the program to do so, "I would have sold my kid's ability to learn Chinese very short."

In a nutshell, students from Chinese-speaking households in Mandarin immersion programs are:

- More likely to embrace Chinese and continue to speak it into adulthood, unlike many immigrant children who reject Chinese and switch to speaking only English so they can 'fit in.'

- Reach, and frequently exceed, the levels of English attained by Chinese-speaking students in English-only programs.

- Learn as much and probably more Chinese as students in English programs who attend Saturday Chinese school (this is highly dependent on the quality of the Saturday Chinese school.)

- Are in classes with children from families who are also very education-minded, so the interest and abilities of the majority of students are often higher than they might otherwise be.

On the downside:

- They do not read and write Chinese as well as similar-age students in China or Taiwan would.

- These programs are seldom as rigorous as Chinese parents wish them to be.

- Students receive an American-style education, with less of a focus on academics than some Chinese parents would wish for.

The Chinese isn't good enough

The main complaint I hear from families who speak and read Chinese is that the level of Chinese taught in immersion programs is woefully low, especially the level of reading and writing. Interestingly, families in which the parents only speak Chinese but do not read it, whose parents or grandparents came from China, are not as concerned about this. But for parents who are literate in Chinese, this is a huge issue and one that isn't going to go away.

"I would say that most of us Chinese-speaking parents, and even those who are not, have extremely high expectations that may or may not be realistic," said Hann-Yu Chang, whose children attend Field Elementary School in Pasadena, California. "Parents do not realize what they are up against."

The reading ability of students in Mandarin immersion programs is generally two to five grade levels below their counterparts in China or Taiwan. (Though note that what families do at home to foster literacy can make a huge difference in this. See *Chapter 17: How To Get Your Child Reading in Chinese* for more information.) That means that an eighth grader in a Chinese immersion program in the United States could be reading at the same level as a third grader in China, though they could also be reading at the same level as a sixth grader. Not surprisingly, students who do all their homework tend to read at a higher level than students who don't. But no programs achieve literacy levels that would be anywhere near grade level in China.

This is unacceptable and frustrating to Chinese parents. However, programs are geared to the needs of English-speaking students and the expectations of English-speaking families, as we live in an English-speaking nation. Mandarin immersion programs typically only teach 20 to 30 new characters a month, whereas many Chinese parents feel their children should be learning that many a week. Programs seem reluctant to push students to do more, especially when they face complaints from English-speaking parents that the homework is already too hard.

Here's an example of even the most basic rigor that these parents want but don't always get: Almost all Mandarin immersion programs send students home with daily or weekly worksheets covering the new characters. These usually consist of the character, its stroke order and radical, and some examples of words that contain it. The worksheet has a line of character-sized boxes and the students write a character in each box.

In China and Taiwan these boxes would all have faint dotted lines through them, breaking them into nine squares or sometimes into eight wedges. The character being taught is also presented in this grid. When students practice writing the character, they use the grid lines to guide them in placing the characters' component parts correctly into a pleasing (and correct) whole. Bunching up pieces of a character, or having them in the wrong proportions, is just plain wrong. It not only looks horrible but also makes the character difficult to read.

However, parents in some programs have had a hard time getting schools to institute something as simple as placing the grid lines on student homework and working with children to correctly compose their characters. Without those lines, it takes more work and more precision to make the characters look right. However that level of detail isn't always a priority for programs. For parents who learned to write in China, it's as if their child was allowed to have the world's worst handwriting the whole way through high school—and no one cared enough to make it better.

Reading

In our grade school, Starr King Elementary, several Chinese-speaking families left the program because they were unhappy with the rigor and level of Chinese being taught. Others worked at home with their children using textbooks and workbooks to increase the number of characters their children can read. A popular series is the 中文 *Zhongwen* books,[2] which are published by the Overseas Chinese Language and Culture Education office in Shanghai. These books are meant for use by Chinese-speaking pupils in Saturday Chinese schools and progress from first through twelfth grade. They systematically introduce 2,500 characters and build a solid reading vocabulary relatively quickly. Much as many American parents send their children to Kumon[3] and other tutoring programs to support math and English, these Chinese parents work through the *Zhongwen* books to raise their children's reading level.

One mother whose son was in a Mandarin immersion kindergarten said:

> I got my hands on *Zhongwen* and saw my child's potential in more than just responding in simple phrases in Chinese. He now has more than 100 character count. And many more 'new' characters from the readings at the end of each lessons.

These families started a weekly study group for their children as they worked through the books at home and overall have been pleased with the results. However, what they really would like is the school to push students harder and have them learn more Chinese.

But there are upsides for Chinese-speaking families

Despite the low level of literacy achieved in most programs, immersion is still valued by many Chinese-speaking families for the simple fact that it helps them ensure that their children will not lose their Chinese.

While it might seem counter-intuitive, immersion can help Chinese-speaking parents who want their children to grow up fully bilingual. Many families ask why, if they already speak Chinese, do they need immersion? But as parent experience and research shows, being in an immersion classroom not only helps children want to keep and improve their Chinese, but gives them access to academic language that they might not get at home.

It won't be anywhere near the same level as the Chinese their parents learned in school in China, Taiwan or Hong Kong, but they will know a great deal more than they would have if they went to an English-only school here in the United States. In addition, there is ample evidence that immersion encourages children to remain bilingual against the push of English. As countless generations of immigrants can attest, maintaining a home language in the face of an overwhelming tide of English is not easy. As one study put it, "without considerable and repeated societal reinforcement," long-term home language development is unlikely."[4]

Dr. Lucy Tse was a professor of applied linguistics and education and is now a senior researcher at the Center for Educational Development in Los Angeles. She has studied the issue of heritage language loss extensively. "Heritage languages vanish from immigrant families as children learn English and prefer it over the home language," she writes, something she and many others consider "one of the most fundamental erosions of a national resource in this country."[5]

Some conservatives have claimed that immigrants resist giving up their native languages. The exact opposite is actually true. Few families are able to keep their native language strong past the third generation, and often lose it by the second. Among Chinese-Americans, cultural assimilation and the shift from speaking Chinese to English starts happening with the first generation to grow up in the United States. By the time the second generation grows up, Chinese is often totally lost. Even if they do speak Chinese, the kids prefer English and feel "considerable pressure to assimilate, both culturally and linguistically, writes Kathryn Lindholm-Leary, an expert on immersion and bilingual programs."[6]

This seemingly inexorable loss of heritage languages, what linguists call "language shift," is a powerful process that always favors the language of the country over the language of the family.[7]

While this was once considered a necessary, and by some even a good outcome, in today's world we know it is an enormous loss. The United States spends billions of dollars each year attempting to teach American college students and adults how to speak foreign languages so we can be a part of the global community. At the same time, each year tens of thousands of children who are fluent speakers of Spanish, Chinese and other languages lose the ability and become monoglot English speakers.

The odd thing about the United States is that while we're theoretically an English-speaking nation, in actuality we're multilingual. According to the U.S. Census, 20% of Americans speak another language at home.[8] But too many people (sometimes our own children) see that as a negative, not a positive. The U.S. view can be very black and white—either you are a native speaker of English or you can't speak English well enough to function. The concept of highly-educated citizens of the world who move effortlessly between multiple languages (including English) is common and indeed expected elsewhere. However it is not one that we as a nation have embraced.

Thankfully, this is beginning to change. There are more opportunities for families to help their children deepen their mastery of their home language while still attaining fluency in English. That's good, because research shows that being bilingual is overwhelmingly a good thing. It has no negative effects on a person's ability to function in society. In fact, people who are fully bilingual do better in school[9] and, according to multiple studies, have stronger, more elastic brains. There's even evidence that being bilingual can delay the onset of Alzheimer's disease symptoms![10] For more on this, see *Chapter 8: Being Bilingual is Better.*

But as parents who speak Chinese know, ensuring that children grow up bilingual and biliterate in both English and Chinese while living in the United States isn't easy.

How immersion can keep Chinese alive

Mandarin immersion can help families who want to keep their children fluent in Chinese by creating "an environment to let the kids know that it is okay to speak Mandarin in this English-dominated society," as one mom from Taiwan put it.

It can be painful for parents when their children reject their own language and culture because they somehow feel they must stop being Chinese to become American. Without having a school where Mandarin is a cool and useful thing, kids who speak Chinese at home begin to see it as having lower social status and less prestige.[11] They start speaking English when they're out with their parents because they are embarrassed to speak differently than their friends. But in an immersion program, their friends, their teacher and everyone around them is speaking Mandarin. Numerous studies also show that students in bilingual programs are less stressed in school, participate more in class, and have better grades and fewer behavior problems.[12]

In many programs, students who speak Chinese at a native level are looked up to by the other children. In fact being part of the "in" group in immersion schools is so much about being Chinese that my hapa, brown-haired daughters at times have wished aloud that they had nice, straight, black hair, "like everyone else."

Why keep Chinese?

It is not uncommon for Chinese-speaking families to be asked by English speakers why, when they've moved to the United States, they want to go to the trouble of retaining Chinese. There are multiple reasons beyond the obvious "Why *wouldn't* you want your children to speak two languages?"

First, any parent wants their children to speak the language of their family, their relatives and their heritage.

There's also ample evidence that students who are fluent in both their home language and English do better in school, have higher grades and get better jobs than students who lose their heritage language.[13]

Also, Mandarin today isn't just a heritage language that helps kids stay better connected to their families. It's a world language used in a country that's a major player on the global stage. Both politically and economically, it's likely to become only more important as our children grow up. Many Chinese parents hope their children will maintain their Mandarin so they can easily move back and forth between the United States and China, Taiwan or Singapore as adults.

In fact, Chinese-Americans who can speak both Chinese and English are sometimes called "tigers with wings" because they are so competitive in the job market.[14]

Most Chinese-American adults are bilingual. In 2008, 83% reported they spoke a language in addition to English at home (Cantonese, Mandarin, Taiwanese or another language).[15] But ensuring that their children are also bilingual is difficult. Children must first believe that Chinese is important and worthy. Though they grow up in Chinese-speaking homes, kids are exposed to English at school, on TV, in movies and even in video games. It's too easy for them to shift from Chinese to English and leave Chinese behind. Plus English is the language of the dominant culture and children hate being different. Parents may be proud of their Chinese identity but children want to be just like their friends.

Research shows that bilingual children in bilingual or immersion classes are much more likely to keep their home language, because it helps them develop a strong sense of linguistic identity. This in turn is protective against the very common experience among immigrant families of children rejecting their family's heritage and language so they can claim an American identity. This is a well-known trajectory for immigrant children and young adults and can result in heartache, dislocation and family disunity.

Dr. Tse writes that for students "how well you speak English determines in large part your status in the school, with the new immigrants at the bottom of the ladder." Studies have shown that "English fluency is a badge to prestige, a membership card for entry into the mainstream. English is one of the primary keys to fitting in and being accepted."[16]

The good news is that in an immersion classroom *both* languages have social prestige so children don't feel that to become "real Americans" they have to give up their home language. In a book on heritage language retention, Tse says that many children go through four stages of embracing their ethnicity:[17]

- *Unawareness*, the period when children don't realize they are any different from mainstream culture.

- *Ethnic Ambivalence/Evasion*, when children begin to feel negative about their home culture and prefer to identify with the dominant culture. This can be permanent and is common among children of immigrants.

- *Ethnic Emergence*, when children begin to explore and embrace their own culture.

- *Ethnic Identity Incorporation*, when children or young adults accept their ethnic background and embrace that they are part of both it and the dominant (in this case, American) culture.

Tse has found that children who retain their home language have a much easier time embracing both their ethnic identity and American culture, and suffer much less self-doubt and self-hatred.[18]

Most kids lose their Chinese

Many children in the United States who arrive at kindergarten fully fluent in their parents' native language end up only speaking English. For Chinese speakers, the younger the child is when they come to America the less likely they are to speak Chinese well when they're older. One study of Mandarin-speaking children found that students who arrived in the U.S. when they were younger than nine switched their preferred language from Chinese to English within a year.[19] Students who came to the U.S. before the age of 12 lost more Chinese than students who came after the age of 12.

Interestingly, the better educated the parent, the less likely their child will continue to speak Chinese. The researchers found that students with lower family incomes were more likely to continue to speak Chinese, probably because their parents didn't speak English as well, so they had to use more Chinese. "Those with higher income, higher educational levels, and better English abilities assimilate more successfully, and subsequently use Chinese less."[20]

So the younger a child is when he or she comes to the United States, the better educated his or her parents are and the higher their family income, the less chance he or she will retain proficiency in Chinese.

It's not simple to keep Chinese alive at home. Often parents are just as busy as the child trying to find their place in an English-speaking world. For Ining Chao in British Columbia, Canada, it was hard enough for her to keep a strong sense of her own cultural identity after settling in Victoria, called "the most English of Canadian cities."

She says, "If the parents can have a strong sense of their own cultural identity, they will have a better chance of being a role model and guiding the children's development. I struggle with this one myself. Being an immigrant, I have forgotten my roots for 10 years. I have to make an effort to find my own voice and my own identity as a bilingual person."

Sometimes parents' eagerness to support their kids' English works against Chinese. Chinese parents are heavily involved in their children's educational development, much more so than many parents in the United States. In China, they focus on Chinese literacy. In the United States they tend to switch those efforts to English literacy—at the expense of Chinese. Researchers and authors of a 2008 study who studied the children of Chinese immigrants in the United States found that the parents focused on English and ignored Chinese.

"To grasp every opportunity for their children to learn English, the parents and sometimes grandparents demonstrated interest in learning English by reading books or being read to by their children. Although they agreed that their home language was important, the parents believe that their children must have good English to go to college and have college degrees to obtain decent jobs. In the home environment, the children's oral use of Chinese gradually decreased and was eventually replaced by English."[21]

In Pasadena, Hann-Yu Chang has seen the same split in her family, depending on whether family members immigrated or were born in the United States. "I observe that even within my family, based on whether or not they had immigrated to the U.S. This is true of my grandparents, uncles, aunts, cousins, household help, caretakers and their children who have immigrated even more recently and are desperately trying to learn and improve upon their English."

It can be remarkably difficult to get family members to speak Chinese with children. I see this with my own girls, whose paternal grandparents are both native Mandarin speakers and who speak Mandarin with each other. However they seldom speak Chinese with the girls. That's partly because, until recently, the girls' Chinese wasn't really good enough to have an easy conversation. It's also because they're used to speaking English with their children and with their other grandchildren, so it just doesn't come naturally to look at a child and switch to Chinese.

They are wonderfully gracious and helpful when reminded, but it feels very disrespectful to be "correcting" them by always saying "*Zhongwen!*" (Chinese!) to the girls when they're with their grandparents.

In Pasadena, Chang has the same problem with her husband's family, who are all native Spanish speakers. "They often do the translation thing, or forget to speak in Spanish because they are concentrating so hard on English that they have a hard time switching between the two."

Here's a long quote from Jim Cummings, one of the leading world authorities on language acquisition and bilingualism, about children losing their home language and how quickly it can go—before parents even realize it's happening.

"Many people marvel at how quickly bilingual children seem to 'pick up' conversational skills in the majority language in the early years at school (although it takes much longer for them to catch up to native speakers in academic language skills). However, educators are often much less aware about how quickly children can lose their ability to use their mother tongues, even in the home context. The extent and rapidity of language loss will vary according to the concentration of families from a particular linguistic group in the school and neighborhood. Where the mother tongue is used extensively in the community outside the school, then language loss among young children will be less. However, where language communities are not concentrated or 'ghettoized' in particular neighborhoods, children can lose their ability to communicate in their mother tongue within two to three years of starting school. They may retain receptive (understanding) skills in the language but they will use the majority language in speaking with their peers and siblings and in responding to their parents. By the time children become adolescents, the linguistic gap between parents and children has become an emotional chasm. Pupils frequently become alienated from the cultures of both home and school with predictable results."[22]

For bilingual families

Many families who have children in Chinese immersion have one parent who speaks Chinese (or at least some Chinese) and one who speaks English. For those families, there's a wonderful book on how to raise bilingual children in a monolingual country by a Finnish educator named Annika Bourgogne. She speaks Finnish, Swedish, English and French, and is married to a Frenchman. They live in Finland and she and her husband have worked very hard to raise their daughters to be bilingual in both French and Finnish (while also learning English and Swedish in school.)

Bourgogne's story will resonate with many families. Her family is part of the Swedish-speaking minority in Finland and her family spoke Swedish in addition to Finnish. But when she was growing up she wanted to fit in with Finnish society so she turned her back on Swedish and quickly lost the ability to speak it. She then had to go to the work of learning it again later in life to reconnect with her roots. That lesson, of how easy it is to lose a language that's spoken at home, pushed her to make sure her daughters spoke not only Finnish with her, but French with their father. She never wanted them to be cut off from their cultural heritage in the ways she cut herself off from hers.

Her 2012 book, *Be Bilingual: Practical Ideas for Multilingual Families*, is full of excellent advice on how to do the day-to-day work of ensuring that children don't lose their parents' languages. I highly recommend it.

What about English?

While making sure their children continue to speak Chinese is nice, the most common questions Chinese-speaking families ask about immersion are:

- Will my child learn English quickly and well?
- Will my child benefit from the Chinese instruction, given that we already speak Chinese at home?

Overall research shows that almost all students who arrive in the United States speaking no English go on to speak English "well" or "very well." Researchers at Princeton and Johns Hopkins University studied more than 5,000 eighth and ninth graders in Miami and San Diego and found that they acquired English "well and with striking rapidity, and they are doing well in U.S. school."[23] Asians did very well; 90.3% of students spoke English well or very well.

The best answer to that question comes from a study published in 2011 by Kathryn Lindholm-Leary[24]. She is a professor of Child and Adolescent Development at San Jose State University and an immersion language expert who had done several of the major, definitive studies of Spanish language immersion programs. Hers was the first study of Chinese immersion programs in elementary and middle schools. She looked at two established Chinese immersion programs in California and found that students in these programs:

- made excellent progress in both languages
- scored at or above grade level in English
- performed at comparable or often superior levels compared to non-two-way-immersion peers
- reported an interest in and knowledge about Chinese culture

In all public Mandarin immersion programs, schools use the same district and state English curriculum standards as the English programs. So for the English portion of the day students use all same textbooks and learn the same things as they would if they were in a 100% English school. The students Lindholm-Leary studied scored higher in English overall. Those who weren't native English speakers became fully fluent in English more quickly and ended up doing *better* than native English speakers in English-only programs, her research found.

Lindholm-Leary's research shows that students from Chinese-speaking families not only learn English as well as or better than English-speaking students but also keep their Chinese—which as we've seen isn't easy to do without some kind of outside instruction supporting it.[25]

The numbers are even more impressive than you might imagine. Students in these two Chinese immersion programs achieved levels much higher than would be expected given their parents' educational backgrounds. Across California, between 62 and 73% of fourth- through eighth-grade students whose parents have a college education achieve Proficient or Advanced, and about a third score as Advanced in English Language Arts.

At the first school, the students had the same scores, but only *half* had parents with a college degree and a third had parents who have a high school diploma or less.

In the second school, the students achieve at very high levels in English Language Arts. Almost all students, 89 to 100%, achieved at least Proficient and most, 65 to 77%, reached Advanced. They did even better in math. All in all, the data show that students in Chinese immersion programs easily match and often surpass the achievements of their English-speaking monolingual peers.[26]

Wouldn't a Saturday school have the same effect?

Heritage schools, sometimes called Saturday schools, have a long history in the Chinese community. The first one was launched in San Francisco, in 1886. In 2009 there were an estimated 1,205 such schools teaching 180,000 students in the United States.[27]

Today, these schools come in many types. In some large cities they offer popular after-school programs for children who may or may not speak Chinese at home. They often teach not only Chinese reading and writing but also give support in other subjects. Vickie Tsui, a Mandarin-speaking mom in Silicon Valley, says among her sons' friends, attending these programs is very common:

> Over the last few years, there has been a huge rise in the interest in Mandarin, leading to increased numbers of competing 'community Chinese schools' throughout the country. I suspect the nature of these schools has also changed somewhat. For example, I have two friends in Boston whose non-Asian kids are all going to after-school Chinese programs. For them, the main reason was actually not so much to learn Chinese. It was because they felt that public schools were teaching math too slowly, and they wanted their kids to be exposed to more advanced math, which these Chinese schools offer.

In fact, several people I know in the Bay area also switched to Chinese after-school programs because the alternative after-school programs were not structured or academic enough.

In areas where there are high numbers of Chinese-speaking families, going to an after-school Chinese program can simply be normal. In her blog, "How to Raise Bilingual Children," Tsui writes that her sons go to Chinese school when their elementary school day ends at 3:00:

> Our elementary school has several vans waiting to pick up students from competing Chinese schools—students no longer feel like they are outliers for going to Chinese school. Two of our son's non-Asian friends have told their parents they also wanted to go to Chinese school, since that's where their best friends were going.[28]

Of course that isn't always the case. For some students going to Chinese school, especially Saturday school, keeps them apart from their friends. They can't play sports that have games on Saturday and have to miss out on many group activities the rest of their classmates can do. Many Chinese-American parents don't have fond memories of Saturday school. Some remember doing everything they could to avoid it. One mom told me this story:

> A friend of mine recently told me that her mom used to drop her off at Saturday school, and she would walk to the back of the school, call her friends to have them pick her up, and she'd hang out with them until it was time for her mom to pick her up.

Saturday schools also are for a much shorter period of time each week than the hours spent studying Mandarin in an immersion school. This affects how much can be taught. Here's what a mom who attended Saturday school herself and now has a child in a Mandarin immersion program says:

> For kids whose primary language is English at home (for the various reasons you discuss), they learn much less in Saturday school than in immersion. They might get a similar number of characters, but with only 2–3 hours of class/week, they get forgotten REALLY quickly (like 10 minutes after the exam is over). Of course, this isn't based on a study, but my personal experience and the experience of my friends. Also, they don't learn academic Chinese at all (math vocabulary like shapes, "odd number," "even number" and science terms).

Tammy Chiang studied in a Chinese-strand school in Singapore and now lives in the United States. For her, Saturday schools aren't the same as actual school.

> In Singapore, we take Chinese language class every day. It just has to be that way. You can't learn a language by going to school once

a week. This also doesn't work for parents who enjoy taking their children outdoors like my husband and I. In addition, a parent has to ask himself/herself, would he/she like to attend weekend school after five days of working? Nobody would, unless they are so motivated, and motivation has to come from oneself, not pushed by the parent.

However, there isn't much data comparing how students in Chinese heritage schools and immersion schools do. The only example I could find that was even slightly similar looked at attitudes towards home language in a group of Italian-speaking eighth graders in Toronto. The study compared students who attended a Saturday Italian school with students who attended an integrated Italian home language program within their regular school day. The students in the program outside of school felt strongly, "that Italian was not a legitimate school subject because it was not part of the 'official' school curriculum."[29] Students in a school-based Italian program embraced the language.

None of this is to say that language schools are bad. For many families they're the only way their children can learn to read and write Chinese, either because there aren't immersion schools where they live or because they couldn't get in. Also, many heritage schools today are changing their curriculum from the older, more formal format to more modern teaching methods.

However, not all schools are up to the task, say researchers:

Chinese community schools are not yet a full-fledged education system but transient gap-filler between home and mainstream school. They are characterized by minimal operation (two to three hours per week), insufficient funding provision (makeshift classrooms and facilities), and out-of-date traditional teaching practices (instructors are mostly untrained volunteers). The majority of the interviews in this study complained about boredom and lack of age/level-appropriate tasks in Chinese community schools.[30]

These researchers interviewed 130 college students from Chinese-speaking homes who were taking Chinese at three American universities. Sixty percent of these students had attended community Chinese schools when they were children. They reported that they normally studied there for two to three hours per week for one or two years and dropped out after kindergarten or grade school started.

When asked why they dropped out, the typical answer was "I hated going to Chinese Sunday school. It was boring!" When asked what they did in Chinese Sunday schools, the answer was "we learned pinyin, wrote names, character strokes, some simple characters, sang children's songs and read kids' stories."[31]

Dr. Keiko Koda, a professor of second language acquisition at Carnegie Mellon University in Pittsburgh, Pennsylvania. has done research on both Japanese and Chinese heritage language schools in the United States. She told me she hasn't seen evidence that "heritage language schools teach more characters [than immersion schools] if that's what people are assuming." The level of character knowledge and therefore literacy is probably about the same, she says. "So I don't think heritage language school learners have an advantage."

How about waiting until high school or college to learn to read Chinese?

Some Chinese-speaking families decide that their children will learn to speak Chinese at home and wait until high school or college, when they can take academic courses in Chinese, to learn to read and write. This can work but has down sides.

One issue is that high school courses are generally not designed for heritage speakers, so students come in at a very different level than the other students. Sometimes they're not even allowed to take beginning Mandarin because they're considered native speakers—but they don't read and write, so they can't take advanced Mandarin. A few colleges, mostly on the West coast, offer classes for heritage speakers but researchers have found that they're often not a good fit.

> Heritage language students are treated either the same as non-heritage language students and then placed in classes they are over-qualified for (and consequently often bored with), or simply dismissed as 'native speakers' who do not need any instruction, or are discussed derisively by administrators, teachers and classmates as people seeking inflated grades, "an easy A."[32]

Linguistics expert Ann Kelleher did an extensive study of students taking Mandarin at a large California university. The majority of students taking Mandarin identified themselves as Chinese-American. While many of them could speak fluently, they couldn't read and write, so they didn't actually feel that they "knew" Chinese. She found the students were frustrated trying to learn to read and write Chinese because the way Chinese is taught in college, for non-speakers, didn't mesh well with their abilities. The courses presumed they needed to learn everything, including grammar, when they knew the grammar and often spoke quite well.

"They also get grief from other students and sometimes from teachers who think they've signed up 'just to get an easy A' when they actually want to become literate in the language they grew up in," she said.[33]

Immersion as a way to combat language shyness

Language shyness may not be a phrase most parents are familiar with but it's something they've certainly seen either in their own families or in those of friends. It's the phenomenon in which people who grew up speaking a language at home are afraid to use it because they don't feel they speak it well enough.[34] This often occurs because the person speaks "baby" or "kitchen" Chinese, as some call it. They never had a chance to develop an adult, educated vocabulary and don't know the formal, polite forms they easily use in English.

The shyness gets even worse as children get older. When they're little it's okay if they speak like little kids, but when they become teenagers adults expect them to speak like grown-ups. Language researcher and University of Southern California emeritus professor Stephen Krashen quotes one university student who grew up speaking Spanish.

> My father still ... interrupts me repeatedly every time I speak Spanish in his presence to correct my grammar or pronunciation. I do my best to speak only English in his company.[35]

Having parents correct them can stop young people from trying to speak their home language at all. "Rather than risk error, they interact less in the heritage language. This sets up a vicious cycle—less interaction means less input, and less input means less proficiency."[36]

Immersion can be a benefit here as well because instruction in Mandarin comes from teachers in a school setting where everyone is learning, not at home in what can be a more emotionally fraught environment. It also helps children acquire more adult, formal forms of the language that aren't normally part of parent-child interactions.

Researchers have studied this phenomenon extensively. Among Spanish speaking students, it's been shown that they require training to be able to move from the informal speech of talking with friends and family to the more formal kinds of speaking and writing required in academic and business settings.[37]

Parents sometimes think the distinction is between children's language and adult language but it's really about education. The parents were generally educated in Spanish in their home countries and know how to use Spanish in formal settings. The children haven't learned that—and it's not something one can pick up just talking to friends and family and watching TV.

It's certainly not only a Spanish issue. One man I know grew up speaking Mandarin at home but didn't learn to speak "grown-up" Mandarin until he went to college and took it as a class there. Yet somehow his parents, especially his father, expected him to be able to:

> magically speak as they did—but they went to college and graduate school in Taiwan, so of course they knew formal, academic Chinese. It wasn't until I had finished two years of college level Chinese that I think my dad finally started to interact with me like an adult, because we could speak to each other using adult language and I wasn't always stuck in the "kid" role.

Parents may think that simply by speaking Chinese at home they're giving their children the same opportunities in the language they themselves had growing up in China or Taiwan. But it isn't really the full language, only a piece of it.[38] Jin-huei Enya Dai and Lihua Zhang did a survey of college students who were Chinese heritage speakers in the San Francisco Bay area. They found that for many of these students, Chinese is something that's only good enough for home use. One student said,

> 中文我只是在家里说得、跟别人不同好意思。　　　　　　　[sic]
> Zhōngwén wǒ zhǐshì zài jiālǐ shuō de, gēn biérén bùtóng hào yì si.
> "I only speak Chinese at home. It's embarrassing to speak it with others."[39]

Enrolling in an immersion program takes away some of this embarrassment, because all the students are learning Chinese and it's expected that they'll make mistakes. It normalizes Chinese as something that exists both at home and out in the world. In immersion classes, both Chinese-speaking and those who don't speak Chinese at home move from grade to grade together, learning year by year how to use more formal, educated and adult forms. And it can be easier to take criticism and correction from a teacher than from a parent.

What can parents do?

Language researchers are very clear on the steps necessary for parents to raise children who are fluent in their home language:

- Speak your language, and only your language, to your children.
- Don't answer them when they speak English to you.
- Don't translate, saying a phrase first in your language and then in English. Research shows that when parents translate into English, children don't bother to listen to the first language—they know they'll be able to understand the English so they tune out the rest.

Vickie Tsui has some nice tips in her blog "How to Raise Bilingual Children 双语教育成功的秘法."[40] And Carmen Cordovez, a mom with a daughter in my daughter's class, has some lovely posts on the topic at "InCultureParent: For Parents raising little global citizens."[41] The blog has a whole section on raising bilingual children. [42]

But to be honest, this isn't that easy to do. I have many, many friends who struggle against a daily tsunami of English, fighting to speak only Chinese or Spanish or Swedish or Dutch with their children. It's easier when both parents speak the language, so at least they can always use it at home. If only one does, it's more of an effort. These parents speak English all day at work, they speak English with their spouse, and then they try to always speak their native language to their child. It's like "juggling dictionaries" as one mom described it to me. Plus her kids hate it when she makes them answer her in Swedish in the grocery store. They think it makes them sound "weird."

All of which is to say that if your kids are in a Mandarin immersion program you'll have some backup. It's another chunk of their lives when they're around adults who speak, read and write Chinese, and expect and require them to use it, and use it properly. That, according to many parents, is a huge help.

1. *Hapa* is a Hawai'ian word that means "part" or "mixed." It's commonly used in Hawai'i to refer to any person of mixed ethnic heritage. In California it's often used to mean someone who is part Asian or Pacific Islander. It's a nice way to say someone is a mix of things and one a lot of families we know embrace. As our girls' dad points out, they are not *half* anything—they are *all* themselves. They're all Chinese-American and they're all white-bread American. (Okay, he doesn't call us that, but given my wife's and my collective Irish-English-German ancestry, I feel pretty comfortable with that description.)
2. http://www.zhongwentextbook.org
   Their ordering program is difficult to navigate. Another option is NanHai Books, which also makes them available.
   http://www.nanhaibooks.com/language-learning/k-6/
   chinese-language.html
3. Kumon is a math and reading program that originated in Japan. It is intended to supplement school lessons. Students progress through the program at their own pace, moving on to the next level when they have achieved mastery of the previous level. Every day they have a packet of problems or reading that takes about 15 minutes to complete.
   http://www.kumon.com
4. Joshua A. Fishman, Michael H. Gertner, Esther G. Lowy, *Ethnicity in Action: The Community Resources of Ethnic Languages in the United States* (Binghamton, NY, Bilingual Press, 1997.)
5. Lucy Tse, *"Why Don't They Learn English?" Separating Fact from Fallacy in the U.S. Language Debate* (New York, Teachers College Press, 2001) 30.

6. Kathryn Lindholm-Leary, "Student Outcomes in Chinese Two-Way Immersion Programs: Language Proficiency, Academic Achievement, and Student Attitudes," in D. Tedick, D. Christian and Tara Fortune (Eds.), *Immersion education: Practices, Policies, Possibilities.* (Avon, England: Multilingual Matters, 2011.)

7. Stephen Krashen, "Heritage Language Development: Some Practical Arguments." in Stephen Krashen, Lucy Tse and Jeff McQuillan (Eds.), *Heritage Language Development* (Culver City, Calif.: Language Education Associates, 1998) 3.

8. United States Census Bureau, "New Census Bureau Report Analyzes Nation's Linguistic Diversity."
http://www.census.gov/newsroom/releases/archives/american_community survey_acs/cb10-cn58.html
Accessed June 6, 2014.

9. Stephen Krashen, "Heritage Language Development: Some Practical Arguments." in Stephen Krashen, Lucy Tse and Jeff McQuillan (Eds.), *Heritage Language Development* (Culver City, Calif.: Language Education Associates, 1998) 7.

10. Claudia Drifus, "The Bilingual Advantage," *The New York Times*, May 30, 2011.
http://www.nytimes.com/2011/05/31/science/31conversation.html?_r=0
Accessed June 6, 2014.

11. Jin-Huie Enya Dai, Lihua Zhang, "What Are the Chinese Home Language Learners Inheriting? *Habitus* of the Chinese Home Language Learners," in Agnes Weiyun He and Yun Xiao (Eds.) *Chinese as a Heritage Language: Fostering Rooted World Citizenry* (National Foreign Language Resource Center, University of Hawai'i at Manoa, 2008) 3752.

12. Lucy Tse, "Affecting Affect: The Impact of Heritage Language Programs on Student Attitudes," in Stephen Krashen, Lucy Tse and Jeff McQuillan (Eds.), *Heritage Language Development* (Culver City, Calif.: Language Education Associates. 1998) 66.

13. Stephen Krashen, "Heritage Language Development: Some Practical Arguments." in Stephen Krashen, Lucy Tse and Jeff McQuillan (Eds.), *Heritage Language Development* (Culver City, Calif.: Language Education Associates, 1998) 9.

14. Na Liu, "The Linguistic Vitality of Chinese in the United States," *Heritage Language Journal*, Winter, 2013, 9.
http://www.heritagelanguages.org/Journal.aspx
Accessed Jan. 23, 2013.

15. U.S. Census Bureau. "More Working Women Than Men Have College Degrees, Census Bureau reports" April 26, 2011.
http://www.census.gov/newsroom/releases/archives/education/cb11-72.html
Accessed Jan. 13, 2014.

16. Lucy Tse, "Why don't they learn English?" *Separating Fact from Fallacy in the U.S. Language Debate* (New York, Teachers College Press, 2001) 19.

17. Lucy Tse, "Ethnic Identity Formation and Its Implications for Heritage Language Development," in Stephen Krashen, Lucy Tse and Jeff McQuillan (Eds.), *Heritage Language Development* (Culver City, Calif., Language Education Associates, 1998) 15.

18. Stephen Krashen, "Heritage Language Development: Some Practical Arguments." in Stephen Krashen, Lucy Tse and Jeff McQuillan (Eds.), *Heritage Language Development* (Culver City, Calif.: Language Education Associates, 1998) 15–27.

19. Gizela Jia, "Heritage Language Development, Maintenance, and Attrition Among Recent Chinese Immigrants in New York City," in Agnes Weiyun He and Yun Xiao (Eds.) *Chinese as a Heritage Language: Fostering Rooted World Citizenry*

(National Foreign Language Resource Center, University of Hawai'i at Manoa, 2008) 196.

20. Gisela Jia, "Heritage Language Development, Maintenance, and Attrition Among Recent Chinese Immigrants in New York City," in Agnes Weiyun He and Yun Xiao (Eds.), *Chinese as a Heritage Language: Fostering Rooted World Citizenry* (National Foreign Language Resource Center, University of Hawai'i at Manoa, 2008) 197.

21. Yun Xiao, "Home Literacy Environment in Chinese Heritage Language Development," in Agnes Weiyun He and Yun Xiao (Eds.), *Chinese as a Heritage Language: Fostering Rooted World Citizenry* (National Foreign Language Resource Center, University of Hawai'i at Manoa, 2008) 152-166.

22. J. Cummings, *Bilingual Children's Mother Tongue: Why Is It Important for Education?*, Sprogforum [Language Forum] #19, 2001.

23. Lucy Tse, "Why don't they learn English?" *Separating Fact from Fallacy in the U.S. Language Debate* (New York, Teachers College Press, 2001) 19.

24. Kathryn Lindholm-Leary, "Student Outcomes in Chinese Two-Way Immersion Programs: Language Proficiency, Academic Achievement, and Student Attitudes," in D. Tedick, D. Christian and Tara Fortune (Eds.), *Immersion Education: Practices, Policies, Possibilities.* (Avon, England, Multilingual Matters, 2011.)

25. Kathryn Lindholm-Leary, "Student Outcomes in Chinese Two-Way Immersion Programs: Language Proficiency, Academic Achievement, and Student Attitudes," in D. Tedick, D. Christian and Tara Fortune (Eds.), *Immersion Education: Practices, Policies, Possibilities.* (Avon, England, Multilingual Matters, 2011.) 22.

26. Kathryn Lindholm-Leary, "Student Outcomes in Chinese Two-Way Immersion Programs: Language Proficiency, Academic Achievement, and Student Attitudes," in D. Tedick, D. Christian and Tara Fortune (Eds.), *Immersion Education: Practices, Policies, Possibilities.* (Avon, England, Multilingual Matters, 2011.) 18.

27. Na Liu, "The Linguistic Vitality of Chinese in the United States," *Heritage Language Journal*, Winter, 2013, 1. http://www.heritagelanguages.org/Journal.aspx Accessed Jan. 23, 2013.

28. Vicky Tsui, How to Raise Bilingual Children. 双语教育成功的秘法. http://mandarin-tiger-mom.blogspot.com Accessed Feb. 3, 2014.

29. G. Feuerverger, "A Multicultural Literacy Intervention for Minority Language Students," *Language and Education 1994*, 8(3): 123–146.

30. Yun Xiao, "Home Literacy Environment in Chinese Heritage Language Development," in Agnes Weiyun He and Yun Xiao (Eds.), *Chinese as a Heritage Language: Fostering Rooted World Citizenry* (National Foreign Language Resource Center, University of Hawai'i at Manoa, 2008) 152.

31. Yun Xiao, "Home Literacy Environment in Chinese Heritage Language Development," in Agnes Weiyun He and Yun Xiao (Eds.), *Chinese as a Heritage Language: Fostering Rooted World Citizenry* (National Foreign Language Resource Center, University of Hawai'i at Manoa, 2008) 159.

32. Duanduan Li and Patricia A. Duff, "Issues in Chinese Heritage Language Education and Research at the Postsecondary Level," in Agnes Weiyun He and Yun Xiao (Eds.), *Chinese as a Heritage Language: Fostering Rooted World Citizenry* (National Foreign Language Resource Center, University of Hawai'i at Manoa, 2008) 15–33.

33. Ann M. Kelleher, "Placements and Re-Positionings: Tensions Around Chinese Home Language Learning in a University Mandarin Program," in Agnes Weiyun He and Yun Xiao (Eds.) *Chinese as a Heritage Language: Fostering Rooted World Citizenry.* (National Foreign Language Resource Center, University of Hawai'i at Manoa, 2008)

34. Stephen Krashen, "Language Shyness and Heritage Language Development," in Stephen Krashen, Lucy Tse and Jeff McQuillan (Eds.), *Heritage Language Development* (Culver City, Calif., Language Education Associates, 1998) 41–49.

35. Stephen Krashen, "Language Shyness and Heritage Language Development," in Stephen Krashen, Lucy Tse and Jeff McQuillan (Eds.), *Heritage Language Development* (Culver City, Calif., Language Education Associates. 1998) 43.

36. Stephen Krashen, "Language Shyness and Heritage Language Development," in Stephen Krashen, Lucy Tse and Jeff McQuillan (Eds.), *Heritage Language Development* (Culver City, Calif., Language Education Associates. 1998) 41.

37. A. Roca and M.C. Colombi (Eds.), *Mi lengua: Spanish as a Heritage Language in the United States.* (Washington D.C., Georgetown University Press, 2003)

38. Jin-Huei Enya Dai, Lihua Zhang, "What are the Chinese Heritage Language Learners Inheriting? *Habitus* of the Chinese Heritage Language Learners," in *Chinese as a Heritage Language: Fostering Rooted World Citizenry.* Agnes Weiyun He and Yun Xiao (Eds.) (National Foreign Language Resource Center, University of Hawai'i at Manoa, 2008) 37–51.

39. I realize this isn't correct Chinese, but it's what the student said.
Jin-Huei Enya Dai, Lihua Zhang, "What are the Chinese Heritage Language Learners Inheriting? *Habitus* of the Chinese Heritage Language Learners," in *Chinese as a Heritage Language: Fostering Rooted World Citizenry.* Agnes Weiyun He and Yun Xiao (Eds.) (National Foreign Language Resource Center, University of Hawai'i at Manoa, 2008)

40. Vicky Tsui, How to Raise Bilingual Children. 双语教育成功的秘法.
http://mandarin-tiger-mom.blogspot.com
Accessed June 6, 2014.

41. Carmen Cordovez, "Traveling to Ecuador for two months of immersion," *InCultureParent.* May 7, 2013.
http://www.incultureparent.com/2013/05/traveling-to-ecuador-for-two-months-of-immersion/
Accessed Feb. 3, 2014.

42. "Raising bilingual children, *InCultureParent.*
http://www.incultureparent.com/2013/06/lessons-from-ecuador-on-raising-multicultural-kids/
Accessed June 6, 2014.

十九 Why Schools
shí jiǔ Choose Mandarin
19 Immersion

So you've decided Mandarin immersion might be something you want for your child. You understand a bit about how immersion works. You've thought about your own motivations and what you hope your child to get out of it. You even know a little bit about how Mandarin functions as a language. Now it's time to go visit the Mandarin immersion school in your area (or schools, if you're very lucky) to see if it's a good fit.

What you'll find will very much depend on where the school is located and why it chose immersion. Schools, like families, have different motivations for their commitment to Mandarin immersion. Yours could be an underperforming urban school that's using Mandarin to bring in middle-class families. It could be a choice school district (or state, if you're in Minnesota) in which parents have the right to choose any school in the district for their children. In these situations, each school has to offer something special to entice families to enroll there. It could be part of a well-organized effort to fit today's students for the 21st century (hi, Utah!). It could be a response to efforts by Chinese families or by parents who adopted children from China.

There are many reasons a school district might introduce immersion. At its heart is a simple desire to give monolingual students (who either speak only Mandarin or only English) the chance to learn both languages well. But there are other reasons in play. For parents, understanding these reasons can help explain something that often seems inexplicable: where these programs are placed and why.

Mandarin immersion is comparatively cheap

One reason public school districts like Mandarin immersion is that it isn't hugely expensive to add. That is because immersion teachers don't get paid any more than regular teachers. An immersion program might have 12 immersion classrooms, two per grade from kindergarten through fifth. That requires 12 immersion teachers. But the school would need 12 teachers anyway for those students, even if they were taught only in English. If that same school decided to add a Mandarin class an hour a day for all the kids, it would have to hire two or three additional Mandarin instructors, at a cost of something like $40,000 to $60,000 per year per teacher, depending on seniority.

When Minnetonka Public Schools in Minnesota added Spanish and Mandarin immersion to its offerings in 2007, it replaced FLEX (Foreign Language Exploration) classes in elementary schools, meant to introduce students to a new language but not actually teach them that much of it. From the district's report:

> The concept of returning to the previous exploratory language program was considered. However, the former model is more costly and less effective for language acquisition than the proposed immersion model. The goal of immersion is language acquisition. The goal of the exploratory model is exposure to the culture and language.[1]

Adding immersion was a more cost-efficient and effective way to add world languages, the district had decided.

> Most people are surprised to learn that the immersion model is **less** costly than our previous model. Many assume that a new program requires a great deal of financial support. This is an unfounded assumption. Language immersion does not require significant additional financial resources.[2]

In fact, immersion programs are "cost neutral," the district said.

- Teachers—students will already be in kindergarten and we will already have a need for a teacher for them. In an immersion program, we are taking an existing teaching position and changing the assignment from teaching in English to teaching in the second language. This is cost neutral.

- Transportation—utilizing the school within a school concept, students attend their neighborhood school without any additional cost.

- Textbooks—there are no textbooks in most K and Grade 1 classrooms; the curricular materials are "consumables" and need to be replaced every year. Therefore, there is no additional cost because materials would simply be purchased in that second language. In later elementary grades and in middle school grades textbooks are used. There is a textbook adoption and replacement cycle so purchases would be part of that regular cycle, when due. Some minor adjustments in the planned replacement and adoption cycle may have to happen as the program grows.[3]

In addition, many Mandarin programs are put in schools that have too many empty classrooms because their student population has fallen. The upkeep to the building is the same whatever the student population. In most public schools, funding is on a per-student basis. Overall, schools save money because a full building is more cost-effective to run.[4]

That said, building a good program isn't free. Districts that have the following supports in place tend to have stronger programs over time:

- Teacher training
- Curriculum development
- Carefully chosen Chinese textbooks/materials and training on how to use them
- Translations of English-language textbooks into Chinese
- Chinese books for the school library
- A Mandarin curriculum coordinator (either part- or full-time) who will work with the district, principals and schools to ensure that the program is rigorous and thriving

Some of this comes automatically if the school is a member of one of the Mandarin immersion school consortia that are emerging as a way for schools and districts to share resources. For a list of the current ones, see *Chapter 22: Immersion Consortia: The Support Schools Need.*

Why two classes per grade

The savings in the early years can be lost, however, if there weren't enough kindergarten students at the beginning to create at least one full class by the end of elementary school and into middle school. For many districts that means there should be between 30 and 35 students still in the program by eighth grade. Programs that use immersion to fill under-enrolled schools can run into trouble if they have only one class per grade in the early years. Because of natural attrition, and because it's difficult to find students with the necessary Mandarin skills to fill in empty slots in the upper grades, Mandarin programs tend to get smaller as they move up through the grades. If a school starts with two or three Mandarin immersion classrooms per grade in kindergarten, by fourth or fifth grade it's likely to have one or two nicely full classes and one solidly full classroom in middle school. This is especially true in school districts that cap the number of students allowed in the lower grades but increase classroom size in third or fourth grade.

Schools that start with just one class per grade in kindergarten or first grade can find that by fourth and fifth grade there aren't enough students to fill a classroom. This can result in underutilized space (and less funding) or the need for split classrooms (including students in two grades in one classroom), which are difficult to teach. Either way, the budget boon they saw in the early years can be lost further on in the program's life.

There are other reasons to have two classes per grade. It's best for families of twins (there are three sets in my daughter's class!) because they can have their children in separate classrooms. It also makes for better social groups among the students in the older grades, as smaller classes get a little claustrophobic for students who've been with the same kids since kindergarten.

Immersion keeps families in district

An interesting natural experiment in Portland, Oregon shows that immersion programs in general aid in student retention. The RAND Corporation began a three-year, $1.7 million research project[5] funded by the U.S. Department of Education in 2012 to see how well dual-language immersion was working in the Portland Public Schools.

Portland was chosen because it provides a built-in control group. To get into one of the 10 immersion schools in the Portland Public Schools when the study began (Spanish, Japanese, Mandarin and Russian), families had to enter a lottery. Researchers will be comparing the English, math and science scores of students enrolled in immersion programs with similar students whose families applied to enter immersion in the district's lottery but didn't get in. This way they'll be comparing similar families with similar motivations.

Results won't be available until 2015. But one thing's already becoming clear, says Jennifer Steele with RAND, who is coordinating the study: students who don't get into one of the immersion programs leave the district at a higher rate than students who do. "We don't know if they're going private or if they're physically moving out of the city," she says.

Immersion as a carrot: Magnet programs in low-performing schools

In school districts with under-enrolled, low-scoring schools, immersion can be used as a draw for families whose energy, tax dollars and fundraising abilities might otherwise leave for the suburbs or private schools. Instead they flood into schools with historically poor test scores or falling enrollment because they want their children to learn Mandarin. The list of schools where this has worked successfully is long and includes Portland, Oregon's now august Woodside Elementary, Los Angeles' Broadway Elementary, Houston's Mandarin Chinese Language Immersion Magnet School, and my own family's Starr King Elementary in San Francisco.

The idea of schools using special programs as magnets goes back to the national push for integration in the 1950s and 1960s, when white, middle-class parents—for multiple and often racist reasons—began the long flight out of urban school districts. Starting in the early 1970s, school districts hit upon a new way to keep those families. They created "magnet" programs that offered special features unavailable in regular schools. The price of admission was sending your child to a school that had higher minority enrollment. Instead of busing children to schools that middle-class families were avoiding, districts enticed them with alternative schools that focused on science, math and the arts. It was a win-win-win system: school districts got better integrated schools and kept middle-class (often white) families from leaving, middle class-families got programs they couldn't get in their neighborhood schools and struggling schools got an influx of well-resourced parents.

Today magnet programs are under pressure from school districts facing budget cuts to raise test scores and meet academic targets. According to Scott Thomas, executive director of Magnet Schools of America in Washington D.C., many districts "are looking to shave any costs they can" and if school superintendents don't support these magnet programs, they're often put on the chopping block. In some districts these programs are seen as elitist as they often draw a higher percentage of middle class families. This makes the discussion about magnet schools a fraught one. In many districts parents are fighting back to protect their programs, up to and including filing lawsuits to keep their schools open.

Districts that have embraced magnet programs have done well. Thomas cites the Miami-Dade public schools, which have gone full-out for magnets. The district added 42 magnet programs in the 2013–2014 year, including schools focused on science, arts and languages. "They've been able to draw students out of charter schools and out of private schools and they've increased student achievement dramatically," he says. "In Miami they understand that creating schools designed around student interests and needs really pays off."

Nationally, arts magnets are the most common, followed by International Baccalaureate programs, then STEM (Science, Technology, Engineering, Math), according to a survey by Magnet Schools of America. However their survey only included eight language immersion schools and we know there are hundreds across the nation, so it's probably not statistically valid for language programs.

Mandarin's more like French than Spanish

Language immersion, as we've seen, began in Canada with the first French immersion elementary school in Quebec in 1965. Beginning in the 1990s, in part because of a growing awareness in the United States that we might need to pay more attention to the rest of the world, and in part as a counter to ugly English-only laws, a few school districts began to apply that same magnet model in a new way. They offered language fluency through immersion, most often in Spanish.

These new programs added another "win" to the tally sheet: they served not just middle-class families looking for enrichment but also language communities that wanted their children to learn the academic speaking, reading and writing of their home languages as well as English. It's one thing to speak Spanish or Mandarin or French with your mom and dad. It's another to be able to write a report or read a novel in one of those languages. It was that level of fluency—academic fluency—that these programs offered to students who spoke those languages at home.

There was an added plus: researchers began to note that children going to bilingual schools did better academically, no matter what their family background or what language they spoke at home.

As the language immersion trend in schools grew, districts hoped that Mandarin would be the same kind of integrating force that Spanish immersion is, bringing native-English-speaking families into schools with large numbers of newer immigrants and allowing both to learn from the other. Sadly, it hasn't quite turned out that way. There are almost no immersion schools in the country with a majority or even high minority of Mandarin-speaking students, so the goal of bringing non-Chinese speakers into majority Mandarin-speaking schools didn't work. Which isn't to say the programs didn't integrate the schools, they just didn't bring in new immigrants in the ways that had been hoped.

Districts have instead come to realize that Mandarin is a lot more like French than Spanish. It's a prestige language that attracts middle- and upper-middle class, non-Chinese speaking parents for whom Spanish isn't that big a draw. I've had parents tell me, "My kid can pick up Spanish by doing an intensive program in Mexico in high school if they want to. Mandarin you just can't pick up in a summer."

So school districts began to place Mandarin immersion programs in schools that needed a boost in enrollment and parent engagement but didn't have a large Chinese presence. These programs are often placed alongside English programs in so-called "dual strand" schools. Some students spend half their day or more learning in Mandarin, others spend their full day in English. In some schools they mingle in classes taught in English, in others they're fairly separate.

Sometimes it works well but not always. The state of Louisiana has long had French immersion programs because of its history of French bilingualism through the Cajun community. Chinese was added in 2010 in Lafayette, Louisiana at the World Languages Academy in Alice Coucher Elementary School.

"At many districts in the state, we've been under a desegregation order for the past 40 or 50 years," says Nicole Bourdreaux, the world language specialist for the Lafayette Parish School District. The decision was made to place Mandarin immersion "in one of the most at-risk schools in the district," she told an audience at the 2013 Asia Society Chinese Language Conference in Boston. "It's funny and sad at the same time that the most affluent people who we thought would be interested in Chinese refused to go to that school, so we ended up serving extremely at-risk students, 99% of them African-American, 99% free or reduced lunch, most of them under the poverty level."

The program has had somewhat rocky times. In the 2014-2015 school year it was moved to Plantation Elementary, though overall it has worked well for the students who attend it, she said. There was also a larger push to broaden immersion into other schools. "I was asked to prepare a project on the expansion of immersion, opening new sites in Spanish, French and Chinese," says Boudeaux. Then in 2013, "we found out that $12 million was going to be cut and this was put on the back burner."

The silver lining is that the existing programs are protected against budget cuts because the academic results for students in immersion have been so good in her district. "We know we're not going to be cut; we know we're going to survive," she says. "Not only because of the waiting lists [of families wanting to get into programs] for different languages, but also because if a school board starts thinking about cutting immersion the public reacts. Immersion in Louisiana is a grass roots movement and the parents will get up and show their support."

An example from Spanish immersion

The story of the Inter-American Magnet School in Chicago is a great object lesson for anyone who might imagine it's only Chinese programs that go through growing pains. The school started in 1975 as a preschool for Spanish-speaking children funded by the Chicago Public School District after a year of work by Adela Coronado Greeley, a community organizer, and Janet Nolan, an early childhood specialist. Both were new mothers who spoke Spanish, wanted their children to learn Spanish in school, and nurtured "visions of an inclusive bilingual school."[6]

They got the go-ahead, though Greeley said, "We were so naïve, it is miraculous we succeeded." It wasn't easy to find a building. The first school they approached "had a very domineering principal who refused the program." The second one, at Mary Bartelme Early Childhood Center, said, "Do what you want, and do it well; just don't bother me."

They launched the preschool with 60 students in two classrooms in 1975. There were two teachers, one Spanish-speaking and one English-speaking.

Students spent 90 minutes a day in Spanish class, the rest in English. They had no books and made do with photocopies and what the teachers and parents could scrounge. When 1977 came around and they had students ready for kindergarten, the school district allowed them to extend into elementary school, although still by first grade they had no books. Finally the parents went to the school board to complain. Greeley says, "The parents have always been the strong arm of our school."

The next year they became a magnet school, a new program begun by the Chicago schools. Because they were being funded by a program to help non-English speakers, the school was only supposed to be accessible to Spanish-speaking children. Their first "illegal" student (because she didn't come from a Spanish-speaking home) was Joan O'Malley's daughter. She said, "Why should my daughter Shannon be learning only one language?" Today her daughter is the head of a bilingual program in a Chicago suburb.

Recruiting parents was difficult. The founding moms went to private school fairs "but at the time they (parents) only wanted their children to learn French," said Greeley.

Eventually the students came and by 1978 they'd outgrown Bartelme and were moved into a new school, LeMoyne School, just east of Wrigley Field. They had 60 students in two classrooms per grade. The principal was busy and ignored them. They kept adding grades and soon outgrew their portion of the building.

Things became tense. "Other teachers felt that Inter-American staff and students were getting more than their share because they had magnet funds as well as Federal Title VII bilingual funds." The board of education was actively trying to find another location for them, but according to Greeley, "no one wanted us because of our active, assertive parents."

Finally in 1983, eight years after they launched their preschool, the Chicago Public Schools decided to invest federal desegregation funds into three new dual-language schools, and Inter-American was chosen as one of them. This brought them to a new building (number three in eight years), Morris School, which had declining enrollment and space for their program.

The plan was to convert it from a regular school into a 100% dual immersion school. Its name changed to Inter-American Magnet School (IAMS), the first time they actually had their own name on a dedicated school building.

The 280 students at the school were told they either could enter the program or transfer to another school. Most stayed, as did the principal. That was a problem as "she was not in favor of bilingual education and did not allow parents into the building," said Greeley. Existing Morris teachers, who were also opposed to dual immersion, told the seventh graders that being taught in two languages was "ruining them."

That principal eventually took early retirement. When the teachers and parents began the hiring process, they thought they wanted a Latino principal. But after they did interviews they ended up hiring a Hungarian woman who had come to the United States as a child after World War II and spoke English, Hungarian and German. As a teenager she was placed in first grade when she arrived in the U.S. because of her English skills. Despite not speaking Spanish, Harding had "the necessary sensitivity and understanding of the realities faced by linguistically and culturally diverse students." In 1985 IAMS graduated its first class of eighth graders.

In 2006 the school got its fourth building, a newly renovated school on West Waveland Avenue. Today AIMS serves almost 700 students from pre-school through eighth grade.[7]

Whole school versus strand

There's compelling data from magnet schools in general that whole-school programs do better than strand-within-a-school programs. School-wide programs are twice as likely to make Adequate Yearly Progress under No Child Left Behind than magnet programs that are strands, says Magnet Schools of America's Thomas. "These schools are more likely to have an integrated theme throughout the day, in all areas. When they do art in a STEM (Science Technology Engineering Math) school, they incorporate STEM. When they do physical education in an arts magnet, they incorporate art."

However, 85% of immersion programs are strands-within-a-school because school districts see that as a better model for diversifying a school. Thomas argues that if districts and school make efforts to widely market their programs and recruit families, and if those recruitment efforts are inclusive, a whole-school program will be diverse without creating strands within a school.

Houston's Mandarin Chinese Language Immersion Magnet School is an excellent example of this. The school is very racially mixed and yet is a whole-school program. For the 2013–2014 school year, the student body was made up of 21% white students, 20% African-American students, 27% Hispanic students and 23% Asian students.

Immersion in high-performing schools, public and private

In thriving school districts immersion is an "extra" that can be added to meet parental demand. Or, as in Utah and Delaware, immersion is supported because of the state government's focus on creating a multilingual work force. It also can be a way to bring in students for schools in an open-enrollment district or even a whole state, in the case of Minnesota. These districts tend to already offer multiple educational options for families. For them, Mandarin immersion is a sought-after plus that parents want for their children. The first public Mandarin immersion program in the country was very much for that reason. It was created at Potomac Elementary in Montgomery County, Maryland, a very affluent community. See *Chapter 21: School Profiles* for their story. Some more recent examples:

Casper, Wyoming

Mandarin immersion programs often come into being after concerted, strong marketing efforts by parents. In Casper, parents pushed hard on the school district. "The parents started a website, they had a Facebook page. They were just relentless," says Ann Tollefson, a world language consultant who works with the Casper program.

Park City, Utah

Park City is a high-income district that thought it was fully meeting the needs of its students as things were. So when the state asked if it wanted immersion programs, the district said it only wanted one. Parents found out and were irate. They started a Facebook campaign to bring Utah's immersion programs to the other schools in their district. In 2013–2014 all four Park City elementary schools will have dual-language immersion programs, in French and Spanish. The program has proven so popular that one school will become 100% immersion, meaning it will have no English-only track. Instead all students will be enrolled in the 50/50 Spanish immersion program. While they don't have Mandarin, it's an instructive example of how parent demand can push a district.

Orange County, California

In Orange County, it took one parent to start the revolution. In early 2011 Thalia Tong started talking to other parents about creating a Mandarin immersion program in the Capistrano Unified School District. By the time she was done talking, a group of 75 parents had come together. Over the course of several months this ad hoc group organized, gathered information and lobbied the school board. The parents arrived at the crucial meeting all arrayed in bright red t-shirts calling for the creation of a Mandarin immersion program. To the surprise of everyone, the board approved it the same evening.

The program was placed at Bergeson Elementary School for several reasons, says principal Barbara Scholl. A popular and highly-regarded school with excellent test scores, its kindergarten classes were shrinking because the population in the local area was aging and there were fewer families with school-age children. It is also centrally located in a school district that covers

200 square miles of southern Orange County just south of Los Angeles and includes eight cities. It's near a freeway, which would allow parents to easily get their children to school as they came from across the county.

Utah

In Utah, it's about building the best possible workforce for the 21st century, says Gregg Roberts, World Languages & Dual Immersion Specialist for the Utah State Office of Education. The state has a huge and growing dual-immersion program statewide in multiple languages. In the 2014–2015 school year, it had 33 Mandarin Chinese dual-immersion schools with enrollment of over 6,000 students. So far the state's most advanced class in Mandarin Chinese will be begin sixth grade in 2014–2015. Overall it has 118 elementary and middle schools offering immersion, including Spanish, French, Chinese, German and Portuguese.

When the *Speaking in Tongues* documentary film blog asked Roberts the reason why Utah had gone all out for immersion, he answered "Economics, economics, economics! Utah is a small state, so for our economic survival and the national security of our country we MUST educate students who are multilingual. In these tough budget times, the only reason why the State Legislature continues to fund this program while all others have been cut or reduced is because this program is tied directly to the future economic development of Utah."

"We want to take immersion education out of the obscurity of boutiqueness and actually make it a mainstream 21st century education for all students in Utah. We want to make this the norm of what we do in Utah," Roberts said at the 2013 Asia Society Chinese Language Conference in Boston.

The United States education establishment needs to "get over its love affair with mono-lingualism. We need to produce students who are multilingual and globally competent," he said.

Mandarin not always welcome

Not all high-performing school districts are receptive to Mandarin immersion. They believe they're already offering a good education, so there's no need to offer anything on top of that. Montclair, New Jersey was the site of a bruising battle in 2011–2012 over establishing a Mandarin immersion charter school there. The charter was rejected after vigorous opposition from some parents and the school district. *Montclair Patch*, an online newsletter covering the area, wrote this on Feburary 3, 2012:

> The application was rejected for the second time last month when eight urban charters were approved while no suburban charters were given the green light. Both Governor Christie and New Jersey

State Acting Education Commissioner Christopher Cerf have made comments indicating their view that charter schools are appropriate for struggling urban districts, not suburban districts deemed successful."[8]

Lake Forest's not-so-happy example

Lake Forest, Illinois offers a cautionary tale of the unintended consequences that can spring from Mandarin immersion. Lake Forest is a small, affluent and attractive suburb about five miles north of Chicago. It's a town with great schools. So great that every year Chicago families with young children nearing kindergarten age pack up and move there. "We're really a white picket fence kind of place," one resident told me.

The school district is small. It contains just five schools: three K–4 schools, one middle school and one high school. Together they serve the communities of Lake Forest, Lake Bluff and Knollwood.

In the fall of 2011, in an effort to provide an innovative program that would better prepare students for work in a global economy, Lake Forest launched a Mandarin immersion program at Cherokee Elementary School. Cherokee was chosen because it is the most centrally located of the district's three K–4 schools. The program began with two kindergarten classes and two first grade classes. Cherokee historically had four kindergarten classes each year, capped at a maximum of 22 students in each. The Mandarin program was so popular among parents that by the 2013–2014 school year it had 150 students.

By the fall of 2013, 42 of the kindergarteners were in the program. That's a whopping 70% of the school's kindergarten class. This is where the unintended consequences come in.

Just as the Mandarin program was ramping up, the recession was doing the same. Suddenly families in Chicago, who in past years could reliably be expected to sell their condos and move to the suburbs for a house, a big yard and great schools, weren't knocking on Lake Forest realtors' doors.

Overall district enrollment began to fall, especially in the lower grades and most precipitously in kindergarten. Which is how, by 2013–2014, the English language kindergarten at Cherokee was just 14 kids. Meanwhile Mandarin had two packed classes of 21 each. In fact by 2013–2014 Mandarin students made up 31% of the entire kindergarten student population district-wide.

Suddenly a school district that had always prided itself on neighborhood schools was faced with a dilemma. An extremely popular program had unintentionally turned the traditional English program into a minority within a school—and enrollment in the English program was continuing to decline.

Things got testy. Parents who chose the traditional English program felt their children were not getting the attention they deserved. A few vocal parents made comments about elitism, fairness and the involvement of the Chinese communist government. A group of residents in the town launched a campaign to have the program ended, saying it took money away from other programs and was inherently inequitable. They claimed the program created hostile divisions between children in it and those in the English track. According to an article in the Chicago *Tribune* in 2013:

"Some parents and taxpayers are advocating against continuing the language program, saying it divides the Mandarin-speaking and non-Mandarin-speaking children. The opponents argue that since the Mandarin-speaking children are removed from the regular English classroom for half a day, children who aren't in the program are ostracized from their peers and cliques have formed."[9]

Laura Rukavina, whose son currently attends Cherokee, was quoted by the *Tribune* saying, "It's so unfair. It's a public school. If you're going to use taxpayer dollars—even one dollar—it needs to be equal among all."

A letter to the editor in the *Gazebo News*, the local paper, read in part:

"The haves (Mandarin students) are taking from the have-not's (non-Mandarin students). We are having a sort of class warfare, again, the haves and have-not's, owing to funding issues and the non-Mandarin students becoming second class students. From the outset, this was not about Mandarin, it was about elitism and bragging rights."[10]

All the while, the immersion program continued to draw Chicagoland parents to Lake Forest, despite the recession, so it was helping the overall student numbers stay up. The district offers one of only four Mandarin immersion programs in the entire state of Illinois.

District administrators began surveying families, trying to understand the underlying issues. But there was nothing they could do about the economy or the dwindling enrollment in the district as a whole—or the demand for Mandarin immersion among parents who were there.

In order to stay on track for incoming kindergarten registration and staff for 2014–15, the school board voted in February of 2014 to decrease the immersion option from the 2014–15 kindergarten program. Instead, students will get a 90 minute block of time (dubbed the "Inspiration Block") during which they will get Mandarin immersion while students in the English track will get advanced social studies and science programs. This means the program ceases to be true immersion, as students are no longer getting half of their academic instruction in Mandarin. The 150 students currently enrolled in the immersion program would continue their 50/50 language learning.

The kindergarten Mandarin immersion teacher at the school, Mengmeng Lyn, told the Chicago Tribune "I think the time will be decreased, but it's still better than nothing."[11]

Private schools

Private schools, too, go for Mandarin because some parents consider it a must-have language in today's world.

The nation's oldest Mandarin immersion school, San Francisco's Chinese American International School, originally began as a school where families with connections to China or Taiwan could maintain their children's Mandarin, with a smattering of non-Chinese families. But today 80% of incoming students come from families where no Chinese is spoken and many cite the desire to raise international children who will be able to move easily in an interconnected, 21st century world.

Avenues: The World School—a private, for-profit school—opened in Manhattan in the fall of 2012. Its target market of parents considers being bilingual so crucial that one of the school's main selling points is that it offers either Mandarin or Spanish immersion for $42,000 a year. There is some question, however, whether the program actually will be immersion. As of 2014, students in the upper grades of elementary school were slated to get only one or two classes in Chinese per day, not the 50% of class time that would make it a true immersion program.

Charters

Mandarin immersion charter schools are often the result of families pushing to get a Mandarin program in a district that for whatever reason hasn't seen fit to create one. All the ones I'm aware of were created by families or staff with a passionate interest in Mandarin. Charters can be an extremely positive way to create an immersion school because they're 100% Mandarin, not a strand within a school. This allows the school to focus solely on Mandarin and create a school culture that embraces and celebrates Chinese. Schools such as Yinghua Academy in Minneapolis, Minnesota, Washington Yu Ying in Washington D.C., and Pioneer Valley Chinese Immersion Charter School in Hadley, Massachusetts, thrive in part because they are able to create a whole-school environment that centers on Chinese.

1. Minnetonka Public Schools, Frequently Asked Questions: Did the School Board consider other models to better enhance the opportunities for all students? http://www.minnetonka.k12.mn.us/academics/immersion/faqs/Pages/Background.aspx
    Accessed Jan. 16, 2014.
2. Minnetonka Public Schools, Frequently Asked Questions: Did the School Board consider other models to better enhance the opportunities for all students? http://www.minnetonka.k12.mn.us/academics/immersion/faqs/Pages/Background.aspx
    Accessed Jan. 16, 2014.

3. Minnetonka Public Schools, Frequently Asked Questions: Did the School Board consider other models to better enhance the opportunities for all students? http://www.minnetonka.k12.mn.us/academics/immersion/faqs/Pages/Background.aspx
Accessed Jan. 16, 2014.

4. Marco Basile, "The Cost-Effectiveness of Socioeconomic School Integration," in Richard Kahlenberg, (Ed.), *The Future of School Integration: Socioeconomic Diversity as an Education Reform Strategy* (New York, The Century Foundation Press, 2012) 133–134.

5. Leslie Maxwell, "Study of Dual-Language Immersion Launches in Portland Schools," *Education Week blog*, July 10, 2012. http://blogs.edweek.org/edweek/learning-the-language/2012/07/dual-language_immersion_study_.html
Accessed Jan. 7, 2014.

6. Kim Potoswki, "Inter-American Magnet School." *Language and Identity in a Dual Immersion School*. Volume 63 of *Bilingual education and bilingualism*. (Albany, NY, Cornell University, 2007)

7. Inter-American Magnet School. http://iamschicago.com
Accessed June 7, 2014.

8. Shelley Emling, "Montclair Charter Founders Move on; Maplewood Charter Founders Give up," *Montclair Patch*, Feb. 3, 2012. http://montclair.patch.com/groups/schools/p/maplewood-charter-founders-give-up-montclair-charter-22c839b601
Accessed Jan. 7, 2014.

9. Kate Jacobson, "Lake Forest Parents Ask District 67 to End Mandarin Chinese Program, *Chicago Tribune*, Nov. 22, 2013. http://articles.chicagotribune.com/2013-11-22/news/ct-district-67-mandarin-program-tl-20131122_1_language-program-immersion-program-language-instruction
Accessed June 7, 2014.

10. Al Boese, "Lake Forest's Mandarin Immersion, a Gift That Keeps On Giving," *Gazebo News*, Dec. 5, 2013. http://gazebonews.com/2013/12/05/lake-forests-mandarin-immersion-a-gift-that-keeps-on-giving/
Accessed June 7, 2014.

11. Kristy MacKaben, "Lake Forest District 67 to continue Mandarin program, but new plan keeps children in English-language homeroom," *Chicago Tribune*, May 5, 2014. http://articles.chicagotribune.com/2014-05-05/news/ct-lake-forest-district-67-world-language-program—20140502_1_mandarin-program-immersion-program-andy-henrikson
Accessed June 24, 2014.

èr shí
20

What You Should Look for in an Immersion Program

No matter what type of Mandarin immersion school you're considering, there are certain things you'll want to look for to see if the program is strong and will be a good fit for your child and your family. You won't find every single thing you want in any one program. But then, you wouldn't in an all-English school either. Mandarin immersion involves tradeoffs. There are only so many hours in the day, even at charter or private schools with extended day teaching. Adding Chinese means other things don't fit. But for the most part your child, with your help, will get a solid education that will match the one they would have gotten in an all-English program. And they'll come out knowing Mandarin as well.

What to look for in a magnet program

First, look inside yourself. Are you comfortable with racial and economic diversity? If you're not, these schools are not for you. Walk out the door and go somewhere else. Districts put these programs in poor-performing, under-enrolled schools to bring middle class, academically-minded families like yours into poorly resourced schools where academic levels lag. It is very much meant to be a give and take. You get Mandarin, the school gets your time, your energy, your money and—I would bet in the end—your love and devotion.

That just isn't possible for some parents. I heard of one mom who went through her child's classroom and made up a list of all the students she felt were bringing her daughter's chances at academic success down and presented it to the principal, saying those students shouldn't be there because they could never learn Mandarin. None of the children on the list were white or Asian. The mom and her daughter finally left the school. The other students are still there and thriving.

Still with me? Okay, let's look at what you *do* want to see.

What to look for in a *new* program

If the program you're looking at is new (and given that each year more than ten new Mandarin programs sprout nationally, there's a good chance it might be), the issues you'll need to think about are slightly different than those involved in considering an established program.

Pushback

Expect a lot of pushback from friends and family members if it's a new program in a school with low scores. I remember hearing lots of "I can't believe you're sending your daughter to Starr King," and "How brave of you," when we first signed up our oldest. People took care to point out to us that it was next door to a housing project and in what some considered a bad part of town. By the time we got to fourth grade the questions were more along the lines of "How did you manage to get a place there?" and "How can I game the system so my kid gets in?"

A *strong principal committed to the new program*

All schools need strong, capable principals, but a school that's adding a Mandarin immersion program especially does. While it's a plus if the principal speaks Mandarin or another Chinese dialect, that's pretty rare and not entirely necessary. What you really want is someone who's committed to the new program and the new parent body that's coming his or her way. A principal whose life mission has been to work in an underserved community may be flummoxed or even annoyed by the arrival of hordes of engaged (pushy), active (busy-body) and education-minded (demanding) parents.

Remember: This is a change for everyone concerned. The first few years are a shake-out period. However if the principal isn't into the idea and is only grudgingly accepting it because otherwise the school might close, you could be in for problems.

There are many constituencies in a school that's adding a Mandarin strand and they're going to be jockeying for attention, funding and time. The principal needs to be on top of all of this and able to deal not just with students, families and teachers, but also the school district. You want a principal who can stand up to parents, teachers and the district. Most importantly, you want a principal whose first question is always, "What's the best thing for my students?"

Long-term support from the school district

There are no "just add Mandarin and bake" kits you can buy at your local School Supply Superstore. Crafting a language immersion program takes time. Teachers are hard to come by and need to be nurtured and supported, especially in their first years of teaching. New books need to be bought and, more crucially, a curriculum needs to be created/translated/bought (when possible). It's a huge job. Simply expecting it to magically happen all by itself, or for teachers to do it in their free time, is unreasonable. Programs that do well from the beginning often join a consortium, hire a Mandarin immersion or curriculum creator, or at the very least retain a consultant who helps schools set these programs up. The Center for Advanced Research on Language Acquisition at the University of Minnesota also leads summer intensive workshops for principals and teachers, some focused specifically on Chinese. Ask if your district is sending anyone.

Connection to a Chinese immersion consortium

These consortia offer new programs a roadmap, curriculum and teacher training, and support. This is really helpful because trying to create an immersion program on your own is very difficult. Thankfully here's no need to reinvent the wheel. The biggest is Utah's Flagship–Chinese Acquisition Pipeline consortium. That's the closest thing there is to "Mandarin immersion in a box." Anchored by the Utah State Department of Education, F-CAP includes six state departments of education and individual school districts in 18 other states. It's a bit like the International Baccalaureate program in that it provides member schools with a roadmap and instructions on how to set up and run a program. F-CAP offers a national model for a K–12 Chinese immersion curriculum, textbooks, support and a yearly teacher and staff training summit in Utah each summer.

There's also one in Minnesota and The Asia Society's CELIN network. More about them in *Chapter 22: Immersion Consortia: The Support Schools Need.*

An instructive example of this comes from the Cambridge, Massachusetts Mandarin immersion program that was placed at Martin Luther King Jr. Elementary School in 2010. The program had had difficulty keeping teachers and in the 2012-2013 school year announced it was going to merge its immersion program with its *Ni Hao* hour-a-day Chinese class program for the non-immersion strand of the school. This provoked an uproar among parents. At the beginning of the 2013–2014 year the program joined the F-CAP consortium, which will hopefully give it the support it needs to thrive.

What to look for in an established program

If your Mandarin program as been around at least five years, here are some things you'll want to look for:

Scores

One of your first data-gathering forays will be to look at a school's test scores. But don't just look at the overall school tests. Fifty years of highly compelling data show that the most powerful predictor of academic achievement is the socio-economic status of a child's family.[1] That means that the information you need is not how good the average student at the school does, but how good a job the school does of educating children who come from families like yours. To get a real sense of that, you want to look at the test scores for students who are socio-economically most like your family.

The problem is that in this country we don't gather data about socio-economics and class—we gather data by race. It's unfortunate because that same mountain of data makes it clear that it's class—not race—that is predictive (but thankfully not definitive) of academic achievement in this country. But that's how we do it, so you've got to use race as a proxy for class. Which means you need to figure out what the socio-economic composition of the school is and then figure out which race maps to that, and then compare yourself to test scores for that race.

If the school is full of the children of double-Ph.D. African-American couples, and you happen to be white but your Iranian wife has a Ph.D. in biochemistry, look at the scores for African-American kids. If the school has a ton of college-educated, Asian-American families but almost no white families, and you're college educated and African-American, look at the Asian-American scores. If it's got a thriving Hispanic middle class population but few Asians and you're middle class and Chinese-American, look at the Hispanic scores.

To find them, and to find this level of specificity, you can look at the school's website, the school district's website and potentially your state's department of education. Check out GreatSchools.org which lists scores and allows you to really drill down into the data. To learn more about how to use test scores, I recommend reading *The Diverse Schools Dilemma: A Parent's Guide to Socioeconomically Mixed Public Schools* by Michael J. Petrilli.

Mandarin achievement

What level of Chinese are students expected to achieve at the end of each grade? What tests are used to gauge that ability? Realize that yearly testing with standardized tests is expensive, so the school may only test a random group of students each year, or only test certain grades. But the administrators should be able to tell you what benchmarks students are supposed to achieve and whether they meet them.

What is the program's expectation for students who go all the way through? Passing the AP Chinese exam in 9th or 10th grade is increasingly becoming the standard, although it's by no means the only possible or acceptable endpoint. But your program should be able to clearly identify its endpoints.

Literacy

Literacy is the elephant in the room in Mandarin immersion. Students typically read Chinese between two and five grade levels below what a student the same age would read in China. Everyone in the field is working hard to figure out how to do better. Don't expect your district to have solved this problem. (If they have, please have them let the rest of us in on their secret.) But you do want them to be honest about it and be able to tell you what they're doing to work on the issue. Are there lots of graded readers in the classrooms? Do they make sure those go home with students so they can read in Chinese at home as well? Do they hold workshops for parents who don't speak Chinese on how to promote Chinese literacy?

If they don't, this might be a project a parent support network needs to take on. Parents are an important part of making this all happen, so don't just expect the school to deliver everything to you on a platter.

Culture and community

Strands-within-schools can quickly become "separate but equal" programs. Does the school community mix and mingle? While the logistics of a multi-strand school often don't allow for lots of classes together, does the school work to make sure kids interact in classes where they can? Is the parent-teacher association a mix of parents from all the school communities? Or if it isn't, do they at least acknowledge it and have plans in place to change it?

Sometimes you have to look outside the box on this one, especially for getting parents to mix. At Starr King the programs are structured in such a way that it's hard to get a lot of mixing during class time. But soccer is huge at Starr King and each grade has several teams. Those weekend hours standing in the freezing fog each week (this is San Francisco, after all) is how lots of parents get to know families from other strands in the school.

How many classes per grade?

When it comes to Mandarin, more is better, at least in terms of the number of classrooms. While some schools have just one class of Mandarin per grade level, two is better and three or more is superb. Most families of twins prefer to have their children in separate classrooms.

What to look for in a private or charter program

Is it a well-designed program that really teaches Mandarin? Some private schools have been eager to jump on the Mandarin bandwagon without putting in the necessary research time to set up a really good program. Public schools do this too, but generally there's some district oversight of the quality. Is the school working with a consultant or Mandarin coordinator to help craft the program? Is there someone who is ensuring that the program builds Chinese competence grade by grade?

What are the qualifications of the teachers?

In some states private school teachers aren't required to be certified, so look hard at their ability to teach immersion to children. Just speaking Mandarin is not enough to make someone a good teacher.

Goals

What is the endpoint? As in public schools, many Mandarin immersion programs seem to be converging on students being able to pass the Advanced Placement Mandarin exam in in 9th or 10th grade.

Academics

Be aware that private schools that offer Mandarin immersion tend also to be very rigorous academically. These schools have chosen to focus on a difficult-to-learn language and expect a great deal of work and perseverance from students. Children who can't keep up are often "counseled out." That rigor is prized by parents who seek out these schools as a good fit for their family and their children. However, it can be instructive to ask what the attrition rate is between kindergarten and fifth or eighth grade, especially if you think your child might struggle.

Final thoughts

In all of this, remember that you're looking for a school where students are cared for, engaged, learning and having fun while doing it. Although the Mandarin part may be a little impenetrable, you'll get a good sense of the school merely by walking the halls and getting a read on how students and teachers interact, as well as by observing the attitude of the principal.

Talk to other parents in the program if you can, especially in the upper grades, because they'll know how the school functions academically. And if you can, attend a PTA meeting or another school event to see the parents in action. School fundraisers are a great way to get the "feel" of a school.

Finally, remember that most kids can do just fine in a variety of school settings. You don't have to find the perfect school, just one that meets your family's and your child's needs. Choosing a kindergarten can sometimes feel as if it's the most important decision you'll ever make in your child's life, but really there's a lot of leeway. Don't fret about it too much. Do your homework, spend some time in the schools you're considering and then trust your instincts.

1. Richard D. Kahlenberg (Ed.), "Socioeconomic School Integration," *The Future of School Integration: Socioeconomic Diversity as an Education Reform Strategy* (New York, The Century Foundation Press, 2012)

School Profiles

èr shí yī
21

In this chapter I profile nine Mandarin immersion programs in the United States and one fledgling school in Germany. I hope it gives a sense of the range of program types, how schools come into being and how they evolve over time. Some schools I was able to visit; for some I interviewed parents, teachers and principals over the phone and via email.

The profiles are in order of the year each program was founded. They begin with the nation's (and perhaps the world's) first Mandarin immersion program, the Chinese American International School, founded in 1981. Next comes the story of Potomac Elementary, 1991, the oldest public Mandarin immersion program in the nation.

Portland Public Schools in Oregon has one of the best-known public immersion programs and one of the most influential. The program began at Woodstock Elementary in 1998. District staff has been very welcoming of visits and have shared information widely, so its reach is felt nationwide.

Minnesota is home to five Mandarin immersion programs. Minnetonka's, founded in 2007, is a nice example of how immersion plays out in a wealthy suburb where it's used to bring in families from a wide area. These programs have been especially popular as a way for schools to draw in students under Minnesota's school choice rules, which allow parents to apply to any school in the state.

An excellent example of a struggling public school that remade itself with Mandarin immersion is found in Los Angeles' Broadway Elementary. That program began in 2007 when the school's Taiwanese-born principal launched it to repopulate her building. It is now so popular the school has four Mandarin immersion kindergarten classes each year and will move to a larger building soon.

How charter schools can be used to create Mandarin immersion programs is illustrated by the story of the Pioneer Valley Chinese Immersion Charter School in the town of Hadley in western Massachusetts. Launched in 2007, the school has proven so popular it has grown to be a K–12 program, with students coming from 39 surrounding communities. It's also one of several Mandarin programs that incorporate the International Baccalaureate. Having an IB program is emerging as a way for many schools, Mandarin including, to distinguish themselves as academically challenging.

The surprising story of how the state of Utah became an immersion giant is instructive in that it shows how a statewide initiative can be a catalyst not just for the state but also the nation. Begun in 2009, the state boasted 33 Mandarin immersion schools as of the fall of 2014.

Another charter school that has become a vibrant and sought-after program is Washington Yu Ying, in Washington D.C. It was created in 2008 by parents who wanted a Mandarin option in the public school system. Once opened it underwent a few rocky years, as many new schools do, but emerged strong and is flourishing today. It, too, is an IB school.

Berlin's *Deutsch-Chinesische Grundschule*, at the Planetarium Elementary School, is an example of the hurdles programs can face to even begin. In Germany, education officials have not yet agreed to allow Chinese to be used as an instructional language. French, English, Spanish, Italian, Russian and Turkish are the only languages in which curriculum may be offered in addition to German. The parents at the school, many of whom have children who already speak Chinese because they have spent time in China, began their efforts in 2011. They are now cobbling together afterschool programs and a "focus" curriculum, while they wait for the Ministry of Education to issue a decision.

Houston's Mandarin Chinese Language Immersion Magnet School is the final profile. Founded in 2012, the school is an astounding success and an excellent example of what happens when all the pieces fall into place. It was launched and supported by its school district from the beginning, a rarity. It was created as a full school, rather than a strand. And from the beginning it was a member of the Flagship–Chinese Acquisition Pipeline consortium. Because of that, it didn't have to reinvent the wheel but began with a solid curriculum and roadmap for future growth and development.

Together these schools give a view of the variety of different forms Mandarin immersion programs can take and how they can flourish.

Mandarin immersion schools

Founded 1981–1982

Chinese American International School
San Francisco, California

Founded 1996–1997

Montgomery County Public Schools
Montgomery, Maryland

Founded 1998–1999

Portland Public Schools
   Portland, Oregon

Founded 2007–2008

Excelsior Elementary
Scenic Heights Elementary
Middle School East
   Minnetonka, Minnesota
   Minnetonka Independent School District
Los Angeles Unified School District
Pioneer Valley Chinese Immersion Charter School
   Hadley, Massachusetts

Founded 2008–2009

Washington Yu Ying Public Charter School
   Washington D.C.

Founded 2009–2010

Utah Department of Education

Founded 2011–2012

Deutsch-Chinesische Grundschule
   Berlin, Germany

Founded 2012–2013

Mandarin Chinese Language Immersion Magnet School
   Houston, Texas

Chinese American International School

San Francisco, California
Founded 1981

San Francisco's Chinese American International School is the oldest Mandarin immersion program in North America and quite possibly the world. Founded in 1981, the private school offers a Mandarin immersion preschool that continues into a kindergarten through eighth grade program. For the school year 2013–2014 there were 520 students enrolled. The school is one-way immersion, designed for students who arrive at school fluent in English.

It uses a 50/50 model through fifth grade. In middle school the model shifts to two classes in Mandarin per day, the rest in English.

Called CAIS [pronounced "case"] the school's story began in 1973 when Carol Ruth Silver, a single lawyer and activist, adopted her son from Taiwan. Silver was a maverick even in a very tumultuous time. She had been a Freedom Rider during the Civil Rights movement of the 1960s and spent 40 days in jail in Jackson, Mississippi. In 1977 she was elected to the San Francisco Board of Supervisors (the city's term for its city council) and was described as "the board's first unwed mother" in the *New York Times*. She served for three terms and was one of the supervisors allegedly targeted by Dan White on November 27, 1978 when he assassinated Mayor George Moscone and Supervisor Harvey Milk "as a blow against liberals who he believed were ruining the city."[1] Silver survived because she was not in her office at the time of the murders.

When her son began to near school age, Silver started looking for a Mandarin-speaking school that would teach him both Mandarin and Chinese culture. "There wasn't any offering in Mandarin in San Francisco at the time, so I turned to my Chinese friends and said 'Well, we'll just have to make one.' "[2]

Silver created a working committee composed of influential San Franciscans from the city's political, professional and Chinese communities. They included then-San Francisco Mayor Dianne Feinstein; Professor Maurice Tseng, head of the Department of Foreign Language and Literature at San Francisco State University; Francisco Hsieh, publisher of the *Chinese Commercial News* and René-Yvon Lefebvre d'Argencé, director of the Asian Art Museum's Avery Brundage Collection, among others.

At the time most of San Francisco's Chinese community spoke Cantonese or other southern dialects and Mandarin was rarely heard on the city's streets. China was still a relatively poor country and its economic possibilities were not as apparent as they were to later become. But those involved could see where the future was heading. "It was obvious to me that Mandarin was going to be the key language and the most important in Asia, and perhaps economically, the world,"[3] said Superior Court Judge Harry Low, one of that original committee. "[O]pening a school like CAIS was a no-brainer to me. But to get it started was a bold adventure."

The group looked to the then 20-year-old French American Bilingual School in San Francisco as a model, and on July 17, 1980 announced that they planned to launch the Chinese American Bilingual School. They faced many hurdles. There were no teaching materials in Mandarin for English-speaking elementary school students. There was no real financial support. They had no building.

What they did have was a director who could bring their vision to life. Shirley Lee was a native Mandarin speaker who had a degree in Chinese

Language and Literature from San Francisco State University. She had taught Chinese language and civilization at several local schools and colleges. In August of 1981 she told *East West Magazine*:[4]

> The era when being bilingual was a mark of status for the elite has long gone by. What we want our students to achieve is a true and profound bilingualism, an increased respect for others, an open-minded outlook and a more adequate understanding of the world around us. In our opinion these things are exactly what is needed to produce good, well-rounded citizens in modern America.

The Chinese American Bilingual School launched on September 11, 1981 in two storage rooms in the basement of a University of California Extension building at 55 Laguna Street that was also the home of the French American Bilingual School. The first year's class consisted of just four students, including Silver's son Jefferson. The parents began a campaign to tell the city about their new program, which used the tagline "Educating children for a world of challenges." They ran ads in local Chinese papers and each year got between five and eight new students.

In 1982 the board discussed changing the school's name as it was felt it appealed mostly to the Chinese community and they meant this to be a school for all children. The name Chinese American International School was chosen.

By 1986 the school had a total of almost 30 students, five to a grade. Tuition was $1,850 a year, teacher pay was low and parents did much of the work. The educational style was predominantly Chinese, with lots of memorization, character sheets and summer homework. The program taught traditional characters and most of its educational materials came from Taiwan.

In the early years there was concern that while the Mandarin-language portion of the day was strong, the English program wasn't as good. Some parents worried that their children wouldn't do well on the tests required to get into private high schools in San Francisco. Around 1985 it was arranged that CAIS students would spend 50% of their time in the English program of the now renamed French American International School upstairs. After several years CAIS launched its own, strong, English program which continues to this day.

By the late 1980s CAIS had 60 students. About 75% were from Asian families, 40% of those Chinese families with Cantonese backgrounds. In 1987 the French American International school wanted its space back to expand, so CAIS was forced to move to a new building, a former military hospital at the far western end of San Francisco at 15th Avenue and Lake Street in the Presidio.

CAIS was using educational materials from Taiwan for the most part, together with other things it cobbled together from Singapore, Hong Kong and China. The school adopted the Bopomofo phonetic system to transliterate Mandarin, used in Taiwan. The school day was conducted 50% of the day in Chinese, 50% in English.

In 1989 the board decided to create the CAIS Institute for Teaching Chinese Language and Culture, which was meant to package the school's curriculum so it could be sold to other schools that wanted to create a bilingual immersion program. It was eventually renamed The Mandarin Institute.

To put this into perspective, it was until 1991, ten years after CAIS was founded, that the nation's second Mandarin immersion school opened. It was Pacific Rim International School in Berkeley, California.

The next year, in 1992, the first CAIS middle school class of sixth graders began with just six students. In 1995 the first CAIS eighth grade class of four students graduated. Interest in China and Chinese was growing nationally and more families were looking for the kind of education in Mandarin that only CAIS provided. The next year CAIS sent its first group of students on a summer trip to China.

By 1994 the school's enrollment had grown to nearly 200 students and the school began to look for a new home. The plan was to create an international campus to be shared by CAIS and the French American International School. The schools formed a joint governing body, the National Center for International Schools, to develop a common campus. They were joined by International High School.

The building chosen was the old California Department of Transportation headquarters near San Francisco's Civic Center, at 150 Oak Street. It was a rather monolithic six-story building from 1949 with an addition from 1964. The two schools purchased it for $3.3 million. After a year and a half of renovation the space was ready for students. On November 3, 1997, 156 CAIS students walked into their new home, a building they shared with FAIS. Some families had left because the move to a new building meant a long drive across town. However, the decision had been made in part because of an awareness that the school's new location, near San Francisco's Civic Center, would make it possible to further increase the student body in years to come.

Today the building is divided into three parts, one side French, the other Chinese and on the top International High School. CAIS's decision proved to be the right one. Its Mandarin immersion program was no longer seen as "experimental" in the words of parent and board member Mary Yen.[5] During the aughts, the school underwent a period of major growth with applications and admissions increasing yearly. Shirley Lee retired as headmistress in 1999.

Andrew Corcoran was appointed Head of School in 2001, leading CAIS through a period of growth and expansion as interest in China and Mandarin blossomed. The school's families were increasingly non-Chinese as the school's immersion program and academics made it one of the city's most popular (and difficult to get into) private schools. Corcoran introduced the Shanghai program of "Read First, Write Later," to raise students' reading ability.

San Francisco's Mandarin immersion scene

With a population that is 30% Chinese-American and a long history of contact with Asia and China, it isn't surprising that Mandarin immersion has taken such a strong hold in San Francisco. CAIS is now one of five schools that offer Mandarin immersion in the city. The San Francisco Unified School District launched its first public Mandarin immersion program at Starr King Elementary School in 2006, followed by a second in 2007 at José Ortega Elementary. In 2012 a second private Mandarin immersion school, Presidio Knolls, launched from a preschool program. That year SFUSD's Mandarin middle school program opened at Aptos Middle School.

Unlike most American cities, in San Francisco parents not only can choose which of the five they want to apply to, but also can and do move between the schools depending on which is a better fit for their children and their finances.

CAIS academics

CAIS developed its own curriculum because at the time it was founded no such thing as a Mandarin-English immersion curriculum existed, anywhere in the world. It has shifted and changed over the years as the school's teachers and administrators worked to develop the best possible program for their students.

Because the school has such a long history, it has used the full gamut of Chinese writing systems. When it first began, it taught traditional characters and used Taiwan's Bopomofo writing system for pronunciation. In 2007 the school shifted to teaching the pinyin Romanization system, though it had begun the shift earlier in the upper grades. In the 2012–2013 school year switched from teaching traditional to simplified characters.

By definition, immersion programs teach language through content, not language itself. Teachers do not walk into a classroom and say "*Zhuōzi* is how you say 'table' in Chinese." Instead, beginning in kindergarten, CAIS students learn the language by experiencing it from teachers, who bit by bit build up their understanding and vocabulary.

There are many philosophies of how immersion should work. Some schools are very content-heavy, others focus more on language. Early on CAIS focused more on content but in recent years has found itself moving more towards language, trying to achieve a balance that will allow its students to gain mastery over both Mandarin and the subjects they must learn.

One example is the way CAIS approaches teaching math—it is taught in both languages. For the first six years of the program students have two math classes per day, one in Mandarin and one in English. CAIS math classes taught in Chinese use materials its staff have created, based on textbooks from Taiwan. The math program taught in English uses the *Everyday Mathematics* textbook. Previously the school had used the *Singapore Math* series, but the shift was made because it was felt Singapore math was more similar to the CAIS math curriculum taught in Chinese.

Both classes cover a steady progression of mathematical material, but not in lock step. "In Chinese they might be learning basic multiplication while in English they might be learning how to count money or how to tell time," says Kevin Chang, the director of the school's Chinese program. That allows students "to transfer the knowledge and skills between the languages." This also means an increase in the time spent learning math compared to many schools. "This helps student think more deeply about math problems," says Chang. Together, these have paid off in very high scores among CAIS students when they take standardized math tests.

Unlike public schools, CAIS is free to design its own curriculum and doesn't have to hew to that of all-English programs. For students in the elementary school the school day is seven hours, from 8:00 am to 3:00 pm. In middle school the school day lengthens to seven and a half hours, from 8:00 am to 3:30 pm.

Elementary students have classes in English language arts, science, math, social studies and art in English. In Mandarin they study Mandarin language arts, which includes thematic units in social studies and health and wellness, as well as math. Music is taught in Chinese from kindergarten through second grade, and in English from third grade on up.

What language non-academic classes are taught in depends in part on what teachers are available and what languages they speak, says Chang. For example in 2012–2013 one of the physical education teachers spoke Mandarin so one-third of the classes were taught in Chinese. That teacher has since moved to a different school and now PE is taught in English.

The decision to teach science in English came because of a feeling among the faculty that a subject which depends so deeply on experimentation and classroom work would be more effective if it were taught by a specialist in science rather than a homeroom Chinese teacher, Chang says. In addition, they found that it was "difficult for the students to retain the science vocabulary in Chinese because they don't get a lot of reinforcement, they don't get enough repeated practice." At times the school experimented with teaching science in Mandarin but wasn't satisfied with what students retained compared to the amount of time necessary for them to learn it.

The same decision was made about social studies, a highly vocabulary-intensive subject that requires a familiarity with American history that may not be present in teachers trained in China or Taiwan. In California the social studies standards include lessons on California history, the Gold Rush, the Mission system and California native peoples. "Our Chinese teachers would have needed to study California history first," to gain the necessary expertise, says Chang.

Instead the school made the decision early on to have two different social studies classes, one taught in English and one in Chinese. The Chinese class focuses on social studies topics related to Chinese language, culture or current events. "That way it has close ties to the language component," Chang says. The school calls the course Chinese Social Studies, which is a separate course from English Social Studies. For example, in fifth grade CAIS students are preparing for a spring trip to a sister school in Taiwan. So in Chinese Social Studies they study the history and culture of Taiwan, including daily life, what people there eat, what Taiwan was like in the past and what kind of a country it is today. The same approach is used to prepare students in middle school for trips to Beijing and southwestern China.

In middle school, for sixth through eighth grades, the school shifts away from a 50/50 model to something closer to the 70% English, 30% Mandarin model used by most immersion programs for middle school. However, instead of teaching social studies and Mandarin language arts in Mandarin as most public school programs do, the school teaches the regular social studies curriculum in English. Social studies taught in Mandarin is folded into Mandarin language arts curriculum. The entire curriculum is blended to insure that appropriate materials are taught in the appropriate language. For example, in seventh grade social studies students study the major world religions in English, but Buddhism is covered in the Chinese culture portion of the day, as many of the original texts are in Chinese.

These extra classes are made possible in part by the middle school's longer day from 8:00 am to 3:30 pm.

In English, students study English language arts, math, science and social studies along with PE, art, music and a technology course. Students experience art, music and dance classes in Chinese and in English, so over the year students rotate through art including brush painting and Chinese calligraphy as well as Western art topics.

CAIS in its 30s

In 2010 CAIS hired Jeff Bissell as its new Head of School. Bissell had spent 11 years living in Beijing as the director of the School Year Abroad-China program. There he coordinated programs for high school students from 47 private high schools in the United States. A fluent Mandarin speaker, Bissell previously taught Chinese at Marquette University and holds a Ph.D. in Chinese from the University of Wisconsin-Madison. Bissell introduced a host of new innovations at CAIS, for example shifting the whole school beginning in pre-K to the teaching and use of simplified characters in 2012–2013. Previously students had only been exposed to simplified characters in middle school.

Bissell also expanded the school's international program in Asia. Today fifth grade students have the option to spend two weeks at the school's partner school in Taiwan. Seventh graders are required to go to Beijing for a three-week intensive language program, living with host families. Eighth graders culminate their immersion experience with the option of a service learning trip to China's southwest.

In 2013 CAIS had 520 students with a student body made up of 38% Asian-Americans, 40% multi-ethnic students, 19% Caucasian, 1% Hispanic and 2% African American. The school has 74 faculty and 37 administrative staff. The tuition is now $23,000 per year. Each year dozens of families apply for the much-coveted seats in CAIS's immersion preschool program at their pre-K Waller Street campus, which begins at age three. The preschool is the main entry point for CAIS. At age five, these children will then continue on to its kindergarten-through-eighth grade program at the main campus at 150 Oak Street.

With the tremendous desire on the part of parents for Mandarin immersion, the school has been expanding. Its preschool program is now housed in a nearby building, and in the fall of 2013 the school signed a lease on a building an additional 33,000 square feet about 11 blocks from the main campus. The middle school portion of the program is expected to move there during the 2015–2016 school year.

Embracing "Embrace Chinese"

CAIS's mission statement exhorts students to:

心怀中华	Xīnhuái zhōnghuá	Embrace Chinese
精益求精	Jīngyìqiújīng	Become your best self
立足世界	Lìzú shìjiè	Create your place in the world

In 2013 CAIS made that focus on "embracing Chinese" explicit when it released new goals and principles of Chinese language immersion instruction. In this one-page document CAIS stated "academic content serves as a vehicle through which Chinese language proficiency is developed."

This represents a shift, says School Head Bissell. "Our success in Chinese class rests largely in the success of our students to develop Chinese proficiency. Our Chinese teachers know that language objectives must be met before core academic competencies can be achieved."

The school isn't putting Chinese ahead of academic achievement, but rather saying that while both are equally important, Chinese competency must come first to *allow* for competency in academic subjects.

Given the high-powered nature of its teachers and the academic prowess of the students it selects, CAIS isn't about to become less academically oriented and no one expects its stellar scores on standardized tests to fall even a notch. But for the first time the school is making explicit that it will focus on producing students who know Chinese first. That's very different from many programs, which focus on Chinese only as long as it doesn't interfere with students' ability to learn the curriculum.

In some ways this represents the next stage of Mandarin immersion. While many schools have embraced immersion in the past ten years, there's been a somewhat uneasy balance between the needs of language acquisition and academic competency. CAIS has drawn a line in the sand and stepped over it. It will be interesting to see whether other programs choose to follow it.

Montgomery County Public Schools
Montgomery, Maryland
Founded 1996

The oldest public Mandarin immersion program in the country was founded in 1996 at Potomac Elementary, in the town of Potomac, Maryland. It is one of eleven schools that offer immersion programs in the Montgomery County Public Schools.

The district has a very long history of immersion. Its French Immersion Magnet Program began in 1974, Spanish in 1977 and Mandarin in 1996. Immersion is popular in the district. It is now home to seven immersion elementary schools out of a total of 133. There are also three middle schools with immersion programs. Of the elementary schools, two offer French, three Spanish and two Mandarin. In 2012–2013 a total of 647 students applied for one of 286 available kindergarten immersion seats, said Michael Herlihy, lead teacher for Chinese immersion and English for Speakers of Other Languages.

The school district's programs are a blend of several different immersion models. Some schools offer full immersion, where 100% of the class day is taught in either French or Spanish. Others offer what the district terms 'partial immersion' though all are at least 50% of the day in the target language. In most other school districts, that 50/50 model is considered full immersion.

French

It all started with *Française*. French immersion in the district began at Four Corners Elementary School in 1974. The program moved twice and ended up at Maryvale Elementary School in Rockville in 1992. That school served students living in the northern part of the county and was so popular that in the 1999–2000 school year a second French immersion program was launched at Sligo Creek Elementary in Silver Spring to serve students in the southern part of the county.

Students receive all their subject matter instruction in French. In kindergarten through third grade, French is the only language used in the classrooms. Remarkably, in part because of the academically charged families they tend to come from, the students figure out how to read and write English at home. Students who struggle with English get help from the school, but few appear to need it.

In fourth grade, students are given instruction in English twice a week for 45 minutes during the second half of the school year. In fifth grade students are given instruction in English for approximately four hours each week. This works out to approximately 80% of the school time spent in French in the early grades, approximately 60% in fifth grade and 30% in grades 6 though 8. Art, music and physical education are taught in English in all grades.

In middle school students get two French-language blocks taught totally in French, one French Language Arts and one World Studies, at either Silver Spring International Middle School or Gaithersburg Middle School. Successful completion of the sequence allows the student to enter French 4 or French 5 honors classes in ninth grade.

Spanish

The Spanish program at Rock Creek Forest Elementary was founded in 1977 with one class of first, second and third graders. It has grown from that one multi-age class to two classes at each grade level for a total of twelve classes of Spanish immersion from kindergarten through fifth grade. Two other schools were later added.

Rock Creek Forest Elementary offers what the school district terms "full immersion." In kindergarten through third grade, Spanish is the only language used in the classrooms. It isn't until fourth grade that students begin to receive English instruction and at that point it's only twice a week for forty-five minutes during the second semester of the school year. In fifth grade they get English four times a week for 45 minutes.

Because art, music, physical education and media center/library classes are also taught in English in all grades, students don't spend 100% of their day in Spanish, however. In kindergarten through third grade it's approximately 72%, in fourth grade it's 67% and in fifth grade 62%. In middle school they get two classes, Spanish Language Arts and World Studies, for a total of 29% of their school time in Spanish.

Upon successful completion of the middle school program, students are usually placed in level 4 Spanish in high school.

The district's other two Spanish immersion schools offer what the district calls "partial immersion," though again, it would be considered full immersion in most other districts. At Burnt Mills Elementary and Rolling Terrace Elementary schools, students get all their instruction in Spanish in kindergarten and first grade. In second through fifth grades, math and science are taught in Spanish, about 50% of the day. Reading, Spanish language arts and social studies are taught in Spanish. In fourth and fifth grades students get math and science in Spanish.

Mandarin

In 1996 there were just two other Mandarin immersion programs in the nation, both private and both in the San Francisco Bay area. That year saw the opening of both Potomac and another private school, the International School of the Peninsula in Palo Alto, California. The next Mandarin immersion programs in a public school didn't come until two years later, in 1998 with the opening of ShuangWen School (Public School 184) in New York City and Portland, Oregon's Woodstock Elementary.

Potomac Elementary School's Mandarin immersion program was founded at the start of the 1996–1997 school year. College Gardens Elementary began a second Mandarin program in 2005–2006. In the Montgomery county program students spend half their day being taught in Chinese and the other half in English. Math and science are taught in Chinese. English reading, language arts and social studies are taught in English.

All Montgomery County immersion programs use the same curriculum for all students; only the language it is offered in varies. "We're just teaching it in Chinese, but it is the MCPS curriculum," said Herlihy. "Our teachers teach a split day. For instance, one teacher will teach kindergarten Mandarin in the morning and then first grade Mandarin in the afternoon," said Herlihy. In addition students receive one hour of direct language instruction in Chinese each week.

The program continues at Hoover Middle School with two classes per day, one in Mandarin language arts and one in World Studies. When students get to high school at Winston Churchill High they can enter the regular Chinese language track, including Advanced Placement courses, Herlihy said.

Potomac and College Gardens both offer just one Mandarin immersion class per grade level, for a total of six classes per school. At Potomac Elementary there are 520 students, with 180 of them in the Mandarin program, which makes up one-third of the student body, Herlihy said.

The demographics at the schools are primarily white and Asian. At Potomac fewer than 5% of students receive free or reduced-price lunch. At College Gardens the figure is 19.2%.

The program uses simplified characters and is meant for students who are not native speakers of Chinese. However, because of its proximity to Washington D.C., with its diplomatic corps and various other international agencies, there are many students who arrive having spent time in China. "We usually have some students who came from Beijing because their families were stationed there. We also have a number of heritage speakers in our classes," said Herlihy.

The program is extremely popular. "It's usually over-enrolled, there's a waiting list," said Herlihy.

Overall, students in the Chinese program do "as well if not better than the general education students. There's a little lag at the beginning but they catch up and often outstrip them by fourth and fifth grade on standardized tests," Herlihy said. The students achieve proficiency in Chinese and have near-native accents, visiting Chinese speakers have told teachers.

"The skill set here is really focused on listening and speaking because it's immersion. When they get to secondary school there is more emphasis on reading and writing," he said. Students get actual Chinese language arts training one hour a week.

Portland Public Schools
Portland, Oregon
Founded 1998

The Rose City is home to one of the most thriving Mandarin immersion scenes in the nation. Portland boasts the second-oldest public program in the country, fully built-out from elementary school through middle, high school and into college, as well as three private schools that offer Mandarin immersion for elementary, middle and high school. The school district added a second elementary school in the fall of 2014. In addition there are Mandarin programs in nearby towns and one just across the Columbia River in Vancouver, Washington.

But the nexus is Woodstock Elementary. It is here, in a graceful wooden building in southeast Portland, that it all began back in 1998. The Portland Public Schools Mandarin immersion program launched with one blended kindergarten/first grade class in September from a grassroots effort by parents and teachers. Many of the parents in those early years were American families who had adopted girls from China and wanted to offer their daughters the chance to learn Chinese and about Chinese culture.

Portland Public Schools early on made a strong and broad commitment to immersion education. In the 2012–2013 school year the district boasted immersion programs in Spanish, Japanese, Mandarin, Russian and Vietnamese. There were 27 schools in the system that house immersion strands. In a district with 47,000 students, 3,794 are in immersion programs, 8% of the total Portland Public Schools student body.[6] This commitment to immersion could help explain why Portland public schools have such a high "capture rate," the term used for the number of school-aged students in a given community who attend public school. In many urban school districts a 60% capture rate is considered good. Portland's was 85% in 2007. In 2011 the capture rate for Woodstock elementary was 88% and the school had 491 students.[7]

The first immersion program created in the district was for Spanish, in 1986 at Ainsworth Elementary School. A Japanese immersion strand was added at Richmond Elementary in 1989. It was so popular that it went from being a one-class strand in the school to a stand-alone immersion program that begins with four kindergarten classes and also includes a Japanese language preschool. The district has since added more Spanish immersion schools, a Russian two-way immersion program at Kelly Elementary School and a Vietnamese immersion program at Roseway Heights K–8 school in 2014–2015. In 2011 the school board voted[8] to allow a French immersion charter school and in the fall of 2012 Le Monde Immersion school launched.[9]

Mandarin

The Mandarin program began with that one mixed kindergarten/first grade class in 1998 at Woodstock, which at the time was an under-enrolled elementary school in a working class neighborhood in the city's southeast. One class per grade was added each year until the program was fully built out in 2004 with students K–5. The original request for the program came from a school board member, then-principal Mary Patterson said in 2007.[10] There was also much support from parents who had adopted children from China, according to Gary Rydout, a former president of ShuRen, the non-profit that supports the Mandarin program.

In the early years it was difficult to fill the classes. However by the mid-2000s parents were moving into the neighborhood to take advantage of Portland's neighborhood school allotment system, which gave them a better chance of getting their child into the program. Because Portland was for many years one of the few public Mandarin immersion programs available, families moved there from across the country to take advantage of it.

The Portland Mandarin program is 50/50 and teaches simplified characters. In 2004 the first group of sixth graders entered Hosford Middle School, where they continued their studies in middle school with Social Studies and Chinese Language Arts taught in Mandarin. The high school Mandarin immersion program began in 2007 with the first group of students arriving at Cleveland High School. There the curriculum offers both face-to-face and blended online courses incorporating language and content-based instruction.

The Mandarin program doubled in size in 2006 when Portland received a million-dollar-a-year National Security Education Program flagship grant to build out its curriculum, testing and instructional strategies. The grant also specified that PPS must make what it developed available to other school districts, which has made Portland a go-to district for new Mandarin programs needing advice.

In 2012–2013[11] Portland's K–12 Mandarin immersion program had 490 students, including 325 at Woodstock Elementary, 92 at Hosford Middle School and 72 at Cleveland High School. They made up 12% of all immersion students in the district. Spanish immersion students were 58%, Russian 5% and Japanese 23%. Portland's Japanese immersion program has a total of 920 students, including 665 at the all-Japanese Richmond elementary school.[12]

Since 2008 Portland's program has had a strong travel element, with students attending a capstone Chinese Research Residency in Suzhou, China in the spring of their eighth grade. Much of the work of the non-profit parent group, ShuRen, is focused on fundraising so that all students who wish to can go on the two-week program to China. In Suzhou, students "utilize their language and cultural skills to navigate day-to-day aspects of living and to conduct research based on student-centered inquiry projects."[13]

The strong connection between Portland and Suzhou includes a teacher exchange with its sister school in Suzhou. The teachers come to Woodstock Elementary where they help to expand students' experience of Chinese language and culture.

But wait, there's more!

Portland's Mandarin immersion program doesn't end when students graduate from high school. In 2005 the National Security Education Program awarded Portland and the University of Oregon at Eugene a large grant to establish the nation's first K–16 Chinese Flagship program. The proposal was to not just graduate students who were professionally proficient in Mandarin at the Superior level based on ACTFL Proficiency Guidelines, but also to create a model that could be replicated at other schools.

In the fall of 2006 the first group of Chinese Flagship Scholars entered the University of Oregon Chinese Flagship. Since then, graduates have studied in majors ranging from International Relations, to Mathematics, to Art History, while at the same time taking university-level academic requirements in Mandarin.

The Oregon Chinese Flagship[14] was unique for its continuity and program coordination from the elementary level through college, though today there are 11 flagship programs at colleges and universities across the nation.[15] Portland Public Schools in the past has worked closely with the

University of Oregon in professional development, curriculum articulation, and assessment, leveraging intellectual and logistical resources from both communities. With the end of federal Foreign Language Assistance Program (FLAP) grant funding it's unclear if that relationship will continue to be as close.

Nationally-known

Portland's Mandarin program has become so well-known and is considered such a trend setter that at least one publisher touts its choices in its catalog. Cheng and Tsui, a Boston-based publisher and distributor of materials for learning Chinese, Japanese and Korean, marks some of its Mandarin books with a special note "Recently Adopted in OREGON."

"It has name recognition, which is really key," says Cheng and Tsui's Megan Norlund. "When more established programs adopt some of our books, and tell other programs they've adopted them, it makes a difference."

Expansion

Parents have long advocated for expanding the size of the Mandarin program, much as the Japanese immersion program was expanded. However, creating an all-immersion school is difficult in a district that uses immersion as a magnet program to diversify schools. Portland's Japanese program was enlarged before that thinking became ingrained. That hasn't stopped parents from trying. In 2010 Dave Porter wrote in a local op-ed piece that the district each year turns away a full kindergarten class worth of students whose families want Mandarin immersion but who aren't able to be accommodated because there are not sufficient places. Each year there are only 60 Mandarin kindergarten seats available for which the district receives between 85 and 110 applications. That means each year between 25 and 50 students are turned away.[16]

In one example of the program's draw, Wahkiakum County Commissioner Lisa Marsyla announced in 2012[17] that she wouldn't seek re-election because she was *hoping* to get her daughter accepted into Portland's Mandarin program. That required that she move to Portland, which is in Multnomah County. Marsyla has an adopted daughter from China. The commissioner gave up her seat because she couldn't know until April whether her daughter was accepted. She told reporters that the possibility was too good to give up and she didn't want to keep other potential candidates from seeking her seat. In a statement she said her family had a "wonderful opportunity to potentially enroll my daughter in a Mandarin immersion program, which, if accepted, would take us outside the county several days a week," because she would have to commute into Portland. Her gamble paid off and her daughter got a space in the program for the fall of 2012–2013.

The district finally decided to add another school in the spring of 2014, announcing that King School in Portland's northeast section would add two kindergarten and two first grade Mandarin immersion classrooms. The school is K–8 and will eventually be home to at least 12 classrooms of Mandarin immersion students. It is also home to an International Baccalaureate program.

More data to come, but it's looking good

Portland's program works both in terms of teaching students Mandarin and teaching them the Portland school curriculum, says Michael Bacon. He is Portland's Chinese Flagship Director and Immersion Achievement Coordinator. "In our program we see our kids' math scores are out the roof and their English language arts performance and (English) reading is meeting or exceeding expectations for almost every single kid, even though they're getting only half of a day in English."

In the summer of 2012, the RAND Corporation kicked off a three-year research project funded by a $1.7 million grant from the U.S. Department of Education to see how well dual-language immersion was working in Portland. The District provides an excellent study site because it has a built-in control group. Researchers will be looking at the academic progress of students enrolled in each of Portland's language immersion programs and will compare them with similar students whose families applied to enter immersion in the district's lottery but didn't get in. This way they can compare similar families with similar motivations, says Jennifer Steele with RAND, who is coordinating the study. They will be looking at student achievement in English language arts, math and science.

Data from the study won't be fully available until 2015. However in a paper presented in 2013 at the Society for Research on Educational Effectiveness conference in Washington D.C., some preliminary information was presented. The researchers didn't break out the different language groups, so this is from Spanish, Mandarin, Japanese and Russian programs combined. Some of their findings:

- Students who "win" the lottery and get a coveted assignment to a language immersion program are much more likely to enroll in kindergarten, as opposed to leaving for the suburbs or private school. Of students who didn't enroll in their kindergarten placement, 13% were students who got their language immersion choice. Compare that with the 37% of those who didn't get their choice who didn't enroll in a Portland Public Schools kindergarten.

- The quality of instruction in immersion classrooms was better than in non-immersion classrooms. Principals described immersion teachers as "star teachers" because of their skills.

- Students in immersion classes did better in math and reading (in English) than English-only students, especially in the upper grades.
- Students who were English Language Learners (i.e. who spoke a language other than English at home) became fluent in English at higher levels than students in non-immersion classes by fifth grade.
- Students in immersion were 10% more likely to stay in the district in first grade and 18% more likely by sixth grade.

Trouble in paradise

However, after being a jewel in the Portland Public School's crown for 15 years, there are cracks appearing. In May of 2013 the district's superintendent Carole Smith announced a new budget that focused on "prioritizing equity"[18] while cutting support for immersion programs. The district put its high school Japanese immersion program, the culmination of a 12-year program for many students, on the chopping block the same year. Only at the last minute was it saved. At the same time, two new programs, in Mandarin and Vietnamese, were announced. As is often the case with Mandarin programs used as magnets, the King School program was placed in a school with low test scores and a high needs population. Currently 93% of King school students are eligible for free lunch. It also had a tiny (2%) Asian student population. The existing Mandarin program at Woodstock is now meant to serve 50% native Chinese speakers, with English speaking families who want Mandarin presumably going to the new program at King.

The new priorities also affected the Mandarin program at Woodstock Elementary. The number of students in its incoming kindergarten class for 2013–2014 was cut from 60 to 52 students. Rather than having three classes of 20 students each, as it has since 2008, it was switched to two classes of 26 students each. The district describes this as necessary to "rebalance allocation" within the school building between the Mandarin program and the regular English program at Woodstock.

The district is also working to make the Woodstock program more of a two-way program that serves the needs of English language learners. In order to "provide equitable access,"[19] in the 2014-2015 school year, the school district reserved 41% of Mandarin immersion slots for native Chinese speakers.

As one admittedly angry parent put it, "So, in 6 months, PPS has pulled bait-and-switch on the Chinese community thinking they were promised a program in a (neighborhood) district where they lived (oh, and no school bus routes exist between there and the new school), put a program in a school (King) with a Spanish English Language Learner program and which doesn't exactly want it, split the alliance of Neighborhood and Mandarin

Immersion Program at Woodstock, and has the Chinese, mixed, white, and adoption families all looking sideways at each other."

Many parents within the program expressed frustration with this move. There is always a waiting list of families eager to get into Woodstock's Mandarin program and it's widely acknowledged that the Mandarin program could actually grow to include many more students, enough to easily fill three or even four kindergarten classes. However that would mean no space for the local program, which is also growing.

Portland's school assignment system gives students from within a school's geographic region first priority. For that reason, families have moved to Woodstock's catchment area to have a better chance at getting into the Mandarin program. According to one parent with a child currently in the program, having fewer kindergarten openings available for families that don't speak Chinese is "a shame because there's a bunch of people who moved into the neighborhood thinking they would have a better chance at getting into the Mandarin class."

Mandarin immersion families protested the new system at Woodside at a school board budget meeting. When they met with a school board member they were told, "appeals to excellence will be useless," according to one parent who was there. They were told that the district's concern was now focused on closing the achievement gap and helping English language learners rather than middle-class English speakers. Hence the addition of a Mandarin immersion program at King School.

The irony in all this is that the Mandarin immersion program was started in part to bring families to Woodstock at a time when it was under-enrolled and had low test scores. It worked all too well. Now the district is moving the "carrot" of Mandarin immersion to another school in need of the same shift.

Portland appears to be an example of a district coming to terms with multiple expectations upon its program from both parents and the district. The district now sees immersion more as a way to serve the needs of English language learners, although it's unclear how many Mandarin-speaking immigrants Portland has. It is also focusing more on reducing the achievement gap between students, in part due to federal education requirements. At the same time, parents want the strongest Mandarin immersion program possible for their children and enough space for everyone who wants it. These two sets of desires and expectations are being to collide and how they will turn out is unclear.

Beyond Portland

PPS's Mandarin program stoked a fire that has only continued to grow in the region. The International School, a private immersion K–8, added a Mandarin strand in 1998. The Northwest Chinese Academy, in the town of Beaverton eight miles west of Portland, launched in 2008. Beaverton got a public Mandarin program at Hope Chinese Charter in the fall of 2012. Just across the Columbia River in Vancouver, Washington, Ben Franklin Elementary began a Mandarin program in the fall of 2009.

Minnetonka Independent School District
Minnetonka, Minnesota
Founded 2007

Minnetonka, Minnestoa is an excellent example of how a school district used language immersion to fill seats that otherwise would have been empty, in a state where every student has the right to apply to any public school. Today students in the district's immersion programs show higher test scores overall than students in general English classes.

Minnetonka is located eight miles west of Minneapolis. In 2002, population projections showed Minnetonka Public Schools losing 1,300 students over the next ten years as its population aged and fewer families had school-age children. The school board and district staff instead set out to make Minnetonka a magnet for families outside the district. Multiple programs were discussed. One was language immersion.

In 2007 Minnetonka launched four Spanish and two Mandarin immersion programs in its six elementary schools—placing a language immersion option in every elementary school in the district.

The gamble paid off handsomely for both the district and families. In 2012–2013 the District had 9,432 students and Minnetonka has the highest percentage growth of any school district in Minnesota. One-quarter of its seats are filled through the open enrollment process. About 50% of students in the district either are in Spanish or Mandarin immersion, half of each elementary school. Families who enroll their children in kindergarten are asked to make at least a six-year commitment to the immersion program and with the launch of its middle school immersion program in 2013 they look to stay on through high school.

Minnetonka's students are already extremely high performing. Ninety-nine percent graduate from high school, 93% are college bound and 80% attend a four-year college. But language immersion offered that "something extra" that has drawn families in from 41 other school districts.

And at no threat to their English or test scores, says Lee Drolet, principal of Excelsior Elementary, one of the district's two Mandarin immersion schools. The other is Scenic Heights Elementary. Not only does the Mandarin immersion program offer language proficiency at a young age, but the district is finding students "show higher achievement in our immersion programs than our other students," she says.

The district has a beautifully produced video on its website for both its Mandarin and Spanish immersion programs. Videos are an excellent way to introduce the program to families who might live far away and need to be enticed to come and tour a school. The Chinese immersion video notes that:

"K–6 Chinese immersion students have performed higher than programs at each grade level in math. By sixth grade, immersion students performed higher than all programs in reading."[20]

Academics are clearly a major draw for families and the district responds with lots of information about immersion and how it affects students' scores. As its website says:

Minnetonka's model is uniquely successful in terms of student achievement. Many immersion schools report that English test scores may dip from grades 2 to 4 and rebound by grade 5 to be equal to, or higher than, the non-immersion classes. However, in Minnetonka Schools this has not occurred. Our immersion students perform on par with their English program peers at all grade levels. A strong commitment by parents to read with children in English at home every night complements Minnetonka's exceptional instruction in English in grades 3 to 5, resulting in outstanding achievement levels by all of our students. By the end of fifth grade, most Minnetonka students are reading in English at the 11th grade level (according to NWEA Measures of Academic Progress).[21]

The district has a wealthy population. Just 7% of students qualify for free or reduced lunch. It spent $9,680 per pupil in 2009–2010, with additional support from multiple parent groups that support schools and the district. The per-student spending level still puts it below the national average of $10,615 in 2010, according to U.S. Census figures. States that spent the most per pupil included New York ($18,618), New Jersey ($16,841), Alaska ($15,783), Vermont ($15,274) and Wyoming ($15,169).

For families who don't choose the immersion programs, afterschool language programs in Spanish and Mandarin are also available in elementary school.

First three years are 100% Chinese

Because very few of the students in the program speak Mandarin, the Minnetonka program is one-way immersion program, focusing on the needs of English-speaking students who are learning Mandarin. Based on its demographics, Minnetonka chose to make its Mandarin immersion program 100% immersion for kindergarten through second grade. The only classes students in the first three years have in English are music and art.

Only in third grade do students begin in English, with one 50-minute class a day in English language arts. The class is taught by a native English-speaking teacher. Almost all students come into the program already reading in first grade, said Principal Drolet. It's expected that they'll learn English reading at home. If a student isn't making progress, they get intervention either in the winter of second grade or in third grade. The district presumes strong parental support. "We tell parents to read to their children in English 30 minutes a day," she said.

In third grade, immersion students get 60 minutes of English instruction a day and in fourth and fifth grades it increases to 70 minutes. The district feels the high concentration of Mandarin time is necessary to really cement the language. And because students are getting the same subjects and material as the English and Spanish language counterparts, there's no net loss of instruction time, she points out. Because so little of the school day is offered in English, "English time is really intense. I tell our teachers they can't waste a second of it," says Drolet.

The District uses the *Better Chinese* textbooks for kindergarten and first grade, and then Singapore's *Chinese Language for Primary Schools* for second through fifth, with the addition of reading supplementation with leveled readers.

"We have resource books on particular themes, so students can work in guided reading groups. They work in differentiated groups based on their level," said Drolet.

One thing teachers have really found surprising is "how wonderful technology has been to support language learning. Interactive white boards have been a big help," in teaching Mandarin, said Drolet. You can see this in use in the district's video.

Middle school

The district has two middle schools, one on the town's east side and one on the west. Both have a Mandarin immersion strand. The middle school program was well planned years in advance. The district spent two years putting together the model, said Peter *Dymit,* principal of Minnetonka Middle School East. "There are very few schools in the entire country that continue immersion into the middle school year, so there were not a lot of middle schools to work with," he said. Thankfully Portland, Oregon's Hosford Middle School has "been wonderful" and helpful, he said.

Middle school students take six classes per day:

- English language arts
- Math
- Science

- Mandarin language arts
- Social studies
- Elective

Mandarin language arts and social studies are offered in Mandarin. Social studies was chosen as a Mandarin language course because it was the only middle school subject that wasn't offered at multiple difficulty levels, said Dymit.

Minnetonka offers highly differentiated courses to meet the needs of students working at different levels. In middle school there are three levels of math, two of science and two of language arts at each grade level. In addition the district offers a Gifted and Talented Education (GATE) program that requires a tested IQ of 145 or over to enroll.

"We could have offered math in Mandarin, but we couldn't offer three levels of math in Mandarin," Dymit said. "Our parents come to Minnetonka because they want a highly differentiated, highly rigorous curriculum that meets where their child is," he said. "If our parents had to decide between accelerated math and Mandarin, they'd say they weren't willing to give up the right math class," he said.

The district was able to offer more instructional minutes in Mandarin for middle school students by taking the social studies class period and adding what English program students would have had as student advisory homeroom class, and by "shaving some time off the minutes they get to go from class to class," said Dymit. That allowed the creation of an 87-minute block of time for Mandarin, he said.

The rest of the school day, Mandarin students are mixed in with students from the general education and Spanish immersion tracks. "Our model is balanced between giving them content time without having them in immersion so much that they become disgruntled because they feel they're giving up too much to stay in the program," he added.

High school

The high school portion of the Minnetonka Mandarin immersion program will begin in 2015–2016 when the first class of students matriculate into ninth grade.

The focus in the middle school Mandarin language arts is getting students ready to have the proficiency to pass the Advanced Placement language program at the end of ninth grade. Here's what the proposed high school program will look like:

- The summer after eighth grade, students will be eligible to take part in a summer abroad program in either China or Taiwan.

- In ninth grade they will take AP Chinese, culminating in taking the AP Mandarin Language and Culture test.
- In tenth grade they will take honors Chinese literature, humanities and cultural studies in Mandarin.
- In eleventh grade they will take honors language cultural exploration with a spring semester study abroad.
- In twelfth grade they will take a Chinese honors language class dubbed "superior fluency," which will bring them to a level that will allow them pass the HSK[22] test at the "Advanced with Honors" level.

In addition, high school seniors may have the option of taking either a core content or elective course in Mandarin. On the ACTFL (American Council on the Teaching of Foreign Languages) scale, students will begin tenth grade at the ACTFL Intermediate-High level and graduate having achieved the Advanced-High level with "a proficiency level that is very close to that of a native speaker," according to a report that the Minnetonka School Board presented on May 17, 2012.

Teacher support and training key

Staffing the program is a key focus of the district, and the schools work hard to ensure that their highly trained teaching staff stay in their positions. To that end, they are offered ample training and professional support, said Drolet. Each new Mandarin immersion teacher gets a one-on-one mentor teacher for his or her first year. During their first three years teaching in the program they also get monthly teaching support, including after-school classes to learn content and instructional methods. The Chinese teachers in the district work very much as a department, with monthly meetings on topics of interest to faculty. "We very much have a team approach," Drolet said.

Because the curriculum taught in the district wasn't available in Mandarin, teachers had to translate it into Chinese. The district now makes that available for sale to other districts beginning such programs.

Minnetonka is an excellent example of a high-performing school district looking to bring in students using Mandarin immersion as a draw. In a state where parents are free to choose any school they can get their children to, schools must offer programs that families want. Mandarin immersion clearly has been that in Minnesota.

Los Angeles Unified School District

Los Angeles, California

Founded 2007

Frank and Mindy Han live in the city of Calabasas, in the hills west of the San Fernando Valley. They moved there specifically for the public schools, which are uniformly rated as excellent. They wanted a high-quality education for their three children and chose the town specifically because it was in the Las Virgenes Unified School District. Yet this is Frank's morning routine:

> The morning sun was just breaking the horizon in the far distance, but it was still dark and cold inside our house. It was time to lift my daughter out of her comfortable bed, still asleep, and place her gently in our car, which was carefully prepared the night before. Morning snacks for the one-hour drive to her school. Check. Lap table, pencils, crayons so she can finish her homework in the car. Check. Clothes, socks, shoes, jacket. Check. Backpack with snacks, lunch, and water bottle. Check.

What could make an education-minded family in a green and lovely suburb with excellent schools brave Los Angeles rush hour traffic for two hours a day to send their daughter to a school in a rough neighborhood that several years ago was dying and the Los Angeles Unified School District (LAUSD) wanted to close?

Mandarin.

Han didn't even know LAUSD offered Mandarin immersion until a week before the school year began in August of 2012. Despite the distance and the investment they'd made by moving to Calabasas, he and his wife were drawn to the possibility of their three children learning Mandarin beginning in kindergarten. Both second-generation American-born Chinese, their own parents went to great lengths to make sure they were fluent in the Mandarin language.

Now the Hans struggle to give their own children the same opportunity. "We speak Chinese at home, we hire Chinese-speaking nannies, and those things all help, but to keep up with fluency, especially learning to read and write, an immersion environment at school is the only real alternative, short of moving to Asia," said Mindy.

After they learned about Broadway Elementary School, they considered waiting a year to enroll their oldest daughter as 2012–2013 already had a long and growing wait list. Then the weekend before school started the school's principal, Susan Wang, called to tell them there was an opening in the kindergarten class and asked if they wanted it.

They jumped at the chance.

It meant "up-ending our lives by foregoing enrollment in our walking-distance, top-rated, well-funded, Las Virgenes district elementary school" but they haven't regretted it, Han says. They're not the only ones. Broadway has other families who every morning launch themselves into the grueling Los Angeles rush hour commute, coming in from as far as Porter Ranch (over 30 miles away), Manhattan Beach, Hermosa Beach, and Hollywood, among many other far-away places.

Han can't say enough good things about the school, the Mandarin immersion program and especially Principal Wang. She's "leading the charge of seeing this program succeed."

Birth of a new program

By the 2013-2014 school year, Broadway Elementary in Los Angeles was full to the bursting. There were four kindergarten, six first-grade and four second-grade classes. Test scores have risen dramatically. In fact, the school has become so popular that it's scheduled to move to a new building within a year or two to accommodate the growth. Principal Susan Wang, whose vision of a Mandarin school made all this possible, is moving with it, together with the school's Mandarin immersion teachers.

It's all a huge turnaround for a school housed in a beautiful 1926 building in the beach town of Venice, California. Broadway had seen its student population slowly shrinking for decades. In the 1980s and 1990s the neighborhood that surrounded it had succumbed to decay and in some areas gang violence. It was home to what one magazine called "a Westside wasteland of burned-out hippies and off-the-grid artists."[23] Families moved away and those that were left tried to send their children to other schools.

"Eighteen years ago there were 17 people shot dead and 58 gun shot injuries, all gang related," in the neighborhood, says Wang. When she arrived in the 2008–2009 school year, students at Broadway barely filled seven classrooms, one for each grade from kindergarten to sixth.

"Three years in a row I was called to the district for a small school meeting where principals were offered to stay where we were but take on two schools" as principal, says Wang.

The neighborhood began to turn around about 15 years ago, becoming much safer and more peaceful. Today it is very diverse, with some of the poorest and also some of the wealthiest households in L.A. But the changes didn't bring students to the school. Broadway Elementary continued to shrink and the Los Angeles Unified School District told Wang that it planned to close the school or merge it with another.

She chose to fight to save it. The Broadway community had worked tremendously hard to improve the school and she believed in her students. "We raised our API by 107 points!" she says proudly of her first years there—

before Mandarin immersion. To attract new families, the Taiwanese-born, Mandarin-speaking Wang tried adding Mandarin classes for students, called FLES for "foreign language in elementary school" among educators. She recognized that "nowadays you've got to have something to sell your instruction," she said. Working with the Confucius Institute at UCLA she made Mandarin classes available for all students. The school hung a big banner out saying it offered Mandarin. "But nobody came here because of that," she says.

Instead, something else happened, something that surprised her. Through her door came a steady stream of parents who told her "I don't want FLES, I want immersion. If you have it, I'll come."

Wang asked them to put the word out on local parent email lists to see how much interest there was in the wider community. A lot, it turned out. In 2009 she was able to go to the district and say 'I've got 40 kids who want Mandarin Immersion at Broadway.'"

Los Angeles already had one Mandarin immersion school, City Terrace Elementary in East Los Angeles. But it was over 25 miles to the east so it wasn't an option for Westside parents to send their children there. Venice, on the beach between Santa Monica and Marina Del Rey, was close. The district gave her the go-ahead.

Wang began with two Mandarin immersion kindergartens in 2010–2011, both of which filled. The program was so overwhelmingly popular that in 2011–2012 the kindergarten expanded to four Mandarin classes of 24 students each. For the first time in memory the school had a waiting list.

The school's Academic Performance Index scores, already on the way up, have since risen dramatically. The API is California's system for measuring school performance and improvement. In 2009, Broadway's API score was 748. By 2013 it had reached 885, well above the coveted 800-mark that is the goal of all California public schools.

For the first time the school has a parent organization, "Friends of Broadway," a parent-run, non-profit organization that raises money to support Broadway Elementary School instruction and student activities. It raises thousands of dollars to support school programs. That's helpful because getting the money to fully equip four new classrooms with the necessary materials as the program grows each year is difficult.

Parents in the Mandarin immersion program also launched a non-profit, DragonSprouts,[24] to support the Mandarin program as it grows.

The English language program at Broadway also has grown. In 2011–2012 there were only 13 students in the English kindergarten. For the 2012–2013 school year "we have a full class of 24," said Wang.

Growing Pains

In Los Angeles, as in many large, urban school districts, middle and upper middle class families have tended to look for either magnet or immersion programs if they consider the public schools at all, although that's beginning to change.[25] Wang knows that were it not for Mandarin, many families "would not have sent their kids to Broadway, or LAUSD." That's a loss for the community, the schools and the city.

The Mandarin program integrated the school, says one school parent. When parents toured the school before the Mandarin program arrived and "they looked on the playground and they saw shades of brown, they didn't want to go here." The Mandarin program helped overcome those prejudices.

Buzz in the community has been "great," says Broadway mom Jean Hsi. A large percentage of the first wave of incoming families were American-born Chinese, often second-generation Mandarin speakers. That's been a surprise to Hsi, who's a Mandarin speaker herself. She thought many first generation Mandarin-speaking immigrants would have wanted the program, but they told her that they're more concerned about their children learning English. "They say 'I'm not really sure my kids really need to learn to speak Mandarin. We prefer they learn at home with us,'" she says.

Second-generation families have been much more committed to having their children learn to read, write and speak Mandarin in school, she says. These families may speak Mandarin or they may have learned some in Saturday school but their grandparents speak it. "Or they're hiring Chinese-speaking nannies," she says. They're working hard to retain the language for their kids and see the immersion program as a great opportunity to do so."

The majority of Asian parents who send their children to Broadway grew up not speaking Chinese and they regret it. Their parents felt that English was what was going to bring them success. "Now they're back so their children can learn Chinese," says Wang.

Han is grateful for the work of those pioneer families who helped pave the way for his daughter and took a chance on an unknown school and a new program in its first two years. Now in its third year, "the Broadway Mandarin Immersion Program has largely settled into a routine," he says. "As is often the case, the pioneering class, now second graders, were the ones blazing the trail, wading into the unknown, trying and failing, trying and succeeding, setting the stage for classes to come and hopefully improve upon the program. And for that, this year's kindergarten class is grateful and indebted to these pioneers."

He's seeing his daughter "blossom under the guidance of Principal Wang and the tutelage of both the English and Mandarin teachers, who together have crafted a wonderful and academically challenging program to mold our children into better citizens of the world."

Immersion popular in Los Angeles

Los Angeles Unified is the second largest school district in the country and has implemented a broad policy of creating immersion schools, both to serve the needs of English language learners and the desires of second- and third-generation immigrants who want to give their children access to their heritage language. These schools also draw in families who might otherwise leave the public schools for private schools or the suburbs. In the 2013–2014 school year LAUSD had 52 language immersion programs in 48 schools.[26] There are several joint Spanish/Korean schools, and a Spanish immersion program was added at Broadway in 2013–2014. District-wide there were:

- 39 Spanish programs
- 9 Korean programs
- 4 Mandarin programs

The oldest Mandarin immersion program in Los Angeles, and the oldest in Southern California, is at City Terrace Elementary School in East Los Angeles. The school's Mandarin program launched in 2007–2008 with one kindergarten class. It is a strand within the school, with one class per grade and another "two or three English language classes per grade" depending on the year, says Principal Elaine Fujiu.

In 2013–2014 the program had expanded through fifth grade and that year the first class moved on to El Sereno Middle School, where District officials opened a Mandarin immersion strand. El Sereno also has an International Baccalaureate Program, as well as a Math Science and Technology Magnet program and a program for highly gifted students.

The program begins using traditional characters and switches to simplified in fourth grade, Fujiu said. The principal at the time "thought it would be an advantage to our students to learn Mandarin, so he and one of our teachers just started the program," says Fujiu.

The school's population is 90% Hispanic. The school is 100% Title 1 students, meaning students qualify for free or reduced-price lunches. Most of the parents in the Mandarin program come from the surrounding community and the students in the program are mainly Hispanic with a smattering of African-American, Korean and other Asians. There are few Chinese families. Those that come want their children to know how to read and write. "Their kids can speak 'playground Chinese' but they want the academic language," Fujiu said. The parents have been very supportive and involved in the school.

The program has been very successful academically, said Fujiu. In the Mandarin program 80% of students are proficient in English reading and math "and we have a lot of perfect scores."

Los Angeles' Castelar Elementary School in Chinatown also has a Mandarin immersion program. The school was built in 1882, making it the second-oldest continuously operating school in Los Angeles. Principal Cheuk Choi helped launched a Mandarin immersion program in the school's kindergarten in 2011–2012 in conjunction with UCLA's Confucius Institute.

Mandarin at Broadway

Wang is a big fan of having at least two Mandarin classrooms per grade. The program is 50% English and 50% Mandarin. That allows her to have one Mandarin teacher and one English teacher per grade—though with the incredible success of the program she's now got two Mandarin and two English teachers per grade for a total of four Mandarin classrooms per grade. "It makes sense to have native speakers teach in their own language and also the power of collaborating in both languages," she says.

The District previously had had some 90/10 Spanish immersion programs, but has now moved to an entirely 50/50, immersion model, in part to ensure that English language learners get enough instruction in English that they can do well on the state standardized tests on which so much school funding depends.

Broadway teaches traditional Chinese characters and uses the *Better Chinese* textbooks for kindergarten then adds the *Mei Zhou* (美洲华语) series from first grade on. "We use both," says Wang. The needs of immersion students are different from those of students taking Chinese as a separate class, so "you can't go page-by-page, lesson-by-lesson. You have to pick and choose, see what matches the grade school curriculum," she said. In addition her teachers work to translate and adapt the LAUSD math, science and social studies curriculum into Mandarin.

Challenges

Wang's biggest challenge continues to be hiring Mandarin-speaking staff. While LAUSD is supportive, the district's human resources department isn't designed for schools that are increasing four classes a year. Like many large districts it isn't able to offer the teachers contracts until late in the year, when a school can prove it will have sufficient students to fill those classes the next year. With Mandarin immersion teachers worth their weight in gold these days, districts that can offer contracts early on are able to lock in teachers long before LAUSD, and San Francisco Unified as well, can even make an offer.

Wang has had the heartbreak of finding a great line-up of teachers, only to see them sign with other school districts that can offer contracts earlier in the year. In addition, Mandarin immersion teaching is a high-energy, high-burnout profession, so each year a few of her teachers decide they just can't keep up with the pace. Once a program is fully built-out and solid it's easier—but in the initial 'pioneer' years the difficulties are enormous. In six years Wang will need to hire 24 teachers in one of the most sought-after and difficult-to-find teaching specialties. She sighs at the thought, but then brightens when she begins talking about the program she's helped create.

New problems

The new program has been so wildly successful that it outgrew Broadway in just three years. By 2012–2013 it was filling four Mandarin immersion kindergartens a year, "and could fill six if we had the space," Wang says. Because of that, LAUSD announced in the fall of 2013 that in the 2013–2014 school year the Mandarin program at Broadway would move to Marina Del Rey middle school, three miles away. The new school would become a K–8 Mandarin immersion community school with an English-language strand in middle school that will also offer Mandarin classes.

Such transitions aren't always smooth. When it was originally announced that the program would move, Wang was to go with it. Then in January LAUSD told parents that Wang would oversee the new Mandarin school *while at the same time* staying at Broadway to oversee three new programs there: a new Spanish immersion program, an arts-infused curriculum, and an hour-a-day Spanish language program for the English program. "Rather than dedicating her time to the sole development of our nascent Mandarin immersion program at Marina Del Rey, she would have been split between *four* programs and *two* locations," is how one parent email put it.

An outpouring of community anger at the proposal, which parents felt would have cut the Mandarin program off at the knees just as it faced its biggest challenge yet, caused the district to re-think its plan. Wang was allowed to continue to lead the Mandarin program's more than 300 students to their new school. A second set-back came when it was announced that the new building they were to move into wasn't going to be ready in time for the 2013–2014 school year. There was also tension with some families in the English program at the school.[27] For a time it looked as if the placement of the other new programs already announced for Broadway would mean cutting the number of Mandarin immersion kindergarten classes for the year. That, too, was rescinded and the school opened the year with four Mandarin immersion kindergartens. "This year, the school is at full capacity. Every single room is taken by a class," says Wang.

By the fall of 2014, plans had changed again. In the 2015–2016 school year the upper grades of the Mandarin immersion program are scheduled to move to nearby Mark Twain Middle School. Construction of a new elementary school to house the lower grades of the program at the Twain site will begin that year. The full program is projected to move to the new site in 2016–2017.

The move to a new, larger building will bring the school community "new challenges to face, new bumps in the road to manage, but also new opportunities to take advantage of," says dad Han. "Whatever the new name of our program will be, we are honored and grateful to be participants, contributors and most of all, beneficiaries of it, and are looking forward to seeing our other two children follow in our oldest daughter's footsteps."

Pioneer Valley Chinese Immersion Charter School

Hadley, Massachusetts
Founded 2007

The Pioneer Valley Chinese Immersion Charter School (PVCICS) is in the town of Hadley in western Massachusetts. The school opened in 2007, as a K–8 regional public charter school. It was the first Mandarin immersion program in the state and one of the first in the northeast. The school expanded into high school in 2013–2014, making it one of only three K – 12 Mandarin immersion schools in the nation. In 2014–2015 it had roughly 390 students. It will expand to its full capacity of 540 students in grades K–12 by 2018. Students typically enter in kindergarten, sixth or ninth grade. Entrance to the charter school is by lottery. As a public charter, the school is tuition-free.

PVCICS is a 'whole school' Mandarin program with an extended day. Students in kindergarten and first grade are in school 8:30 AM to 3:30 PM and students in second grade and higher are in school 8:30 AM to 4:15 PM Kindergarten and first grade students spend 75% of their day in Mandarin and 25% in English. At second grade it becomes a 50/50 model and then a 25/75 model starting in sixth grade, roughly two hours per day of class time taught in Chinese in later grades. "We have almost an eight hour day and we still feel sometimes we don't have enough time," to do everything we'd like to, says Kathleen Wang, the school's principal.

It is a one-way immersion program, meaning almost all students come in with no background in Chinese language. Most are native English speakers although for some Mandarin is a third language. The school uses simplified characters as the foundation, but in calligraphy classes students are exposed to traditional characters as well. The school introduces *pinyin* in third grade.

The school was co-founded by Wang and her husband Richard Alcorn, the school's executive director. In the spring of 2013 it received permission from the state of Massachusetts to extend into high school and is a candidate school for the International Baccalaureate (IB) Diploma Programme. This school is pursuing authorization as an IB World School. These are schools that share a common philosophy—a commitment to high quality, challenging and international education.

Hadley is about 100 miles west of Boston in an area known both for farming and college, including the University of Massachusetts at Amherst, Smith College, Mt. Holyoke College, Amherst College and Hampshire College. There is a small population of Chinese speakers in the area but the school's students are always "very diverse," says Wang. PVCICS has some students from families affiliated with the area colleges but most are not. They come from all over its region of service, an area that spans three counties encompassing 39 different communities. One of the counties is the poorest in the state of Massachusetts and two of the poorest cities in western Massachusetts are in its region of service. "The school's students come from a geographic area roughly 50 miles across. We're a Title I targeted assistance school," she says.

That diversity is one of the things that made the school attractive to the federal government and helped it get a $1.5 million, five-year Foreign Language Assistance Program, or FLAP, grant in 2008. These grants were crucial to the founding of many Mandarin immersion schools nationwide. When Congress eliminated the FLAP grants due to federal budget cuts in 2011, it was a surprise to PVCICS and many other programs because the FLAP program had been in existence for decades. "It's tiny to the federal budget but to schools it's a lifeline. We're very thankful to have had the funding because it was very important to help us build the program," says Wang. Thankfully PVCICS had its program in place when the grant ended, so it was less of a blow than it was to other programs.

When the school opened in 2007, it had 42 students in one cohort of kindergarteners and one cohort of first graders. Each year grades and staff were added and facilities were renovated to accommodate growth.

Since the program began, interest in Chinese immersion has grown enormously. "When we started there were fewer than 20 Chinese immersion programs in the country," said co-founder Alcorn. In 2010 the school was named one of the first of twenty in the Hanban-Asia Society Confucius Classrooms Network. Today its students are meeting and surpassing all the benchmarks its charter has set for English, Mandarin and mathematics.

PVCICS got its start because Wang and Alcorn were interested in a bilingual education for their children and because they had been working on a Massachusetts state initiative to promote improving international education in the state's schools. "We felt strongly that international education include high proficiency in world languages, of which we were focused on Mandarin," says Wang.

They began researching Mandarin programs and worked with local school districts to start one but found little interest in the early 2000s. "We talked to hundreds of parents and found there was interest throughout Pioneer Valley," says Wang. They decided to apply to open a regional charter school, something possible under Massachusetts state law, because they wanted to offer a public Chinese immersion program to a wide range of families in the area. Families come from almost every socio-economic, linguistic, racial and ethnic background. Being a regional public charter school gave the school an area that included a large enough population to support the program.

Washington Yu Ying Public Charter School
Washington D.C.
Founded 2008

Washington Yu Ying is a preschool through eighth grade Mandarin immersion charter school in Washington D.C. The school has four classes per grade in the lower grades, two in the upper grades. It began with 130 students in 2008 and in 2013–2014 had approximately 700 through sixth grade. It will expand fully through eighth grade in 2015–2016.

The school is also an International Baccalaureate school. The Yu Ying school day is an hour longer than local public schools, from 8:30 to 3:30, allowing it more time to work with students. They also have a half-day off every Friday to use for teacher planning and staff development.

The school's name, 育英, Yùyīng, means "nurturing excellence." It is used with the permission of a groundbreaking girls school founded in 1911 in Beijing established by a former Imperial Lady-in-Waiting, Madame Tzen-Kuei Wang. Her school offered classroom education at a time when the centuries-old tutorial system was still the norm in China. The school was a powerful force for educational change in China. Because it has the same name as the Beijing school, it's called Washington Yu Ying to distinguish between the two.

The school uses simplified characters and *pinyin* is introduced in third grade.

The decision to make it a public charter school was taken to allow it to create a unique focus on Mandarin immersion and to build a curriculum and environment that wasn't possible within the constraints of the D.C. public school system. Charter schools are independently operated public schools that are open to all District residents, regardless of their neighborhood, socioeconomic status, academic achievement, or ethnicity. There are no admission tests or tuition fees.

Many of Yu Ying's teachers are from local universities. There are also some from China. Most, if not all, of the teachers have an H1B visa. The school is located in northeast Washington D.C. in a beautifully renovated former seminary. Students come to the school from all eight wards of the District. Parents have created a network of chartered buses to bring students to school from around the city.

The student body is approximately 47% African-American, 30% white and 18% Asian. While the number of Asians might seem low to some schools, it's actually very high for Washington D.C. schools, which on average have only 9% Asian students. There is also a small Latino population. Overall the families are solidly middle class. The school is very popular among District families.

The Head of School, Maquita Alexander, is a former reading specialist and administrator who does not speak Chinese, but is "learning it now" as she says. Her three children attend the school. "Not only do they learn Mandarin, but their English is solid. They get things at this school that I couldn't find in public schools and couldn't afford in private," she says of the school.

Because she does not speak Chinese, Alexander considers it "critical" that the school has both a Chinese-speaking administrator and a Chinese Curriculum Consultant. The program consultant is Elizabeth Hardage, a fluent speaker of Mandarin who taught in China and is the Chinese curriculum consultant to multiple Mandarin immersion schools. She began as vice principal at Washington Yu Ying. "We needed someone who could solely advocate for Chinese," says Alexander, "Elizabeth does that." Having a consultant also allows the Chinese teachers to *teach*, while Hardage works on lesson plans and curriculum, and provides professional development, she says.

Hardage also works with teachers to "up their game," as she says. For example, Pearl You, the Chinese Program Coordinator, might have Hardage Skype into a classroom to observe a teacher giving a lesson. Later she and You will discuss the lesson and decide how best to help the teacher or the students. The school also focuses on leveraging its resources. For example, flash cards are common to all classes in a grade, so they only have to be made up once. There are also lots of games and other flash card activities posted on the parent portal so parents can work with their kids at home.

The first years of the program were somewhat rocky, as with many new programs. But after two years "it suddenly clicked," says Alexander, and parents across D.C. began clamoring to send their children there. Today it is extremely popular and very difficult to get into, with most of the school's 640 students entering in preschool. In the 2014–2015 school year there were over 1,000 applications for 14 kindergarten slots. Students who are Mandarin-proficient may test in in upper grades.

The average class has 15 students. "Our teachers voted to have small class size rather than larger classes with a classroom aide," says Alexander.

Yu Ying uses an uncommon immersion model that provides equal instructional time in each language. One week a given class has classes in Chinese on Monday, Wednesday and Friday and in English on Tuesday and Thursday. The next week they have English on Monday, Wednesday and Friday and Chinese on Tuesday and Thursday. This gives them 50% time in both languages. The model allows Mandarin-speaking teachers to teach only in Mandarin and English-speaking teachers to teach only in English. Students get a double-dose of material in both languages.

"Our goal is to have students perform at the Advanced level[28] upon graduating high-school and be able to take college level courses in Chinese," said Hardage.

Just as schools in Asia are beginning to do, Yu Ying follows a Read-First, Write-Later model. Students must be able to read, pronounce and recognize all characters but are only required to be able to write some of them. "We make the distinction between handwriting and writing," is how Hardage puts it. For the ones they don't have to be able to hand write, they use computers to write (as is common in China now). This allows students to more quickly ramp up their reading ability while still maintaining a strong link to written Chinese.

Families at Yu Ying are typically very engaged in their children's education, sometimes too much so, says principal Alexander. "They get stressed out because they can't help their kids with homework." To lower those stress levels, the school has built a strong infrastructure of support for non-Chinese speaking families. This includes an impressive amount of education for parents on how immersion works. Parents get yearly workshops and webinars so they know how to work with their students at home. There's also a series of graded readers that go home with students each week, tied to their current Chinese reading level. These books are also available on the school's parent website, so students can listen to them be read aloud at home. "This lets parents be engaged," Alexander says.

One issue the school, like all Mandarin immersion schools, has struggled with is helping students who fall behind. For some students the pace of a Mandarin immersion classroom can be too much. Students who fall two years behind in either English or Chinese are moved to the school's small English track, where all classes are in English but a daily 45-minute class in Mandarin is offered. "That way they can stay with their peers, but they're not in the Mandarin immersion program," says Alexander. This gives these students, some of whom have Individualized Education Programs or IEPs, an education suited to their needs while not requiring that the Mandarin classes become too simplistic for the bulk of students.

Yu Ying is very focused on setting clear goals for the school, for teachers and for students and then testing and assessing constantly to see what they've mastered and what they still need work on. "We have to be very clear on how to assess those targets and then be very clear on how to get students to move in the right direction to meet those targets," says Hardage.

The school also makes clear to parents that choosing Mandarin immersion is not something to be done lightly. "They're taking on a responsibility themselves, for a lot of years. In some schools you can leave your kid at the schoolhouse door and they'll be fine. But you cannot do that in a Chinese immersion program. You're signing your whole family up for immersion— for nine years!" she says.

The school asks that all parents dedicate 30 minutes a night to doing something related to their child's Chinese studies. This is in addition to homework. It can be playing games with flash cards, it can be watching a Chinese cartoon or TV show, it can be listening to a book read aloud or on the computer. "It just has to be something every single day for 30 minutes," says Hardage. "Yes, they're in an immersion program, but they're in school only six hours a day and only half that is in Chinese."

Middle school and beyond

Yu Ying's charter to continue through twelfth grade was approved in 2013. For middle and high school, Yu Ying helped create the District of Columbia International School, which will offer both a middle and high school. The new school will be located in Delano Hall, a 1933 nurses' residence at the former Walter Reed Hospital in Washington D.C. There are four member elementary schools including Washington Yu Ying:

- DC Bilingual Public Charter School (Spanish)
- Elsie Whitlow Stokes Community Freedom School (French and Spanish)
- Latin American Montessori Bilingual charter school (Spanish)
- *Mundo Verde* Bilingual (Spanish)

The school opened in the fall of 2014 and enroll up to 1,200 students when it is fully built out.

Utah Department of Education
Founded 2009

In 2014–2015, Utah had 33 Mandarin immersion schools, making it the biggest Chinese dual language immersion network in the nation. It was the first state to begin a statewide initiative to implement immersion programs in Chinese, French, Spanish, Portuguese and German. Over 20,000 students across all languages are enrolled in over 20 Utah districts, half of the state's total number of districts. Even with this kind of statewide effort, Utah educators are having a difficult time keeping up with parent demand for immersion seats.

It all began in 2008 when then-governor John Huntsman, a fluent Mandarin speaker, urged the state to launch a Dual Language Immersion initiative. It was the first such program in the nation. Since then the model has been followed by Delaware, and other states are looking into it.

That year Huntsman also initiated the Governor's Language Summit and the Governor's World Language Council, both with a goal to create a K–12 language roadmap for Utah.[29]

The Utah senate passed the International Initiatives in 2008, creating funding for Utah schools to begin Dual Language Immersion (DLI) programs in Chinese, French, and Spanish. Dual language immersion means students are taught in two languages, the 'target language' and English. In Mandarin immersion, for example, students are taught in Mandarin and English.

Extensive planning and research by Utah educators also prepared the way for the statewide implementation. Before any classroom instruction began, Utah DLI leaders worked with national immersion experts to consider important questions about DLI curriculum and teachers.

Memorandums of Understanding were put in place to welcome international guest teachers from China, Taiwan, Spain, Mexico, Brazil and France to help support instruction in the DLI classrooms. Leadership from the Licensure Office at the Utah State Office of Education worked with Gregg Roberts, the Languages and Dual Immersion Specialist, to create pathways for all of the potentially qualified local DLI teachers that would be needed in DLI classrooms. Plans for extensive immersion-specific training for all teachers were made.

District and school administrators visited immersion programs in the United States and many traveled to China as part of the College Board's China Bridge trips. DLI language directors looked at immersion curricula that would sustain the fast-paced language learning that students would experience in an immersion classroom. Where curriculum didn't exist, the DLI directors and teams of teachers began to create their own.

Through this coordinated effort, Utah's DLI teachers are supported by the largest collection of curriculum and teacher training materials available in the United States. The materials are delivered by websites and through teacher training conferences. Materials are also standardized to insure that quality and equitable instruction is available to students across the state. All of this preparation has paid off handsomely.

In 2010, Governor Gary Herbert challenged Utah to implement one hundred immersion programs in the state by 2015, with a goal of enrolling 30,000 students. The program has been so successful and there has been such demand by Utah parents that the target completion date was moved to 2014 and it is highly likely that Utah will meet and surpass Governor Herbert's challenge.

For the 2014–15 school year, Utah has 118 Dual Language Immersion schools:

- 63 Spanish
- 33 Chinese (almost 30% of all Chinese public programs in the nation)

- 14 French (the second highest number of French immersion students in the country, after Louisiana)
- 6 Portuguese (to support a large and growing Brazilian community in Utah)
- 2 German (in response to parent requests)

Utah doesn't spend a lot of money on education. In fact in 2013 it ranked dead last on the list of per-pupil spending, at $6,212.[30] New York led the nation in spending at $19,076[31] per student. The economic advantage of a 50/50 immersion model appealed to Utah's frugal educators, as no additional funding is needed for DLI teachers.

Utah districts are eligible to receive limited funding to help them purchase language-specific curriculum through Senate Bill 41 sponsored by Utah Senator Howard Stephenson. This funding for DLI programs was threatened in the Utah legislative session of 2011 and within three hours of the announcement over 10,000 emails flooded Utah legislators from concerned parents. Full funding was reinstated.

The state also has advantages that help make their programs successful, even with limited per-pupil spending. In 2013 it had a relatively homogeneous and English-speaking population that was 76.5% white. Latinos made up the largest minority group, 16%. About 33% of its students receive free or reduced-price lunches.[32] In 2011 it had the lowest number of single-parent households nationally,[33] which can be a marker for lower student achievement. This gives it fewer hurdles than many states face and lessens the impact of lower spending.

The focus on immersion education and language instruction comes because Utah realizes its strength is the education of its workforce. It's already known as a hub of language ability because of the number of Mormon missionaries who return after spending two years abroad fully fluent in the languages of the countries they worked in. The state decided to capitalize on that existing expertise and its citizens' strong awareness of the importance of bilingualism and biculturalism.

"Utah is a small state and for our future economic survival, we must educate students who are multilingual and culturally competent," says Roberts. Most of Utah's parents are involved in some way with international trade or relationships and they understand the important economic skill their children are receiving in DLI classrooms.

Parents are embracing the possibility. While few in the state speak Mandarin, many speak another language. That can make having children study in a second language less intimidating. Sherilyn Hopper is bilingual and has a daughter in her second year of Mandarin immersion. "It is exciting to see my daughter picking up on this new language, children can learn so quickly. I believe as a parent, it can be intimidating if you let yourself get overwhelmed; however; take it one day at a time and the possibilities can be endless."

Immersion parent organizations are forming around the state, mainly to encourage conversations about immersion programs and ways that parents can support their school and their children, especially when schoolwork is done in a language most of the parents don't understand. Utah's Mandarin immersion families have quickly taken up the parents' side of the equation, launching the Utah Mandarin Immersion Parent Council in 2012–2013 to provide parent support to students, families and schools statewide. Their website, at http://utahimmersioncouncil.org, offers online resources, thoughts and general information for families who embark on Mandarin immersion.

The growth of Utah's dual language immersion programs is largely due to the parent demand for more. Most immersion schools have waiting lists of students that didn't make it through the lottery process of student selection.

The Portuguese immersion program came about because of the state's 30,000 Portuguese speakers. Of those, 15,000 are Brazilian and 15,000 are returned missionaries. There are now 3 million Mormons in Brazil, which adds to the economic interchange between the nation and the state. Two other Portuguese-speaking nations, Angola and Mozambique in Africa, are also economically important, with Angola being the continent's second largest oil producer.

French is popular because it's still considered a language of culture and it's the most important business language in the world after English and Chinese, according to the latest Bloomberg report released in August 2011.

Parents are excited by the opportunities immersion offers, says Hopper. "I feel like it is a real golden opportunity to introduce our young children to not only a new language but a new culture. We have had the opportunity of having exchange students come and stay at our home for short periods of time and all of my children love it! Being able to learn about how people in other countries live and learning a foreign language in an immersion pro-gram such as this is invaluable."

Although the state teaches multiple languages through immersion beginning in elementary school, it is in Chinese where the Utah experience most directly impacts the nation. In 2011 Utah helped create a national Mandarin immersion consortium. Called the Flagship–Chinese Acquisition Pipeline, or F-CAP, the consortium allows participating states and schools to share resources, curriculum and expertise. Currently Mandarin immersion schools in 20 states are F-CAP partners. You can read more about the con-sortium and how it works in *Chapter 22: Immersion Consortia: The Support Schools Need.*

Deutsch-Chinesische Grundschule
Berlin, Germany
Founded 2011

Germany's first Mandarin immersion program is struggling to get the German educational establishment to recognize Chinese as a language in which academic subjects can be taught. The school, which launched in the fall of 2011, has been forced to settle for offering a Chinese language class to its students three times a week, rather than the immersion they had hoped for, says parent Jianqiu Wang.

Germany is awash in immersion schools. In Berlin alone there are 17. But they are called *Europaschule* (European Schools) and they focus on European languages. In Berlin, students can study 50% of their day in English, French, Spanish, Italian, Portuguese, Russian, Polish or Greek. The one exception to the European language rule is Turkish, used because of German's large Turkish immigrant population

The German Ministry of Education allows these schools to teach core academic subjects in the school's target language. Programs that want to teach in Chinese and Arabic have been proposed but not yet authorized, said Wang. "It is frustrating. If you don't have the status, then all the subjects must be taught in German."

The school is called the *Deutsch-Chinesische Grundschule*. It was launched in September of 2011 at the Planetarium Elementary School in Berlin.

In Germany a school must get permission from the German Senate to teach content subjects such as math or science in a language other than German. So far the school hasn't been able to get permission. Instead they're making do with a program which has an "emphasis" on Chinese, Wang says. Students get three hours of Mandarin instruction per week. The school currently has three classes of 13 students for now, one of five-year-olds, one of six-year-olds and one of seven-year-olds.

The country's educational establishment only recently began offering a teaching certificate in Chinese. Prior to that it was presumed that Chinese was only taught as a foreign language, at the high school or university level. "So we still have a way to go," Wang said.

One concern has been the *Abitur*. That's the exam all German students who want to attend university must take at the end of high school. Scores on the *Abitur* determine whether one can attend university and which one. The exam is given in German and the state educational ministries are concerned that students taught in a non-European language would be at a disadvantage.

In Germany, each state controls its educational organization and requirements. So far Berlin is the only state even considering allowing Chinese to be used as a language of instruction.

Lots of immersion, no Chinese

Parents certainly want the opportunity to have their children educated in Mandarin. When the school's director, Günter Urban, held a meeting of all the school's parents, he explained that only six children had enrolled in the Mandarin program. He asked the other parents in Grade One (the equivalent of the U.S. kindergarten) if they would like their children to participate in the four-hour-a-week Mandarin classes.

All the German parents raised their hands. When Herr Urban asked again "Are you sure you don't want to think about it?" they all raised their hands a second time.

"It really surprised us," says Wang, who was one of the parents that helped start the school.

Immersion preschools, but not in Mandarin

Berlin has many preschools that offer immersion. Because of this, Wang thought there would certainly be a Mandarin preschool for her son and daughter. But when she went looking, she realized that there was not a single Chinese preschool. Or in all of Germany, for that matter. There were Saturday Chinese schools but nothing that was immersion in the way the *Europaschulen* were.

Wang is from Shanghai and is married to a German. She speaks Mandarin, German and English fluently and her children are being brought up bilingually in both German and Mandarin. But she knew "if they don't learn to read and write, they'll lose their culture."

So she and a small group of Chinese and German parents in Berlin set out to first create a Mandarin preschool, called a *Kindergarten* in German. There were also two students from German-speaking families who had gone to preschool in China because their families were living there for work. Their children left China speaking Mandarin fluently but when they returned to Germany, "they had no possibility to speak Chinese again at home or in school, so they forgot their Chinese. It was very sad," Wang says.

Starting a parent-initiated preschool isn't that difficult in Germany, so the families were able to create one, says Wang. It begins, as *Kindergartens* do in Germany, at age 1 and continues through age 4.

But when students turn 5 they begin *Grundschule*, or elementary school. And there was no place for them to continue Chinese. Inspired by the co-founder of a French *Europaschule,* the families began discussing starting a public Chinese immersion elementary school. "People told us that it's not possible, that Chinese is too difficult a language for German students to learn. They can learn European languages, but not Chinese," Wang says.

The parents knew better. They reached out to the public schools. Herr Urban, the principal of the Planetarium School, located next to Berlin's planetarium, gave them a very positive answer and support. "He was very open-minded," she says. Perhaps as importantly, he had the flexibility to take on more students because his school did not have enough students to fill all its classrooms.

About 50% of the families have at least one Mandarin-speaking parent, the rest are German speakers. "Chinese is very popular here now," says Wang. "We just heard from the Chinese embassy that China is the second most popular place for German students to want to do an exchange program with, after the United States. That surprised us."

The school has benefited from San Francisco's experience creating one of the country's first Chinese immersion programs, the now-30-year-old Cantonese immersion program at West Portal Elementary School in San Francisco. "We've been talking to Jenny Lee, the teacher at West Portal, and she's been helping us," says Wang. The program uses the *Better Chinese* books, which are used at many Mandarin immersion programs in the United States. There are no German-Mandarin textbooks for elementary schools available.

"The American experience has been really helpful to us, because otherwise there wouldn't be anywhere for us to go to ask questions," says Wang.

Chinese immigrants in Germany are primarily Mandarin-speaking, says Wang. The country does not have the historical connection to Cantonese that many immigrant communities in the United States have. For that reason they chose to use simplified characters, as that's what most families in the program already read.

As in the *Europaschule*, they plan to teach math and German in German while science, social studies and Mandarin will be taught in Mandarin. As in all German schools, English classes will begin at age 7.

There's a small bit of tension between the German and Chinese educational styles, though it's not that big a problem, says Wang. Chinese families want higher levels of Chinese because the language is part of their culture. But German parents are against pushing kids hard to learn. "They say 'It should be fun, we don't need too much pressure.' But we'll find a way to balance both," she says.

Mandarin Chinese Language Immersion Magnet School
Houston, Texas
Founded 2012

To the rest of the country this might seem like an odd statement, but here goes. If you were going to design the best public Mandarin immersion school you possibly could, it would probably look a lot like the one that launched in September of 2012—in Houston, Texas.

Houston? Really?

Yes, Houston. Really. When the Houston Independent School District (HISD) decided to create a Mandarin immersion school it didn't do what many districts do:

- Houston didn't make Mandarin a single strand in a larger school, making it impossible for the school's culture to focus on Chinese.

- Houston didn't put in just one classroom per grade, which makes for tiny classes in the upper grades as students move, often requiring a difficult to teach fourth-fifth split class.

- Houston didn't place it as a small strand in a low-performing school to bring in active parents, launching a school with a host of tensions between the strands over funding and emphasis.

- Houston didn't make the school K–5 and then jump to a middle school where the Mandarin students would be a tiny proportion of students in a much larger school.

- Houston didn't start from scratch, expecting its newly hired teachers to somehow create a program out of whole cloth as they also taught full time, burning them out in the process.

Houston did it Texas-sized.

In August of 2012, Houston opened a 100% Mandarin immersion school, the district's first. It began with kindergarten, first and second grade. The program began with 250 students its first year and had 307 by the second. The school will add one grade per year until it reaches eighth grade in 2018–2019. When it is fully built out it will be home to 836 students. This year's kindergarten had four classes totaling 88 students, an extremely lucky number in Chinese—and clearly just as lucky for the families who got in on the ground floor as well.

The school has been wildly successful, especially for a new, untried program in a language that's never been taught in a Houston elementary school before. "It's been phenomenal," said the founding principal Bryan Bordelon. Because the entire school is focused on Chinese, it has given the opportunity to learn Mandarin to a large number of students in the district. That's much better than a strand in a school, which would have made Mandarin a "neat little quirk we can offer for 25 to 50 kids."

There's certainly demand for the program. In 2013 the school had "more people on the wait list for our entire school than we have total enrolled students," said Bordelon. For the 2014–2015 school year there were more than 400 applications for the school's 88 kindergarten seats, said new principal ChaoLin Chang.

In fact pretty much the only thing Houston did that seems even a little off is the ungainly name they saddled the school with. It's officially The Mandarin Chinese Language Immersion Magnet School. Even its acronym, MCLIMS, doesn't really roll off the tongue. The school community is already discussing what it will take to change the name, and the first Shared Decisions Making Committee (SDMC) meeting of the 2013–2014 addressed it.

As to why Chinese in Texas, Bordelon says that while Texas may seem a more likely home for Spanish immersion, Houston is actually an extremely international city. It has a very large business population that works with Asia, so much so that Houston has a Chinese consul in the city. With so many international oil and energy companies headquartered there, businesses are clamoring for multilingual workers. The school is already talking to large corporations about support for its program.

Keeping the middle class in public schools

One of the really wonderful outcomes of the way the district created the Mandarin immersion school was that it has become a true magnet for a large number of families who otherwise would have sent their children to private schools or moved to the suburbs. As multiple other schools nationwide have found, immersion is a powerful carrot to keep families in the public school system. In fact the school sits across the street from two private schools, an Episcopal high school and the Post Oak School, both of which cost in the $30,000-a-year range.

But instead parents are knocking down the door to get into Mandarin immersion. "The waiting list is long and getting longer," said parent James Troutman. "Which is like 'Hello, Houston? You need another school!'"

Far from creating a segregated school that was primarily white and Asian, as many districts fear will happen, the Mandarin school is extremely mixed. For the 2013–2014 school year, the student body was made up of 21% white students, 20% African-American students, 27% Hispanic students and 23% Asian students.

That's a far cry from the rest of Houston's schools. While Houston itself is about 25% non-Hispanic white, white students make up just 11% of the students in the school district. District-wide, Asians make up just 3.3% of students while the city's Asian population is 6% according to the 2012 Census. The program is clearly pulling in a high percentage of white and Asian families, two demographics that all too often leave the public schools.

Schools that make major shifts like this have to find their own way. Here's one example: In Houston schools are allowed six "Foods of Minimal Nutritional Value" (FMNV) days. Those are days when things like candy and cake are allowed in school. Traditionally schools use those for holidays such as Halloween, Thanksgiving, Valentine's Day and the Last Day of School. In

October of 2013 the school's SDMC voted to change one of its FMNV days from Valentine's Day to Chinese New Year, so students could indulge in sweet Chinese treats.

Active parents

Houston is a zoned school district, meaning students are assigned to schools in their local zone. But the Chinese school is not zoned, so families must apply to get in. No one is automatically assigned there. That makes for "a very willing parent body," says Bordelon. "They made this choice. No one is zoned to us—everyone has to apply."

The families who come are engaged and active in the extreme. The school's newly created Parent-Teacher Organization hit the ground running. It held a large fundraiser in the spring and ended its first year with $16,000 in the bank, impressive for a new organization.

Placement

The most complex part of the endeavor has been the placement of the school. It took over the building of an existing but very poorly enrolled school called Gordon Elementary. Gordon was an overflow school. When there were too many students from a nearby zone to go to their zoned school, they were sent to Gordon.

Now the English program that was at Gordon is being phased out and for the 2013–2014 school year there are fewer than 50 students from it who will finish out fifth grade there, says Bordelon. While they're there "we're working hard to make sure that it isn't two separate campuses." Those students learn about Chinese cultures in physical education and music classes. They are also immersed in the Chinese language and culture during daily morning assemblies.

Setup

To create its first Mandarin immersion program, Houston chose to join the Flagship–Chinese Acquisition Pipeline (F-CAP) consortium. Joining the consortium "has been a phenomenal connection for us," says Bordelon. "We're not reinventing the wheel. The professional development opportunities for our teachers is amazing."

Remarkably, Bordelon was able to hire all the teachers he needed from within the Houston school system. The sprawling and enormous district includes 273 schools and 11,000 teachers. It turned out that there were a surprising number who spoke Mandarin fluently. Bordelon had to hire six Chinese teachers in the program's first year and had 65 applicants. "I had one teacher who's trilingual. She was born in China, raised in Costa Rica and then spent 17 years teaching in a Spanish bilingual school."

Moving into high school should be easy. Bordelon said he's already had multiple Houston high school principals approach him about how they can get ready to attract his graduating eighth graders come 2019.

The school was also lucky with its first principal. Bordelon's father worked for an oil company and he spent much of his childhood overseas, in Indonesia, Qatar and Venezuela. He then studied Mandarin at the University of Texas, went on to attend a summer immersion program at Middlebury College in Vermont and lived in China for a year.

Getting the program up and running is, "one of the things I'm most proud of," he says. "I can't lie and say it wasn't hard work. They announced the school in December of 2011. They started taking applications in January of 2012 and there was literally nothing. I was named to the position in February 2012 and basically told, 'Create a Mandarin immersion school. Go!'"

Bordelon proved to be so good at his job that HISD moved him to a new position, launching a college readiness program across the district. The new principal is ChaoLin Chang. An educator in Austin school for 12 years, Chang grew up in Taiwan and is a fluent speaker of Mandarin. He's also working on building the school's sister school relationship with an elementary school affiliated with People's University in Beijing, Renmin Elementary School.

How it got started

Houston also is extraordinary in how it got its Mandarin program. In most schools, parents are the ones who want Chinese immersion and they spend years trying to convince their school district that it's a good idea. Often the most committed parents give up when their children have to enter kindergarten or first grade and become too old to join whatever program eventually gets created. That leaves the core group constantly working to attract new members while the school district ponders the idea.

In Houston the biggest champion has been the school board itself, whereas in many districts it's the major stumbling block. Board member Harvin Moore had focused on the idea since taking two education-related trips to China. He also visited a Mandarin immersion program in San Diego, where Houston Superintendent Terry Grier used to work. "Much of the push to create an immersion school was based on those two individuals," says Bordelon.

The future

Clearly Houston's model only works in a large school district with enough schools that turning one into a full-immersion program leaves enough space in English programs. A small school district with just a handful of elementary schools would be hard pressed to make a case for creating an all-immersion school, simply because it would restrict family choices far too much. But in a large district like Houston, which has 276 schools, turning one or more all-immersion creates rather than restricts choices.

The school is beginning to think about building out its middle school. It is seriously considering keeping its Chinese/English ratio at 50/50 in middle school, unlike most programs, which typically go to 20/80 for middle school. The minutes of the August SDMC meeting say, "To prepare students for success on AP Chinese in ninth grade, the school needs to continue its Chinese immersion model."

The school has proved so popular that it's getting a new building. The Bellaire building where it began wasn't big enough to hold the anticipated 900 students the school will have when it is fully built out. There had been plans to renovate the building. However in February of 2014 the school district's Board of Trustees voted to move the school to a new campus about three miles west of the current school, in Houston's Westside.

The new campus will be eight acres and include a new building that is expected to cost $32 million, a project that was part of a school bond election in 2012.

The Houston Independent School District also has two Spanish immersion schools as well as multiple Spanish bilingual programs. The Mandarin program is on the west side of town and it has proven so popular that there is talk of opening another Chinese immersion school on the east side. But others have suggested opening another immersion school in another language.

Principal Chang said, "I cannot speak for the district regarding Mandarin Chinese immersion programs. However, based on the number of applications we have received (more than 400) for the limited spots next school year (88), it is popular. Hopefully, our school will prove immersion works, which leads to other Mandarin Chinese immersion programs elsewhere in HISD."

Whether another immersion school will open and what language it would teach remains to be seen. But clearly Houston is a school district that has put itself on the map by creating a robust, popular and high-performing Chinese immersion program with none of the baggage that causes so many programs to struggle. Other large urban school districts would do well to learn from their example.

1. Michael Weiss, "Killer of Moscone, Milk had Willie Brown on list," *San Jose Mercury News*. September 18, 1998.
2. Megan Wyman, *Standing Strong: Celebrating 30 Years of Chinese American International School*. (San Francisco, Blurb Press, 2013)

Available for purchase at
http://www.blurb.com/b/4290404-standing-strong-softcover

3. Megan Wyman, *Standing Strong: Celebrating 30 Years of Chinese American International School*, (San Francisco, Blurb Press, 2013) 5.

4. Megan Wyman, *Standing Strong: Celebrating 30 Years of Chinese American International School*, (San Francisco, Blurb Press, 2013) 12.

5. Megan Wyman, *Standing Strong: Celebrating 30 years of Chinese American International School*, (San Francisco, Blurb Press, 2013) 70.

6. Portland Public Schools. Program Models and Definitions.
http://www.pps.k12.or.us/departments/immersion/7189.htm
Accessed June 8, 2014.

7. Portland Public Schools, Long range facility plan, "Issue Paper #5.3 School Utilization."
http://www.pps.k12.or.us/files/facilities/Issue_Paper_5_3.pdf
Accessed June 8, 2014.

8. Betsy Hammond, "Portland may get its first public French immersion school," *Oregon Live*, Dec. 13, 2011.
http://www.oregonlive.com/portland/index.ssf/2011/12/portland_may_get_its_first_pub.html
Accessed June 8, 2014.

9. Le Monde French Immersion Public Charter School
http://www.lemondeimmersion.org/pages/Le_Monde
Accessed June 8, 2014.

10. *Scholastic*, "Year of the Chinese Language," August 2007.
http://www.scholastic.com/browse/article.jsp?id=3746848
Accessed June 8, 2014.

11. Portland Public Schools. PPS Mandarin Chinese Immersion.
http://www.pps.k12.or.us/departments/immersion/1138.htm
Accessed June 8, 2014.

12. Jennifer Steele, Robert Slater, Gema Zammarro, Jennifer Li, "The Effect of Dual-Language Immersion on Student Performance in the Portland Public Schools: Evidence from the First Year Study," Presented at the Society for Research on Educational Effectiveness fall conference, Washington D.C., September 28, 2013.

13. Portland Public Schools, "Immersion Chinese/中文."
http://www.pps.k12.or.us/departments/immersion/4379.htm
Accessed June 8, 2014.

14. University of Oregon Chinese Flagship Program.
http://chineseflagship.uoregon.edu
Accessed June 8, 2014.

15. Language Flagship Chinese.
http://www.thelanguageflagship.org/content/chinese
Accessed June 8, 2014.

16. Dave Porter, "Mandarin immersion capacity: Portland Public Schools annual decision has global impact," *Blue Oregon*, April 19, 2010.
http://www.blueoregon.com/2010/04/mandarin-immersion-capacity-portland-public-schools-annual-decision-has-global-impact/
Accessed June 8, 2014.

17. Natalie St. John, "Wahkiakum County Commissioner Marsyla won't seek re-election, *The Daily News Online*. Feb. 27, 2012.

http://tdn.com/news/local/wahkiakum-county-commissioner-marsyla-won-t-seek-re-election/article_06b5cf52-61d8-11e1-a434-001871e3ce6c.html#ixzz1nsn17HhX
Accessed Jan. 16, 2014.

18. Nicole Dungca, "Portland Public Schools budget draws both outcry and support," *The Oregonian*, May 1, 2013.
http://www.oregonlive.com/portland/index.ssf/2013/05/portland_public_schools_budget.html
Accessed June 8, 2014.

19. *Portland Public School News*, "PPS expands dual immersion," January 27, 2014.
http://www.pps.k12.or.us/news/9412.htm
Accessed June 8, 2014.

20. Chinese Immersion Program, Minnetonka Public Schools. 2010.
http://vimeo.com/14073402
Accessed June 8, 2014.

21. Minnetonka Public Schools. Chinese and Spanish Language Immersion.
http://www.minnetonka.k12.mn.us/academics/immersion/pages/default.aspx
Accessed June 8, 2014.

22. The Hanyu Shuiping Kaoshi, (汉语水平考试, *Hànyǔ Shuǐpíng Kǎoshì*), is the Chinese proficiency test used by the People's Republic of China to test the standard Chinese language proficiency of non-native speakers. The Advanced with Honors designation is for "learners who can easily understand any information communicated in Chinese and are capable of smoothly expressing themselves in written or oral form."

23. Degen Pener, "Venice Spotlight: Is the coolest neighborhood in L.A. overheating?" *Hollywood Reporter*, Oct. 19, 2012.
http://www.hollywoodreporter.com/news/venice-coolest-neighborhood-la-overheating-380132?page=show
Accessed June 8, 2014.

24. Broadway Elementary School, *DragonSprouts*
http://www.broadwayelementary.org/dragonsprouts
Accessed June 8, 2014.

25. If you want to read about what it feels like on the ground, Sandra Tsing Loh tells a great story. She's got a book out, *Mother on Fire*, and a piece from *The Atlantic* that many of us recognize parts of our own schools in.
Sandra Tsing Loh, "Tales Out of School: How a Pushy, Type A Mother Stopped Reading Jonathan Kozol and Learned to Love the Public Schools," *The Atlantic*, March 2008.
http://www.theatlantic.com/magazine/archive/2008/03/tales-out-of-school/306645/
Accessed June 8, 2014.

26. Los Angeles Unified School District, Dual Language Program.
http://notebook.lausd.net/portal/page?_pageid=33,230293&_dad=ptl
Accessed June 8, 2014.

27. Gary Walker, "Moving school's Mandarin program ignites fierce community debate," The Argonaut, March 14, 2013.
http://argonautnews.com/moving-schools-mandarin-program-ignites-fierce-community-debate/
Accessed June 25, 2014.

28. On the ACTFL scale. See *Chapter 14: How Much Chinese Will They Learn?* for more information on how this scale works and what it means.

29. Governor's World Language Council, "Utah Language Roadmap for the 21st Century,"
http://www.schools.utah.gov/CURR/dualimmersion/Home/
Utah-Language-Road-for-the-21st-Century.aspx
Accessed June 8, 2014.

30. Michael Sauter, "States Spending the Most (and Least) on Education, 24/7 Wall St.
http://247wallst.com/special-report/2013/05/31/states-that-spend-the-most-on-education/5/
Accessed June 8, 2014.

31. Michael Sauter, "States Spending the Most (and least) on Education, 24/7 Wall St.
http://247wallst.com/special-report/2013/05/31/states-that-spend-the-most-on-education/5/
Accessed June 8, 2014.

32. Kristen Moulton, "Utah's Schools Educating 11,566 More Students This Year," *The Salt Lake Tribune*, Nov. 10, 2013.
http://www.sltrib.com/sltrib/news/57101542-78/percent-students-district-enrollment.html.csp
Accessed June 8, 2014

33. Lisa Schencker, "To exit last place in per-pupil funding, Utah would need to spend $365 million more a year," *The Salt Lake Tribune*, May 22, 2013.
http://www.sltrib.com/sltrib/news/56351636-78/utah-education-state-task
.html.csp
Accessed June 8, 2014.

二十二 Immersion Consortia:
èr shí èr The Support Schools
22 Need

Mandarin immersion programs in elementary school are growing at a tremendous rate. In the 2014–2015 school year alone 18 U.S. schools began programs. Most of those schools start from scratch with nothing but the desire to teach in Mandarin. They are often just one school in a district that has few Mandarin speakers, with no staff who have experience setting up a Mandarin immersion school, no Mandarin-speaking principal and sometimes no Mandarin-speaking teachers to start.

Until recently, there's been no road map for these programs, no "Mandarin immersion in a box" that could tell them, step-by-step, what was needed to create a vibrant, academically strong Mandarin immersion program. Each school has had to work out for itself how to go about creating what many in the world of education believe to be one of the most challenging types of school programs that exists.

If they were lucky, program administrators were able to attend a Chinese language conference before they launched. Until 2012 and the publication of *Chinese Language Learning in the Early Grades: A Handbook of Resources and Best Practices for Mandarin Immersion* by the Asia Society, there wasn't even a book that discussed effective practices for starting and maintaining Mandarin immersion programs.

Thankfully this is beginning to change. Multiple conferences offer insight and techniques including:

- The American Council on the Teaching of Foreign Languages (ACTFL)
- The Chinese Language Education Forum
- The Center for Advanced Research on Language Acquisition (CARLA) Conference on Language Immersion Education[1]
- The National Chinese Education Conference
- The National Chinese Language Conference

The Asia Society's China Learning Initiative, which runs the National Chinese Language Conference, has lots of information on its website.[2]

The Center for Advanced Research on Language Acquisition at the University of Minnesota also does several summer teacher trainings specifically for Chinese immersion teachers that are very helpful.[3]

Education professionals with experience in Mandarin immersion are now also beginning to be available to consult with newer programs. However, probably the most helpful guides for schools nationwide come from Mandarin immersion consortia that provide support and guidance for programs. There are several:

- Confucius Classrooms
- The Minnesota Mandarin Immersion Collaborate
- Utah's Flagship–Chinese Acquisition Pipeline (F-CAP)
- The Chinese Early Language and Immersion Network (CELIN)

Confucius Classrooms

These are Chinese language programs supported by Hanban, the Chinese government agency that works to establish Chinese language programs overseas. According to its website, there were about 70 such classrooms in K–12 schools in the United States in 2014.[4] These programs support language and culture. Most are not immersion programs but simply offer Chinese classes. The schools are linked with partner schools in China and get support through newsletters, professional development seminars and conferences. The Asia Society also has a network of "exemplary Chinese language programs" that are part of the Confucius Classroom Network; some of these are immersion programs.[5]

The Minnesota Mandarin Immersion Collaborative

This is an ongoing but diminished partnership between five Minnesota K–12 Mandarin immersion program schools, and two entities at the University of Minnesota, the Center for Advanced Research on Language Acquisition (CARLA) and the Confucius Institute. The MMIC was originally formed through a federal Foreign Language Assistance Program (FLAP) grant. The grant that supported the collaboration ended in 2012, so the consortium is now more informal. Dr. Molly Wieland, program coordinator for Hopkins Public Schools' XinXing Academy, and Dr. Tara Fortune, the immersion program director at CARLA, are the lead partners for the immersion programs in the consortium.

Schools in the collaborative include:

- Excelsior Elementary Mandarin Immersion Programs, Minnetonka Public Schools
- GuangMing Academy (a strand Madison Elementary School), St. Cloud Public Schools
- Jie Ming Mandarin Immersion Academy, St. Paul Public Schools
- Scenic Heights Elementary Mandarin Immersion Program, Minnetonka Public Schools
- XinXing Academy (a strand in Eisenhower Elementary), Hopkins Public Schools

As part of its work, the MMIC curriculum team developed curriculum for Mandarin immersion programs that included a third grade science unit called "Just Passing Through: Designing Model Membranes."[6] The MMIC assessment team adapted and piloted oral proficiency assessments for students in grades K–5 using tools initially developed by the Center for Applied Linguistics (CAL): Student Oral Proficiency Assessment (SOPA) and CAL Oral Proficiency Exam. Dr. Tara Fortune, lead University of Minnesota partner and director of CARLA's Immersion Projects, is carrying out research that examines the Mandarin language and literacy development of K–5 students participating in early total immersion programs. It is available online at CARLA's website.[7]

Flagship–Chinese Acquisition Pipeline (F-CAP)

In 2011 Utah, which has the largest number of linked Chinese immersion schools in the nation, launched a consortium led by Brigham Young University and the Utah State Office of Education. The project was funded by The Language Flagship, a federal program that supports K–16 language learning and links students from immersion programs with appropriate-level courses when they reach the college level.

F-CAP is made up of multiple state departments of education and individual school districts in more than 20 other states as well as Chinese Flagship universities.

The goal of the consortium is aligned to the goals of the Language Flagship; to create "a national model of well-articulated and replicable K–16 pathways for Chinese language study" that results in students' superior level of proficiency by the time they graduate college, said Gregg Roberts, World Languages & Dual Immersion Specialist with the Utah State Office of Education in Salt Lake City.

To translate that for parents, this means that experts in the field familiar with the constraints placed on public schools in various types of settings (urban, rural, suburban, etc.) have put together a proven curriculum for Mandarin immersion that your school can use. This means really nitty-gritty stuff like putting together over 1,400 daily lesson plans covering math, science, social studies and Chinese. When a new teacher walks into an F-CAP classroom, he or she walks in prepared. This is in sharp contrast to many programs where teachers are expected to "fill in the blanks" between their school district's curriculum and teaching that same curriculum in Mandarin.

F-CAP also includes a substantial amount of teacher and principal training, including summer workshops, websites and on-going support. In short, it's a one-stop shop for school districts that allows them to take advantage of the collective wisdom of hundreds of teachers and administrators.

The consortium outlines two pathways. The first is for students entering immersion programs in either kindergarten or first grade. The second is for students beginning their Chinese instruction in middle or high school. The goal of each is to have students reach an advanced level of proficiency[8] by high school graduation. Students coming out of either of these pathways will be primed to enter a Chinese Flagship university in the United States offering advanced Chinese training here and in China. The list of these universities can be found at http://www.thelanguageflagship.org/chinese.

These goals and the model for the two pathways come directly out of Utah's Language Roadmap, an initiative started by Utah Governor Jon Huntsman in 2008. Leaders from Utah's government, education, and business communities were invited to attend three summits in 2008 and 2009 to provide the Roadmap with input on the language skills students need to contribute to Utah's global economy and how to give them those skills through the immersion and secondary language pathways.

Utah's schools implemented the Roadmap plan in 2009[9] by starting immersion programs in Chinese, French, and Spanish. It also opened discussions with the Utah State Office of Education (USOE) about their plans to support stronger secondary language programs. School districts were encouraged to apply to the USOE for a small grant to help them start immersion programs, funding that was made available through Utah Senate Bill 41, the Critical Languages Bill sponsored by Senator Howard Stephenson.

Since 2009, Utah has become a model in how to implement, support and sustain replicable programs in Chinese, French, Spanish, Portuguese and German across over 20 Utah school districts. Each is autonomous in how it implements curriculum. However, to be a part of the state system there are a few requirements that must be met. So while individuals programs will look different, they have a backbone of similarity.

Much as the International Baccalaureate program has become a recognized leader in education, the Chinese K–12 consortium is creating an easy-to-replicate program that can be implemented at any school anywhere in the country. It is being funded in part by a grant from the Language Flagship,[10] a federally-funded component of the National Security Education Program at the U.S. Department of Defense.

F-CAP has an executive committee and advisory board to guarantee effective use of resources, equal opportunity for all consortium members, plans for national dissemination, program evaluation, and program quality control to ensure consistency in the pedagogical philosophy, goals, and approaches throughout the program consortium. In addition to the executive committee and advisory board, Sandra Talbot directs the immersion strand for the F-CAP consortium.

The state of Utah has done a great deal to support the F-CAP consortium. Two national F-CAP meetings held in Utah in 2012 and 2013 brought together the executive committee and advisory board and leaders from participating F-CAP institutions. Utah's efforts to support Chinese immersion teachers and curriculum via the internet were shared and discussed. The consortium has created teacher training videos, student online learning and curriculum maps, just to name a few.

The Brigham Young University Chinese Flagship and the Arizona State University Chinese Flagship are also developing teacher training and curriculum support for Chinese language secondary programs to be delivered via the internet. This will give smaller school districts that might not have the staff or funding to provide appropriate high school level classes in Chinese a way to ensure that immersion students don't spend their high school years twiddling their thumbs waiting to get to college where they can find courses at their level—and forgetting their Chinese in the process.

Although curriculum-specific information is password protected for members of the consortium, the open websites for both the immersion and secondary programs provide a wide range of information that is helpful to administrators, teachers and parents. The Utah Chinese immersion website can be found at http://utahchineseimmersion.org and the secondary website can be found at http://www.clt7-12.org. The F-CAP website, which has links to both of these and provides more information about the consortium, can be found at http://www.f-cap.org.

Programs in the consortium

- Utah State Office of Education
- South Carolina Department of Education
- Delaware Department of Education
- Georgia Department of Education
- Oklahoma Department of Education
- Kentucky Department of Education

  School districts include those from:

- Arizona

- California
- Delaware
- Georgia
- Illinois
- Idaho
- Kentucky
- Massachusetts
- Michigan
- Mississippi
- New York
- Ohio
- Oklahoma
- Oregon
- Rhode Island
- South Carolina
- Tennessee
- Texas
- Utah
- Wyoming

What the "Utah model" looks like in the classroom

50/50 Chinese/English instruction and a minimum of two classes per grade level

This allows schools to hire one Chinese-speaking teacher for each grade level and one English teacher. In the morning half the students are instructed in one language and in the afternoon they switch to the other, which means that two full classes of students are able to participate. "Our target language teachers are never required to teach in English," says Roberts. This makes hiring and teaching easier. There are also economic benefits to the 50/50 model that give it sustainability. Because both the Chinese teacher and English teacher are sharing two classrooms, both are supported as part of the school's regular full-time faculty. No additional funding is necessary to support a Chinese teacher.

Dual language

All programs work on the dual-language model, meaning they are meant for both Mandarin-speaking and English-speaking students. In dual-language programs, Mandarin speakers and English speakers aid each other in learning both languages. Some immersion programs are one-way, meaning all students are expected to be fluent English speakers who are new to Mandarin. While many of the schools in the Utah program have low levels of Mandarin-speaking students (as is the case nationally in almost all Mandarin immersion programs) they are designed to offer the chance for Mandarin-speaking students to learn English and English-speaking students to learn Mandarin.

All schools use the same progression

In K–3, the Chinese curriculum includes Chinese, math, science, and social studies. The English curriculum focuses on language arts.

In fourth and fifth grades, math and social sciences are taught in English. In sixth grade, social science shifts back to Chinese and science shifts to English.

In seventh through ninth grades, student have two classes a day in Chinese: one in Chinese language arts and one in another subject.

In ninth grade students take the AP Chinese exam and a class in world geography in Chinese.

In tenth through twelfth grade, students will be offered university-level course work through blended learning with six major Utah universities. Students are also encouraged to begin study of a third language in high school.

A state program of teacher recruitment

Utah sponsors J-1 work visas for teachers from China and Taiwan and has a well-organized guest teacher program that licenses the teachers for three years. The state has a Memoranda of Understanding with China and Taiwan to bring in teachers. Hanban[11] in China is developing immersion teachers for Utah's needs. Beginning in 2013, Hanban guest teachers targeted for immersion classrooms were given elementary level immersion-specific training for eight weeks in China prior to their coming to the U.S. The training focused on how to teach in an immersion classroom and to help them adjust to the challenges of teaching subjects many of them have never taught before, like math and science, and how to work in American classrooms. The Hanban is also recruiting more elementary teachers to be interviewed to come to the U.S., as the demand for elementary immersion teachers is now outpacing the demand for secondary teachers.

There is also a strong system of support for the teachers. In addition to their visa, they get a week of education at the Annual Utah Dual Immersion Institute as well as four meetings a year for the entire team. There is a state-wide Chinese Dual Language Immersion director who oversees the Chinese Dual Language Immersion (DLI) program along with a team of state coordinators who support all of the 97 Chinese teachers currently teaching in 2013 in Utah's Chinese immersion classrooms. Among the state's coordinators is He De, a national Hanban coordinator who shares his responsibility between Utah and the rest of the U.S. supporting Hanban teachers. Since joining the USOE Chinese dual language immersion leadership team in 2011, He De has been critical in raising awareness with the Hanban about the needs of Hanban teachers in immersion classrooms, helping facilitate recruitment and training.

Training for administrators

The Utah Dual Language Immersion Advisory Council, made up of district administrators, principals and instructional specialists from all DLI schools and districts, is brought together four times a year for training and sharing of information. The USOE Chinese dual language director and coordinators also give personalized support to administrators, as needed, for challenges unique to their school and district.

Cross-coordination among all DLI programs in all languages

Teachers in all Utah DLI languages (Spanish, Chinese, French and Portuguese) are sometimes trained together, except when there is language-specific information to be conveyed. This allows a larger community of teachers to share knowledge and experience. A successful example is the STARTALK teacher training programs held for both the Chinese and Portuguese immersion programs in Utah each year. This collaboration allows the teachers from both languages an opportunity to "test" their immersion teaching skills on a non-fluent audience of teachers from another language and provides them with feedback before they enter a classroom full of students.

No English allowed after January of first grade

As was mentioned before, F-CAP has a few required policies for schools that join the consortium. One of them is that no English is allowed in the Chinese portion of the day after the winter break in first grade. "Kids must start doing all their group work in the target language. It's all about expectations of teachers, students and parents," says Roberts. To help with that, Utah focuses on teaching students not just academic Chinese but also social language. "They teach them how to say, 'It's my turn,' 'Move over,' 'What do you think?' etc.," adds Roberts.

Reading is still the wildcard

Utah, like all Chinese immersion programs, is very aware of the difficulties of getting students to read more in Chinese. Students in this country face the difficulty of having to first learn Chinese and then learn to read and write it. The sheer number of characters that must be memorized to be able to read at grade level (Chinese grade level, that is) is daunting.

Co-chaired by Gregg Roberts and Sandra Talbot, Utah has convened two meetings so far to talk about literacy and what came out was a great big question mark: "There is no definitive answer. We don't have enough data. It's a big open area to do research on," says Roberts.

For kindergarten and first grade, Utah uses the *Better Chinese* textbooks from the Palo Alto-based company by the same name. For second through sixth grade, Utah has adopted the textbooks Singapore uses for Chinese education in elementary school, *Chinese Language for Primary Schools*. These are the same textbooks used by Portland's well-known Chinese immersion program.

Singapore is actually one giant immersion program itself, so it's a good match for immersion students here. More than 50% of children in Singapore live in homes that speak a Chinese dialect, the rest speak English, Malay, Tamil or other languages at home. The main language of instruction in elementary school is English but all students must also learn one of the others as their second language. Just as the Singapore Math textbooks are considered among the world's best, Singapore's Chinese textbooks for elementary school are also considered excellent. "We've had a lot of issues with teachers and parents saying 'It's too hard,' but we say 'Better hard now than later,'" Roberts said.

Utah's Chinese Dual Language Immersion classes work about one to two semesters behind what students would be doing in Singapore, so in 2nd grade they do textbooks 1B and 2A, then in 3rd grade 2B and 3A, he says.

"We have learned one thing—we know that without having rigorous literacy materials, your kids aren't going to go anywhere. Literacy is the key to everything and the sooner you get kids literate so they can read, read, read," the sooner they will be able to progress in the language, Roberts says.

Like other Chinese DLI programs nationally, Utah is always on the lookout for a better solution to Chinese literacy curriculum and reading materials. "I am constantly being contacted by publishers who want to talk to us about new Chinese curriculum and reading materials they believe will work for immersion students but we see a big gap in the reading materials available for students, especially in grades 3 to 6," says Talbot.

Chinese Early Language and Immersion Network

This group, called CELIN, was established through the Asia Society's Chinese Language Initiatives program in 2012. Its director is Dr. Shuhan Wang. CELIN aims to:

> Support the growth and sustainability of Chinese early language and immersion programs in and outside the United States to ensure that students have the opportunity to develop high-level multilingual

and intercultural competency for advanced study and work in an interconnected world.[12]

CELIN[13] plans to create several supports for programs nationally, for both immersion schools and for schools teaching Chinese. Its goals are to:

- Distribute a CELIN website and newsletter
- Create a directory of Chinese early language and immersion programs
- Identify and develop model Chinese early language and immersion programs, including Confucius Classrooms
- Work with professional organizations, teacher preparation programs, state certification agencies and local education institutions to cultivate effective Chinese language teachers for elementary schools and immersion programs

Long term, CELIN plans to:

- Create curriculum frameworks for K – 8 immersion programs
- Make reading materials for immersion teachers available
- Write a guide to language assessment resources for Chinese immersion programs
- Produce instructional videos with exemplary teachers
- Post online lesson plans
- Disseminate resources and best practices through the web, publications, conferences and seminars

The group also hopes to create a network of up to 30 "high-quality" Chinese immersion Confucius Classrooms that can serve as models for other programs. In addition, CELIN is considering working to develop a multi-state alternative certification route for Chinese immersion teachers. This would be very helpful as currently there is no nationally recognized certification for immersion teachers.

I serve as a parent representative on CELIN's advisory board.

1. This international conference was first hosted by CARLA at the University of Minnesota in 1995, with partial funding from the U.S. Department of Education Title VI Language Resource Center grant. CARLA hosted the conference again in 2004, 2008 and 2012. CARLA invited state leaders in Utah and North Carolina as partners so that the conference can take place once every two years and involve other states that are also experiencing significant growth in immersion programming. Thus, Utah will host in 2014, and planning is underway for CARLA to host again in 2016, and North Carolina in 2018.

2. Asia Society, "Start a Program."
http://asiasociety.org/education/chinese-language-initiatives/
start-program
Accessed June 8, 2014.

3. Center for Advanced Research on Language Acquisition, Summer Institutes
http://www.carla.umn.edu/institutes/index.html
See especially:
Immersion 101 for Chinese and Japanese: An introduction to immersion
teaching.
http://www.carla.umn.edu/institutes/2014/imm_chnjpn.html
Accessed June 8, 2014.

4. Confucius Institute/Classroom.
http://english.hanban.org/node_10971.htm
Accessed June 8, 2014.

5. Asia Society Confucius Classroom Network.
http://asiasociety.org/education/chinese-language-initiatives/
asia-society-confucius-classrooms-network
Accessed June 8, 2014.

6. Engineering is Elementary, "Just Passing Through: Designing Model
Membranes."
Repurposed for Mandarin immersion by the Minnesota Mandarin
Immersion Collaborative (MMIC)
http://www.carla.umn.edu/immersion/mmic/IPAdesign.pdf
Accessed June 8, 2014.

7. Engineering is Elementary, "Just Passing Through: Designing Model
Membranes."
Repurposed for Mandarin immersion by the Minnesota Mandarin Immersion
Collaborative (MMIC)
http://www.carla.umn.edu/immersion/mmic/IPAdesign.pdf
Accessed June 8, 2014.

8. See *14: How Much Chinese Will They Learn?* for information about what this
means.

9. Utah Language Roadmap for the 21st Century.
http://www.schools.utah.gov/CURR/dualimmersion/Home/
Utah-Language-Road-for-the-21st-Century.aspx
Accessed June 8, 2014.

10. The Language Flagship.
http://www.thelanguageflagship.org
Accessed June 8, 2014.

11. Hanban, 汉办, is the commonly-used abbreviation for the Chinese National
Office for Teaching Chinese as a Foreign Language. It is governed by the Office of
Chinese Language Council International. Hanban is a non-profit affiliated with
the Chinese Ministry of Education and it works to provide Chinese language and
cultural teaching resources and services worldwide. Hanban is the sponsor for
Confucius classroom programs and donates books to many Chinese programs. It
also has an extensive program to bring Chinese teachers to the United States.

12. CELIN Goal, Objectives and Plans: Year 1- and 5-year.

13. Chinese Early Language and Immersion Network at Asia Society
http://asiasociety.org/files/education-celin.pdf
Accessed June 8, 2014.

– 341 –

二十三
èr shí sān
23

Going to School in China

Packing up and moving to Asia, whether for language acquisition, a job or to be near family, is a form of immersion that's becoming more common. For those who make the leap, it can be an adventure, a mind-expanding experience and a time for families to come together. The journey requires grit, flexibility and openness to really make it work. For many families their time in China, whether brief or long-term, is deeply treasured.

The vast majority of families who move to China or another Chinese-speaking country end up placing their children in international schools where Chinese is taught as a foreign language for an hour or less a day. These students tend not to learn much Chinese as they're generally in an English-speaking environment and don't have much need to use the language outside of class. The exception are children who have a Mandarin-speaking nanny (阿姨, *āyí*, "Aunty") who only speaks Mandarin with them. In general, families who have moved to China and chosen international schools with the hope that their children will become fluent Chinese speakers are often disappointed.

However, an increasing number of families are placing their children in entirely Chinese schools or the few bilingual international schools that are beginning to appear, especially in larger cities. Here are some of their stories.

80ᵗʰ Middle School, Beijing

Elaine Wang and her family moved to Beijing in July of 2011. Her husband had a new job there and the family was excited about the possibility of truly immersing themselves in China and the Chinese language.

Both Elaine and her husband grew up in Taiwan speaking Mandarin before they moved to the United States as teens. Their children were born in the United States and the family lived in San Francisco. Their son and daughter both attended a Chinese immersion program for one year, her son at West Portal Elementary School and her daughter at Starr King Elementary School.

Despite the fact that the family had always spoken Mandarin at home, and both her children were fluent, her older son didn't like speaking Chinese once he started school in San Francisco. That changed when they got to Beijing.

When they arrived, he was 12 and going into sixth grade. Elementary schools in China go through sixth grade, so his first year was spent at Fang Cao Di International School. The school has an international section for students who hold foreign passports. It offers support for students getting up to speed in Chinese although all classes are taught in Chinese except an hour of English a day.

"That one year transition was helpful since the school had a policy where your math class is your actual grade. So my son went to sixth grade math, seventh grade English (or advanced) and second grade Chinese," Wang says.

The first year was the hardest. "We did hire tutors to help and I also stayed at home to help them." Because she's a fluent Mandarin speaker and can read Chinese, Wang was able to give them strong support at home as they made the leap into the Chinese educational system.

The next year her son moved on to the 80th Middle School in Beijing, where he went into the regular Chinese program. Everything was taught in Chinese except for one hour of English every day. Although it was a public school with an international section for children who hold foreign passports, no Chinese support classes are available. "Students come from Asian countries such as Mongolia, South Korea, Hong Kong, Taiwan as well as from the U.S. and Canada. However, most students come from Mandarin-speaking families," Wang says.

"It was very difficult, but he survived. We hired a tutor to help and I have to say Lucas is quite a smart kid. He can adapt quickly to different circumstances. I think if we stayed in the U.S. he might not have had as much challenge and fun," she says.

When they arrived in Beijing, their daughter was six and she also began at Fang Cao Di International School, in first grade. Because her children had only attended Chinese immersion for a single year, Elaine can't tell if it made that much of a difference in their ability to transition into school in China. To a certain extent "it's like comparing apples to oranges," she says, because they came from a Mandarin-speaking home. "In the U.S., immersion programs seems best suited for kids who don't have prior knowledge in Chinese."

After two years, both of her children were doing well and were almost fully literate. Her son still prefers to read in English, though he also reads lots of graphic novels in Chinese. Her daughter's Chinese is actually better than her English, "so it's easier for her to read in Chinese," Wang says.

By the spring of their second year, "my son is now in eighth grade and he is doing okay. His Chinese definitely improved significantly." Her daughter is also doing well at Fang Cao Di elementary, "even though I still have to help her catch up at times."

The difference in educational philosophy and structure between China and the United States is enormous. Because she and her husband were both educated in Taiwan, Wang says she and her husband are more comfortable with it than friends in China who attended U.S. schools.

To begin with, the school day is very long by U.S. standards. Grade school starts at 8:00 am and ends at 3:15 pm. Middle school begins at 7:30 am and ends at 4:30 pm. In third grade her daughter spent about an hour on homework every day while her son has about an hour and a half, she says. School consists of much more rote learning than would be considered acceptable in the United States. Academic standards are high and there is rigorous testing. "Teachers text or call parents right away if they notice a child is not doing well," she says.

She echoes a sentiment expressed by many families with roots in both the United States and China: They are far more comfortable with the Asian educational model than many Americans. For them, it works. "Putting my kids in the Chinese programs not only enhances their Chinese literacy, but it also teaches them the 'Chinese way' of doing things and the subtle cultural elements that are hard to get in the U.S.," Wang says. "Because I grew up in this system, I don't think it's a big deal. Students are supposed to work hard, aren't they?"

For her "there's no right or wrong way, the Chinese way is just different from the American way. Things like absolute respect for the teacher, filial duty to your parents and group conformity can be seen as negative in the U.S. But we want our kids to at least know about them so they don't grow up to be so different from us."

Being in China has allowed her to give her children choices about their future, "but right now we are giving them the Chinese perspective that they won't get in the U.S."

The family expects to stay in China another year or two. By that time, both children will be fully literate and they hope maintaining the language in the U.S. will not be too hard. "We might send them to a Saturday program or hire a private tutor," she says.

As for advice about moving to China, she says every parent has different goals so she can't compare her experience to others. "We are a native Mandarin-speaking family so we expect our children to be fully literate and functional in Chinese. This may not be the goal for others. Parents should simply follow their own instincts and assess their own needs when choosing a program."

One thing she's noted is that while she and her husband felt comfortable with the level of rigor and memorization required in ordinary Chinese school, "most Westerners seem really troubled by the rote learning aspect. So again, parents should follow their own hearts."

Dalian Maple Leaf International School

Not everyone moves to Beijing or Shanghai when they go to China. The Gustafsons of Portland, Oregon moved to Dalian, where their three children, Clara, Anna and Peter, spent two years attending a large Chinese boarding school with thousands of other students. They were the only American students at their school. The only other Westerners came from Eastern Europe.

Clara says her parents had known since they got married they wanted their children to have the opportunity to live abroad. Their father had worked internationally for 27 years with lots of time spent in Asia and China. Their mom is a retired lawyer. "What ended up happening is they were thinking, 'Oh, Clara's going into high school so if we're going to do this, we better do it now'," says Clara.

When they began looking for a country to move to, their father's career in the wood products industry in Oregon led him to a position in Dalian, a seaport in Liaoning province, just north of Beijing across the Bohai Sea. "It's a 'small' city of seven million people where they speak Mandarin," Clara says with a laugh. They began to prepare for the move about six months before, taking some "very basic Chinese lessons," in her words. In July of 2005, they packed up their house and moved. Clara was going into ninth grade, her sister Anna into eighth and their brother Peter into second.

For Anna, then 14, one thing really helped her through the process. "My parents made it clear to all of us kids from the beginning that if it was really awful and we all really hated it, and were crying every day, we could go back. That gave me a more generally positive outlook and meant that it never felt really scary."

When they arrived, Clara and her sister were enrolled in the Dalian Maple Leaf International School. A Chinese-Canadian joint school, it caters almost entirely to Chinese families seeking a better education for their children along with some expatriate families. Despite the school's name, none of the foreigners in the Chinese immersion program were from Canada.

Chinese families who can afford to send their children to boarding schools, because they are perceived to be easier than public school and because students get more attention. "Public schools in China frequently have 50 kids per classroom. In our school it was 25–30 kids per class, so we got more teacher time," Anna says. It was also a place for students who struggled with the strict conformity and discipline of a Chinese public school and had trouble behaving in class. Sometimes they were good students, especially some boys. But "they'd just gotten lost in the big schools." Those same boys probably would be considered paragons of virtue in a U.S. public school, but in China things are different.

The first hurdle was that the school was 45 minutes from the family's apartment. After much discussion, their parents decided to have the two girls board there during the week so they didn't lose two hours a day commuting. "My parents were realistic," says Clara. "They said 'If you come home every day you'll just speak English. If you stay there you'll learn Chinese.'"

It helped, a little, to realize that many of the students in the school came from far away and saw much less of their parents than the Gustafsons did. "My roommate was from the way far south of China so she only went home for Chinese New Year and a few holidays," says Anna. The girls' other roommates were girls younger than 10 from Russia who saw their families about as frequently.

Clara and Anna first lived in the grade school dorm. After a semester of introductory Chinese in the immersion program for non-Chinese speakers, they moved to the middle school dorms, which had 1,500 students. Only 100 were not Chinese, most of those Korean. "My sister stood out during morning exercises because she has blond hair and she's tall," says Clara.

Chinese educational mores, even in a private school, came as something of a shock to the girls. The sisters had spent their entire school life at Portland's Franciscan Montessori Earth School, a Catholic Montessori school focusing on ecology and "the study of the interconnectedness of all living things," according to its website. Dalian Maple Leaf International School "was the opposite," Clara says. School went from 7:00 am to 7:00 pm every day. It was intense. Clara was placed back a year, into eighth grade, so she could learn Chinese. Her sister Anna went into seventh grade.

Learning Chinese

That first semester was "extreme immersion," Anna says. "Every semester they would take all the new foreign kids, regardless of your age or your first language, and put you all in a big class." Students ranged in age from 5 years to 17. All the students in the introductory Chinese semester lived in the elementary school boarding dorms. The girls both had non-Chinese foreign roommates, but neither of them spoke English.

After that semester, students were placed in whatever class was age-appropriate for them. However, they spent half their time in Chinese-as-a-second-language classes. These had the same curriculum as the Chinese students, but it was taught at a slower pace and with time for explanations of vocabulary—very much like a U.S. Mandarin immersion program.

By the end of those first four months, Clara describes her conversational Chinese as excellent. "The first semester we went through one whole book, it had a lot of pictures. As we got more advanced, we were able to read paragraphs and then whole pages and two page stories." But then the second semester began and she moved to the middle school. There instruction in all subjects was in Chinese. She realized how much of her communication included hand gestures and facial expressions. That worked when chatting with classmates, but not when she had to suddenly take math, physics and Chinese literature—in Chinese.

For their second semester, the sisters moved to the middle school campus where all their roommates were Chinese. "It was all Chinese, all the time," Clara says. In the second semester, "we graduated to the Chinese textbooks [used in a normal Chinese middle school] which was awesome and super intense."

Socially, the transition was difficult. Clara describes herself as a naturally "fairly emotionally connected person." She'd also spent eight years at a Montessori school, where such empathy was prized. Chinese students had been focusing on an entirely different set of abilities, mostly academic, and she didn't find it easy to connect with the Chinese girls in her class. "It was hard to make friends," she says. She and her sister gravitated especially to two other immigrant students, one from Kazakhstan and one from Mongolia. "They were the oldest, and they'd been studying English the longest so we all became best friends," Clara says.

After a year in China, the family held a vote on whether to stay a second year and the decision was made to stay in their new home. That second year, Clara and her sister continued on middle school. Clara was in the ninth grade and Anna in eighth. By the end of the second year, Clara's Chinese was pretty proficient and she could have a conversation with anyone. She studied physics, chemistry, math and advanced Chinese literature with her classmates, with some tutoring help from the Chinese-as-a-Second-Language Department.

Clara says she's "still in awe" of people who learn to read and write Chinese while living in the United States. "I don't understand that. It's so hard to memorize all that stuff. Being surrounded by it every day makes it easier. It's out of necessity that you remember. If I learned it in the United States, there's no way my Chinese would be this fluent."

Anna says it took her a year to be able to speak easily with teachers even though they "tried to speak clearly." It wasn't until the end of her second year that she could speak easily with her classmates. "Before that, I was the annoying girl who was asking them to repeat themselves and I didn't understand their slang. By the end of my second year, I knew the catch phrases, and I could follow the classroom gossip."

By Anna's second year, she was good enough to take the school's classic Chinese literature class. That means studying texts written in the Chinese of between 500 BC and 200 AD. While the characters are the same, the meanings are elusive and complex. Many would-be Chinese majors in the United States break on the rock that is Classical Chinese. Anna took it when she was 15.

Anna says she "worked really hard in my Chinese classes, because I figured it was why my parents put us there." She liked Chinese because it was simple. "It doesn't have verb tenses; it doesn't have conjugations. It's very straightforward. It just requires lots of hours to learn the characters. But after you get that out of the way, it's easy."

One of her proudest moments was when she almost passed—just one point shy—the final Chinese literature exam, which consisted mostly of writing essays in Chinese.

At the end of two years, with all three children speaking Chinese fluently as well as reading and writing it, the family moved back to Portland. Clara and Anna enrolled in St. Mary's Academy, a Catholic high school and Portland's oldest secondary school. Social re-entry into a U.S. school went well for the most part, though Clara was more aware of cultural nuances than some of her classmates. It wasn't that the other students were narrow-minded, but they "hadn't had the valuable opportunity to be as exposed to the world as I had," she says.

To keep their Chinese up, the family hired a Chinese tutor, as there were no classes at the appropriate level for them at St. Mary's. One regret was that they couldn't easily stay in touch with friends in China because at school they had all used the Chinese instant messaging program QQ to communicate via phones. QQ wasn't available in the United States. "My last couple of weeks I went around getting everyone's QQ numbers," only to find that the QQ network wasn't available in the United States, Anna says. Since then several of her friends have been able to find her on Facebook, despite the fact that it's blocked in China, so she's been able to reconnect with some of them.

Academically, re-entry went well. The only class Clara had to re-take was world history. "In science, I was all caught up. I didn't have to take any in high school, because I'd already had physics and chemistry. In math, I was fine." Anna transferred in as a sophomore and had already fulfilled the school's language requirement four times over.

Clara says their experience "hugely influenced" what colleges she looked for. She knew she wanted to continue in Chinese, even if she didn't major in it, so she only looked at schools that offered a Chinese major. "Otherwise, they wouldn't have had courses advanced enough for me." At the time, in 2008, the Flagship University program at the University of Oregon hadn't been fully developed so there weren't many choices. The experience also sparked an interest in international studies. She got into Georgetown where she took Chinese for three years, as well as Spanish. "I tested into third-year Chinese my freshman year" at Georgetown, she says.

Clara majored in Science, Technology and International Affairs and graduated in the spring of 2013. In the fall, she began her first job at a cyber security company, Riskive, in Baltimore and hopes to go back to Asia as soon as possible.

Anna wrote her college application essay about living in China and was accepted at the University of Chicago, where she is taking a double major in English Language & Literature and East Asian Languages & Civilizations. She tested into third year Chinese, but regrets not pushing harder to be placed into the more challenging fourth year level. After her freshman year, she got a scholarship to do a two-month language intensive program in Kunming in China. She's also worked at Concordia Language Village camps as a Chinese counselor and as a Chinese tutor. Now a senior, she is currently applying to graduate programs to become a Chinese teacher.

A lot of plusses

One thing Clara says she treasures from her time in China is the experience of being a minority. "White people in the United States don't get that and it's super valuable," she says.

Another result of their family's years abroad has been a much closer connection with her family than she thinks she would have otherwise had. "We would be close no matter what, but not as deeply if we hadn't done this. My sister is my best friend, and I'm not sure we would have been as close if not for China." Her respect for her parents grew and continues to grow as she realizes what it meant that they were willing to put themselves in a completely new environment where they didn't have all the answers and had to rely on their children for help. "The humility of learning and pushing their comfort zone" was an inspiration, she says. Looking towards the future, "if I ever have kids of my own I definitely plan to take them abroad to live."

As she looks back on the experience, Clara says she is deeply grateful for their time in China, even if at times it was painful. "My life would be a lot tamer, and I'd be a lot more risk averse, if we hadn't gone to China."

Peter's experience

The experience of one sibling isn't necessarily the experience of the others. As an example, Clara and Anna's younger brother, Peter, had a very different trajectory in China and Chinese than his older sisters.

When the family moved to China, he had just finished first grade in Portland at the same Montessori school his sisters attended. When the family got to China, his parents decided that because he was so young they would go for full-on immersion and placed him in the local public school—DongBeiLu Elementary School. He spoke almost no Chinese at the time. "I don't remember a lot of it, since I was pretty young," says Peter, but "I do remember it being fun. The language part came pretty easy since I had friends to play with who spoke Chinese."

The Chinese public school experience was challenging, though, in part because there were over 50 kids in a classroom with one teacher. After his first semester, they decided to move him to the English-language elementary school branch of the Dalian Maple Leaf International School. It was mainly expats and offered some Chinese language instruction rather than being the full Chinese program his sisters had attended.

After their first year, the family voted on whether they would remain in China for another year. Peter was the only one out of the five to vote to return home to Portland. But with the vote four to one, the decision was made to stay. The point of being in China was to learn Chinese, so for his second year of school he transferred to the same Chinese as a second language program his sisters had completed. From there, he went into his grade at the school. During the entire time he had a private Chinese tutor several times a week. By the end of the family's two years, Peter was fully fluent and could read and write at close to grade level in Chinese.

When the family returned to Portland, Peter was in fourth grade. He enrolled at Portland's private International School in the Mandarin immersion track. After his time in China he was able to easily do the Mandarin language. For middle school, he attended a Catholic school that didn't offer Chinese, so he kept up his Chinese with private tutoring during the week.

When the time came for high school, he also chose a Catholic high school. Unfortunately, the school didn't offer Chinese at his level since the school was just starting a Chinese language program. Peter enrolled in the Chinese 1 class and actually reviewed a lot of grammar rules that hadn't been taught when he was in school in China because they were obvious to native speakers.

The family also hosted a Confucius Institute teacher from Anhui province for the year, who worked with Peter as a tutor. In the summer, he attended the Confucius Institute's high school summer bridge program in Beijing and Tianjin. While he was there, he found it easy to chat with people. His time there also strengthened his reading and writing ability.

Peter says he plans to continue his Chinese studies at La Salle Catholic College Preparatory high school in Portland, taking Chinese 2. He hopes to return to China soon. Overall the now 15-year-old says he's happy he learned Chinese. "I think it will be useful in my later life." While he doesn't know yet what his future holds, "I'd like to go into some area of work using Chinese," he says.

Chinese International School in Hong Kong

Steve Tennant, a British national living in Hong Kong, chose to place his two daughters in the Chinese International School in Hong Kong. The school was founded in 1983 by three Wellesley College graduates. They wanted a school for their children where they would learn both English and Chinese and have a Western-style curriculum. The school has become one of the most sought-after in Hong Kong.

Tennant's daughters learned to speak, read and write both English and Mandarin in their years there. His eldest daughter, now an attorney in Hong Kong with Baker & McKenzie, "uses Chinese on a daily basis in Hong Kong, including preparing legal advice in traditional or simplified Chinese characters," he says

"Learning the characters was not easy and led to many tearful nights at home, not just in our household but many other school families. Chinese homework was considered by many of the Western families to be excessive and could amount to several hours a night, in addition to other subjects' homework. The use of home tutoring in Chinese by parents, two to three times a week, whilst not officially approved by the school, was in practice common."

This was at a private school where most students had at least one parent who spoke a Chinese dialect and yet they *still* spent hours at it each night. They were not having the fun students in the West see as their birthright. Eventually they came around though, he says.

"Almost all of the kids would have dropped Chinese had they been given the choice at school (which they were not) because the program was really tough and demanding. It probably wasn't until about the age of 15–16, as kids started thinking about university and careers, that the commercial benefits of having had a bilingual education started to become apparent." He's now seen the advantages they gained in university admissions. "CIS graduates are highly sought after by North American, European and Asia Pacific Universities because of the kids' ethnic diversity, language skills and plain old hard work ethic."

Both his daughters tell him that it was easier to graduate from college than from the Chinese International School. But his family "got what we wanted, which was to have happy, well-educated kids who fully understand their English and Chinese cultures and heritages."

二十四
èr shí sì
24

Going to School in Singapore

When talking about Mandarin education, Singapore makes for an interesting study. While the nation's schools are all taught in English, about three-quarters of all students are in a strand of the national education system that requires them to become fluent in Mandarin in order to graduate.

"Singapore is quite different from the rest of the world because we make the learning of Mandarin compulsory" for all students with Chinese heritage, said Dr. CheeKuen Chin, who is executive director of the Singapore Centre for Chinese Language at Nanyang Technological University. The goal is to create "bilingual citizens of the world."

In the past, only the most capable people, those who were able to master two languages, truly became bilingual. Now it's a simple "part of life" and necessary for the 21st century. Singapore has built its educational system around ensuring that its students are ready for that future, Dr. Chin said.

Singapore is an island nation situated between Malaysia and Indonesia. In area, it's about 3.5 times as big as Washington D.C. It was founded as an English trading colony in 1819, which is why English is one of its official languages and why all school is taught in English. It became an independent country in 1965.

One of the four Asian Tiger countries (Hong Kong, Singapore, South Korea and Taiwan) with free, developed and industrialized economies, today it has the third highest per capita income in the world. The population is 5.26 million, made up of multiple diverse groups:

- 74% of Chinese descent
- 13% of Malay descent
- 9% of Indian descent
- 3% Eurasians and other groups

Singapore's educational system is considered one of the world's best. Its students consistently score at the very top of international measures of science and math ability.

The nation has four official languages, based on the main language communities of the island: English, Chinese, Malay and Tamil. All children are enrolled in a 'mother tongue' strand within the school system depending on their ethnicity, which is determined by their father's ethnicity. This language remains one of their core subjects as they move through school. The breakdown is

- 72% to 75% of students in the Chinese strand
- 12% to 15% in the Malay strand
- 10% in the Tamil or other minorities' language strand

Just because students come from ethnically Chinese families does not mean that they speak Mandarin. Among Chinese families, 37% speak only or mainly Mandarin at home, 25% speak both Mandarin and English at home and 38% speak only or mainly English. The use of Mandarin as a home language is declining in Singapore as English slowly supplants it, Dr. Chin said. Many Chinese families speak a dialect other than Mandarin.

The Singapore school year runs for 40 weeks and the school day goes from 7:30 am to 1:30 pm. Most students do extracurricular activities or special projects at school after the academic day ends, or attend tutoring programs where they do more studying. Singapore schools embrace tracking. Students are tested and assigned to a top, mainstream or vocational track according to their academic ability.

All subjects but the mother tongue are taught in English, so up to 90% of the day is in English and the rest is in Chinese, Malay or Tamil depending on the student's background. In Chinese, students get more Mandarin time in elementary school and then the level drops slightly as other subjects are emphasized. The amount of time students in the mainstream program for elementary school spend studying Mandarin in first through sixth grade varies between 4 and 6.5 hours a week, depending on their grade.

In secondary school, the U.S. equivalent of middle and high school, students in the mainstream program study Chinese 3.75 hours a week. There is also a track for students who have done very well in Chinese or who are interested in pursuing Chinese studies. These students get an extra 30 minutes of Mandarin per week.

Singapore has its own national examinations, taken at the end of grade 6, grade 10 or 11 and grade 12 or 13. Chinese language is one of the compulsory subjects for all Chinese students in these examinations. Students in the Chinese track in middle school need to pass a Mandarin test in the General Certificate of Education (GCE) 'O' (Ordinary) Level examination in order to enroll in high school. They also must pass a Chinese test to get their "A" (Advanced) level certificate, necessary to attend local universities.

How good their Chinese is depends on their interest and how hard they work. It's impossible to directly compare their Mandarin ability with either Chinese and Taiwanese students on the one hand and American immersion students on the other, says Dr. Chin. However students who truly apply themselves are able to enter Beijing University in China. "We have some students whose Mandarin standard is really comparable to mainland China. We have some families who do not speak Chinese at home and I think they are learning the language from the ground up," so the level they reach is not as high in general, Dr. Chin says. And some speak it very well. As in all schools "there's a big difference here between individuals."

However, all students must pass the Chinese language at A Level examination to be able to enter university in Singapore. This makes students and parents "take learning of Mandarin in school seriously," says Dr. Chin.

Read-First-Write-Later

Singapore has been a leader of the read-first-write-later strategy of Chinese education. Students are expected to read and recognize more characters than they are able to write. This allows them to read most complicated material more quickly. A distinction is made between the number of characters students must be able to read and recognize and characters students must 'master,' i.e. be able to read and write.

By the end of second grade, students will have learned between 600 and 650 characters, 300 to 350 of which they must be able to write. By the end of fourth grade they must know between 1,200 to 1,300 characters, including 700 to 750 they must master. By end of sixth grade they know between 1,600 and 1,700 characters, of which they must have mastered between 1,000 and 1,100. By the time they take their O Level Examination when they're 15 or 16, they will have mastered between 2,400 and 2,500 characters, 2,000 to 2,100 of which they must be able to write.

Despite this, most students still read for pleasure in English, with which they're more comfortable, but that depends on their family and the students themselves, says Dr. Chin.

The Mandarin taught in Singapore's schools is very close to standard Beijing Mandarin, and simplified characters are used. In Singapore it's called 新加坡华语, *Xīnjiāpō Huáyǔ*, Singaporean Mandarin. The Mandarin spoken on the street is called Colloquial Singaporean Mandarin and contains loan words from Malay and from Chinese dialects spoken in Singapore. It is quite natural for people in Singapore to "mix up the vocabulary between Mandarin and English. They might say a Mandarin sentence but have an English or Malay word," said Dr. Chin. However, in formal settings where Chinese is the main or one of the main languages, formal Mandarin is used.

Singapore doesn't have actual immersion classes in elementary school but some preschools are beginning to experiment with the idea. As families shift to speaking English rather than Chinese at home, immersion programs are seen as helpful to introduce children to the language they will study in school.

The Chinese textbook series used in Singapore schools is called 华文, *Huáwén, Chinese Language for Primary Schools* or *Chinese Language for Secondary Schools.* Several U.S. Mandarin immersion programs use these textbooks as well.

An American in Singapore schools

So should we all just move to Singapore? Maybe not. I asked an American mother whose job took her family to Singapore when her daughter was still a toddler to tell me about their experience. She found while there were many excellent aspects to the education her child received, there was quite a bit of downside, too.

Her daughter began learning Mandarin at a bilingual preschool when she was two-and-a-half. When it came time to start first grade, her Chinese was good enough for entry in the neighborhood primary school's Mandarin track. She attended Raffles Girls Primary School, which was one of the better public schools in the city-state.

She did well in her coursework during her six years in Singapore, thanks to extra tutoring, and thrived in the structured environment of the school system. When the family arrived back in the United States for seventh grade, her daughter was able to get a place at a Mandarin immersion school and has had no trouble keeping up.

The schools in Singapore had well-funded music and sports programs. Intellectualism was encouraged and all children got to participate in a variety of activities as part of their school day. "The biggest benefit of life in Singapore was the experience of living abroad—meeting new people, having new experiences, etc.," the mother said of their time there.

Still, there is no magic bullet to creating the Perfect School—even in Singapore, often touted as the best country in the world for education. Despite identical government funding and curriculum, students who attend schools in the wealthier districts tend to outperform those in the less affluent. "Even if the Singapore government doubled or tripled funding for low-performing schools, I bet children in the wealthier neighborhoods would still get better test scores," the American mom said.

Children from wealthy families have access to expensive, high-quality tutoring to supplement their education and are better able to transport their children to study centers. Über-competitive parents also gain status from their child's school placement and exam scores, she said. Families are highly motivated for their children to excel.

The test scores touted internationally refer to students in the most academically demanding courses, many of whom have been nurtured since pre-K by academically-minded families. Sixth grade students take an especially grueling test, the Primary School Leaving Exam, that determines what type of secondary school they will enter. According to the Ministry of Education, in 201?, students' scores broke down like this:

- Advanced   67%
- Academic   20%
- Technical   11%

Many Singaporean school children struggle with spoken English despite the fact that much of the curriculum is taught in English. Teachers throughout the city-state speak a pidgin version of the language known as Singlish and writing assignments often reflect a lack of proper sentence structure. The government's "Speak Good English" campaign did little to encourage fluency.

The pressures put on students in high-performing schools in Singapore are ones many American parents might find unreasonable or even damaging. When her daughter scored 94.5 in English, 95.0 in Chinese and 87.0 in Math on her first report card, the teacher wrote at the bottom, the student "needs to be more meticulous so as to attain better results."

The grading curve in Singapore is 85–100 for "Band One," so her daughter's grades were the equivalent of straight A's. "I don't know about other parents, but that means 'Ice cream sundaes for all!' at my house," the mom said.

Unreasonably Rigid?

The school system also can seem unreasonably rigid. Singapore's school year beings on January 2. Everyone born in 1999, for instance, is in the same grade and expected to be at the same level. Brutal mid-terms are given at the beginning of May. They often contain new material that won't be introduced until the second-term, if at all. When the American mom asked about this, the teacher responded, "We like to challenge them." Bad grades for the mid-term often mean students spend their four-week break in June studying.

Finals occur in October and there's a week off when kids are expected to cram with their private tutors. All extracurricular activities are suspended in September/October, which is "not a joyful time," the mom said. After finals, the students do nothing until the year ends in mid-November. The American mom's take-home: They may have a longer school year but they're not maximizing learning.

Each class has 30 or more kids. Her daughter's sixth grade math class had 42 students. "Her teachers didn't cover all that much in the classroom and the homework load was often freakishly light because the teachers assumed kids got assignments from tutors.

According to the American mom, "the number one difference between Singapore's education system and that of the U.S. is the expectation that children will have hours of private tutoring every week. And it's not cheap."

"Teachers often moonlight as tutors. Our Chinese tutor was an 'education mother' from the Mainland. She had accompanied her brilliant daughter, who was on a scholarship. The tutor came two times a week for 90 minutes. She charged 45 Singapore dollars per hour ($37 US). Starting from fourth grade, my daughter had a math/science 'homework helper' for two hours every Sunday morning."

Rote memorization is often prized over true learning

Singapore students may score highly but that doesn't necessarily mean the students have actually learned anything. Here are some of her observations:

The first time my daughter asked me to help her study for an English spelling test I was impressed with the vocabulary. But guess what? The kids weren't expected to know what the words meant—only to spell them! I asked the teacher about this and she gave me a blank stare. She then told me I could teach my daughter the meanings if I wanted to, but because it's a spelling test, she only needed to spell the words.

My daughter was once asked to read a composition about orangutans and then fill in a worksheet. First question: How tall is an orangutan? She parroted what was in the composition, which was around 1.4 meters or so. I asked her—what's a meter? How tall are you? She had no idea so I got out a measuring tape. It turned out an orangutan was about the same size as my daughter, so she added that into her answer.

Another question: How long does an orangutan stay with its mother? The answer was six years, which was a year younger than my daughter at the time. She wrote, "Six years" and added, "I'm seven and I'm not ready to leave my mother yet!"

The teacher handed back the assignment and crossed out my daughter's added comments, writing "irrelevant" in red pen. I mentioned this to the principal. "Oh well," she said.

My daughter failed her science midterm one year. Most of her class failed it. Einstein might have failed it. The teacher was incompetent and they learned nothing. Instead of conducting a simple experiment in front of the class, the teacher showed a YouTube video of it. Guess what was needed to do the experiment? A bowl of water, a plastic cup and some cotton.

Because of the massive failure, the school offered a "remedial" class given by local high-school students. It was so fun and hands-on that parents of the kids who passed called to complain that their kids were being punished by the exclusion. My daughter aced the final. Happy ending!"

Overall, the American mom says, the experience was a good one. Since moving back to the U.S., her daughter's English has gotten better and her Mandarin worse, as would be expected moving from a Chinese-speaking to an English-speaking country. Her main message to parents is that despite the hype and the test scores, Singapore isn't an educational paradise. But perhaps, she says, nowhere is.

Another parent's take on how the system works

Judy Shei and her family moved to Singapore in the summer of 2013 from San Francisco, where their oldest son had been a student in the Mandarin immersion program at Starr King Elementary School. Two months into the school year she sent this note back to the Mandarin immersion email list in San Francisco.

Just wanted to let you know that we just started tutoring with Emmett here in Singapore as he's been struggling a bit in school and I'm afraid just one or two hours a day wasn't enough to keep up and improve his speaking skills.

Good news on 2 fronts... I found out from the tutor that Emmett is in a "higher Chinese" class which progressed more quickly and is more difficult than "normal Chinese." From a reading and writing perspective Emmett is constantly telling me that he "hasn't learned" that character before. But with the higher expectations, I've noticed his reading has improved by leaps and bounds! So, although the level of reading and writing has been more difficult than what he encountered in second grade at Starr King, he has a strong enough base from Starr King Mandarin immersion that making the leap hasn't been insurmountable.

Also the tutor told me he was really impressed with Emmett's listening and speaking ability. Although he is not on par with a "rice" family (a family that speaks Chinese at home), Emmett is far ahead of the kids in a typical "potato" family (a non-Chinese family). With the tutor speaking at normal speed, Emmett understands about 70% to 80% and he has no problem expressing basic ideas and communicating, although he does lack vocabulary. This is entirely due to Starr King. As you know, although I occasionally speak to my kids in Mandarin (maybe 10% of the time), they always answer in English.

Now my worry is our second son, and that Singapore might not be up to the standards of SFUSD Mandarin Immersion program!!!"

Shei wrote up this Singapore schools cheat sheet to answer all the questions she'd gotten about how the system works. It's instructive to read how very different schools there are, and yet how similar.

There is a lot of information online regarding Singapore Public Schools at www.moe.gov.sg but most of it is geared toward Singaporeans who already know the system and just want to brush up on the latest MOE (Ministry of Education) rules and changes. Very little of it is geared toward Americans and what is different between a typical American public school and typical Singaporean Primary School.

Quick facts

The school year runs from January 1 through mid-November, with a one-month break in June, a one-week break in March, and one in September, as well as public holidays throughout the year.

Preschool/kindergarten is private. Kindergarten is divided into K1 (5-year-olds) and K2 (6-year-olds)

Primary school ages: Primary 1 (P1)—for all kids who turn 7 that calendar year—through Primary 6 (P6). So for the school year starting January 2014, all children born in the year 2007 must enroll into P1. Red-shirting (the American term for holding back children who are near the cut-off so they enroll the following year) requires special permission from the Ministry of Education.

P1 expectations: Children entering P1 are expected to know how to read. For children who don't, most schools will provide after-school support.

P1–P3 class size: maximum 30 students

P4–P6 class size: maximum 40 students

Primary school size: Typically 6 to 8 classes per level, so most schools have 1,100–1,400 students.

Vocabulary list

MOE: Ministry of Education

Local school: Public school. Singaporean citizens must attend local schools and require special permission to attend international schools. International students who are Permanent residents or on dependent passes may also attend local schools, although are not guaranteed a spot.

International schools: Private school. Typically most students are from other countries. The Singaporeans who attend either have one parent who has a passport for another country or received special permission from the MOE allowing them to attend for a specific reason.

Level: Grade. Instead of saying "I'm in 2nd grade," you say "I'm in P2."

SAP school: Special assistance plan schools. Contrary to what it sounds like to an American, it is a school that has enriched Chinese language and culture. These schools are very difficult for international students to enroll in, as they are very popular with locals. They typically have a more high-pressure environment.

GEP school: Gifted Education Program. All children take an exam at the end of P3, which determines whether they qualify for the program, which starts in P4. GEP is only in select primary schools so a child may switch schools at this time.

Elite vs. neighborhood schools: Although the MOE officially states that all primary schools are "good schools," in reality in many Singaporean minds there are the "elite" schools (Raffles, Anglo-Chinese School, Henry Park, Nanyang Primary School, etc.) and "neighborhood" schools. If you don't have $1 million to donate, as an international student it is next to impossible to enroll into an elite school. These schools are highly coveted by Singaporeans.

PSLE: Primary School Leaving Exam. This is an exam all students take at P6, and the results of this exam, and their grades, determine which secondary schools a student can enroll in. That in turn determines which university/polytechnic (technical school) they qualify for. It's not unusual for Singaporean parents to take time off to assist their children in preparing for this. The closer it gets to P6, the higher the pressure and the more likely students will attend tuition on the weekends and during school holidays.

Tuition: The Singapore term for tutoring, usually in an after-school or weekend class. Many Singaporeans send their children to tutoring over the weekend. I have heard anecdotes that in elite primary schools there is an expectation that all children have tuition. There is less of an expectation, if at all, in neighborhood schools.

MT: Mother tongue (Mandarin, Malay or Tamil). MOE is realizing that many students of this generation use English as their primary language at home and is scaling back expectations, particularly in P1 and P2. For non-SAP schools, mother tongue is taught more like a foreign language with a lot of emphasis on vocabulary and grammar. It is not an "immersion" environment for those coming from an immersion program in the States. The teachers will speak in English to students if they don't get it. However, for international students with no background in a mother tongue, they can get a foreign language exemption. Theoretically, that means the child will still participate in class and take exams. The tests, however, will not count toward their grades. In my son's school, his Mandarin class is further divided by levels with some students in advanced Chinese, most in regular Chinese, and a few in beginning Chinese.

PAL: Physical active learning

PE: Physical Education

CCA: Co-curricular activity. In order for students to be more "well rounded," the MOE has decreed all students P3 and above must have an extra-curricular activity. Each school has many to choose from, such as sports, music, theater, etc. Typically one or two afternoons a week, and during school breaks, students stay late and attend a CCA. Once in P6, CCA activity stops so children can focus on studying for the PSLE.

FTGP: Form teacher guidance period—as described to me by a local, it's a class used to teach "values"—such as being nice to each other and social-emotional skills. My child is not able to articulate what exactly he is learning in this period, although he has a textbook just for this!

HE: Health education

CME: Citizenship & moral education (taught in mother tongue). Often described as a class that everyone blows off.

Canteen: Cafeteria. The Canteen is like a mini hawker center and there is a stand to cater to each major population of Singapore—Vegetarian for the Tamils, Halal for Malay, Chinese food and Western food. Children are expected bring cash to school in their wallet and purchase their own breakfast/lunch.

International student: As an American, in my mind's eye, I was thinking relatively well-off expats from North America, Europe, Australia/New Zealand. But there is quite a mix: Those from other Southeast Asian countries (Malaysia, Indonesia), but also quite a large contingent from Korea and China.

Balloting: Basically, if more students want to attend a school than there is space, the school does a random drawing (balloting).

Kiasu: Singlish term that literally means "scared to lose." It can be loosely translated as the need to "keep up with the Joneses." It has been described to me as a "typical" Singaporean mindset, particularly in regards to education and children. Singaporeans openly compare their children to others and will ask you questions about your child's test scores and grades, what school he or she is applying to, and what after-school programs he or she is attending.

Cost

Primary school is not free. There are school fees and more add-on fees than a typical American school, especially for international students. On the flip side, most schools do not have PTAs whose task is to endlessly fundraise for basic supplies.

School fees: For Singapore citizens, typically just a few dollars a month. Permanent residents (PRs), a bit more and international students much more ($500/month in 2013 in Singapore dollars). When you enroll, you have to fill out a form so fees are automatically deducted from your bank account. http://www.moe.gov.sg/education/school-fees/faqs/

Busing: Although the MOE is trying to encourage folks to enroll in their neighborhood schools, many people enroll their children in schools that are not within walking distance. Usually schools will have a contract with a private busing company and you can arrange for pick-up and drop-off. A couple things to note: The farther away you are from the school, the earlier your child will be picked up. Most schools start between 7:00 AM and 7:45 AM, so that means your child might have to be up and out of the door by 6:00 AM. Also, drop-off is typically after the school day ends, so if you child is staying late for an afterschool activity you will have to make other arrangements.

Uniforms: You will be required to buy at least three sets of shirts, athletic shorts, regular shorts/skirt, a tie or hat (depending on the school), socks, shoes, and name patches, which have to be special ordered and sewn on the shirt. Uniforms are required every day. Each school has its own uniform so you must buy them at the school store. You need to check your child's schedule to determine whether it's a PE day (athletic shorts) or a regular school day (regular shorts).

Snack/lunch: Your child will need a wallet to hold his or her money to purchase food at the canteen. Typically the food is about $1 per portion; drinks are about 50 cents. Because food is so inexpensive, most kids purchase at school.

Water bottle: All kids bring their own water bottles for sports class and for lunch/snack.

Textbooks: You will be given a list of textbooks, workbooks and supplies to purchase at the school bookstore. The school does not provide textbooks! Sometimes the teacher will ask a class to purchase an extra book that is not on the list.

Report card: Students do not take home a paper report card generated by a computer. There is a report book, which parents must purchase, in which grades are recorded.

Backpack: Some books are kept at school, but many are taken home. The class schedule changes every day, so students have to remember what books to bring on what day.

School schedule

Primary schools can be either **single session** or **double session**. Single session means all grades have the same start and end time. Double session means P1–P3 is either in the morning and P4–P6 are in the afternoon, or vice versa. All schools are supposed to be single session by 2016.

Schools start EARLY. If you take public transportation any time around 7:00 am, you will be surrounded by students. Most primary schools start anywhere between 7:00 am to 8:00 am.

School ends anywhere between 1:00 pm and 2:00 pm and can differ on different days depending on grade and whether your child attends a CCA. For example, my son, who is in P2, not in a CCA, ends school at 1:45 pm on Monday and Tuesday, but 1:15 pm on all the other days.

Every morning there is a school assembly. There is a show about current events, rules, etc., and then they sing the Singapore national anthem (in Malay) and say something akin to the Singapore Pledge of Allegiance.

In P2, my son has **multiple teachers** (MT, music, PE, art and a head teacher who teaches English and math). Typically students stay put while teachers come in and out. The schedule is different every day. You must refer to a schedule to know what clothes to wear (athletic or regular uniform) and what books to bring and what test to study for! When a teacher arrives, the entire class stands up and says, "Good morning, teacher" and when the teacher leaves, the entire class stands up and says, "Thank you, teacher."

It's not all academics. In a week, in addition to English, math, and mother tongue, there is has music, art, PE/PAL, social studies and CME.

School infrastructure

Schools are **not air conditioned**, but are usually designed for maximum airflow. There is a fan in the classroom and my son has not complained about the classroom being hot.

Every school I visited had really **nice computer rooms**. My son currently uses computers for Chinese on Mondays. He also has access to an online Mandarin website for use at home.

My son's school also has a large **library** and a separate **music room**.

Each school I visited also had a very **large gym**, sometimes also a large assembly room, and an **outdoor sports field** and **play structure**.

In terms of **administrative infrastructure**, in addition to the principal, there is typically an assistant principal, academic advisor and a support staff for children who need extra support for dyslexia or other special needs.

How to Enroll

Beginning of school year

Detailed instructions here: http://www.moe.gov.sg/education/
admissions/international-students/

To apply directly at school of choice:

- Enrollment begins in July and takes place in phases described here: http://www.moe.gov.sg/education/admissions/primary-one-registration/phases/
- In all phases, Singaporean citizens are first priority and then Singaporean PRs.
- International students cannot apply until Phase 3, the last phase, which means that international students tend to cluster in less highly coveted neighborhood schools. At one of the schools we looked at, 25% of the P1 class was international.
- For international students with an older sibling already enrolled, there is no sibling preference until Phase 3. That means all Singaporeans and PRs get first crack at the school and if there are any spaces left in Phase 3, those international students with an elder sibling at the school get priority over an international student who does not have an elder sibling.
- Participate in admissions exercise for international students
- For those wanting to enroll in P2 or higher, you can go through a centralized exam process and the MOE will pick a school for you.
- http://www.moe.gov.sg/education/admissions/international-students/admissions-exercise/

Mid-year

Although this is described extensively on the MOE site, reality is a bit different. This is what happened to us, and based on discussion with others our experience is fairly typical.

I looked on various map sites and the MOE site to find schools close to where I work. Primary schools by location:
http://www.moe.edu.sg/education/admissions/primary-one-registration/listing-by-planning-area/

We also contacted the MOE for schools which had openings in P2.

I also looked on Kiasuparents (http://www.kiasuparents.com/kiasu/content/singapore-primary-1-registration-school-balloting-history) to find schools that have historically been under-enrolled, as those schools would most likely have openings. Note, there is a forum for each local school on

Kiasuparents, so it was useful for me to read up about each school I was targeting to get a sense of the parent community.

During our preview trip (about a month before we were to move permanently), I literally emailed each school I targeted, addressed to the assistant principal or the generic address on their school website, with a picture of our family, copies of my son's report card and why I thought their schools would be prefect for us. I made it clear that I was an American on an employment pass and the kids would be on a dependent pass.

All the schools said they were full. Some suggested we fill out the wait list. Some were open to us stopping by and touring the school.

For the schools where the email response was friendlier, we tried to arrange a school tour. No one would promise anything, but some hinted that if we were to apply upon our return to Singapore, it would be more likely there would be a space.

In the end there were three schools that were strong possibilities. After discussion with local Singaporeans, we ended up in the school with the best reputation of the three.

We contacted the school we liked best and we arranged to have my son take some assessment exams (English and math only, no mother tongue). He did fine, although he was confused by some of the math problems as they were presented differently than he was used to.

He got a spot!

二十五
èr shí wǔ
25

Tips from Parents

Over the past few years I've collected suggestions from parents on how they help their kids and what parents should know starting out. Here they are.

No school is perfect

It's easy to see the problems in the school or program your child attends:

- It's not academic enough. / It's too focused on academics.
- The program is too small. / The program is too large.
- The teachers are too Chinese. / The teachers aren't Chinese enough.
- The principal doesn't have a firm hand. / The principal is a control-freak.

The list can go on and on. I've spent a lot of time in many schools researching this book and what I've learned is that *no* school is perfect. Each has its own problems and its own strengths.

You may imagine there exists some perfect school, somewhere, where everything goes smoothly, nothing is lacking and there is no strife. You'd be wrong. Even at ultra-expensive private schools with astounding academics, beautiful facilities, amazing teachers and excellent curriculum, parents complain about the feelings of entitlement their children can develop in such an environment.

So embrace whatever Mandarin immersion school you might have access to. You'll supplement the things the program doesn't do. You'd do this at whatever school you choose, whether it had immersion or not. It might mean Kumon[1] for math, it might mean more reading at home for English. It might mean music or art lessons for a school short on those. It might mean a tutor from Shanghai to beef up Chinese literacy. It might mean more time volunteering at the local food bank.

Let's be honest here: Immersion parents are a special breed. We're more involved in our kids' educations, more intense and, truth be told, a little more controlling than most parents. Please remember that you cannot make your school perfect. You can do your best to make it better, and supplement at home what it can't do. Know that your child will be fine either way—kids a lot more resilient than we give them credit for.

Homework

You can't learn Chinese if you don't do the homework. In English you've got to learn to read 26 letters and then you can sound out most words. In Chinese your child will memorize literally thousands of characters over the years, most of them by writing them again and again to get the "muscle memory" of each character's composition stuck in his or her brain and body. Homework in Chinese is a given and can't be skipped.

Almost all students need a little coaxing to get their homework done, whether they're in an English-only classroom or in immersion. Remember (as you're in the middle of yet another frustrating battle of wills over homework) that students in all schools go through this, not just ones in Mandarin immersion. Figure out what time of day works for your child and resign yourself to spending a lot of time sitting next to him or her while he or she copies out characters and look up words. I use this time to read the newspaper and catch up on the magazines that build up around the house. I am actually now current on both *The New Yorker* and *The Economist*!

One guardian at our school realized early on that his grandson was just too tired after school to do anything but whine. Instead they moved bedtime up an hour and then both got up at 6:15 am and did homework from 6:30 am to 7:00 am. He told me his grandson could do in 30 minutes in the morning what it took him two hours to do at night.

I know many families go to the trouble of buying their children desks that they put in their rooms for homework, but I know few families where the kids actually do homework anywhere except at the kitchen or dining room table, often with a parent sitting next to them.

A few things will make homework easier:

- Dictionaries: Ask your teacher/school what dictionary they recommend.
- Scratch paper: Really helpful for writing characters out while not messing up the homework.
- A computer or tablet for looking words up online. Popular programs include:
  - » YellowBridge
  - » Pleco
  - » Google Translate (though this can get you into real trouble so use it cautiously)

Watch out—Siri speaks Mandarin!

It didn't take long for Mandarin immersion students to realize that Siri, the voice recognition software on iPhones and iPads, speaks multiple languages—and one of them is Mandarin. If they took their parents' iPad or iPhone and spoke into it in Mandarin, Siri would write out everything they'd said. This is a good thing for their ability to write quickly (they still have to check and make sure it is correct) but not always the educational objective their teacher was setting when she asked them to write something. So check in with your teacher if you find your children are making use of this technological marvel and see if it's considered appropriate. I will say that it's caused my older daughter to develop very clear and crisp diction when she speaks Chinese, as Siri can't understand if you mumble.

Poetry

Here's one perk (or detriment, it depends on the parent) of signing your children up for immersion—you'll become very familiar with Tang dynasty poetry.

China holds literature and the written word in extremely high regard in ways the United States hasn't for at least a century. Up until the 1920s it was expected that educated children here would learn dozens of poems by heart, some of them in older forms of English. That tradition has died out in the U.S. but not in China. Chinese students still memorize dozens of poems during their elementary school years and the ability to recite poetry by heart is considered the mark of an educated person to this day. The poetry of the Tang Dynasty (618 AD to 907 AD) is especially beloved. (It *is* lovely poetry, even in English translation.)

Mandarin immersion students inevitably end up memorizing at least a few poems during their school years. If you live in a city with any kind of a Chinese community, you might also find your child taking part in a poetry recitation contest. It might be sponsored by the local Confucius Institute or by other civic institutions. These competitions generally break students into groups for native speakers and for non-native speakers. Sometimes there are also sections for Cantonese and Mandarin speakers. Each grade level is usually assigned one required poem and one poem the student themselves can choose. Students memorize them and then at the competition stand before a panel of judges and a roomful of parents and other students to do their recitation. In some schools teachers help students choose poetry to recite. If your teachers aren't up for it, ask a parent from China or Taiwan.

The recitations typically include hand motions to convey the meaning of the poems. Written in Classical Chinese, they're unintelligible to modern speakers of Chinese, just as a poem from the Old English used in 800 AD would be unintelligible to us today. Awards are given based on fluency, tones, hand motions and comfort before the audience.

If you go on YouTube and search on "Chinese poetry recital" you'll find multiple examples of students here and around the world, often reciting the same Tang poems.

In larger cities these competitions can also include other Chinese cultural pursuits such as:

- Painting
- Chinese calligraphy using a brush
- Chinese calligraphy using a pen
- Chinese composition (timed essay writing)
- Chinese translation

Be aware that China has not fallen into the "everyone's a winner" mindset. These competitions have first place, second place and third place awards, and sometimes a few honorable mentions. Most children walk away empty handed.

Stick around until at least eighth grade

Immersion programs require a long-term commitment. You can't drop in for kindergarten and then pull your child out in third grade and have them be fluent. All immersion programs presume students will start in kindergarten or first grade and continue at least through eighth grade. If students leave mid-way, they won't have learned much Chinese and they'll quickly forget what they learned.

Language acquisition expert Jim Cummins[2] has written about the two kinds of language proficiency children acquire, one social and one academic. Many children can develop native speaker fluency (i.e. basic interpersonal communication skills) within two years of immersion in the target language. That's how newly immigrated children in the United States so quickly begin sounding like they were born here. But Cummins also found that it takes between five and seven years "for a child to be working on a level with native speakers as far as academic language is concerned."[3]

Parents looking at Mandarin immersion for their children don't want merely social language, they want academic proficiency. And that takes until at least the end of middle school to develop. Most programs would say it really takes through high school and then into college, taking classes in Chinese all the way through. After all, you wouldn't expect someone who dropped out of school in the sixth grade to be able to write a quality research paper in English, would you?

Find a way for your child to spend time in China

Many programs report that even students who end at eighth grade "blossom" when they spend time in a Chinese-speaking country. In some ways, educators say, Mandarin immersion students end up being much like children raised in Chinese-speaking homes in the United States:

- They have native-like accents, because they learned to speak Mandarin so early in life.

- They have a native sense of how the language works and of its grammar. So while they might not have the vocabulary to build elaborate sentences, they known at an intuitive level how a Chinese sentence is constructed.

- Because of these two factors, when Mandarin immersion students go to China, Taiwan or Singapore, their Chinese "blossoms" much as young adults from Chinese-speaking homes in the United States do when they first go to China.

"There's such a connection," says Jeff Bissell, head of school at the Chinese American International School in San Francisco. "They're actually springboarding to higher levels of Chinese." Once in an all-Chinese environment, their language abilities seem to appear almost miraculously. They remember things they didn't even know they'd forgotten. The language makes sense on an unconscious level they weren't aware of. While other young adults new to the language are struggling to express their basic needs, immersion students find their language ability grows by leaps and bounds because the basics are very firmly stuck in their heads.

Be nice to your teachers

Immersion teachers are like gold. Finding trained, high-quality Mandarin immersion teachers is not easy, as any principal can tell you. While there are lots of Mandarin speakers in the world, not that many of them have the training to become immersion teachers in the United States. Immersion has been called one of the most difficult types of teaching because it requires being totally "on" all the time. Teachers spend their days acting out concepts, emphasizing and exaggerating their facial expressions so they can help students understand not just new concepts but new vocabulary every moment of every day. One parent described it as "like watching someone play charades for four hours straight."

Not only that, but in much of the United States Mandarin immersion teachers must not only be fully fluent and literate in Chinese, but also in English, enough that they can complete an education degree at a U.S. university and pass multiple state tests.

Anyone with that level of English and Mandarin has a lot of possible job opportunities, so the ones who choose teaching are dedicated and truly love the language—which is great for students. The problem is, there just aren't enough of them.

Some programs bring in teachers from China, for short- or long-term teaching assignments. Working through Hanban and the Confucius Institute, schools can bring Mandarin teachers in from China for one- or two-year contracts. Other school districts sponsor teachers from China and Taiwan through H1 visa programs. This can be expensive and requires the teacher to make a multi-year commitment to the school.

Teachers coming straight from China and Taiwan can also have a hard time culturally. U.S. teaching and learning styles are very different from the more formal and rote-based teaching common in Asia. U.S. classrooms can seem chaotic and uncontrolled to someone used to the more disciplined classes of China. And in many school districts there are only a few Mandarin speaking teachers coming to a given school, often living in areas where there's no Chinese community for them to become a part of.

Be your school's ambassador to new teachers

One mom in our school took it upon herself to give each year's new crop of teachers an introduction to the neighborhood around our school in the weeks before school started. She'd pick them up, drive them to school and then they'd set off on a day-long walking and driving adventure. She showed them where the nearest library was, the bus stops, the coffee shops and the grocery stores. As she did, she gave them a running cultural commentary on what an American neighborhood looks like. For some teachers who have spent little time in the United States, a neighborhood with lots of Hispanic and African-American families, such as our school is in, can seem intimidating even though it's actually a very welcoming place. Having a tour, and a cultural introduction, went a long way towards making them comfortable and a part of our community.

The Asia Society, which is an excellent resource for Mandarin immersion programs, has created a booklet on preparing Chinese language teachers for American schools. It's available at http://asiasociety.org/files/chineseteacherprep.pdf.

1. Kumon is an after school math and reading program intended to supplement rather than replace school lessons. Students progress at their own pace doing daily worksheets. Mastery is defined as speed and accuracy. More at http://www.kumon.com

2. Second Language Acquisition/Literacy Development.
   http://iteachilearn.org/cummins/converacademlangdisti.html
   Accessed July 4, 2013.
3. Frankfurt International School. *Second language acquisition—essential informa-tion.* http://esl.fis.edu/teachers/support/cummin.htm
   Accessed Jan. 17, 2014.

二十六
èr shí liù
26

Things Teachers and Principals Wish They Could Tell You

Over the past few years, I've been asking Mandarin immersion principals and teachers, "What do you wish you could tell parents, but you can't, or you do, but they don't listen?" Here are some of their replies:

Look in your child's backpack

Teachers and schools spend a lot of effort sending home information about what's going on in the classroom. Students don't always remember to give it to you. Rummage around. You might be surprised what your school is telling you that you haven't been hearing—and some of it might be about the Mandarin program.

Remember that children aren't always reliable narrators

One teacher put it this way, "If you believe everything they say about what I'm doing in class, I'll start believing everything they say about what you do at home." Remember, these are children. Check with other parents and your teacher before you take a nine-year-old's word for something.

Remember that parents don't set curriculum

Teachers, principal and staff set curriculum. Parents do not.

Don't presume that if your child is having trouble, every child is

Teachers call this the "soccer sideline scrum." Parents start chatting during a soccer game and if one or two of their children are having troubles, suddenly a rumor starts that the entire class isn't learning and there's a major problem. Check with your child's teacher first before your make pronouncements about the entire class or school.

Don't ask your child to translate

Translating is a different skill; it's acquired later in life and it's not taught in immersion schools. Just because your child can't translate something from Chinese into English doesn't mean they're not learning.

Immersion students really do lag in English

Every study anyone's done ever says they catch up and frequently exceed their English-only peers by fifth or sixth grade. But they do lag behind early on. One principal told me "Parents nod and say 'I get it.' But if they see their child lagging, they say, 'What is the school doing wrong?'"

Don't be too boastful about your child being in immersion

It's hard not to be proud of your child and everything they're accomplishing in school. But sometimes that can veer into a boastfulness that can contain an element of "My kid's going to do better in the world than your mono-lingual kid." This is especially true in districts where there's a lot of compe-tition to get into immersion schools, so only a few lucky families have the opportunity. This is enough of a cultural meme that Cheetos made an ad[1] about it. Don't be that mom!

Talk to your child's teacher early and often

If you child is frustrated or discouraged, talk with him or her about it. Under-stand why he or she is feeling that way. It might take several chats over a few days to get the full story. Then talk to the teacher right away. Don't let it sit until everything's falling apart.

Take your child's needs and desires into account

Not necessarily in kindergarten, but by middle school and high school stu-dents start to get some sense of what motivates them. It may be your dream to have them be bilingual and end up owning half of Shanghai, but is it theirs?

The school needs your help to get the program running

Form a parents group.

Raise money to buy Chinese books for the library.

Help educate parents about Chinese and immersion (to take some of the burden off the school staff).

Don't force your kids to speak Chinese to show them off

Remember that younger children especially have much stronger passive Chinese ability than they do active—they can't say anywhere near as much as they can understand.

Don't ask them to read menus in a Chinese restaurant

The language used in Chinese menus is highly poetic and not very meaningful to elementary school students. For example, one of my favorite dishes is a spicy pork and tofu stir-fry that goes by the name 麻婆豆腐 or *Má pó dòufu*. This reads as "Pockmarked Crone's tofu"[2] which isn't really something most kids can easily translate. And when they see 龙虾, or *lóngxiā*, they might or might not realize "dragon shrimp" means lobster.[3] Or that 凤爪, *fèngzhǎo*, which reads as "Phoenix talons," is what chicken feet are called on dim sum menus. You can have them pick out characters they know, of course. But don't expect them to be able to read and translate the names of dishes.

Don't ask them to read the newspaper in Chinese

Chinese newspapers use lots of contractions and vocabulary that elementary school students simply don't know. For example, if you translate 目前全国经济形势很好 word-for-word, the way a student might, it's something like "eye before whole country scriptures help shape power very good." You need to know that 目前 means "currently," 经济 means "economic" and 形势 means "situation" and then you can figure out that it actually means, "The current national economic situation is very good."

Trust your teachers

One long-time principal said this: "We're partners. We need you to trust that we're the professionals here. Start with the teacher if you have a problem. Don't go straight to the principal just because he or she speaks English or answers your emails right away."

Talk to your teacher in person

"Please, please emphasize this," one principal emailed. Most Mandarin immersion teachers speak Mandarin as their first language. They speak and write English as well, but often not as easily. For some, writing even a simple email in English can take three or four times as long as it would if they were writing in Chinese. They want to make sure the tone is correct and they want to make sure there are no errors.

This is why meeting with teachers is a *much* better way to communicate about your child and his or her schoolwork than doing it via email. Some teachers feel comfortable with email, but most don't. Also, your child's teacher has 20 or 25 other students. If each parent wants a "quick email" once a week, that's something like 14 hours of time to write (if each takes 30 minutes, which it easily can).

If you must email, ask Yes or No questions

If you're emailing to a non-native speaker of English, it's helpful to ask yes or no questions. You can describe your concern, but make it easy for the teacher to reply by giving them easy-to-answer questions.

Support your program financially

Unless you live in an insanely wealthy school district, most Mandarin immersion programs don't get any extra support from their District. That means the extras that teachers need, such as dictionaries, maps in Chinese, books, props for play-acting so they can explain words, all of that has to come out of the school's budget. And most of it actually comes out of the teacher's pockets. Find out how much teachers make in your school district and see how much of a bite it's taking.

Also remember that a new teacher arrives to a bare room with nothing at all. Look at an established teacher's classroom and you'll see pictures, books and materials like rugs and cups and plants that he or she has built up over years. A new teacher walks into four walls and some desks. If you know you're getting a new teacher, get in touch with your principal and the teacher and ask what he or she needs.

Should you take a Chinese course?

It's not a bad idea, if only because you'll realize how difficult the language is and you'll be aware of how much your child is learning. It will also give you a realistic sense of the challenges they face when it comes to reading and writing. But don't expect to keep up with them; they'll outpace you by first grade. In many ways that's a good thing. Your kids will get a huge kick out of being better at Chinese than you are, and they'll have fun lecturing to you about how to do things.

Most Chinese teachers are ... Chinese

This is a tough one. It's about culture and expectations, and it can be difficult to discuss, in part because parents don't always even understand exactly what they're feeling. At baseline, most Mandarin immersion teachers were raised in either a Chinese-speaking country or a Chinese-speaking household and they tend to have certain cultural traits in common.

One administrator said it can be difficult for American parents to embrace Chinese cultural practices in the classroom. "When you completely deconstruct the conversation you're having with them about their child's teacher, you realize that what they're *really* saying is, "I wish my kid's Chinese teacher wasn't Chinese."

It helps to realize that the Chinese cultural practices students encounter in their classrooms are also Chinese cultural practices they'll encounter in China. While some things just aren't acceptable in the U.S. (shaming students who do poorly, for example) others will stand them in good stead when they go to China. Some examples:

Formal interactions

Chinese teachers typically expect more formal interactions. For example wanting to be called Zhou Laoshi (Teacher Zhou) rather than Anne. This extends to class-room discipline, which can be less freewheeling than tends to be common in American classrooms. Teachers may insist on a level of strictness that's more old-school than many Americans are used to.

Teachers as respected professionals

Across Asia teachers are highly respected professionals and teaching is considered an honorable job. The idea of parents demanding to be part of classroom planning or curriculum development is alien to most teachers in China, where parents are expected to support the teacher's decisions rather than challenge them.

Competition is okay

A willingness to acknowledge academic success is not common in American classrooms, where student scores are kept closely guarded lest anyone feel judged by their academic prowess. In China it's perfectly acceptable and considered appropriate to post everyone's test score and praise students who did well, just as we might praise students who ran the fastest mile in a track meet and post their names. This is something that horrifies American parents, to the surprise of Chinese teachers.

Parent Jackie Chou Lem tells the story that this is so much a part of Chinese culture that it's actually how her parents met. "My parents were elementary school classmates in Taiwan, but my father's family moved away after a few years. My father reconnected with my mother after he saw her name in the newspaper in an article reporting on college entrance examination results!

1. Cheetos Soccer Moms ad, 2009.
    http://www.youtube.com/watch?v=UgoDcCQZzIg
    Accessed Jan. 17, 2014.
2. Wikipedia. Mapo doufu.
    http://en.wikipedia.org/wiki/Mapo_doufu
    Accessed April 7, 2014.
3. A great book for adults to read on this is *Swallowing Clouds: Two Millennia of Chinese Tradition, Folklore and History Hidden in the Language of Food* by A. Zee. (Touchstone, 1990.)

二十七
èr shí qī
27

How to Start
a Parents Group

Any school that has a Mandarin immersion program can probably use a parent support network. That's how ours, 金山中文教育协会/ Jinshan Mandarin Education Council, started in San Francisco. We realized our teachers, kids and parents needed help and the school district couldn't do it all. That's where parents came in.

We began very simply, just a meeting of parents with kids in Mandarin immersion about how to help with homework. We created a Yahoo email group so we could share information with each other. We called ourself the Mandarin Immersion Parents Council.

We had a few more meetings covering basic things like how to look up words in a Chinese dictionary (a real skill unto itself, if you don't speak Chinese) and what summer programs were available for kids in our area. We also started a blog where we could post some of the stuff we came up with.

That was back in 2008. It took us four years, until May of 2012, to become big enough that we needed to be a non-profit that could raise money to support our programs. We chose a fiscal sponsor, a non-profit that allowed us to be a program under them, as we weren't large enough to deal with the legal fees and paperwork necessary to become our own at that point. We also got a new name: 金山中文教育协会/ Jinshan Mandarin Education Council, and a new website, http://www.jinshaneducation.org.

So my message here is this—parents play a huge role in making a Mandarin immersion program work, and you can start very simply. Don't let worries about not being big or official or bilingual enough stop you—your kids, your teachers and the other families need you! So here are some basic suggestions.

First, create an email list. Yahoo worked for us because it was free and easy to switch the person who runs the list, which you'll need to do every few years. However there are many options out there.

Give the list a simple name that will cover all the schools in your school district that are likely to get Mandarin. You may just have kindergarten and first grade now, but eventually there will be a middle school and high school component. So Houston Mandarin Immersion works better than Gordon Elementary Mandarin Immersion. The list will give a chance for families to share resources, ask homework questions and generally support one and other.

If you've got both English- and Chinese-speaking families in your program, try to start out bilingual. It will make your group welcoming for everyone. But if you don't have many Chinese-speaking families, don't let being primarily English-speaking stop you. Everything can happen in time. Better to start now and build over time. As Voltaire said, "Don't let perfect be the enemy of good."

In addition to the program list, create a list for each grade. For example, at Starr King we had SKMI2014 as an address. That was the Starr King Mandarin immersion graduating class of 2014. That way, the email stayed the same for the entire six years students were at the school and parents didn't have to unsubscribe from one list and subscribe to a new one each fall. This is the list you turn to if it's 7:30 PM and your child can't figure out what the character on page 3 of the homework means, or isn't sure exactly what they're supposed to do.

Remember that email lists need someone to watch over them. As we all know, sometimes people post without thinking, or let their frustration or anger spill over into words they would never say to someone's face. Email lists are powerful, useful tools, but it also helps to lay some ground rules and have a list coordinator to enforce them. Simple rules you can start with are:

- Play nice.
- Be polite.
- If someone can't play nice, give them a time out.
- Never say anything in email you wouldn't say face-to-face.
- Never say anything in email you wouldn't stand up and say at a PTA meeting.

Website

If you've got a parent that's handy with the internet, start a website for your group. A Facebook page is also a possibility. All you need to start out is something simple and easy, a place where current parents and families considering your program can come for information. Having an internet presence makes you much more "real" to families outside the school, which will help your program over time.

Especially if you're a strand in a larger school, a separate site can be a place where you can place information specifically about Mandarin.

Remember to make it program-specific, not school-specific. Over time your program will be in at least three schools—elementary, middle and high school. Wordpress.com is one place that offers free websites and it's easy to figure out, but of course there are many other options.

Here are some examples you can use as a starting place. Borrow freely; none of us has to reinvent the wheel here:

CLIPCO
Cupertino, California Language Immersion Program
http://www.cusdclipco.org

Jié Míng Mandarin Immersion Academy
St. Paul, Minnesota
http://www.facebook.com/pages/Jié-M%C3%ADng-Mandarin-Immer-sion-Academy/228497720538807

Jinshan Mandarin Education Council/ 金山中文教育协会
San Francisco Unified School District
http://www.jinshaneducation.org

Quan Ren
Vancouver, Washington public schools
http://www.mipofvancouver.org

ShuRen of Portland
Portland (Oregon) Public Schools
http://www.shurenofportland.org

Utah Mandarin Immersion Parent Council
http://utahimmersioncouncil.org

Second, get parents in the program together for a meeting. It doesn't have to be fancy or formal, just informational. It can be at school in the evening or at someone's house on the weekend. Even at a local coffee shop after morning drop-off, if that works best. Some topics parents have presented over the years:

- Welcome to Mandarin immersion and our program. How Mandarin immersion works in your school district and what you can expect your child to learn. (Get someone from the district or a teacher to present if you can.)

- How to use a Chinese Dictionary/Chinese 101: A basic introduction to how Chinese works. Ask a teacher or bilingual parent to present this.

- Parent-tested suggestions on how to help your kids with homework. Share tips and ideas. Have one of your teachers walk parents through a sample homework packet, so parents can figure out how it's structured so they know how to help their kids at home.

- Extracurricular and summer programs in Mandarin in your area. These may or may not exist—they'll come eventually as the community realizes there's a market.

- Prospective parents roundtable. Publicize this far and wide. This is a chance for families with kids in the Mandarin immersion program to answer questions from parents considering signing up for the program. This will help you get a strong turnout for the following year. Do it at the beginning of the enrollment season in your school district.

- Taking your kids to China—parent suggestions and tips. If no one in your school has yet gone to China, you can reach out to local Chinese adoption groups. Most lead trips back to China for families who have adopted children from China and can offer advice (many are probably also parents in your school).

  Other possible events for your parent group:

- Find a local Chinese bookstore and see if they will hold a book sale at your school, with books appropriate for your students. Tell them whether you use traditional or simplified characters and let them choose books that might work. Parents can also meet to share and swap videos and CDs they got in Mandarin.

- At the end of your first year, find a local Chinese restaurant and hold a banquet to celebrate how far the students and your program has come. Have families underwrite the cost of dinner for the teachers and the principal and let the kids write short speeches thanking them for what they have learned. Pat yourselves on the back!

Grant writing

Parents can also help with school-specific needs that your staff may simply not have time to do. One example is the realm of educational grants. There are many of these but writing grants is a specific skill and they take time to put together. Better to have parents do that work and have teachers teach.

One parent suggested:

All teachers have trouble finding time to do these things, but I think it is especially hard for brand-new teachers for whom English is their second language. Our school district's foundation gives small grants out to teachers, and my daughter's teacher wrote a draft asking for money for books, especially science content. (We had none.) Two parents helped give important feedback, but the deadline was looming. Even for me, as a native speaker of English, it required staying up late to incorporate the changes. She was awarded the grant. Her English is fluent, but she would have taken much longer to do the writing, something she did not have time to do.

Non-profit status

In the long-term, you might want to consider creating a non-profit group. This will allow your group to take tax-deductible contributions. That might mean more Chinese books for the school library, dictionaries for the classrooms or a class trip to China at the end of eighth grade. As I write this, the Jinshan Mandarin Education Council (JMEC) in San Francisco is holding a blitz 10-day online fundraiser to send one teacher from each of our three schools to a Chinese literacy conference in Salt Lake City. (Update: we raised enough to send five!)

If you choose the non-profit route, consider looking first for a fiscal sponsor. In many cities there are community or education groups that will serve as an umbrella non-profit for smaller groups for which the work and expense of getting non-profit status is too much. JMEC uses the San Francisco Study Center as its fiscal sponsor.

Other schools have parents who are lawyers who can help set one up. There are many books and websites to help guide you.

Remember that you don't have to start off as a non-profit! Sometimes parents get so caught up in the work it takes to create a non-profit they don't actually create an organization. Everyone is so exhausted simply by trying to decide what to do that nothing gets done. Your program will exist for many years, so beginning at the beginning is fine. Non-profit status can come when there's sufficient need and energy on the part of parents. In San Francisco that process took four years.

A final suggestion from Portland's Shuren organization, always have the vice president of the group be the president-in-waiting. This way there's continuity across the years. Otherwise you can spend half a year reinventing the wheel while a new board gets up to speed.

You Know You're a Mandarin Immersion Parent* When...

- the birthday cake comes out at a party and you start singing 祝你生日快乐, *Zhù nǐ shēngrì kuàilè,* and then quickly realize everyone else is singing "Happy Birthday To You."
- you reach into your purse for Kleenex, and come out with a handful of flashcards.
- you can explain to a kindergarten parent what a measure word is, and get it right.
- you can pick out your child's handwriting on the bulletin board outside his classroom, even though the papers are all in Chinese.
- you have seriously considered moving to another state for a Mandarin immersion program.
- all the CDs in your car are in Chinese.
- you are ridiculously excited that your child can read some of the characters on the back of the hot sauce bottle at a Chinese restaurant.
- your child runs up to anyone who looks even remotely Asian and tries to start up a conversation in Mandarin.
- your third grader is starting to lose it over homework, so you offer to race him looking up characters by stroke order. You beat him.
- you learned to belt out the entire chorus of *"Gong Xi Gong Xi"* or *"Liang Zhi Lao Hu"* long before you could say basic phrases in Chinese.
- you forget that *"hongbao"* is not an English word, and that non-Chinese or Mandarin immersion friends may not know what's inside the little red envelope you're handing them.
- you know what Yellowbridge.com is and you know how to use it.

---

* A non–Chinese speaking MI parent, that is.

- you have strong preferences in moon cakes, and know how to answer the question, "One egg yolk, two or none?"
- your kid says "I have to *fuxi* for my *kaoshi*, but after that I'm done with my *gongke*," and you understand her.
- you know who the biggest Mando-pop stars are and have their songs, with Chinese subtitles, bookmarked on your computer.
- you own more Chinese dictionaries than English dictionaries.
- you forget that in most schools, teachers will speak to you in English even when there are students around.
- you discover that your eighth grader sometimes texts with her friends in Chinese to keep you from reading what she's saying.
- other parents dream of Harvard and UCLA. You find yourself considering the relative merits of Beijing and Tsinghua universities.

二十九
èr shí jiǔ
29

Moving Forward

Those who have worked to build Chinese immersion programs to their current state deserve a standing ovation. They have given their time and spent their days—as well as nights and weekends—creating the curriculums used in our classrooms. They have found ways to get schools and school districts interested. They have built programs from nothing but blood, sweat and tears while placating parents and motivating students. And yet even the most dedicated proponents of Chinese immersion will tell you it is not yet perfect. In this chapter I share some of my own thoughts about how Mandarin immersion might look in the future.

The basic question is this: Is immersion as it is currently structured the best way to produce American students who speak, read and write both Chinese and English? My answer after two years of research is that the way we currently do things probably isn't the best. However, given the current structure of the U.S. educational system, it's one of the few ways possible.

"Dear heavens! This woman can't make up her mind," you're mumbling to yourself. "First she says Mandarin immersion is the best thing since sliced bread and now, 29 chapters in, she's saying maybe it's not such a hot idea after all."

Actually, having spent a lot of time talking to the people on the front lines of these programs, two things stand out to me:

- We're deploying Chinese immersion without much data on how best to make it work.

- We'll see lots of changes in the coming years as a wave of data begins to arrive and educators use it to construct even stronger immersion programs.

That data will come from large studies currently underway in Portland, Oregon, work Utah is doing, and information gathered through the two big Mandarin immersion consortia, F-CAP (Flagship–Chinese Acquisition Pipeline) and CELIN (Chinese Early Language and Immersion Network). Administrators, academics and teachers will use it to refine and design programs, curricula and lessons.

But parents have a different set of questions, ones school officials aren't always eager, or even able, to answer. So I'm going to put myself on the line here and try to answer them myself, as someone who has trusted her children's education to immersion and plans to continue doing so through high school if at all possible.

Questions, answers, and some more questions

Do students in Chinese immersion programs sacrifice content (i.e. the things they learn in classes like math, science and social studies) when those subjects are taught in Chinese?

Yes. Students' language ability is almost never as high in Mandarin as it is in English, so they're getting somewhat simplified material. However, it should be noted that in many schools the teachers teach in Mandarin but the textbooks are in English. This allows students to be exposed to more complex material when they read, which is good. But overall the level is less advanced in Mandarin than it would be in English.

Effectively we're putting English-speaking students in the same position that students who arrive in U.S. schools not speaking English find themselves. Except that our students are fluent in English, so they've got a huge leg up. There is some evidence that immersion students gain empathy for what English language learners go through—not a bad thing. But perhaps not the lesson their parents thought they were signing up for.

A Mandarin immersion teacher, who didn't want her name used, told me that almost all students need learning support at home. "Students will not get everything the teachers said in the class. That is a for sure! Therefore, parents will provide personal tutors at home or extra help if needed to cover the learning gap. Next day, they will go to school with everything covered from extra help, so they will not be behind."

Are those sacrifices worth it, given the reward of learning Chinese?

Yes, for me and for my family and for many families who prize language ability, it is. But there's a crucial caveat: *We know that we can fill in any blanks in our children's education if they don't understand what they have been taught because it was in Chinese.* It means we do a sort of home schooling. At times you have to sit down and go over what was taught in Chinese class to make sure your child understands the concepts.

This isn't necessarily Chinese-specific. Many immersion families would probably do a fair amount of homework support no matter what language the material was taught in, because that's the kind of educationally minded families they tend to be. However parents need to know this up front. Not all families would make this choice. Many don't realize they have.

Is the accent that immersion students get really native-quality?

Sometimes, but not always. Schools rely on having students be exposed to Chinese from their teachers. However, in many programs the teacher is the only person speaking to these students in Chinese. So they're not getting a lot of input. And there is not always enough focus on correcting student errors, especially when it comes to tones. These are the kind of corrections that Chinese-speaking parents do unconsciously with their toddlers simply by emphasizing the correct way of saying a word when their child has used the wrong tone or pronunciation. In a class of 25 or 30 students it's difficult for teachers to do that and most children who mispronounce a word don't automatically correct themselves if they are understood. Without correction, errors can become fossilized. Students end up speaking Chinese, but they don't sound quite native.

One way to deal with this is to ensure that children get *lots* of exposure to Chinese outside the classroom through videos and movies and by playing with kids who speak Chinese. There is some controversy about whether exposure or correction is the best way to go. Probably a lot of exposure and a little correction are best.

Could students do just as well just taking Chinese in high school?

No. Their accent and their internal sense of the grammar wouldn't be anywhere near as good. It's true that in terms of reading and writing, AP Chinese students in a rigorous class get pretty far in four years. Still, it's only one hour a day of class. I'd go with immersion as the better choice. My 13-year-old knows more Chinese at this point than many high school seniors. And when she went to China this year and lived with a Chinese family for three weeks, she communicated with them almost solely in Chinese. She was functionally fluent. Immersion really does work!

Do these programs truly serve the needs of Chinese-speaking students in terms of the level of Chinese writing and reading they could attain if they were in a Chinese-only program?

No. But here the rub: There *are* no high-quality immersion programs designed for Chinese speakers in this country. So it's really a moot point. The only way to find a Chinese-only school is to send your child to school in China or Taiwan.

As for weekend or Saturday Chinese schools, immersion is probably a better bet because students have a peer group that also uses Chinese, normalizing the language despite the fact that they live in an English-speaking country. For a host of reasons I go over in *Chapter 18: For Chinese-Speaking Parents*, immersion appears to work better than these weekend schools for most students (though many families will want to supplement with more reading in Chinese, just as English-speaking parents do in English).

Another option many Chinese-speaking parents ask about is having their child take Chinese as a class in high school. However, it's generally not a good fit for Chinese-speaking students because they're so bored. They can speak Chinese already, while the students around them are still wrapping their brains around "*Ni hao.*" Only in areas with very high concentrations of Chinese speakers are there high school level Chinese classes specifically designed for heritage speakers.

The ideal Chinese immersion program

After two years or research, here is what I think an ideal Chinese immersion program would look like. I'll explain my reasoning after the list.

- A whole-school environment, not a school-within-a-school

- A workshop for families *before they sign up* for the program explaining what their children will learn and exactly how much work would be required of them and their child. They would sign a contract that clearly outlines what's expected of them and their children in terms of effort and participation—and what they can expect from the school.

- Yearly or semi-yearly testing to ensure that students' Chinese is good enough to master material taught in Chinese. For students who fall behind, intensive support *must* be made available. For those for whom Chinese is not working, the possibility of shifting to a separate hour-a-day Chinese class while staying in the school is optimal.

Why is a whole-school environment so important?

A school that's all Chinese immersion can focus on its uniqueness and strengths and not have to contort itself in a constant struggle to honor the needs of two (and sometimes more) very different programs, one taught in English and one taught in Chinese. It is able to fill important staff positions with bilingual Chinese speakers so that the entire school is focused on the language and culture. In all-immersion schools, the principal, secretaries, art and PE teachers are often Chinese speaking, adding a whole social element that's impossible in a school that must meet the needs of two different programs.

All-immersion schools also are able to celebrate their Chinese-ness in a way that dual-strand schools can't without seeming to leave out the English-program students. Sometimes when you walk into a school that has a Chinese immersion program, it's very hard to tell that there's a Chinese program there at all, because the school wants to be inclusive of all its students. You can usually tell an all-immersion school because it has a Chinese name. Dual-program schools never do.

A Chinese immersion teacher told me this works very well for students' Chinese in her experience. In the school she taught in, all the staff used Chinese. "When kids go to school, they are going to a different country. They learn academic terms in the class, social terms in other times. Does it work at least for speaking and listening? It works great!"

This is something Spanish immersion schools do well. These programs strive to create a space where "the status of the Spanish language and the status of Latin cultures are 'consciously elevated' within a school," in the words of Deborah Sercombe, a principal at Amigos School in Cambridge, Massachusetts "It's important that when anyone walks into our school, they are aware that they are entering a Spanish-speaking environment and entering into a particular culture that is valued here."[1]

That said, it's not always politically possible to have a whole-school program because it can mean pushing out neighborhood students from a neighborhood school. The lesson of what happened in Lake Forest, Illinois in *Chapter 19: Why Schools Choose Mandarin Immersion* is telling. Having a Mandarin program is better than not having a Mandarin program, so if a strand within a school is the only thing possible in a given district, that's better than nothing. But it does create issues a whole-school program doesn't have.

If a strand within a school is the only option, it should have at least two classes per grade level taught in Chinese in the younger years. That provides a critical mass of students and a large enough group of teachers so they can provide support and backup for each other. In addition, this ensures that in the upper grades there are enough students to fill at least one class, as there will inevitably be some attrition. Without at least two classes per grade level in the younger grades, split classes, which are difficult to teach, are often required in the upper grades.

Setting expectations

I once wrote in a flyer for prospective families looking at Starr King Elementary that learning to read and write Chinese is difficult and requires more work than learning to read and write English. I was promptly told by another parent I needed to remove that sentence—it wasn't "welcoming."

Let's just say we disagreed (and I didn't remove it from the flyer, either). Chinese *is* harder to learn to read and write (though not to speak) and it *does* take more work. Families need to know that before they sign up for these programs. No school should be a total walk in the park, but Chinese requires extra work, more homework and a deeper commitment, especially on the part of families that don't speak it at home. There's just no getting around this.

But many schools are leery of admitting this. They don't want to seem unwelcoming, they don't want to scare families away from the program, and they feel that every child should be able to succeed in every program *with no special support*. But I maintain that what they're doing is setting students up for failure by not being honest from the beginning.

This is especially an issue in public schools, because they must be accessible to all students regardless of ability or family circumstances. So students whose families aren't able to sit with them for an hour or two each night making sure they do their homework, armed with a couple of dictionaries and a computer, or students whose families can't afford to hire a tutor, are still presumed to have the same ability to succeed as those whose families have access to those things.

This is a difficult and touchy question. The best-functioning schools manage it by honestly acknowledging that there are demands placed on Mandarin immersion students above and beyond English-only programs. One successful ploy is to create afterschool homework clubs that give all students the chance to do their homework in a quiet, focused place with access to help from teachers or teachers' aides and all the dictionaries and other materials they might need.

Three examples I know of:

- At the public José Ortega Elementary School in San Francisco, an afterschool Gongke Club (功课 *gōngkè*, homework) was created to ensure that all students have the support they need to excel in Chinese.

- San Francisco's Alice Fong Yu Alternative School, a well-established Cantonese immersion K–8, has an afterschool homework program. Teachers are paid for an extra class period a day to allow it to be staffed, with the money coming out of the Parents Association fund. There is also extra mandatory tutoring for kids who are falling behind before and after school.

- At the Chinese American International School, a private K–8 school in San Francisco, a high percentage of elementary school students attend the school's fee-based afterschool study hall. Students get a snack and then are required to do their Chinese homework first, before they move on to their English homework, with Mandarin-speaking teachers available to help them if they run into trouble. "CAIS would have been a lot more daunting for us if there were no study hall," said a parent from a non-Chinese speaking family.

Programs also need to intensively teach parents—early on—how to help their children with homework. This includes training in how to look up words in Chinese, how to use online Chinese dictionaries like YellowBridge and Pleco, and how to foster general time-management skills that the students might otherwise not need until middle school.

Some programs deal with the issue (or, really, don't deal with the issue) with a hodge-podge of student pull-outs and unspoken expectations of private tutoring. Students who are struggling get extra help, but only after they've fallen behind. Private Chinese tutoring is rampant in many public school programs, because most of the parents don't speak Chinese and they realize that after a certain point it's harder to help their children with homework. The problem, of course, is that this is only available to families with the economic and logistical wherewithal to pay for and organize private tutoring. This creates inherent inequities within the school between families that can afford the time or money required for this type of support and those that can't. The gap only gets worse as students advance through the grades.

Testing and why it's so important

Which leads us to testing. In all programs, the range of Chinese ability starts out relatively similar and over the years begins to widen. That's an important point, so let me say it again: *Even Chinese-speaking students arrive in kindergarten not being able to read, so all the kids are basically starting from the same place in terms of literacy.*

However, over the years the amount of time they spend doing homework, the amount of time they spend in Chinese environments outside of school, and the amount of time they spend reading in Chinese outside of school create a sharp divergence in how well students are able to understand Chinese material presented to them orally and in written form.

Most students in most programs do just fine. They may not all be at the same level, they may not be totally fluent speakers or readers of Chinese, but they understand what their teachers are saying to them. They can read the assigned written material, and they grasp the subjects they're being taught in Chinese.

There are also some students who really excel, either because they come from Chinese-speaking families, have parents who are very focused on academics or simply have a natural talent for languages. These kids often do far more in Chinese outside of school than their classmates. One family I know specifically bought the Chinese language cable package from their local cable TV company, even though both parents would have preferred to watch TV in English. The mom kept the TV tuned to Mandarin programs and pretty much any time the kids were in the living room there was Mandarin happening there. When the dad wanted to watch sports he had to go upstairs to a much smaller TV, because it was in English. But the kids got hours more Mandarin exposure each week than their peers, and their Chinese ability showed it.

Clearly not all families are going to be able to or even want to do that. Again, *most kids will do fine*. But there will always be a small subset of students who are going to struggle. They may be struggling in English as well, but in Chinese it's worse. Sometimes their Chinese listening comprehension is just fine, sometimes it's not. But often their reading ability is at a much lower level than the rest of the students. Some of these students literally can't read the Chinese language material being presented in class and at a certain point they just give up trying.

It's not such a big deal in the younger grades, but towards fourth and fifth grade it begins to be an issue because students start learning crucial material in Chinese. If you can't understand what the teacher is teaching and if you can't read the homework, you miss a lot of math or social studies concepts. These are concepts you're not learning anywhere else so they're just gone.

This *must* be addressed with a strong, school-based support program so that students who need extra help get it, even if their parents don't realize there's a problem or aren't comfortable demanding help from the school or don't have the ability to pay for outside tutoring.

If these programs don't exist, these students fall further and further behind with every year that passes. But in several programs I've encountered, the staff doesn't want to "give up" on any students, so they continue to be pushed through the grades. Each year they are less and less able to follow what's happening in class because they don't have the language for it. For them, school "harms them instead of giving them another chance," one teacher told me.

We would never thrust a mono-lingual Chinese-speaking student into a sixth grade social studies class taught in English and expect him or her to succeed, but that's what we're doing with some of our Chinese immersion students—because we're not willing to admit that the program has failed them.

Yes, this is also an issue in English and of course we have decades of stories about students who were socially promoted through the grades without mastering the material. Sometimes, tragically, without even the ability to read and write. But I would honestly say that in Mandarin immersion it's more common for this cohort of lower-achieving students to be illiterate in Chinese. Generally their parents speak, read and write English, and they're surrounded by spoken and written English in the culture.

But Chinese is a different matter. If you haven't been doing the homework, if you only hear or see Mandarin the few hours you have Mandarin at school, if there wasn't a homework club or tutoring available to you, it's hard to have a fighting chance.

Sharon Carstens speaks Mandarin. Her daughter was in the first graduating class of Portland, Oregon's Mandarin immersion program. Carstens says the problems she saw by the time students got to middle school are common in many Mandarin programs.

> Skill gaps between the best and worst students increased yearly, making it difficult for teachers to adjust lessons to appeal to a wide range of student abilities. Students also seemed frustrated with their limited abilities to express themselves in Mandarin, and often seemed to give up entirely, falling back on English (or Cantonese) for even simple expressions learned in early primary grade.[2]

Programs deal with this in different ways. In private schools the answer is usually quite simple—the teacher or the counselor draws the parent aside and says, "We don't think this program is working for your child and we think you should go elsewhere." I've heard of schools where up to a quarter of the incoming kindergarten class is gone by fifth grade because the students simply couldn't keep up. Those are programs that pride themselves on their rigor and have a parent body that supports it.

Some all-immersion schools deal with the issue by creating a Chinese-as-a-foreign-language track for students who really struggle in both English and Mandarin. Washington Yu Ying in Washington D.C. has done an excellent job of this. The school realized that for whatever reasons, full immersion didn't work for some of its students. They also realized that those students and families didn't want to just walk away from Mandarin, often after years of study. Instead Yu Ying created a separate, smaller track at their school that keeps those students in the English language classes and offers something closer to the traditional U.S.-style language class, in this case Chinese, for one period a day.

In schools that have two strands, one Mandarin immersion and one general education, students who are really struggling sometimes have the option of moving to the general education strand. However, I've noticed that those families are more likely to move their child to another school entirely, possibly so their son or daughter doesn't feel that he or she has failed by being around his or her immersion classmates all the time.

The worst way to deal with this problem is to ignore the students who are struggling. And unfortunately that practice can disproportionately affect students from disadvantaged backgrounds. When students from more privileged families start to falter, the parents quickly barge in and demand schooling that will serve their children. Or they hire tutors. Or they sign them up for afterschool programs to bolster their Chinese. And if Mandarin immersion really isn't working then they demand a place in an English language program.

Students from less advantaged families are sometimes quietly counseled out. One first grade teacher at a public school told me teachers in her program feel they honestly can't do anything except counsel the students out because their cash-strapped school doesn't have a tutoring program in place. She told me her fellow teachers know from experience that without extra support, some of their most struggling students won't be able to gain the necessary Chinese skills to follow material in fourth and fifth grade. "If a family can't afford tutoring and their child is really struggling, and has been for a long time, we sometimes suggest they might want to think about another school." She wasn't happy about it, none of the teachers were, but they could see what happens when kids without support stay in the program and "they're simply not getting a quality education."

It's for this reason that I suggest some sort of testing at least at third and fifth grades, to ensure that students are on track to meet whatever expectations the program has set. Third grade because students are beginning to get important material presented in written Chinese at that point, and fifth grade because middle school is much more demanding on all levels. Testing is crucial to ensure that all students in the program have the necessary Chinese speaking and reading ability to understand the material they're being taught. If it turns out a large proportion of students don't have that ability, or a significant proportion of one group doesn't, *then the school needs to put interventions in place to support struggling students*, the earlier the better. Immersion shouldn't be sink-or-swim.

One problem is that many schools don't have good assessments in place to know what progress looks like. Love it or hate it, No Child Left Behind made it abundantly clear what success and failure looks like in math and English in U.S. schools. We don't have anything like that for Chinese (hardly surprising so early on), so schools cobble together what they can, and sometimes they don't do any real testing at all. We're starting to get it, but testing is expensive, so many schools don't do it. But without benchmarks, how do we know how students are doing?

Don't pretend learning in Chinese is the same as learning in English

This is perhaps my most controversial statement. I've spoken with multiple Chinese professors, Chinese immersion program administrators and Chinese-speaking parents who all say the same thing: In the higher grades it would make more sense to focus Chinese time on topics specific to Chinese culture, especially because it would give more time for reading and literacy in Chinese.

Unfortunately, for most programs that's not an option. In public schools, Chinese immersion programs must closely follow the English curriculum required by their school district or state, giving them little extra time to add Chinese culture. Immersion programs must be able to say that they offer exactly the same content as regular English programs and that students get exactly the same education, with the addition of Chinese. It's almost impossible for these schools to add Chinese culture or history as a class. As soon as they begin to offer different courses to different groups of students, immersion programs can be attacked as being inherently unequal because those students are getting something more than students in an English-only program get. In this age of budget cuts that pit school against school, that doesn't go over well.

Unless you're going to substantially lengthen the school day, you can't teach those subjects in English and then tack on a bunch of Mandarin classes at the end of the day. That was the model originally used by Shuang Wen Academy, a public Mandarin immersion school in New York City. Early on in that program's history, the New York City school district told them they couldn't change anything about their curriculum. To get around that, they added another three hours to the school day, in Mandarin, and taught what they felt was appropriate then. In the end that caused other troubles and they've moved to a more common immersion model today.[3]

Still, it all works relatively well. In many programs, as students move into late elementary school and middle school a substantial amount of the curriculum is taught in a hybrid of English and Mandarin. Much of the written material is presented in English. The teachers teach it in Mandarin. From quizzing my own children and other students, I get the sense they retain the English and easily follow their teachers as the American Revolution or the concept of plate tectonics is described in Chinese.

For example, in the Utah immersion program students might be given the Declaration of Independence to read as homework in English and an essay about freedom to read in Chinese. In the classroom they discuss the concepts and issues *in Mandarin.* This allows them to be exposed to necessary vocabulary in both languages.

In my daughter's fifth grade social studies class, the final big project of the year was to write a multiple-page report on a state. She chose West Virginia (my birth state, Go Mountaineers!). She read multiple books from the library about West Virginia and set in West Virginia, all in English. She poured over maps of the state and went online to find images of the state bird, state flower and listen to the state song. After she'd done all the research in English, she sat down and wrote her paper in Chinese. I started out skeptical, but by the end felt she'd grasped the material in English quite well and has also learned how to organize and present the same material in Chinese. There was a lot of useful vocabulary in it, words such as coal, industry, originally, ceded and Civil War.

All of which she got in both languages. However while she retained the ideas easily, whichever language she'd learned them in, the vocabulary that stuck with her was in English. A month later she had forgotten most of the Chinese terms for those words. They might still be there passively, if she watched a documentary in Chinese that used them I expect she would understand them without thinking about it. But she couldn't bring them to mind when I asked her about them.

This is why I wonder if the time spent on 西弗吉尼亚州 *Xī fújíníyǎ zhōu* (West Fu jin ya) might have more profitably been spent on reading material in Chinese and increasing her Chinese literacy. I know I keep harping on this, but the more they read, the more the language is reinforced. You simply run into a lot more words, and a broader palette of words, when you read than when you speak. Instead they did all the reading in English, because all the materials available on West Virginia are, quite naturally, in English. And because their Chinese literacy is nowhere near their English literacy.

I spoke with a middle school Mandarin immersion teacher, who asked for anonymity, who felt quite strongly about this:

> In the upper grades, they learn new Chinese terms for every single subject every day. It feels like they are only doing Chinese class, instead of math, science and social studies. We know we are teaching different subjects, but they don't feel the same. It's Chinese and Chinese and Chinese. Academic Chinese is meaningless for the students, they will maybe remember today but they will forget tomorrow.

Because students don't read much in Chinese, this vocabulary is not being constantly reinforced, as it would be if it were in English. Those who go to China to travel, study or work will find that it comes back to them, which is good. For those that don't it tends to quickly evaporate. The same teacher went on to say:

Social study in Chinese is just a joke, pointless. Why do students need to know all those terms in Chinese? Sometimes there are even no Chinese for those terms. Why does a fifth grader need to know how to say all 13 colonies' names in Chinese?

Another way of going about it would be to focus on teaching about Chinese history and modern day culture in Chinese, because all the materials would be "authentic texts," as educators like to call them, and the vocabulary would all be absolutely relevant. This is what happens at some charter and private schools because they have the luxury of setting their own curriculums. Unfortunately few public schools are able to do this. Instead they must teach ancient history, modern world history and U.S. history, in an English-Mandarin hybrid.

I don't mean to say that we should give up or that this kind of immersion doesn't work. It does, as my daughter's written and oral report on West Virginia showed. I do mean to say that it might not be the absolute best way to achieve our desired goal, which is bilingualism and biliteracy in both languages.

What we should teach that we don't

Which brings me to another point. For the most part, Chinese immersion students in the United States learn the same set of classic stories about China, whether they're in elementary school or college. They learn the pantheon of myths and legends from China's past, including the Monkey King, the Journey to the West, the Legend of the White Snake, and a host of other wonderful tales. They learn about the Four Great Inventions of Ancient China: paper, printing, gunpowder and the compass. They probably learn a bit about Confucius and memorize some Tang dynasty poems. And that's generally where it ends.

I would propose that if we're going to spend nine years at least (kindergarten through eighth grade) teaching our children Chinese, we should give them a working cultural knowledge of China and the Chinese as well. My children weren't sure who Mao was and they only knew there was something called the Cultural Revolution because there are a ton of kids books out about it now. They didn't know why Taiwan was a separate country and they didn't know that Singapore is an island.

And shamefully, they knew nothing at all about the history of oppression that Chinese-Americans have suffered in this country. They had never heard of the Chinese Exclusion Act and were shocked when I told them that it would have been illegal for most of their friends' parents to get married before 1948 in California. One flat out refused to believe that in my hometown of Seattle, in 1885, white residents burned the homes of Chinese, beat them, killed some and drove the rest out in an ugly incident called the Chinese Expulsion.

That might not be appropriate for grade school but certainly by middle school it should be included in the curriculum. Any student going through Chinese immersion should come out with at least a basic grounding in these topics, taught at the appropriate time

- Ancient Chinese history
- Modern Chinese history
- How Hong Kong, Taiwan and Singapore fit into that history
- The history of Chinese-Americans in the United States

One model doesn't fit all

Still, they do this in French and Spanish and it works just fine, doesn't it? Ah, but remember I said Chinese is different? In French immersion as done in Canada, learning social studies in French worked fine first off because it is, after all, a bilingual country. A good 25% of Canadian students learn science, history and social studies in French because they speak French. Across Canada you're likely to run into people who've learned both in both languages. Not only that but French and English academic vocabulary are very similar.

As for Spanish, this is one of those instances where it's "Cognates to the rescue!" Sedimentary rocks are *rocas sedimentarias.* Igneous rocks are *rocas ígneas.* Miwok is *Miwok*, Salish is *Salish*, Navajo is *Navajo.* Much of our scientific and academic vocabulary originally came from Latin, so Spanish and English are pretty close.

For this reason, some Chinese experts have suggested that it would make a whole lot more sense to restructure immersion to focus on learning English content areas in English and Chinese content areas in Mandarin. Forget teaching science and social studies in Mandarin. Teach Chinese history and literature in Mandarin. Math is the wild card—some say teaching it in Mandarin works fine, some think doing it in English makes more sense. Interestingly, the nation's oldest Mandarin immersion program, the Chinese American International School in San Francisco, teaches math in *both*. Students have Mandarin math and English math. With the strong math and science emphasis demanded by parents at the private school, devoting that much time to math works well. That might not be the case elsewhere.

In Portland, Carstens has written a book outlining how this type of a curriculum might work. She is a professor of anthropology at Portland State University in Portland, Oregon. Her daughter's Mandarin immersion program offered an education both "exhilarating and uneven," she says. Problems became especially apparent as the students moved up through the grades and their ability to read lagged behind their cognitive abilities. Her daughter finished the program and went on to do a "gap year" in Nanjing, China, which allowed her Chinese to bloom, but Carstens felt that immersion in general could have worked better.

She launched a study of Mandarin immersion schools in San Francisco, Beijing, Hong Kong and Edmonton, Canada, analyzing what did and didn't work in those programs. Next she began meeting with Mandarin elementary school teachers in Portland to outline how Mandarin might better be taught in an immersion setting. The resulting book, *Language Through Culture, Culture Through Language: A Framework for K–8 Mandarin Curriculum,*[4] came out in 2013.

She suggests that immersion programs focus on Chinese language and culture in the Mandarin portion of their day, and teach subjects such as math, science and social studies in English. This would allow programs to focus on Chinese and on the aspects of Chinese history, culture and society that will both make Mandarin relevant and be most interesting to students, she suggests. The Chinese culture she proposes is not the "classical" subject matter often taught in heritage schools: calligraphy, poetry and Chinese classical literature. Instead it would focus on contemporary China, Taiwan and Singapore, as well as a history of China in the world, in ways that root students' understanding of the country, culture and language they are studying. Think TV, videos, microblogs and newspapers—the real stuff of today's China.

In addition, she advocates teaching art, physical education and music in Mandarin. This offers a great way to get more Mandarin into students' school time without requiring them to learn important vocabulary in a language they won't have occasion to use it in. This has the added plus of giving students social language in a school setting. Knowing how to say "No fair!" or "Hey, wait up!" in Chinese will be useful to them if they spend time with Chinese speakers, and they're not the kind of things you often hear in social studies class.

Less speaking more reading

Another suggestion, somewhat heretical in the immersion world, is that the emphasis on speaking might be toned down a bit to focus more on reading and culture. Carstens says:

> There needs to be more emphasis on reading and less on speaking in the environment that we have here. I know this flies in the face of what foreign language pedagogy teaches at the moment, but I think that building the more passive reading skills will give students more satisfaction and they can draw on this eventually when

they are in a more conducive environment for oral communication. Building reading skills means memorizing more characters and making this a priority. But there should also be some neat games that could move this along! It also means searching for and possibly creating more appropriate reading materials that will keep our kids interested.

It takes lots of reading time and no small amount of work to learn enough characters to become a fluent reader in Chinese. In many programs the time that's spent in school teaching subjects that students won't have much use for in Chinese, such as social studies, might be better spent on focusing on Chinese literacy skills. Several professors of Chinese at universities across the country have told me they feel immersion programs could get students to a self-supporting level of reading if they focused on literacy. And as we know, reading begets more reading, which begets stronger language skills. These professors didn't feel comfortable attaching their names to this in part because there's such a strong pro-oral contingent in the language education community. But some of their suggestions included:

- Work hard to teach students a lot of characters, focusing on the most used ones in written material, in the first four or five years of school.

- Get students reading as much as possible, early on. Make it a priority. Several pointed out a pilot program at San Francisco State University[5] that worked with middle school students and got them reading graphic novels (also known as manga or comic books) in Chinese for fun. After one summer the kids were devouring manga at the rate of up to five a week. Suddenly reading in Chinese wasn't an impossible chore that involved looking up dozens of characters per page, but a page-turning pleasure. See *Chapter 16: Chinese Literacy Issues*.

- Realize that the ability to read Chinese builds on itself. The more you read the easier it is to read. Putting a strong focus on Chinese literacy *early* opens up a whole new world for students that they're currently cut off from because so much written Chinese is beyond them.

- Use computers more for writing in Chinese, so the ability to write by hand does not limit literacy.

So is all lost?

Not at all. Granted, I've come to believe that the way most Mandarin immersion programs teach is not the absolutely most logical course. However it is what works within the rules of our current public school system, and it is within those rules that it's got to function. Much like No Child Left Behind, schools do what they can to create a rich and rewarding experience for children within a sometimes dizzying set of rules and requirements. What's so astounding is how well they succeed. I see this every day in our daughters' Chinese ability, which is quite good despite having been in a new program that went through some pretty wild times in its early years.

While not perfect, the current system is the best we've got if you want to raise a child who speaks both English and Mandarin. Few heritage school programs after school or on Saturdays teach anywhere near as much Mandarin as students get in immersion. And if you don't happen to speak Mandarin at home, those programs generally aren't open to you anyway.

And while it's certainly possible to learn a lot of Mandarin in high school, it's not the same thing. By high school, an English-speaking student's thinking about sounds is pretty set. It's a source of constant amazement to me that my English-speaking kids don't think in English when they see Chinese. When I see the word 东西 *dōngxi* (things) in pinyin, my English-programmed brain thinks "dong like 'ding-dong,' she like 'she done him wrong.'" I can't help it; I learned to read and think in English first and when I see the Chinese word for "things," 东西, I don't hear *dōngxi* in my head, I hear "dong she."

But my daughters don't hear dong, they hear *dōng*. And to them, *dōng* and *dǒng* and *dòng* all sound like totally different words, whereas to me they all sound like subtle variants on the word in ding-dong. It's that kind of bone-deep knowledge of Chinese that you can't get if you start learning it when you're 15 or 18. My daughters think like Chinese-speakers. For every reason I've stated in this book, to me that is an excellent reason to have chosen Mandarin immersion, warts and all.

I realize these musings may seem heretical, especially after an entire book about the positive aspects of Mandarin immersion. But I'd be remiss if I said that I didn't think it could be done better as we gain more knowledge. As Mao so famously said, "Let a hundred flowers bloom; let a hundred schools of thought contend."[6]

And, as he unfortunately didn't go on to say, "Then let's collect the data, see what works best and spread that knowledge far and wide."

1. She is quoted by Susan Eaton in an article titled, "Have We Learned Our Language Lesson?" in Poverty & Race, November/December 2012 issue. http://www.prrac.org/full_text.php?text_id=1413&item_id=13894&newsletter_id=126&header=Immigration&kc=1 Accessed June 18, 2014.

2. Sharon Carstens, *Language Through Culture, Culture Through Language: A Framework for K–8 Mandarin Curriculum* (Bilingual: English and Chinese). (Beijing, Peking University Press. 2013)

3. Sharon Otterman, "At English-Mandarin Public School, High Test Scores, but Also Strife," New York Times, Nov. 1, 2010.
http://www.nytimes.com/2010/11/02/nyregion/
02shuang.html?pagewanted=1&_r=2&hw
Accessed June 18, 2014.

4. Sharon Carstens, *Language Through Culture, Culture Through Language: A Framework for K–8 Mandarin Curriculum* (Bilingual: English and Chinese). (Beijing, Peking University Press. 2013)

5. More on this in *Chapter 17, How to Get Your Child Reading in Chinese.*

6. 百花齊放，百家爭鳴, *Bǎihuā qífàng, bǎijiā zhēngmíng.* Okay, so he used it as a way to flush out dissidents in 1957, which isn't my thought here at all. Rather I'm thinking of the non-ironic meaning: "Don't interfere with promising developments in their early stages."

Not all Kumbaya and Chardonnay: Mandarin Immersion at Starr King

sān shí

30

This is the last chapter I've sat down to write because in many ways it's the hardest. Our Mandarin immersion public school program here in San Francisco is something I, and hundreds of other parents, have spent years working to birth, support and encourage. We've experienced the joy of seeing our children grow up speaking two languages and felt the terror of being in a program so new that no one knew how, or even if, it would work.

I've tried to be brutally, painfully honest as I've written about our school and our journey with Mandarin immersion, acknowledging both the pitfalls and the amazing and wonderful experiences we've had. Lest you imagine it was all *Kumbaya* and white wine, it wasn't. As you embark upon your own immersion journey I hope my openness will be of use.

For me, it all goes back to college. It's been said that parents want to give their children the things they never had. That's certainly true in my case. I only made it to third year Chinese in college by the skin of my teeth and never did become fluent or even readily conversational. So perhaps it is not surprising that I wanted it for my children. Plus, between the time when I studied Mandarin at the University of Washington and our elementary school search, China's star had only become more ascendant.

Why Chinese? There was my first infatuation with characters in high school, as I describe in chapter one. Writing the character 馬 (horse) over and over during algebra after my classmate Tim Louie taught it to me launched my love of the language and characters.

What it meant to be truly bilingual came years later when I spent two years studying at the University of Lund in Sweden. I think for most people it feels as if the world is truly real only where they live. Everything else is a *National Geographic* article, fascinating but not fully alive. When I was living in Lund I had the epiphany that for the Swedes around me, Sweden, not the United States, was that truly real place. My first thought was, "Silly them, don't they know America's the center of the universe?" Next came the more humbling "Silly me..."

How I perceived the world changed fundamentally that day, and I hope I became less insular. I wanted my children to grow up that way. Short of moving abroad, being bilingual seemed an excellent way to do it.

When my wife Lisa and I married, we knew we wanted a family. It was a happy accident that the man we asked to be our children's father, a close friend of Lisa's from her medical residency, was Chinese-American and spoke Mandarin. He claims he doesn't speak well, though I beg to differ. But he grew up speaking it at home and going to Saturday Chinese school. So when our oldest neared preschool age, it didn't seem entirely out of left field that we looked at San Francisco's Chinese American International School, the nation's first Mandarin immersion program.

CAIS (pronounced "case") has a preschool through eighth grade program. When our oldest daughter, *Zhou Qing* (周情, her Chinese name) was 2½, I signed up for a tour and spent a morning getting to know the school.

Despite my love of Chinese and my burning desire to raise bilingual kids, the program at CAIS at that time felt too structured for us for preschool. The father of an older student at the school led the tour I was on. At one point he said rather proudly, "By third grade a lot of the kids wash out and it's only the really smart ones who stay in." We weren't looking for a school where 8-year-olds routinely "washed out," so despite the school's dedicated teachers, strong curriculum and long history, regretfully we crossed CAIS off our list.

Instead we applied to and were accepted at a Montessori preschool that fed into a private K–8 called The San Francisco School. Our daughter was deliriously happy there, delighting in the "manipulables" beloved by Montessori schools, the songs, the stories and the school's sheer joy in learning.

Test scores and race by the swing sets

At that time, word on the playground among middle class families (of all colors) was that San Francisco had several "good" public schools, some "okay" schools and a lot of schools you wouldn't send your kids to if you could help it. This was partly based on test scores, partly on class, partly on culture and partly on race. How much of each is difficult to tease out, and I'm not sure the parents themselves could tell you. One mom told me that the year she toured schools looking for a kindergarten for her son, no white parents she knew would even have considered three of the schools she looked at, "even though those schools had very good test scores, not even accounting for demographics. But they were happy to consider whiter and more middle class schools with lower test scores."

I saw some of that myself. In San Francisco, schools on the west side of town have a high percentage of Asian, mostly Chinese-American, families. These schools have some of the best test scores in the city and are considered academically stellar. But many white families I knew didn't apply to these schools because they were culturally too alien, "too Chinese." Many moms told me, "I don't want my kid to be the only white kid in the classroom."

The lottery

The San Francisco Unified School District uses a lottery system to assign kindergarten slots. At the time we were beginning to think of kindergarten, families got to choose seven of the city's 72 public elementary schools to apply for, listing their first through seventh choices. The applications went in and each was weighted using an opaque formula that took into account the educational level of the mother and whether the family had received social service aid.[1] It was all a proxy for race, as SFUSD was committed to integrated schools but under California law it couldn't use race as a factor. Sadly, poverty is a good proxy for race in San Francisco, as it is in far too many communities.

The system was pretty fair. Prior to the lottery the only way to get into sought-after schools was to literally camp out for days to be first in line to sign up. I have friends with fond memories of those street-side campouts, but it wasn't a very fair way of allocating school places, as not all families had a parent who could take two or three days off work to sleep in front of a school as my neighbors did.

Under the lottery everyone had a relatively equal shot at the schools they listed, with some weighting given to encourage low income families. Of course there was a tremendous amount of teeth-gnashing and analysis of how the algorithm worked, because there was no way everyone who wanted in could get a seat at a "good" school. There simply weren't enough kindergarten seats at those schools for all the families who wanted them. Many parents felt as if they were being personally punished when they were assigned a school that served children from primarily lower socio-economic groups, when in fact it was just the luck of the draw given the scarcity of places at schools that had a majority of middle-class families.

Gather together any group of middle-class parents in San Francisco with preschool age children and sooner or later the "school question" will come up. Will they move to the suburbs when their oldest turns 4? Will they try for one of the tough-to-get seats at a private school? Or will they test their luck with the public school system? Many families do a combination of all three, looking at public and private schools, doing spreadsheets to assess costs (of moving, of paying for private school, of commuting, etc.) and then waiting to see where they get in. The week in March when kindergarten acceptance letters go out for both public and private schools in San Francisco is one of high drama for thousands of families with 4-year-olds.

A relatively high percentage of families get assigned to a public school they don't want, one that's too far away, too high-poverty, too low test scores, too culturally different, too whatever. However, eventually many, though not all, get a slot in a public school they like.[2] Especially if they can handle the knuckle-biting wait for more seats to open up. That can take until the first or second week *after* school starts. It's not for the faint of heart. And many find they come to love a school that originally they couldn't imagine liking.

Still, there's no way around the fact that we have a lot of students in private schools here and one reason the school district is focused on creating "equity"—which really means having racially and economically integrated schools. It would be an easier thing to do if 27% of San Francisco's school age children didn't go to private schools, because a high percentage of those families are white, Asian and middle and upper-middle class.

It's a bit of a chicken and egg problem. San Francisco is a city with a high number of smart, highly educated families (there's a reason the tech boom is happening here) and they want the best possible education for their kids. While they like the idea of integrated schools (private school brochures always feature how "diverse" their school is), when it comes right down to it they don't want to send their kids to a school with low test scores or a culture they feel isn't academically focused.

San Francisco has the smallest number of children of any major city in the country: only 13.4% of the city's 837,422 residents are younger than 18.[3] The city's racial breakdown overall as of 2013, according to the U.S. Census[4], was:

White (non-Hispanic)	41%
Asian	34%
Latino	15%
African-American	6%

That's not the composition of the San Francisco Unified School District. It serves 55,000 students, and in 2014–2015 the demographics of the student body were[5]:

White (not Hispanic)	11%
Chinese	33%
Other Asian	8%
Latino	23%
African-American	10%
Other	10%
Decline to state	4%

While on paper San Francisco looks like a racially mixed city, the overall public school population isn't. Actually the school district is pretty racially mixed except for whites, who are wildly underrepresented.[6] That's even accounting for the fact that there are fewer white children than the number of white adults might indicate, as we've got a large population of white adults with no kids (all those young folks coming to work in the tech industry and a large gay community). As you've read in previous chapters, school districts like to use Mandarin immersion as a way to get white and Asian families to go to schools with low test scores, and that's exactly what happened here.

All of which is to explain that getting a space in a San Francisco public school was a fraught and highly unpredictable process with many variables. Around this time a mom with a 4-year-old started a blog called *The SF K Files*[7] to vent some of the anxiety she was feeling. It has become a rather astounding sounding board for the anxieties of middle class parents in the city. Because people could post anonymously, they were brutally frank. It was fascinating and horrifying and totally addictive for anyone with young kids in the city.

So that was the situation as my family accepted our slot in The San Francisco School's preschool program. We didn't particularly want to go to a private school, both for financial and social reasons. But what pushed us over the edge was a discussion with the director of another preschool we'd been seriously considering, a nearby cooperative. She said, "That's a great school. If you have a spot, take it."

She told us that not one of the eight kids at her preschool moving on to kindergarten that year had gotten into a public school their parents had applied for. Instead they'd been assigned to low-performing, struggling schools where the focus was on catching students up with middle class kids.

So we found ourselves with a 3-year-old who was in love with her school, a happy 1-year-old at home and a fairly calm place from which to contemplate our choices moving forward. We started thinking about where our oldest would go for kindergarten, aware that we had a remarkable gift because one option was simply staying put until eighth grade. It would cost us a huge sum of money but at least we would know our girls were in a school that really worked for them. So let me be the first to admit that we had an unfair advantage in the whole process.

Not that it kept us from fretting. When I'd first come to San Francisco, long before marriage or children, I was thrilled to learn that the city contained not one but two public Chinese immersion schools. However, I later discovered that the schools, West Portal Elementary and Alice Fong Yu Alternative School, taught not Mandarin but Cantonese, and had been founded to help Chinese-American children retain their heritage language. When they were originally founded, most Chinese families in San Francisco spoke Cantonese at home. Both schools had amazing test scores and were highly sought-after, but I couldn't imagine having my children learn Cantonese. Of course there's nothing wrong with Cantonese as a language, but I wanted Mandarin. It was something like wanting your children to learn Spanish by sending them to a Portuguese school, on the theory that later it would be easier to learn Spanish.

San Francisco had started a chapter of Parents for Public Schools (PPS) in 1999.[8] This stellar non-profit began in Jackson, Mississippi, in 1991, as a way to convince white families who'd turned their backs on the public schools to reconsider them. It's the cheerleading group for public schools that many public school systems lack, a one-stop shop for information and hand-holding for families contemplating actually enrolling their kids in public school. In some cities and some social circles, that was the equivalent of saying you planned to lock your kids in a dungeon and feed them only bread and water until they were 18, so PPS was very needed.

I'd heard about PPS from the minister at our church, who was from Jackson and knew the founders. We immediately signed up. Their email list was awash in interesting and useful information about the 72 elementary schools in San Francisco and an antidote to the fear-mongering I heard from parents at the park.

Mandarin immersion comes to the San Francisco public schools

And so it was that in the fall of 2005 a message went by on the PPS list that riveted me. The San Francisco Unified School District was holding a meeting for families interested in Mandarin immersion. Even though we were a year away from even applying to kindergarten, I signed up. I still remember that cold, wet night, the drive to an anonymous school district building down-town, and the big conference table that the parents and school officials sat around as they told us what had been proposed.

The backstory, which I didn't know at the time, was that earlier in the year a group of Mandarin-speaking families had begun meeting to talk about the possibility of creating a Mandarin immersion public school along the lines of the city's two Cantonese immersion public schools. They'd had some political connections and made a case both to the city council (called the Board of Supervisors in San Francisco) and the school board. At the time Mandarin was offered only at one high school in the District, as a foreign language.

The families circulated a petition that was sent to the District. It was time, they said, for San Francisco to look to the future. Cantonese, a strong part of the city's immigrant past, was not the language of the future. Man-darin was.

After much work and multiple meetings, the District decided to open a Mandarin immersion elementary program for the 2006–2007 school year. It would have two classes per grade moving forward, starting in kindergarten and going through fifth, and would join the District's ten Spanish immersion, two Cantonese immersion and one Korean immersion schools.

Here's where things got sticky. The Mandarin-speaking families who'd done the lion's share of the work getting the whole idea going were thrilled. They wanted the program to be placed in the brand new, as-yet-unopened Dianne Feinstein Elementary School in the city's west side. It was a middle-class neighborhood with a high percentage of Chinese-American families.

The District had other ideas. As I discussed in *Chapter 19: Why Schools Choose Mandarin Immersion*, the motivations of school officials are often at odds with those of parents. Many of the families who'd worked to convince the District about the need for the program wanted an all-Mandarin immersion school in a middle class neighborhood they would feel comfortable in. The District wanted to steer a group of committed, well-resourced and highly-motivated parents to a school that needed help. The fact that the District was not straightforward about those motivations to the parents only made the clash worse.

So it was announced that the new Mandarin immersion program would be placed as one strand at Starr King Elementary School on Potrero Hill, literally across the street from one of the city's larger public housing projects. The school is on the eastern side of the city, far from neighborhoods with large concentrations of Chinese families. The Mandarin immersion program would play a role in "naturally diversifying the school and spreading out enrollment in the district," as the *San Francisco Chronicle* put it the week before the program launched.[9]

Named for a Civil War-era Unitarian minister named Thomas Starr King, known for his fiery abolitionist speeches and sermons, the school had low test scores, was only half full and had been on the possible school closure list for two years running. Few families sought it out and its enrollment had been falling for years. In fact, it was down to just 151 students in 2005–2006, though the building could accommodate at least 350. That meant it had the necessary 12 empty classrooms to accommodate a full immersion program with two classrooms each for kindergarten through fifth grade. The school had a general education program (as San Francisco calls its regular English program), a Spanish-bilingual program and a well-regarded special day program for children on the autism spectrum. All three programs would remain in place.

Most of the original group of Chinese families declined to send their children there. Although one side of Potrero Hill had experienced phenomenal growth and boasted many million-dollar homes, the east side, where Starr King was located, was still pretty run-down. The projects were poorly maintained by the city, and families who drove up to visit the school the back way, from the highway, saw a side of the city that doesn't show up on postcards. It does, however, have some of the most amazing views of any school I know of in the city, with San Francisco Bay and the Golden Gate Bridge beyond clearly visible from the school yard, a sweeping vista of the city from the front door and a beautiful, protected open green space right across the street.

The 30 or so families involved broke into two groups. Many who'd started the petition didn't end up sending their children to Starr King. Several went to the Chinese American International School. One mom who'd done a tremendous amount of work gave up on Chinese immersion all together and sent her kids to a Catholic school that had a strong after-school Chinese program.

However, the second group was willing to give it a try. These were the "Mandarin or die" families, as my friend Renée Tan put it. Her husband grew up speaking Burmese and Chinese and they were determined that their kids would speak Mandarin, whatever it took. Their friend Marie Ciepela was an American who had grown up in Panama speaking Spanish and English. She wanted to give her sons the gift of bilingualism.

One thing that really launched the program, I often think, was that Renée and Marie both had kids in a cooperative preschool, or co-op. There are several in San Francisco and they're, quite frankly, remarkably powerful incubators for involved parents. Parents do much of the work and organizing at these preschools. When those families arrive at kindergarten they hit the ground running. Renée and Marie knew how to organize, they knew how to get the word out, and they were willing to do whatever it took to make the program work. Together they and others formed a core of parents who worked to build up the school's relatively new PTA and create a system of tours to bring new students into the school that first year.

Here's the brutal truth about my family. I'd been to those meetings and I'd drunk the Kool-Aid. But we also had a nice, safe perch to watch from. Starr King's principal was a charismatic leader who had started there as a teacher and had been principal for eight years. That spring I toured the school almost 10 times. I brought my wife. I brought our daughter's father and his husband. I brought my wife's sister, an inner-city school teacher for over 30 years. I brought our girls' grandparents, the Chinese ones. At one point the principal took me aside and said, only slightly in jest, "Beth, would you like me to arrange a private tour just for your family so you can get everyone here at once?" By the end I could have led the tours myself. (Later on I did.)

We applied for the program in the lottery, the only SFUSD school we applied to and the only one we wanted. Friends asked me if I wasn't afraid, putting all our eggs in one basket, but I knew there was no way all 40 kindergarten seats were going to fill up that first year. I'd been on the tours; I'd heard the fearful questions families asked about the neighborhood and the new program. I knew it would take a few years before Starr King became a school with a waiting list.

Our letter arrived one fine spring day. We'd gotten a seat. Our daughters could attend a free, public, Mandarin-immersion elementary school program a 12-minute drive from our house. It was just three blocks up the hill from the hospital where my wife worked as a doctor, so she could run up for performances and sudden illnesses. It was everything I'd ever dreamed of.

And then the discussions began. I wanted us to take the slot. My wife was worried the teaching would be too regimented and rote. Their dads weren't sure that being early adopters was worth risking the education of our oldest daughter. Their Chinese grandparents were worried the girls wouldn't learn English. My sister-in-law was worried about the academics at the school. Friends expressed concern about the safety of the school given its location. We talked. We processed. We discussed what we wanted for them and tried to be honest about how much of it came out of what we'd wanted for ourselves as children (which is what so very much of the kindergarten discussion is really about; kids mostly do fine everywhere). We went around and around and around.

And in the end we decided to wait a year.

To this day I am embarrassed by that decision, although the rest of the family was fine with it. We wanted to see how things shook out. We had the option of keeping our daughter where she was for kindergarten because in San Francisco, students who don't speak the target language are allowed to begin in immersion as late as first grade. We were in a position of privilege— we had a place at a highly desirable school, which gave us the enviable option of waiting. So we sat out the program's first year. There are those who've suggested to me that my gung ho attitude about public schools stems in part from the guilt I feel about skipping that first year. They might be right.

But that's what we did.

Year one: 2005–2006

Things at Starr King continued along just fine without us. SFUSD decided to use a "dual-immersion" model, meant for both Mandarin- and English-speaking students. Just as Spanish immersion programs presume students will learn from each other, the Mandarin program was meant to aid Mandarin-speaking students in learning English and English-speaking students in learning Mandarin. It was also decided that just as SFUSD does with Spanish, the Mandarin program would start with 90% of the day in Mandarin in kindergarten, gradually moving year-by-year to 50% in Mandarin and 50% in English by fourth grade.

San Francisco had West Portal Elementary and Alice Fong Yu to use as models for Chinese immersion. West Portal is a K–5 school with one class of Cantonese immersion per grade alongside two general education classes, for a total of three classrooms per grade level. Alice Fong Yu is a K–8 school that is all Cantonese immersion; at the time it was one-way, meaning every student had to enter as a proficient English speaker. West Portal was two-way, meaning students could come in who spoke either only English or only Cantonese.

Therefore the Starr King curriculum was based largely on the Cantonese immersion and bilingual programs at West Portal. The one shift was which characters it would use. The Cantonese programs used traditional characters, but the decision was made to use simplified characters for Mandarin at Starr King because those are the ones used in China. But that meant that the Mandarin program couldn't use the same textbooks the Cantonese program used. Still, the West Portal teachers shared tremendous amounts of information and were hugely supportive of the Starr King teachers.

On August 28, 2006, the inaugural two kindergarten classes of the Mandarin immersion program opened. There were 26 students total, two classes of 13. That was a far cry from the 40 available seats, but it *was* the first year. Things got off to a slightly rocky start. The principal had hired two teachers the spring before. Both quit the month before school started so he had to scramble to find new ones. Thankfully, one of them was Angelica Chang, a stellar young teacher who spoke both Cantonese and Mandarin and who had been a student teacher at West Portal Elementary. Today she's a seasoned immersion educator.

Using a series from a new Palo Alto company called *Better Chinese* as their textbook, the immersion program launched with two classrooms. The kids blossomed, the parents were thrilled, and the school was suddenly the talk of the playground wherever preschool parents gathered.

The program was successful enough that in the spring of 2006 the District announced it would extend the Mandarin immersion program to a second school, choosing José Ortega Elementary School in the OMI (Ocean View-Merced Heights-Ingleside) neighborhood. That program was to have one Mandarin class per grade alongside its two general education classes per grade. Once again, the decision as to why that school and why that configuration wasn't communicated to parents; it was merely presented as "here's your second Mandarin program."

Spring rolled around and my extended family once again made our yearly pilgrimages to Starr King. This time what I'd been able to see in my imagination was there in front of us all: bright, clean classrooms full of art and happy children babbling away in Mandarin. Teachers chatting away with the students, in Mandarin. Books and posters and white boards full of

Chinese. Adorable 5-year-olds laboriously writing their first characters on worksheets, proudly holding them up for us to see. All in Chinese.

Our entire extended family was finally ready. We applied for a first grade slot and got in.

Leaving The San Francisco School was fraught. We'd loved the school but realized that the income disparities there (between the very wealthy and middle class families) were problematic in their own way. Our daughter once asked me why we didn't go to Bora Bora for spring break like her friend had. When I told another mom we were contemplating going public, she asked why. I said it was partly the expense. "Can't you get a job that pays more?" was her puzzled response. And as much as we loved the warm, nurturing spirit we found there, we also wondered about academics. Too many parents told us they 'supplemented' the math with outside tutors. "Why," we asked ourselves, "would we pay $23,000 a year and have to hire tutors?" But even so, it was difficult to leave such a great environment and families that had come to be such good friends. And our oldest was heartbroken to leave.

Year two: 2006–2007, we take the plunge

Still, when our daughter started first grade in August she quickly grew to love her new school. She made friends, liked learning Chinese, enjoyed writing characters and was generally happy. If I'm to be perfectly honest, maybe not as happy as she would have been at The San Francisco School, but then school isn't always about being happy; it's also about learning useful things, and for us, Mandarin was one of those things.

We weren't the only ones who were starting to come around about Starr King. That second year, the kindergarten Mandarin classes enrolled almost 40 students and the first grade Mandarin classes picked up 13 new students. People moved from as far away as Los Angeles to send their kids to Starr King, including Natalie Chu, who went on to become our PTA treasurer and then president. Suddenly, instead of parents gasping in surprise when you said your child went Starr King or José Ortega, they were asking, "How'd you get in?"

The families at Starr King were education-minded but San Francisco-easy. We enjoyed Moms' Nights Out, some really fun "let's all meet up at the wine bar" nights, PTA meetings that were for the most part fun, and the thrill of creating something new and wonderful for our kids. I spent so much time at Starr King in those years it felt like a second home. We led tours, attended programs, helped at Thanksgiving parties and threw Chinese New Year parties in the classrooms. At the school's international potluck I brought my "culture's" signature dish—tuna noodle casserole. It sat beside plates of Chinese *jiaozi*, Filipino *lumpia*, Samoan BBQ and everybody's pizza.

Year three: 2007–2008, finding new teachers every year

We were well launched, but it wasn't all beer and skittles. Finding two new Mandarin immersion teachers each year was a huge hurdle. We had a fair number of parents who traveled to China for work. One dad in particular ended up doing multiple interviews with possible teachers in Beijing and Shanghai. I'm sure they thought we were some amazingly high-powered school, to be able to send representatives all the way to China to interview them.

The year our daughter was in second grade, one of the new teachers fell through and our principal had to quickly hire a replacement. After much beating of the bushes, he found a young Teach for America teacher. It didn't turn out well. She was, I'm sure, a nice person. But her elementary school education in Taiwan and lack of teaching experience meant she wasn't ready to deal with a classroom of squirming, very American (read: not very sedate) 7-year-olds. She threw things at kids and told them they were stupid. Parents freaked out. Kids started crying at home, wetting the bed and refusing to go to school. It was not a pretty picture.

We had so few Chinese-speaking parents at that point that our principal asked me and some other parents to spend some time in the classroom just to give him a sense of what was happening in Chinese. That's pretty sad when you consider how dreadful my Chinese was. But there really weren't many options so I sat there and took notes, cringing all the while. Thankfully, our principal was a my-way-or-the-highway kind of guy and by Thanksgiving she was gone. However, that left us with only one Mandarin teacher for the second grade. The second graders didn't learn a lot of Chinese that year.

The curriculum was bumpy at best. The newly hired teachers didn't get much more than textbooks and some outlines from West Portal and were told to create a new program on their own. But there were also wonderful things. The teachers were warm and loving, rug-time work (when they all sat on a rug at the front of the room and worked in a circle) kept everyone riveted and the classrooms were alive with learning.

As anyone who's in a new program knows, the newer upper grades may be a mess but things really smooth out in the younger grades after the teachers have had some time to settle in. Our younger daughter, *Zhou Yi* (周忆), started kindergarten and had a wonderful experience. Thankfully SFUSD's lottery has sibling preference, so this time around there were no worries about getting in. She got Ms. Chang for her teacher and settled in happily. Ms. Chang was a superstar—no doubt about it. She was featured in a series of articles by Jill Tucker in the *San Francisco Chronicle*[10] that over the years have highlighted our program. She's also in the film *Speaking in Tongues*.[11] Ms. Chang and the original team of kindergarten and first grade teachers, Ms. Helen Tong, Ms. Ina To and Ms. Sandy Sung, were really the anchors that allowed our program to be so successful.

Year four: 2008–2009, the good, the bad and the ugly

By our program's fourth year, both schools had waiting lists for Mandarin immersion. The number of Mandarin-speaking students, originally very low, was starting to increase a tiny bit. But it wasn't fulfilling the District's other goal, of giving Mandarin-speaking students a route to learning English that supported their home language.

Recruiting Chinese-speaking families into the school was difficult for several reasons. First, Starr King is located at the top of Potrero Hill with poor access to public transit and school bus routes that didn't come from neighborhoods with large numbers of Chinese speakers. Mandarin-speaking parents were concerned (and still are) about whether a program that began with 90% Mandarin would do a good job teaching their Mandarin-speaking children English. Those that came were often distressed that the level of Mandarin taught wasn't high enough. And with no Chinese-speaking staff in the office, it was difficult to get information about the program if you didn't also speak English.

We were also experiencing growing pains. Note: There will be lots of gory details and airing-of-dirty-laundry here. In writing this, I talked to multiple parents, went over notes from tons of meetings and then went back and double-checked my memories with other moms and dads who were there. That said, this is ultimately one person's viewpoint, my own. My hope is to give as honest a picture as I can, so that it doesn't seem as if other schools have this wonderful, perfect trajectory and it's only *yours* that is bumpy and difficult and frustrating. So I'm including the good, the bad and the ugly.

Things got ugly for our principal. Myself, I liked him a lot. He was a straight shooter, an excellent educator and supported his teachers well. But he had also devoted his professional life to working with underprivileged kids and saw many of the Mandarin immersion parents as annoying, unreasonable and entitled. He also wasn't used to having to share leadership of the school with the PTA and the School Site Council or be accountable to those two groups. In the past they'd been little more than rubber stamps. He was willing to put up with us because otherwise the District was going to close his school, and then the kids who lived in the projects wouldn't have a school they could easily walk to. But beyond that he wanted us to raise money and chill out so he could focus on the kids who really needed help—and for the most part that wasn't the kids in the Mandarin immersion strand.

As he was fond of pointing out, our kids were going to do fine. He was right. Most students in the Mandarin program had all the support and love in the world, along with tutors and classes and sports and everything else that middle- and upper-middle class families shower upon their kids. Heck, my kids alone had probably gotten more enrichment by the age of 5 than I had gotten by the end of high school.

He was also right that not everyone had those advantages. I spent a lot of time in classes around the school, and there were children who weren't going to do okay. They didn't all have parents with the time or ability to shower them with love. Sometimes they didn't have parents at all. These children faced challenges many of the *adults* I knew couldn't have overcome. At home there was drug addiction, sexual abuse, violence, lack of money, lack of English, lack of decent food, lack of transportation. You name it, these kids had to deal with it. Kids who no one ever put to bed at night, who just conked out wherever they were. Kids who never once were asked if they'd done their homework. Kids who didn't have backpacks or pencils or pens or erasers or anything else. Kids whose families just weren't up to the task of making sure they got those things. Those kids deserved just as excellent and wonderful an education as mine did. Considering what they were up against, they deserved it more.

By comparison, most of the students in the Mandarin immersion program lived in pink, sugar-coated bubbles. Yes, they were going to do just fine. However we didn't want them to do just fine, we wanted them to excel and reach their full potential, preferably at an Ivy League college or at least UC Berkeley. Telling us to chill out and accept middle-of-the-road academics, or possibly no teacher for a year, did not cut it.

Our principal was right in that the Mandarin immersion parents included a fair number of high-powered, involved and yes, entitled, individuals. But that wasn't the full reality by any means. The vast majority of families in the program had chosen Starr King *because* we were committed to building a great school for everyone. Our principal made a point in his talks on tours to emphasize that we were one school with several programs and that the Mandarin program was not, and never would be, a school within a school. That kept many families out who couldn't get with the program from the get-go.

There were many, many families who worked hard to improve the school for everyone, not just for students in the Mandarin immersion program. Soccer teams were started for the younger grades, coached by parents. My wife coached for four years running. These teams provided a nexus for all of the programs to come together. That often meant coaches had to pick up kids at home for games and drive them home afterwards. Those homes could be in the projects or at homeless shelters or require a couple of calls to figure out whose couch the family was sleeping on that week. It wasn't discussed and it wasn't a big deal, it's just what the coaches and parents did to make sure that every child who wanted to play soccer was able to. Sign-up and uniform fees, and charges for the after-season pizza parties were always on a sliding scale, if cost was mentioned at all.

The soccer program was so successful that in February of 2014, Starr King received the President's Award from San Francisco Youth Soccer for its extensive and inclusive extracurricular soccer program. Starr King has soccer teams at every grade and over 50% of students play on a team. The award came in part because of the work parents had done to make sure soccer was as inclusive as possible, so all students who wanted to could play. Several Starr King teams were honored for "extraordinary" sportsmanship during the season as well.

When various adopt-a-classroom programs started, all the classes, not just the Mandarin immersion ones, got adopted. The Mandarin immersion classrooms each had a parent coordinator. When it became clear that some of the general ed classrooms didn't, parents from other classes signed up. Parents also launched an Academic Volunteers program that supported all students who were struggling in either English or Mandarin. For the most part, with a few exceptions, parents in the Mandarin program were committed to the entire school succeeding, not just their kids.

The balance of the school was shifting and we were all trying to figure out how to make it work for everyone. And while we were trying to figure this out, we were getting no support or direction from the school district on how to do it. I've always thought things might have gone much more smoothly had someone at the District level helped us navigate those first, fraught years as the entire school community learned to work together while the demographics shifted under our feet. Certainly the District must have seen it happen at enough schools in the past to have some insight into what worked and what didn't. The realities of what our new program meant for an old school remained unspoken, and perhaps unspeakable. So as a community we were left to muddle through as best we could.

It got nasty, more than once. There was a group of parents who went to the school district to ask that our principal be removed and who claimed they were speaking for all of the parents in the Mandarin immersion program. There was another group—and this took chutzpah—who posted an ad on Craigslist for a Mandarin immersion principal for our school, even though our principal wasn't planning on leaving.

Add to all of this the fact that our school district says its primary focus is "closing the achievement gap" between white and Asian students on one hand and African-American and Latino students on the other. For the District, Mandarin immersion was a means to an end. We were a way to bring well-resourced parents to struggling schools. By having fewer high-needs kids in a school, the school could do a better job of taking care of the kids that really needed help.

It was not subtle. There was one meeting during which some Starr King parents and PTA board members met with a high-up school district officials and the topic of test scores came up. A parent started to tout the rise in scores for kids at Starr King and one official stopped him cold. "I don't care about test scores for white and Asian students. Show me the scores for Latino and African-American students. That's what matters," she said.

Funding and Title I

Much of this is a problem that money, lots of it, could totally have solved. Yes, we have high-needs kids at our school. But good teachers with lots of support, quality programs and infrastructure to back them up make a huge difference in children's lives. Unfortunately, during the time our girls have been in school, the education budget has drastically shrunk due to the economic crisis. California's schools have been hit harder than most because our schools are funded in part by property taxes, and in 1978 Proposition 13 capped increases to property taxes.

California went from having the best-funded, and simply the best, public schools in the nation in the 1960s to some of the worst. In 2012, California's per-student spending was $8,482, putting us at forty-ninth in terms of school funding. The national average is $11,824. Only Nevada, at $8,419, and Utah, at $7,042, spent less.[12]

The Mandarin Immersion Parents Council is born

It was in this, the fourth year of the program, that parents from both Starr King and José Ortega first came together to create a parent and program support group for Mandarin immersion, originally called the Mandarin Immersion Parents Council.

We founded the group in part because of the history of Spanish immersion in the District. There were seven Spanish immersion elementary schools in San Francisco at the time. Each one had been launched with little connection to the others, and when the students reached middle school, each school's students had learned different vocabularies, had different subjects taught in Spanish and different emphasis on grammar or reading or speaking. It was a nightmare that resulted in a lot of anger and frustration when sixth grade arrived. We wanted to avoid it.

Our motto was "Two Schools, One Program."

We also realized that the District, our principals and teachers were busy creating a Mandarin program out of whole cloth so they didn't have a lot of time to focus on holding parents' hands. We knew that anxious parents made for obstreperous parents and decided that the more information they had, the calmer and more productive they could be. This wasn't all that easy as none of us spoke Chinese.

We had a long debate about whether we could in good conscience put out materials only in English. We decided that since we couldn't pay to have them translated we'd just do what we could, trusting that eventually the program would attract enough Chinese-speakers that we'd be truly bilingual. (Today half the board speaks Chinese.)

The MIPC started very simply. We looked into becoming a 501(c)3 non profit and realized it was far too much money (about $3,000 at the time) and not what we needed because our goal was primarily to provide information and education for parents. Our origins were very basic, just a small group of parents from both schools who met for dinner to talk about what parents needed.

One of the first things we did was write a FAQ (frequently asked questions) about Mandarin immersion. I got drafted to do it because I make my living as a reporter, so I've got experience gathering information and writing it up in an accessible form. That FAQ was really the genesis of this book. As I began pulling together information, I realized how much there was available that would go a long way to helping parents—but there had been no way for them to easily find it.

We kept updating the FAQ as more questions and information came in. We passed the hat at a meeting and got about $100 to print it up as a little booklet that we could hand out at school fairs.

Year five: 2009–2010

This was the year the MIPC started doing educational workshops for parents. Our first was just the basics: How to help your kid with homework when you neither speak nor read Chinese (the experience of 95% of our families).

None of this was particularly high powered. We made up a flyer and copied it using someone's work copy machine so we didn't use up school resources. We made up a batch for each Mandarin classroom, and parents went into each school's office and stuffed them in the teachers' mailboxes. It was very low-tech.

That spring Scott Olson, a parent at José Ortega who is an Internet wizard, suggested that we start a blog so we could post some of the information we were putting together. I didn't know a thing about blogging but said I'd be happy to help out. Scott's wife Beth is a writer and a pretty great designer, so they did the work; I just sent them copy. Eventually Scott taught me how to post. I remain hugely grateful to them for not giving up on me and making the Mandarin Immersion Parents Council blog possible. Without them this book never would have come into being.

Year six: 2010–2011

Our program really started to hit its stride this year. Our girls both were having a great time in school, learning lots and having fun. The PTA's fundraising was beginning to have a profound effect on the entire school. One example was an amazing program called Playworks that took place on the school's play yard. Its goal was to get each and every kid taking part in activities and games. Where before the girls would often just sit chatting on the sidelines while the boys played various ball games, they now all got up and enjoyed rousing games. Some were traditional, some new-fangled and some simply hysterical. We got long descriptions at night about the rules, the players and how everyone had acted. The focus was getting kids to be physically active and interact well, and it worked.

Still, there were difficulties. Every year the oldest class moved up a grade and had a new teacher, a new curriculum and a steep learning curve. Being the pioneer class wasn't easy. Each year we lost a few families. Some worried their children weren't learning enough English and fretted that the academic levels overall weren't as high as they could have been. Some simply got tired of always dealing with untrained teachers and an untried curriculum.

In the midst of all this, a broader perspective helped. I'd become friends with Carol Lei back when the initial group working to bring Mandarin immersion to the school district had begun. Carol spent the same years I had on the committee, and the District had always framed it that the program would begin with a kindergarten and a first grade class. When the District finally decided to go forward, the decision was made to begin only with kindergarten. Carol's daughter, one year older than ours, was one year too old. That one year meant my daughters speak Mandarin and hers don't. I tried to keep that in mind when things got bumpy for our pioneer class.

We lose our Title I status

This was also the year we lost our Title I Title I status. That's a federal program, first begun in 1965 as part of the War on Poverty, which allocates extra money for schools with high concentrations of low-income students. It's an issue for schools that contain immersion magnet programs that started with a high proportion of low-income students. When the student population begins to shift as the result of an influx of more middle class families, the money goes away.

The federal rules say that any school with 40% or more students in poverty is eligible for Title I funds. SFUSD has made the sometimes controversial[13] choice to allocate them in an all-or-nothing way rather than on a sliding scale. The reasoning is that schools with a large population of children in poverty really need help while schools with fewer poor kids need less help. So schools are allocated extra money based on the percentage of their students who qualify for a free or reduced lunch. If your school's percentage of low-income students is the same or greater than the District's for that year, you get Title I. If it isn't, you don't. In 2011–2012 the percentage was 61%.

That means that a school with 62% of its students in poverty could get $1 million or so extra for more staff, support, counselors and interventions. A school with 60% of its students in poverty gets no extra money.

From a funding standpoint, schools are penalized for having too many middle- and upper-middle class families. In this system, the ideal mix is about 65% poor/35% middle class—enough low-income students so you qualify for Title I but enough middle class families with the means and wherewithal to raise funds and provide all the support that poor families generally aren't able to supply.

Magnet schools usually have a nice sweet spot for a couple of years when they start out because the number of middle-class families hasn't yet risen above 35 percent. The sweet spot only lasts a few years if your program is successful and attracts a high proportion of middle-class families. Although the number of children in poverty at our school stayed about the same, the percentage of students they represented dropped because of the influx of middle class families into the Mandarin immersion program. In 2010 we 'flipped' and fell below the 61% mark. The District cut us a deal and allowed us to keep the extra money and staff that we'd had that year, but the hand-writing was on the wall.

Staff changes

After several contentious years during which the entire school achieved a tremendous amount and the overall test scores rose (they'd already been on the way up before the Mandarin program got there), it didn't come as a surprise that our principal decided to move to a school that really needed him. John Muir Elementary, near San Francisco's Lower Haight/Western Addition neighborhood, looked a lot like Starr King had when he first arrived. He was following the path he had dedicated his life to and the students at Muir have benefited enormously from his expertise.

In his place Starr King got a new principal who came from an educational non-profit. He had a hard row to hoe but his calm demeanor helped soothe some of the tempers that had flared over the preceding four years. He came without baggage, something that really helped us all get off on a new footing.

In general, the students thrived. They learned English, they learned Mandarin, they learned math. They wrote book reports and had Music in the Schools Today (paid for by the PTA and later a grant) and they had a great drama program called StageWrite (paid for by a grant). They loved school and they loved learning. We loved our school, adored our teachers and tried to stay under the radar of the District.

There were still troubles, of course. One ongoing source of contention was for families who wanted stronger and more rigorous academics, something teachers frequently hadn't ever dealt with before. I remember going in to meet with an English language arts teacher to see if we could get some more challenging work for our daughter, as the assignments were far too easy for her and she was bored. The teacher was very nice but clearly unused to dealing with this issue. She told us quite honestly that she was amazed to have a class that actually sat still and listened to her when she read them a book. She never was able to come up with more challenging assignments. We eventually took to giving our daughter "reading log addendum" essays to write, alongside her normal English language arts assignments.

This wasn't just an issue for the English-speaking families. Chinese-speaking parents flocked to Kumon[14] after-school classes for more practice in math, followed by many of us English-speaking families. We all felt our kids needed more math fundamentals that there wasn't time for in the school day. Saturdays at the Kumon storefront near our house were like a mini-Starr King reunion; I usually saw two, three or even four families from our school there. It clearly wasn't just a public school issue, there were plenty of families from private and Catholic schools there as well. One Mandarin-speaking mom told me that among her friends the expectation was that all their children would be doing work at least a year above grade level, and Kumon helped ensure they were.

Wow, they really *are* learning in Chinese

With my fading college Mandarin, I found that my daughters' Chinese classes were becoming more and more impenetrable. I could catch maybe a third of what was going on. While I could sort of follow what was happening in English by reading the homework and the worksheets that came home, Chinese was a blank spot. I knew the characters they were learning and had to memorize, but who knew what else was happening in class?

The gnawing worry was that nothing *was* happening. That they were just spinning their wheels there in Chinese class, hearing the same old Chinese folk legends again and again. However, every once in a while we'd get a glimpse inside and realize how very much was going on that was invisible to us. One night at the dinner table *Zhou Yi*, then in second grade, was using a pencil to make dots on the table cloth. I told her to stop. She argued that it was a kind of homework because she was making a picture like that guy they'd learned about in school that day.

"What guy?" I asked.

"You know, that Shew-la guy. He's really famous. You know! Our teacher put his pictures up on the board and we looked at them close up and then far away and they were really pretty. You know."

Somehow Shew-la wasn't ringing any bells for us. Schuler? Schiller? Shurrer? We were throwing out every name that we could think of that sounded vaguely arts-oriented.

"No, he was..." she turned to her fourth-grade sister and said, "He was 法国人 *Fàguórén*. What's that?"

"French, he was French," *Zhou Qing* translated.

"Yeah, that's right. He was French. And he painted paintings. He was really, really famous," *Zhou Yi* told us. "It was really sad, he died when he was 30."

"Picasso? Monet? Matisse?" None of them fit. Finally my wife asked, "What did the pictures look like?"

"Like this!" *Zhou Yi* said, dotting the table cloth with her pencil. "You get up close and it's just dots but when you get far away it's a picture. Point pictures."

Finally the light dawned. "Pointillism! You were learning about *pointillism!*" we cried. We knew her teacher loved art and painting. We hadn't realized how much she shared that love with the students.

"I don't know what it is in English. We were learning about 点画 *diǎnhuà*. Point pictures. They're really cool," she said. "We got to make some with colored pencils in class but the green one was broken so it was hard to make the bushes right..." and she launched into a long description of the class's artistic process.

"What class were you learning this in?" my wife asked, still not quite sure.

"Art class," *Zhou Yi* answered.

"But in what language?"

"Chinese," she said, as if it were a given.

So our second grader was learning about Pointillism and Seurat in class. Only in Chinese that was 点画 *diǎnhuà* and 乔治·修拉, *Qiáozhì·Xiūlā*. And if she hadn't started making pencil dots on the tablecloth we never would have known it.

The middle school debacle

The MICP was working hard to live up to our pledge of "Two Schools, One Program" when the District threw us a curveball. In 2010, SFUSD made good its promise that there would be a Mandarin immersion program for middle school students. We'd always been a little worried about it, because the District's lone Korean immersion program stopped at fifth grade, unlike Cantonese and Spanish. Now we were told that our middle school students would get two classes out of six or seven[15] in Mandarin and the rest in English. Using the Spanish and Cantonese immersion model, we knew that those classes would be Mandarin language arts and social studies.

Just as this was being decided, SFUSD was in the midst of creating a new neighborhood assignment program for schools. The lottery stayed in place but became slightly weighted towards a family's local elementary school. One of the components of the new plan was a middle school feeder program in which a group of five to seven elementary schools fed into a single middle school. The schools were carefully chosen to create a mix of races and socio-economic groups all feeding into each San Francisco middle school.

It was a good idea in many ways, creating a sense of connection and continuity for school communities. Up until then you just applied to one of the District's 13 middle schools in the lottery and hoped you got a good one. They broke down into two groups, several large, heavily Asian, high-scoring and underfunded schools; and some smaller, mostly Latino and African-American, low-scoring but better funded schools.

Unfortunately, in a stroke of utter insanity (from our standpoint), the District somehow decided to send Starr King's two Mandarin immersion classes to one middle school and José Ortega's one class to another.

José Ortega fifth graders, when they got that far, were to go to Aptos Middle School. Starr King fifth graders were to go to Horace Mann Middle School. This created a huge rift among families at our two schools because Aptos was a high-performing middle school and Mann was not. The "Two Schools, One Program" coalition we'd worked so hard to create almost broke under the pressure. Our MIPC meetings were heated with the clear majority of parents at José Ortega favoring a high-achieving middle school over staying together with Starr King students. We spent months having meetings that tore us apart until the District finally realized what a colossally bad idea it was and decided to send both schools' students to Aptos.

Then we faced a new hurdle: Aptos didn't want us. Specifically, it didn't want the Mandarin immersion program. As we were told in multiple public meetings and by both staff and parents, inserting a language immersion strand in their school would destroy the carefully crafted schedule they'd created that allowed them to offer honors classes, band, chorus and multiple other programs. Although Aptos had lost its Title I funding a few years before our arrival, the 200 or so mostly middle-class students we would add to the mix would make it impossible for the school to ever get it back.

I can still feel the visceral shock of sitting in a classroom during one of what ended up being multiple "community listening meetings" when a mom practically hissed at a group of Starr King and José Ortega parents: "We don't want you here. We don't want your program here. You're going to ruin Aptos!" We walked out feeling blindsided and assaulted, stunned by the ferocious anger the District's plan had engendered, all of which was directed at us.

Talk about a zero-sum game. Together the staff, principal and parents had created an amazing school with a strong honors program, in a school that a decade ago was considered poor and strife-ridden. In the 1990s, when families got assigned to Aptos it meant a quick search of the real estate listings to get out of town. By 2010, it was eagerly sought after and parents fought to get in.

They didn't want the capricious demands of the District to destroy what they'd worked so hard to create. I could understand that, as hard as it was to be on the receiving end of those feelings. It must be said, though, that Aptos' principal was not among those who didn't want us. He knew what battles he could win with the District, and this wasn't one of them, so he embraced us. But it took months for the feeling of being so hated to dissipate.

Year six: 2011–2012

During the 2011–2012 school year the District put the hammer down and Starr King lost its Title I money. Thankfully this wasn't as contentious in our school as it's been in some in the District, where working-class parents have yelled at middle-class families for "ruining" their school by coming in and messing up their numbers.[16] Even so it was hard. The District specifically created our program to attract middle class families but then set it up so that the mere fact that we were there made it difficult to support the kids who needed it, by taking funding way from them.

The PTA was doing the best it could. In 2011–2012 our PTA raised a total of $90,000. In 2013–2014 we raised $150,000. But we could only ramp up so fast and there was no way it could make up for the money and staff we lost with Title I. That included multiple positions:

- the nearly full-time nurse
- the social worker
- the parent liaison
- the wellness center coordinator
- the resource specialist (who managed students who had special needs)
- the reading recovery specialist (someone who works intensively with kindergarten and first grade students who have shown difficulties learning to read)
- the literacy specialist (a teacher who works with older students who are lagging behind in reading)
- the instructional reform facilitator (a master teacher who works to train other teachers in techniques especially meant to serve historically underserved students)

Some of those positions came back as part-time or quarter-time in the next few years, but the overall level of support the school could offer struggling students was significantly diminished.

And frankly there was a certain amount of tension over fundraising. The PTA supported the whole school, not just the Mandarin program. But that didn't stop the quiet conversations in the hallways about just how much of the PTA money was coming from families in the Mandarin immersion program and how much of it went to Mandarin immersion classes. Some parents in the general ed program felt too much was going to the Mandarin program. Some in the Mandarin program felt too much was going to general ed when numerically they were now a smaller percentage of the entire student body—about one-third general ed, two-thirds Mandarin immersion. Truthfully the PTA benefitted the entire school—music, sports and cultural programs were for everyone. Other PTA-supported programs focused more on kids who were struggling, but those kids came from all our programs, not just general education. Thankfully most of our families embraced the need to support the kids who needed it the most, whatever program they were in.

But not all. There were a few families who argued, strenuously and for years on end, that they should be allowed to donate to the PTA but have the money only go to their child's classroom. That way they'd get the tax benefit but not have to support any children but their own. The PTA said no. It was suggested to them that you couldn't even get away with that in a private school. They didn't care. They only wanted to fund things that would support their own children. Eventually several of those families left, either to suburban or private schools.

You can imagine the PTA meeting and the School Site Council[17] meetings. The people who took on those jobs had the patience of saints and I salute them. I soldiered on as the PTA communications chair, writing the school newsletter each week and trying to avoid meetings where people yelled at each other.

The 金山中文教育协会 is born

After the middle school mess of the previous year we were finally on track to become "Three Schools, One Program." The Mandarin Immersion Parents Council did some serious searching among kindergarten and first grade parents to bring on some new board members who hadn't been traumatized by the whole middle school issue. We were revitalized and calmer, with the energy of new parents who hadn't spent the past few years being put through the wringer. In the spring of 2012, we finally became a non-profit under the umbrella of the San Francisco Schools Alliance. We launched ourselves with a new name, 金山中文教育协会. For those who don't read Chinese, that's:

金山 *Jīnshān*, San Francisco (Gold Mountain, because 旧金山 *Jiùjīnshān, Old Gold Mountain,* is a common name for San Francisco)

中文 *Zhōngwén*, Chinese

教育 *Jiàoyù*, Education
协会 *Xíehuì*, Council

So the *Jinshan* Mandarin Education Council (JMEC) was born. We had an almost all-new board with many new faces from all three schools, including lots of parents from kindergarten and first grade.

Staff woes and stage triumphs

We'd hoped this year would be calm after the torture of the middle school feeder fiasco, but it wasn't. We'd already experienced not having a second-grade teacher. Now our younger daughter's third-grade Mandarin teacher quit six days after school began, leaving the other third-grade teacher to take over for both classes. That was not ideal. Rather than having 70% of the day in Mandarin, they were getting 50% or less and the teacher was overwhelmed. It was *not* a good year. There were meetings: official, unofficial and hysterical. There were proposals. There were petitions sent to the school board, the school district and probably the President. None of it made a bit of difference. We finally got an un-credentialed (but heroic) Mandarin-speaking aide in the classroom who did what she could for our kids. But that class spent much of the next year catching up. We also lost several students that year as their families jumped ship for what they hoped were more stable and less chaotic programs. This would create problems in the years to come because the school's funding was based on the number of students in the school, and it's difficult to back-fill an immersion program as most potential incoming students don't have the requisite abilities in both Mandarin and English.

Despite everything, our daughters' Mandarin was pretty good. We went to China as a family for the first time during spring break and both girls did well, understanding most of what they heard. We felt we'd definitely made the right decision in choosing Mandarin immersion.

The school as a whole was thriving. While there were some staff issues, most students were in classes with teachers who now had a few years of Mandarin immersion under their belts. For our oldest, the level of work in fifth grade was good and the class really covered a lot of ground. Mandarin, English and math were all great.

It wasn't all just reading, writing and Chinese by any means. The arts have always been a huge part of Starr King, from long before the Mandarin program arrived. One program that really shines is called StageWrite. Beginning in kindergarten the students had worked with StageWrite staff to act out ideas and write short skits. Each year the work went deeper and became more complex. In fourth grade each student wrote a short story, and in fifth grade every student wrote a one-act play. The level of support and artistry by the StageWrite staff was amazing.

Just after winter break, six students were chosen from among the fifth grade class to write plays that would be performed by professional actors. Together they went on a field trip to San Francisco's de Young museum where they each chose a piece of art. They spent the next month writing a one-act play based on it.

The students, who came from Starr King's general education, Spanish bilingual and Mandarin immersion strands, all worked intensely with mentors to craft their stories. It culminated in a grand gala event at the museum, attended by the entire school, where all the plays were performed by a cast of adult actors. The next night several hundred parents and families took over the Brava Theater just down the hill from Starr King for an evening performance of the plays. It was an astoundingly moving experience for us adults to get to see deep into the hearts of the kids at our school, from all the programs. The audience laughed, wept and was astounded with what these children, whom we had known since they were toddling little kindergarteners, had inside of them.

Aptos ascendant

Middle school was looking good too. The angriest parents at Aptos had moved on to high school, so the level of animosity towards the Mandarin program had diminished noticeably. The principal at Aptos reached out to the Mandarin immersion fifth grade families and brought us in for meetings and to help hire the new sixth grade teacher.

The clear standout was an immersion teacher with several years under her belt in Silicon Valley, who wanted to move to San Francisco, where she lived. She had a Masters degree from Taiwan and was one of the most organized and hard-working teachers I'd ever seen. She was a dream come true. Aptos's principal immediately realized that and got her to sign a contract in April, months earlier than usually was allowed by the District.

In one of those annoying rules that makes life hard in a new program, the District wanted to know how many students would be in the newly created class before it allowed a teacher to be hired for that class. That information wasn't available until late in May, so even if a principal really wanted to hire a teacher he or she could only promise to do so. With Mandarin immersion teachers scarce and highly prized nationwide, we saw many excellent candidates reluctantly go to districts that could offer them definite contracts months before SFUSD could.

On May 22, 2012, we held a banquet to honor the first class of Mandarin immersion students to be promoted to middle school. And on May 24, the school's auditorium was filled as parents in all four of our school's programs—general education, Spanish bilingual, Mandarin immersion and Special Day—watched our fifth graders be handed their diplomas. *Zhou Qing's* grandparents flew in from Orange County for the event and spent much of the afternoon thanking all the teachers for giving their two granddaughters the gift of Chinese. Memories of all the touring and anxiety and discussions our entire family had had in those same halls six years before kept floating through my head as I cried watching our oldest proudly walk across the stage.

Where we don't ride off into the sunset

After all this, you'd imagine we sent our oldest to Aptos for middle school and lived happily ever after, wouldn't you?

Would that it were so simple.

In the midst of *Zhou Qing's* fifth grade year, the District started throwing out trial balloons about dropping honors classes in middle school. As I explained above, SFUSD has 12 middle schools: several big ones with honors classes, and many little ones that serve mostly Title I students and which offer smaller classes and have more funding for educational intervention to support struggling students.

The smaller schools have never had honors classes. Given their smaller class size, teachers are expected to "differentiate" (in education-jargon), meeting the educational needs of different students at different levels all in the same class.

In larger schools with larger class sizes (up to 35 students), students with high test scores, good grades and (sometimes) a Gifted-and-Talented-Education (GATE) designation in their file, were placed in honors classes. In some schools, honors classes made up between 30% and 50% of the classes. If you looked at test scores, honors ended up being slightly above grade level and up, while regular classes were grade level and remedial.

We knew families whose children had been put in schools with honors but gotten assigned to general education classes by mistake, and they said they were doing fourth and fifth grade work. At schools that didn't have honors it was the same. I toured one sixth grade class where an English teacher was reading a paragraph aloud to students and having them circle the nouns and underline the verbs. There's nothing wrong with that; it was a skill the students in that class were struggling to learn (from the discussion I observed). But it was also what our third grader was doing at Starr King in English.

There was a strong push by some administrators in the District to do away with honors as "inequitable" because honors classes tended to be made up of higher income students and tended to skew Asian and white. The expectation was that everyone should learn together. Teachers were expected to figure out how to differentiate in a class that could have up to 35 students, in which some students might be reading at a third grade level and others at a high school level.

When we didn't know which middle school was going to get the Mandarin program, several parents toured the likely ones. That included Hoover Middle School, where West Portal's Cantonese immersion program continues for middle school (Alice Fong Yu, the other Cantonese immersion school, is K–8). There a vice principal told me that it would be "impossible" for her teachers to properly differentiate and that they shouldn't be asked to. Without honors, the kids able to work above grade level were just left to doodle while the teacher worked with those who needed more help, she said.

No one listened to her. Word came down that Hoover was going to disband honors. The reason was that it made scheduling too difficult because Hoover had both Cantonese and Spanish immersion strands, as well as general ed. And a packet of articles about the basic unfairness of honors classes in middle school was quietly circulated among District staff. Articles about the discussion began to appear in local newspapers.[18]

This all happened in the middle of December, and we went from being excited at the prospect of being at Aptos, which was going to have an excellent Mandarin program and had a strong honors program, to worried. We're academic-minded parents, no ifs, ands or buts. And putting our daughter in a class where she would just be bored wasn't an option. So with heavy hearts we started looking at private schools. We just didn't trust SFUSD.

Visiting private schools was fascinating. Suddenly I knew where all the white kids in San Francisco were hiding. Surprisingly we found that at many of these schools, the academics weren't that much better than Starr King's. Granted, we were only looking at the private schools on our side of town, all of them relatively "progressive" in their leanings and no Catholic schools. It's possible that the older, more moneyed private schools in San Francisco focus more on content. I don't know.

What you did get at these schools was a lack of troubled students, as those kids are pretty quickly asked to leave. I could see how the teachers had more time to teach, simply because they didn't need to focus on children who couldn't sit still or who kept talking or bothering their neighbors. So the learning was more intense and in depth. But we weren't going to give up Chinese just to get a classroom of kids who could sit still doing the same work they'd be doing at a public school.

Did I mention we care about academics? One school we'd been quite taken with was Nueva, a school for gifted students south of San Francisco. Its curriculum was amazing, the school grounds nicer than my university and the level of teaching superb. And yet walking away from six years of

Mandarin was hard. It was clear that there would be no way to keep up *Zhou Qing*'s Chinese with a weekend class. But there weren't any other options.

Or were there? Because we felt we had to do due diligence, we made an appointment to tour the Chinese American International School for middle school. CAIS historically got so few new students for middle school that it didn't actually have tours at that level. The staff simply took us around and let us peek into classrooms. At the time pretty much only kids moving to San Francisco from Asia applied. As you may recall, we didn't have a good take on CAIS back before preschool. The required morning calisthenics that the summer camp began with in those days hadn't gone down well with our girls. But we didn't feel we could dismiss the school as a possibility based on summer school and preschool all those years before without going in for a second look. After all, we hadn't actually looked at its academic program since 2004.

So we walked in and promptly fell in love.

Academics? Check.

Mandarin? Check.

Goofy, geeky kids just like our daughter? Check.

Whatever hadn't worked for us in preschool had transmogrified into something that worked really well for middle school. The school had changed and we had changed, probably us more than CAIS. All I know is that the one school we were sure we would never send her to became the one we most wanted her to attend.

We applied. *Zhou Qing* tested in just fine in Mandarin, English and math and was offered a place at CAIS. After much discussion, tears, pondering and anguish, we decided to take it. And after six years of being the most pro-public school parent you could imagine, I found myself with one foot in both worlds.

You'll note that we didn't move our fourth grader, *Zhou Yi*. We love Starr King and she was getting a fine education there, in Mandarin and English. Better, actually, than *Zhou Qing* had gotten. By *Zhou Yi*'s year the teachers had gotten the hang of the Mandarin curriculum and dealing with a cohort of kids who could work at more advanced levels. There had always been those kids, of course, but now there were lots of them. English homework started coming in three levels each at a slightly differentiated level. There was a Math Club on Fridays where she spent the afternoon solving fiendishly complex problems and loving it. Her school experience was very different from what her sister's had been. From what other parents tell me, for kindergarteners now it's like a whole different school from the one we toured back in 2006.

But for *Zhou Qing*, as much as we loved our public school, we didn't trust the District not to make a political (well, I call it political, they would call it something else) decision and disband honors. And without honors we weren't going to Aptos.

Year seven: 2012–2013

This was the year Starr King lost the last of its Title I funding and also its District-paid parent liaison and half-time master teacher whose job was to work with all the school's teachers to raise their level of classroom teaching. But despite that, the school was amazing. After a turbulent third grade, *Zhou Yi*'s fourth grade was the best by far of any of our years at Starr King. Her Chinese teacher had been teaching in the Mandarin program for several years, so she had had time to establish her classroom and her lesson plans. The curriculum was in place, so she knew what needed to be covered and had two years of it under her belt—and she had a good sense of what her students were capable of.

The fourth grade's classwork was interesting and challenging. For years, students have done reading response journals in English language arts. They read a book (or a chapter, as they get older) and then wrote a response to it. In the early grades it was just questions but later on it become a more formal essay style.

In fourth grade, for the first time, students were being assigned a book a week to read in Chinese. Then they were required to write an essay about it. At the beginning of the year it was very intimidating. But *Zhou Yi* quickly realized that she could actually follow most of the books her teacher was putting out for them to choose from. I cannot tell you how happy it made me to see her sprawled on her bed, immersed in a book in Chinese, reading for the story's sake! In fact it was the first year I'd found Chinese books scattered around on her floor and bed where she's dropped them after reading them. For too many years the Chinese books just sat on their shelf in the hallway, ignored as the girls grabbed books in English to read for fun.

The books were still picture books, but they were not easy ones. Sometimes I asked *Zhou Yi* to tell me what they were about. The stories she told me were complex and the vocabulary she knew surprised me, though of course it shouldn't have.

I showed a few months' worth of her Chinese essays to a professor of Chinese at a local university and she was impressed at the complexity of the writing, and the humor. (*Zhou Yi* has a great sense of the absurd, which comes through even when she's writing in Chinese.) She told me, "That's not bad for sixth grade."

"Sixth grade? This isn't my sixth grader. This is my *fourth* grader!" I told her. The professor picked up the packet of essays again and thumbed through it, "Fourth grade? Really? I'm impressed."

Although as any family with kids in school knows, what goes on in your child's classroom isn't necessarily the picture for the school as a whole. The third grade teacher who'd had to bear the weight of two classes the year before had an even more difficult year this time around. It became clear early in the school year that she was struggling and eventually she went out on disability, leaving the third grade Mandarin immersion students in her class with no teacher at all. Rather than having the other third grade teacher take on both classes, which hadn't gone well, the teacher-less class had to do with substitutes and teacher's aides. For reasons having to do with union rules, District funding and things I (and the parents in that class) never understood, simply hiring a new teacher wasn't possible. They suffered that year and what was remarkable to me was that only two or three families left.

That said, attrition was always a problem. We got a few kids coming in from CAIS and Presidio Knolls, another Mandarin immersion private school that had recently started up in San Francisco. But mostly we lost kids when parents grew frustrated with the bumpiness of the ride and moved to other, less fraught, schools.

Middle school

Zhou Qing was tearful all summer at the thought of not being with her friends for middle school. However, once school started she did fine at CAIS. She quickly found a group of good friends. I would describe them as quirky and somewhat geeky but she assures me they are not. The academics were good, which we wanted, and the expectations strict, which she needed. At times the stress level over grades was higher than we might have liked. We made clear to her that perfect grades weren't what we wanted from her; effort and a well-rounded and happy person were, and things got better.

One area where I realized CAIS had an advantage over public schools was that it had the freedom to teach Chinese as Chinese language and culture. Public schools have to follow a set curriculum, part of which they teach in Chinese and part of which they teach in English. But there isn't much wiggle room in terms of what is taught. CAIS has the luxury of teaching Chinese language arts and Chinese social studies, in addition to English language arts and English social studies. The cultural context of what they were learning made a great deal more sense. *Zhou Qing*'s Mandarin improved greatly.

And so did the Mandarin of the students in sixth grade at Aptos Middle School. The new teacher was amazing, fulfilling and exceeding everyone's expectations. She took to the District's newish computer network like a fish to water. She quickly saw its possibilities and early in the year had her students participating in on-line book clubs, in Chinese, about novels they were reading in class. That forced them to write, but allowed them to do it on the computer, which they loved.

An unexpected bonus was the addition of students who had recently emigrated from China into the class. Middle school classes in SFUSD can have up to 36 students but only 24 students from the Mandarin program at Starr

King moved up to Aptos. One student transferred in from CAIS, which left 11 open seats. JMEC worked with Aptos' principal to send a letter to every incoming sixth grade family in the entire District that had checked "Chinese" as a home language on their application form, telling them these seats were open. Lured both by the draw of having more Mandarin instruction and the chance to get into a highly sought-after middle school, the places filled quickly. For the first time the program was truly two-way immersion, with students fluent in English and students fluent in Mandarin working together in a Mandarin-only classroom.

The influx was great for the English-speakers. They quickly became friends with the kids from China and hung out at lunch and after school, using only Mandarin to communicate because these students didn't yet know English. Suddenly their social language blossomed.

And for the Chinese-speakers, their Mandarin social studies class gave them one class out of six where they were working well above the level of other students. For the rest of the day they were in special English Language Learner classes. But every day when the bell rang for social studies in Chinese, they came into class together as a group. The sixth grade Mandarin teacher would announce, "Ah, our Mandarin experts have arrived!" and they beamed. It was a remarkable educational experience for both sides.

Year nine: 2013–2014, an established program

This was year nine of the Great Mandarin Immersion Experiment in San Francisco, except that it wasn't much of an experiment any more. The program continued to grow and change. Starr King's sister school José Ortega Elementary School has stayed a much calmer and less fraught community than ours, perhaps because of the strong leadership of its long-time principal.

The lottery applications for kindergarten places in SFUSD went out and when the results were announced in May for 2013–2014, both Starr King and José Ortega's incoming kindergarten classes had checked in full—and for the first time one-third of the incoming students were Mandarin proficient. The initial dream, of a truly dual-language program where children who spoke both languages learned from each other and not just the teacher, was beginning to come true.

It turned out that many of those students didn't actually come from Chinese-speaking homes. San Francisco by this time had several Mandarin immersion preschools where families who wanted their children to grow up bilingual could send their children. After two or three years of preschool, these children were comfortable enough in a fully Mandarin environment that they were easily able to pass the test used by SFUSD to indicate Mandarin proficiency, even the ones who came from English-speaking homes.[19]

Parents chose these programs because they're excellent preschools and also because they wanted their children to become comfortable with Chinese early on. It worked. One family I know has three sons, two of whom are at Starr King in the Mandarin immersion program and one at an immersion preschool founded by the sister of a Starr King teacher. The mom told me that their youngest son was somewhat puzzled that his parents—who between them speak English, French and Creole—didn't speak Chinese. After all, he and his two older brothers do. "Why don't you?" he asked her.

However, this eagerness for Mandarin has also had the effect of allowing families to game the system, getting their kids into the Mandarin immersion program in the Chinese-speaker kindergarten seats, which historically haven't filled up and have at times been left empty by the District (much to the frustration of English-speaking parents who really wanted their kids to get into the Mandarin program). I don't know that many parents deliberately chose their preschool with an eye towards having a leg up when it came time to take on the public school lottery in San Francisco, but that's how it has worked out. Whether the District will change its criteria in the future isn't clear.

For families who speak Chinese, other issues had arisen. Many felt the level of Chinese their children were taught wasn't sufficiently high, especially in terms of reading and writing. Given that their children enter already fluent, they expected more. They organized weekend groups using the *Zhong Wen* textbooks to build their children's reading ability. Some of the Chinese parents felt their children could do just as well going to an all-English school and taking Chinese at a Saturday school.

Some English-speaking parents pushed back against calls for more memorization of characters and more worksheets to bring up the level of literacy. Probably the larger issue was what level the program was aiming for in terms of Chinese reading ability, which isn't known. The Chinese families had no intention of leaving their children's literacy to chance. Imagine if someone told English-speaking parents their children might never read at grade level and they should be patient and not expect too much. What if your principal told you, "Maybe by high school your child will be able to read complex material". It wouldn't go over well. This is an on-going discussion, one that's happening nationwide as Mandarin programs mature and expand.

Towards the close of the previous year, the second principal at Starr King during its Mandarin immersion years announced he would be leaving. After three years and an enormous amount of work at healing some of the rifts that had grown up, it had become clear to him the next stage for Starr King required a principal who spoke Chinese. The school has a growing cohort of Chinese-speaking families, yet no one in the office spoke Chinese. The school was originally staffed to support a Spanish bilingual program, which was being phased out. So after much consideration our principal decided to move to another school so we could hire a new principal.

That turned into a kind of homecoming for Starr King, though we didn't realize it at the time. The new principal had immigrated to the United States from China as a child and arrived in San Francisco speaking little English. After a short stint at SFUSD's Chinese Education Center Elementary School, for English language learners, she transferred—to Starr King! She completed her elementary school years at our school and it was in the same lunchroom auditorium on whose stage we'd seen our first fifth grade class walk across for their promotion to middle school that she, too, had moved up to middle school. After high school she went on to college and became an immersion teacher in the Cantonese immersion program at West Portal Elementary School, the same one that had helped birth our Mandarin program. Eventually she spent two years as the District's Mandarin immersion coordinator before she moved on to pursue a credential as a principal, and then two years as an assistant principal at Gordon Lau Elementary in Chinatown. In 2013–2014 she returned to her old stomping grounds as our new, trilingual (English, Cantonese and Mandarin) principal, and Starr King entered into a new era.

For 2014 we got word that Starr King's Academic Performance Index score was 812. That's on a scale of 200 to 1,000, with 800 being the number the state has set as the goal for all schools. It's a magic number for California schools and many families won't even look at a school with an API below 800. We have arrived. What the future will bring no one knows, but Mandarin immersion has a strong, solid grounding and looks to thrive in the years to come.

So, would we do it all over again?

In a heartbeat.

1. You can read more than you'd ever care to know about the system here.
    San Francisco Unified School District, *History of the Student Assignment Method.*
    http://portal.sfusd.edu/apps/departments/educational_placement/
    HistoryStudentAssignment.pdf
    Accessed April 4, 2014.
    If you want to see how much social engineering the District is doing, read this:
    San Francisco Unified School District, *Student Assignment: Annual Report: 2011–2012 School Year.*
    http://www.sfusd.edu/en/assets/sfusd-staff/enroll/files/2012-13/annual_
    report_march_5_2012_FINAL.pdf
    Accessed April 4, 2014.

2. For the 2014–2014 school year the District said that 82% of families got one of their choices. That doesn't meant it was a school they particularly wanted, merely that it was one they included on their list, which can include up to 25 schools.
SFUSD Enrollment Stats, The SF K Files. March 19, 2014.
http://www.sfkfiles.com/2014/03/sfusd-enrollment-stats.html
Accessed May 14, 2014.

3. Heather Knight. "Families' exodus leaves S.F. whiter, less diverse."
San Francisco Chronicle June 10, 2012.
http://www.sfgate.com/bayarea/article/Families-exodus-leaves-S-F-whiter-less-diverse-3393637.php
Accessed April 4, 2014.

4. United States Census Bureau, *State and County Quick Facts, San Francisco County.*
http://quickfacts.census.gov/qfd/states/06/06075.html
Accessed June 24, 2014.

5. San Francisco Unified School District, *Our District in a Snapshot.*
http://www.sfusd.edu/en/employment/certificated-careers/teaching-careers/why-teach-with-sfusd/our-district-snapshot.html
Accessed April 4, 2014.

6. This is changing as housing costs continue to rise, pushing poor and middle class families out of San Francisco. Though some middle class families would say that, after housing, the difficulty of finding a good public school is also pushing them out as they can't afford private school.
Heather Knight, "Families' exodus leaves S.F. whiter, less diverse," *San Francisco Chronicle*, June 10, 2013.
http://www.sfgate.com/bayarea/article/Families-exodus-leaves-S-F-whiter-less-diverse-3393637.php
Accessed April 4, 2014.

7. The SF K Files.
http://www.sfkfiles.com
Accessed April 4, 2014.

8. Parents for Public Schools' national website is
http://parents4publicschools.org.
If your city doesn't have a chapter, *start one!*

9. Jill Tucker, "Starr King Elementary talks the talk (in Mandarin)," *San Francisco Chronicle*, August 21, 2006.
http://www.sfgate.com/education/article/SAN-FRANCISCO-Starr-King-Elementary-talks-the-2490791.php
Accessed April 4, 2014.

10. Jill Tucker, "Starr King Elementary talks the talk (in Mandarin.)" *San Francisco Chronicle*. (Aug. 21, 2006).
http://www.sfgate.com/education/article/SAN-FRANCISCO-Starr-King-Elementary-talks-the-2490791.php
Accessed April 4, 2014.

Jill Tucker, "Kindergarten Mandarin / Language Immersion at Starr King Elementary / Not a word of English, not one little peep," *San Francisco Chronicle*, Oct. 15, 2006.
http://www.sfgate.com/education/article/SAN-FRANCISCO-Kindergarten-s-big-triumph-2587451.php
Accessed April 4, 2014.

Jill Tucker, "Kindergarten students learning Mandarin fast in immersion class / Speechless as school began, they're now amazingly proficient," *San Francisco Chronicle*, April 1, 2007.
http://www.sfgate.com/education/article/
SAN-FRANCISCO-Kindergarten-students-learning-2606032.php
Accessed April 4, 2014.

Jill Tucker, "Kindergarten's big triumph / Starr King students ace their Mandarin immersion program," *San Francisco Chronicle*, June 12, 2007.
http://www.sfgate.com/education/article/
SAN-FRANCISCO-Kindergarten-s-big-triumph-2587451.php
Accessed April 4, 2014.

Jill Tucker, "Chinese language program a stunning bilingual success," *San Francisco Chronicle*, June 11, 2008.
http://www.sfgate.com/bayarea/article/
Chinese-language-program-a-stunning-bilingual-3280795.php
Accessed April 4, 2014.

Jill Tucker, "Mandarin masters: Starr King's 1st class grows up," *San Francisco Chronicle*, April 17, 2012.
http://www.sfgate.com/bayarea/article/
Mandarin-masters-Starr-King-s-1st-class-grows-up-3486786.php
Accessed April 4, 2014.

11. An amazing documentary about immersion schools in San Francisco. The graduation scene will make you cry.
    http://speakingintonguesfilm.info

12. Note that Washington D.C. is included in this, so it's 49th out of 51.
    EdSource, "California drops to 49th in school spending in annual Ed Week report," January 14, 2013.
    http://www.edsource.org/today/2013/california-drops-to-49th-in-school-spending-in-annual-ed-week-report/25379#.UYaUOb_OvcY
    Accessed April 4, 2014.

13. Lisa Schiff, "School Beat: Title I funds for all Title I students," *Beyond Chron*, May 3, 2012.
    http://www.beyondchron.org/news/index.php?itemid=10123
    Accessed April 4, 2014.

14. Kumon is a math and reading program that originated in Japan. It is intended to supplement school lessons. Students progress through the program at their own pace, moving on to the next level when they have achieved mastery of the previous level. Every day they have a packet of problems or reading that takes about 15 minutes to complete.
    http://www.kumon.com

15. This is another funding issue. Title I middle schools typically had the money to fund seven periods a day. Non-Title I middle schools only had six. Some real powerhouse fundraising schools like Alice Fong Yu managed to pay for an extra period a day through their Parent Teacher Organization, but that was in part because they're K–8 so they had the full fundraising efforts of nine grades to pull from.

16. Carol Lloyd, "When the Melting Pot Boils Over," GreatSchools.org.
    http://www.greatschools.org/school-choice/

7282-melting-pot-diversity-at-schools.gs
Accessed April 4, 2014.

17. These are the elected boards that officially run public schools in California. They vote on the budget and decide on the focus of the school each year.

18. Amy Crawford, "SFUSD veers away from honors classes," *San Francisco Examiner*, February 12, 2012.
http://www.sfexaminer.com/sanfrancisco/
sfusd-veers-away-from-honors-classes/Content?oid=2194848
Accessed April 4, 2014.

19. The test involves having the child, who is between four and five years old, go into a room alone with one of the District's testers. The tester asks simple questions such as "What color is that ball?" and "How many people are in your family?" while chatting away in Mandarin.

三十一
sān shí yī
31

Afterword

I hate it when I've read an entire book, I get to the end and it just … stops. After spending so much time with the author, I want a good-bye.

So here's my good-bye. Thanks for reading my admittedly idiosyncratic take on Mandarin immersion. I hope, parent-to-parent, it's been helpful.

In all of this, remember that your child is getting a remarkable opportunity to learn one of the crucial languages of the 21st century. As they say in Beijing, 加油 — *Jiāyóu!*, which means "Give it the gas!"

It will take work on your part, and your child's. But it's worth it. So settle in for the long haul and get ready for a fascinating ride into what, for many of us, is a whole new culture and language.

You're in for an incredible journey.

sān shí èr

32

Resources

American Council on the Teaching of Foreign Languages
http://www.actfl.org

Asia Society
http://asiasociety.org/education/chinese-language-initiatives
Their Chinese Language Initiatives holds the yearly National Chinese Language Conference, which is a major source of information about immersion and Chinese education. They also have a mailing list that's quite helpful.

The Chinese Language Association of Secondary-Elementary Schools
http://www.classk12.org

Chinese Language Teachers Association
http://clta-us.org

Chinese Language Teachers Association of California
http://www.cltac.org/

Chinese Schools Association in the United States
http://www.csaus.org
Weekend Chinese schools.

Confucius Institutes
http://www.chinesecio.com
Based at more than 60 U.S. universities, these support Chinese language and cultural studies.

eChinese, Inc.
http://www.echineseworld.com/
A Chinese teaching and learning program based on a successful Singapore Mandarin Chinese program.. The company is focused on delivering quality educational digital contents, resources and online learning systems for schools, corporate, and individual customers. This is a fee-based subscription service.

Flagship—Chinese Acquisition Pipeline
http://f-cap.org
A consortium effort led by the Utah State Department of Education and the Brigham Young University Chinese Flagship Center to develop and improve K–12 Chinese language instruction. The model includes two pathways toward high levels of student proficiency in Chinese: A full articulation for dual immersion programs in elementary schools, followed by enhanced language instruction in middle and high schools and a secondary sequential study pathway. The consortium works on curricular standards, teacher training, and proficiency assessment issues.

Hanban
http://english.hanban.org
The non-governmental organization affiliated with the Chinese Ministry of Education. It supports the Confucius Institutes as well as many other programs that foster Chinese studies.

Mandarin Immersion Parents Council
http://miparentscouncil.org
A website that tracks news about Mandarin immersion worldwide, edited by Elizabeth Weise, the author of this book.

The Mandarin Institute
http://www.mandarininstitute.org
The Mandarin Institute is a national K-12 Chinese language and culture education advocate, providing resources for students to prepare for global opportunities. Founded in 1989 at the Chinese American International School, the Mandarin Institute is a nonprofit dedicated to growing and strengthening Chinese language and culture education in schools throughout the United States.

National Council of Chinese Language Schools
http:// http://www.ncacls.org

Read Chinese
http://readchinese.nflc.umd.edu
A project funded by the U.S. Department of Education which provides e-learning reading lessons aimed at beginning and intermediate students of the language. The materials may be easily used by individual learners studying on their own or by teachers assigning them for individual or group study.

Speaking in Tongues
http://speakingintonguesfilm.info
A fantastic movie about immersion education which features students at two Chinese immersion schools in San Francisco, Starr King Elementary

and Alice Fong Yu Alternative School. Well worth watching, though beware, afterwards you'll feel that immersion is the *only* option worth considering for your child. Their website also features lots of excellent information and resources on immersion.

STARTALK Resources and Teacher Workshops
http://startalk@umn.edu

Utah Dual Language Immersion: Chinese
http://utahchineseimmersion.org

Glossary

sān shí sān
33

Dual language immersion
Schools or programs in which students are taught literacy and content (i.e. math, science, social studies, etc.) in two languages.

FLES
Foreign Language in the Elementary School. This is the one-period language class of your high school. In elementary school the learning is much less formal than you might remember from high school, but the idea is still that students are learning the language during this period. Sometimes the teacher only speaks in the language they're learning, sometimes the teacher also uses English.

Hanban
Hanban, 汉办、is the commonly used abbreviation for the Chinese National Office for Teaching Chinese as a Foreign Language. It is governed by the Office of Chinese Language Council International. Hanban is a non-profit affiliated with the Chinese Ministry of Education. It works to provide Chinese language and cultural teaching resources and services worldwide. Hanban is the sponsor for Confucius Classroom programs and donates books to many Chinese programs. It also has an extensive program to bring Chinese teachers to the United States.

One-way immersion
In these programs, all incoming students are fluent English speakers. They're all learning Mandarin (or another target language). So the program presumes that everyone's starting at zero.

Pinyin
The Romanization system used to write Chinese in the People's Republic of China and Singapore.

Simplified
The simplified form of Chinese characters, first adopted in 1958 in China. They are based on handwriting conventions for the most part and are used in China, Singapore and increasingly by overseas Chinese.

Strand
When immersion is just one of multiple programs offered in a school. For example many schools have a Mandarin immersion strand, which is one or two classrooms of students per grade and then an English strand, which is one or two classrooms of students per grade. Schools can have multiple strands. Starr King Elementary began with four: English, Spanish bilingual (for Spanish-speaking students who were learning English), Mandarin immersion and an Autism/Spectrum Special Day Program.

Traditional
The traditional or complex form of Chinese characters, used in Taiwan, Hong Kong and throughout much of the Chinese Diaspora.

Target language
The language that's being taught in a given program. If your child speaks English, then Mandarin is their target language. If they speak Mandarin, then English is their target language. In one-way Mandarin immersion programs the target language is Mandarin. In two-way Mandarin immersion programs the target language is Mandarin during Mandarin time and English during English time.

Two-way immersion
In these programs, half the class is supposed to be made up of native speakers of Mandarin (or another non-English target language) and half native speakers of English. The Mandarin speakers learn English, aided by the English speakers, and the English speakers learn Mandarin, aided by the Mandarin speakers. In some schools the target is one-third English speakers, one-third Mandarin speakers and one-third students who speak both.

Language terms you're likely to hear

Balanced bilingual
A person who is equally proficient and comfortable using two languages. This is rare.

Bilingual
The ability to speak two languages. Usually bilinguals are more comfortable in one or the other language, or are more comfortable in certain circumstances in one or the other language. For example a Swedish scientist might be socially proficient and comfortable speaking Swedish but more

proficient discussing biomechanical engineering in English. That's because English is used in technical journals and to discuss the field at conferences, so the vocabulary she knows is in English, not Swedish. So while her social English might not be as good as her social Swedish, her technical English in her field is better than her technical Swedish. This is especially true of professionals who did graduate school in an English-speaking country where they've never really used their native language to discuss technical topics.

Biliterate
The ability to read two languages fluently or nearly fluently.

Community language
The dominant language used by the majority of people outside the home. In the United States the community language is English.

Fluency
The ability to communicate clearly and easily in a language. See *Chapter 14: How Much Chinese Will They Learn?* for an in-depth discussion of language ability levels.

Minority language
A language spoken at home that is different from the community language.

Minority language at home
A language acquisition strategy in which the minority language (for example, the minority language would be Korean if you live in the United States, but in Korea English would be the minority language) is spoken at home by everyone in the family. So a family might only speak German at home, but the parents and the children would speak English with each other when they're outside of the home.

Multilingual
The ability to speak multiple languages fluently or nearly fluently.

One parent-one language
A language acquisition strategy used by some families in which each parent speaks a different language to their children. So if the mother speaks Cantonese and the father speaks Spanish, the mother will always speak Cantonese to the children while the father always speaks Spanish. Sometimes called OPOL.

Passive bilingual
A person who can understand two languages but only speaks one. Sometimes called a receptive bilingual.

三十四
sān shí sì
34

Bibliography

Asia Society, *Creating a Chinese Language Program in Your School: An Introductory Guide* (New York: Asia Society, 2006.)

Bourgogne, Annika, *Be Bilingual: Practical ideas for multilingual families* (Seattle: Amazon Digital Services, 2012)

Carstens, Sharon. (Editor) *Language Through Culture, Culture Through Language: A Framework for K-8 Mandarin Curriculum.* (Beijing: Peking University Press, 2013)

Chinese Language Learning in the Early Grades: A handbook of resources and best practices for Mandarin immersion (New York: Asia Society, 2012).

Cucchiara, Maia Bloomfield, *Marketing Schools, Marketing Cities. Who wins and who loses when schools become urban amenities* (Chicago: The University of Chicago Press, 2013.)

DeFrancis, John, *The Chinese Language: Face and Fantasy* (Honolulu: University of Hawai'i Press, 1984)

Diamond, Jared, *The World Until Yesterday* (New York: Viking, 2012)

Fortune, Tara and Menke, Mandy. *Struggling Learners and Language Immersion Education: Research-based, Practitioner-informed Responses to Educators' Top Questions* (Minneapolis: Center for Advanced Research on Language Acquisition, 2010.)

Kahlenberg, Richard D., *The Future of School Integration: Socioeconomic diversity as an education reform strategy* (New York: The Century Foundation Press, 2012).

Lindholm-Leary, Kathryn, "Student Outcomes in Chinese Two-Way Immersion Programs: Language Proficiency, Academic Achievement, and Student Attitudes," *Immersion education: Practices, policies, possibilities* (Avon, England: Multilingual Matters, 2011)

Petrilli, Michael J., *The Diverse Schools Dilemma: A Parents Guide to Socioeconomically Mixed Public Schools* (Washington D.C.: Thomas B. Fordham Institute, 2012.)

Ripley, Amanda, *The Smartest Kids in the World and How They Got That Way* (New York: Simon & Schuster, 2013.)

Trelease, Jim, *The Read-Aloud Handbook* (New York: Penguin Books, 2006.)

Schmidt, William H. and McKnight, Curtis C., *Inequality for All: The Challenge of Unequal Opportunity in American Schools* (New York: The Teachers College Press, 2012.)

Tse, Lucy, *Why Don't They Just Learn English? Separating Fact from Fallacy in the U.S. Language Debate* (New York: Teachers College Press, 2001.)

Wyman, Megan, *Standing Strong: Celebrating 30 Years of Chinese American International School* (San Francisco: Blurb Books, 2013.)

三十五
sān shí wǔ
35
Author Biography

Elizabeth Weise [it rhymes with "geese"] is a mother of two daughters who attend Mandarin immersion schools in San Francisco. She was on the committee that helped start a Mandarin immersion program in the San Francisco Unified School District in 2005. Both her daughters graduated from Starr King Elementary school and now attend the Chinese American International School.

She was a founding member of the Mandarin Immersion Parents Council and was on the board of the non-profit it became, the Jinshan Mandarin Education Council (金山中文教育协会) for three years. The organization supports Mandarin immersion in SF public schools.

She writes the Mandarin Immersion Parents Council blog at http://miparentscouncil.org.

In her day job, she covers technology and Silicon Valley for USA TODAY, based at the paper's San Francisco bureau.

There are few things she enjoys more than speaking and learning languages, which she likens to a four-dimensional crossword puzzle for the brain. Weise speaks English and Swedish fluently, Spanish eagerly yet poorly. Despite years of study in college, her Mandarin is now so dreadful her daughters cover their ears when they hear her try to speak it.

三十六
sān shí liù
36

Acknowledgements

Writing this book has been a fascinating journey that's introduced me to dozens of amazing people—and taught me that the passion for language and education runs deep in many Americans, despite our reputation as monolingual louts. As kids today say, "That's such 20th century thinking!"

To begin with, I must thank the San Francisco Unified School District. As much as the District sometimes drives me crazy in how it implements programs, without the commitment to language immersion it has shown since the 1980s, our daughters would be monolingual and I'd have spent the last eight years reading novels and eating bonbons. So, hats off to SFUSD for making this all possible.

But a District is not a school, and the real learning has taken place at Starr King Elementary, high atop Potrero Hill in San Francisco. It was home to our daughters for seven years. It is where they learned their first 一, 二, 三's, where they mastered stroke order and Tang poetry along with math, social studies, science, how to play fair and the art of four-square. The teachers and staff at Starr King were truly *in loco parentis* for the six hours a day they spent there, and they were in excellent hands.

While they were learning, our family became part of an extended community of parents, guardians, friends and family who supported our kids, our program and our school. Choosing a school is choosing not only a social group for your children, but also a social group for yourself (a surprise to many of us.) We were so lucky to find such a wonderful, congenial group of families. The Moms' Nights Out parties, the brunches, the dumpling fests, the PTA meetings and Principal's Talks, the soccer games, the spring concerts and just hanging out chatting in the play yard after morning drop off were wonderful.

Two staffers at Parents For Public Schools–San Francisco were endless sources of support, information and at times a shoulder to cry on. Kellyn Dong, a partner (er, parent)-in-crime at José Ortega Elementary, was a lifeline as our two schools jointly tried to figure out what in the heck it was we needed to make this Mandarin immersion thing work. Her calming emails and phone calls in the early years were a light in what at times felt like darkness. When she got hired on at PPS, parents across San Francisco gained— but oh how we missed her.

Carol Lei. Well, what can I say about Carol except that she knows more about how the San Francisco Unified School District works that the District itself? She was in on those early meetings to launch our Mandarin immersion program and then, at the last minute, the District decided to begin only in kindergarten and not also in first grade. Because her daughter was already in kindergarten, Carol's family was locked out of immersion. But despite that, she remained a staunch and steady supporter over the years. During times of trial herself, she still found the energy to come to evening meetings and workshops even while doing multiple jobs, including one at Parents for Public Schools. She now directs San Francisco's Kindergarten to College program, a great fit. But I miss her cheery morning emails popping into my inbox.

Gary Rydout, in Portland, Oregon, was the first Mandarin immersion parent outside of San Francisco I connected with, a marvelous boon. He was president of Shu Ren, the non-profit that supports the Mandarin immersion program in the Portland public schools and a huge help as we created a similar group here in San Francisco. He even took a summer day off to tour me around Woodside when work took me to Portland—and kindly mailed my camera case back when I left it in his car.

My analysis of where we stand with Mandarin immersion schools wouldn't have been possible without the heroic efforts of Joan Fang, whose son is in the Mandarin immersion program at Bergeson Elementary in the Capistrano Unified School District in Orange County. She volunteered to input the schools I had collected on the Mandarin Immersion Parents Council blog into a spreadsheet. That made it possible to analyze information about the programs. Thanks also to the database of the Center for Applied Linguistics in Washington D.C., which contributed to the list. You can find the full, frequently updated, list of Mandarin immersion schools on my blog, the Mandarin Immersion Parents Council.

Parents locally and nationally came forward when I asked for stories of what it's like to have kids in Mandarin immersion. Many sent thoughtful emails and you'll find their comments throughout the book. Four wrote so eloquently that I asked them to turn their thoughts into essays, which you will find in Chapter 11. They are Sarah Beth Chionsini, Carmen Cordovez, Jamila Nightingale and Frank and Mindy Han. Their stories will give you insights that I could not and I'm thrilled they agreed to take part in this project.

The same goes with students. I put out a call for stories of what it's like to go to school in Mandarin and got four great ones. Thanks to Madeleine Adams, Day Chionsini, Anya Hauptmann, and Katie Stern-Stillinger for giving parents pondering these programs the inside scoop. Keep their names in mind, I have no doubt they'll go far.

One thing I kept hearing from people was that maybe we should all just move to China if we wanted our kids to learn Chinese. To get a sense of how well that works, I put out another call, and a group of parents responded with honest assessments. Thanks to Elaine Wang in Beijing, the Gustafsons of Portland in Dalian, Steve Tennant in Hong Kong and Judy Shei in Singapore for their stories.

Educators have also been extremely supportive of this book, freely giving of their time, their thoughts and their expertise to make it useful to parents.

Discussing Mandarin immersion over beers in Washington D.C. with Michael Bacon and Kojo Hakam from Portland Public Schools and Jeff Bissell, head of school at the Chinese American International School, was the Vulcan mind meld I needed to get things off and running.

Tara Fortune at the University of Minnesota's Center for Advanced Language Acquisition in Minneapolis is a treasure beyond measure in this field and should be listened to by all and sundry whenever she has anything to say on these topics.

Language acquisition expert Stephen Krashen in Los Angeles offered a wealth of wisdom, with links and research to back it all up. Having him treat me like a colleague (or at least a promising student) was an honor.

In Los Angeles, Susan Wang, principal and founder of the Mandarin immersion program at Broadway Elementary, has been a constant go-to person despite being in the midst of creating a new program out of whole cloth.

In New York and New Jersey, Sharon Huang, founder and director of Bilingual Buds, was always quick to reply to emails and graciously met me at the train station in Summit so I could see her lovely school in action.

Myriam Met, an independent language immersion consultant and former director of the National Foreign Language Center at the University of Maryland, was hugely important in the early years of our program in San Francisco. She helped us understand how immersion works and what's required. I was fortunate enough to hear her speak at several workshops, which significantly deepened my understanding of the complex and difficult type of teaching this is. I was honored to have her take time from a very busy schedule to offer comments.

When I started writing this book, Chris Livaccari was the Senior Advisor for Chinese Language Initiatives at Asia Society in New York City. By the time I had finished, he'd moved on to be the upper elementary principal and Chinese program director at the International School of the Peninsula in Palo Alto, California. Throughout that time, he offered thoughtful critiques of various chapters and much helpful advice.

Ann Tollefson, a world language consultant based in Casper, Wyoming, was most giving of her time and understanding of how programs are evolving nationally.

Annika Bourgonge, a linguist, bilingualism expert and author in Finland, was a big source of wisdom and understanding around how language acquisition plays out within families and how hard it is to hold on to a language that's not spoken in the country you're living in. Plus she and her family were charming dinner guests when they came through San Francisco.

Christy Lao, a professor of education and expert on second language acquisition at San Francisco State University, was gracious with her time, showing me the marvelous Chinese reading program she created for middle school students. She also kindly allowed me access to her extensive library of books on language acquisition. Her incisive critiques and deep understanding of Chinese, biliteracy and Chinese literature strengthened this book immeasurably.

Chinese immersion consultant Elizabeth Hardage spent more time than I'm sure she had answering my questions and talking me through how reading strategies work in Chinese. Her kindness and help were a boon.

Two theses were very helpful as I researched what's known about Chinese immersion. They were Hope Schlicht's "A Critical Appraisal of the Chinese Immersion Program in St. Cloud" in Minnesota and Heidi Smith's "Chinese Immersion: A Study of Effective Elementary School Programs" in San Francisco. Both deepened my understanding of these types of programs, their history and how they function.

Shuhan Wang, the director of the Chinese Early Language Immersion Network at the Asia Society, was most helpful. I am very honored that she asked me to be on CELIN's national advisory committee.

Kathleen Wang, founder and director of the Pioneer Valley Chinese Immersion Charter School in Hadley, Massachusetts, offered helpful criticisms and talked me through the creation of her school and its program.

At the Chinese American International School in San Francisco, Chinese Director Kevin Chang was a thoughtful and patient reader of several chapters, minimizing my errors and helping me to understand the development of the school's three-decade–old program.

At the Center for Applied Linguistics in Washington D.C., Nancy Rhodes was one of my earliest interviews, setting me on the correct path as I began to research immersion. Later on, her colleague Lynn Thompson spent a very patient hour on the phone talking me through language assessment tools.

The staff of Starr King and José Ortega Elementary schools here in San Francisco were of course an ongoing graduate level course in immersion. Perhaps more importantly, as a parent I got to see up close and personal what truly fine teaching is. My respect for them, for their professionalism and deep understanding and love for teaching is immeasurable.

Gregg Roberts at the Utah Department of Education has answered more questions than he should have had to, but was always gracious and helpful—especially given as Mandarin is just one of *six* languages he's in charge of.

Invisible at times but very much here are stories from people who chose not to be named. They include a mother whose daughter went to one of the fanciest schools in Singapore, a teacher from a much-lauded Mandarin immersion school, a professor in a well-known Chinese department and many others. They offered insights that significantly aided my understanding.

Dr. Eleanor Drey not only helped deliver our two girls, but sent her own son to Starr King's Mandarin immersion program—*and* read the whole darned book when it was still a work in progress. I know my stance on the serial comma caused her endless anguish but she soldiered on, offering great suggestions.

Our youngest daughter's godfather, Ted Weinstein, has been a constant support and sounding board about everything from the nature of e-publishing to the wackiness of Word margins. Our near-daily phone calls are something I look forward to. If only world leaders would listen to our suggestions, much global conflict could be averted.

Her godmother, Sherry Boschert, gave me one of the most wonderful birthday presents ever when she offered to read the full manuscript early on in the process. A reporter by trade and published author, her input was invaluable.

As the manuscript was close to done, I realized it needed a good going over. I am grateful beyond words that my long-time editor at *USA Today*, Sue Kelly, agreed to read it through. Sue's since gone on to better things, but was still willing to give up nights and weekends to read every single page. In the years we worked together in the paper's science section, I knew Sue could not touch my words without making them sing. Having her eyes on these chapters in this non-work realm was a gift beyond compare.

Next came copyediting, unsung and yet vital for any book. I priced out professional copy editors and realized this labor of love could quickly become a very high priced hobby. Which is how I came to crowd source the feedback and copy editing. I sent a note out to the various Mandarin immersion emails lists and posted one of the Mandarin Immersion Parents Council blog and parents came forward and offered to read one or more chapters. Some read for English, some read for Chinese. All caught embarrassing errors and made excellent points. Thanks to Alex Akin, Hann Yu Chang, Tammy Chiang, Sarah Beth Chionsini, Ining Chou, Tracy Hilton, Eric and Christina Hsia, Patti Huang, Katie Jiang, Sarah June, Lewison Lem, Jackie Chou Lem, Marjorie Diaz, Lelan Miller, Marcelo Rodriguez, Lee Shu, June Tai, Vivian Tam, Renée Tan, Kathleen Ting, Caryn Tsagalis, Lynna Tsou and Vickie Tsui.

The final pass was made by a mom from CAIS, Jill Kustner, who came to the project like an angel from heaven. A meticulous and precise line editor, she found problems and mistakes that all previous eyes had missed. And she read the entire danged thing, from beginning to end, with that eagle eye. Any mistakes that are left are mine and mine alone but without her there would have been so many cringe-worthy more of them.

Of course, despite everyone's efforts on behalf of this project, any errors in the resulting work remains my own.

When the time came to turn the files on my computer into a book you could hold in your hands (whether on paper or as electrons) I turned to the internet. I found a great book jacket designer in England named James Smith. You can see his work at GoOnWrite.com. I sent him some text and photos, answered a page of very thoughtful questions and got back a great cover in about a week. I highly recommend him.

Of course, you can't have a cover without the pages to put beneath it. I started out imagining I would lay the book out myself. But a chapter or so in I realize that between the block quotes, bullet points, pinyin and characters, this one was bear of a book to design. One of my other great loves in life is the Glen Park Parents email list here in San Francisco, a digital home for close to 1,500 neighbors. I sent out a query, asking if there was anyone on the list who knew someone who designed e-books and felt comfortable working with a multi-lingual manuscript.

In the small world way of things, one of the emails I got was from Craig Johnson, a dad from the next neighborhood over, Bernal Heights. Not only did we share a love of Chinese, but also an obscure online hangout (The Well) and a long history of folk music and dancing. He even knew one of my oldest friends from Seattle. So the book was in excellent hands, as the pages you're now reading clearly show.

Our girls' dads, Calvin and Craig are very much a part of their lives and have embraced this whole notion of a bilingual education. Calvin claims his Chinese isn't up to par but when I listen to him bent over homework with the girls at the dining room table, I have to disagree. His parents, our girls' *Yeye* and *Nainai*, have been loving and supportive. *Yeye* came to school to teach the kids calligraphy, *Nainai* found old friends to help coach the girls as they learned their recitation poems. Both have shared with our girls their deep and abiding love of their birth language.

Here at home, words fail me. My wife Lisa knew of my fascination with languages when we married but I don't think she realized quite how deep it went. Still, she was game when I said I thought we should raise bilingual kids. She went along when I became one of the founding members of the Mandarin Immersion Parents Council and got increasingly involved in parent education. I think when I said, "I'll just put everything I've written about all this stuff together and then I'll be done with it!" she believed me—or at least thought

I believed it myself. Her Christmas present, "A month's dinners cooked by someone other than YOU," really made a difference. She has endured this process with good grace and good cheer as it became the project that ate my free time.

And, as the end drew near, her free time as well. My physician/scientist wife is far better at details than I will ever be. When she saw me flailing with Word templates and style sheets, she stepped in and set the whole thing up in one marathon week of coding that took my breath away and resulted in a manuscript that could go to Craig to be designed.

All told, this has been a wonderful and very fulfilling project. But with a full-time job and two kids with busy schedules, it's meant a lot of times when the family would have liked Mama to be somewhere other than glued to her computer or on the phone doing yet another interview about Mandarin. As my daughters note, "If you'd spent all that time studying Mandarin you'd *speak* it now!"

So thank you to Lisa for giving me the time to work on this labor of love. And I promise not to start another one until the kitchen remodel is done.

Finally, to our beloved daughters, *Zhou Qing* and *Zhou Yi*. They have put up with my using them as guinea pigs, experimental subjects and examples over the last three years. They've answered questions, translated things and cringed over my Chinese. But most importantly, they've learned to speak, read and write this language without (much) complaint. We are so proud of them and their hard work. Wherever their lives take them, they are truly citizens of the world. It is a pleasure and an honor to watch their progress.

CPSIA information can be obtained at www.ICGtesting.com
Printed in the USA
BVOW09s1937241114

376538BV00014BA/244/P